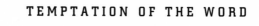

TEMPTATION OF THE WORD

TEMPTATION OF THE WORD

The Novels of Mario Vargas Llosa

EFRAÍN KRISTAL

Vanderbilt
University
Press

Nashville

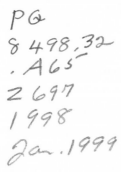

This publication is made from recycled paper and meets the minimum requirements of American National Standard for Information Sciences—Permanence of Paper for Printed Library Materials. ∞

Library of Congress Cataloging-in-Publication Data

  Kristal, Efrain, 1959-
    Temptation of the word : the novels of Mario Vargas Llosa / Efraín
  Kristal. -- 1st ed.
      p. cm.
    Includes bibliographical references and index.
    ISBN 0-8265-1301-8 (alk. paper)
    1. Vargas Llosa, Mario, 1936- --Criticism and interpretation.
  I. Title.
  PQ8498.32.A65Z697 1996
  863--dc21   97-21194
                                        CIP

Manufactured in the United States of America

Je suis devoré maintenant par un besoin de métamorphoses. Je voudrais écrire tout ce que je vois, non tel qu'il est, mais transfiguré. La narration exacte du fait réel le plus magnifique me serait impossible. Il me faudrait le broder encore.

—Gustave Flaubert, letter to Louise Colbert, August 26, 1853.

More than others the artist is a child of his age, a vulnerable child, responsive to all the changes of its weather, cheered by its promises, riddled by its doubts, seduced by its fashions, infected by its vices.

—Stanley Kunitz, "The Temptations of the Artist"

CONTENTS

ix   Acknowledgments

xi   Introduction

3   Chapter 1: The Writer's Commitment

25   Chapter 2: The Novels of the 1960s

69   Chapter 3: The Transition

99   Chapter 4: Against Wind and Tide

124   Chapter 5: The Novels of the 1980s

185   Conclusion

201   Notes

238   Bibliography

249   Index

ACKNOWLEDGMENTS

I would like to thank my friend the Peruvian philosopher Alberto Cordero for his intellectual generosity in long conversations where I rehearsed my basic ideas and for a careful critical reading of an advanced manuscript. I tried to write a book that I could hope would come close to meeting his exacting standards of intellectual rigor. Of equal importance to this book was the support of Christopher Maurer. He is the model for my aspirations as a literary scholar, and I am fortunate to count him as a friend.

I wrote the first version of this book in Spanish while a fellow of the Alexander von Humboldt Foundation during my 1991–1992 visit to the Iberoamericanisches Institut in Berlin, where I took ample advantage of its extraordinary library collections for Latin American studies. I am grateful to my host Prof. Dr. Dietrich Briesemeister, director of the Institut, for his hospitality and encouragement. I was lucky and fortunate that Mario and Patricia Vargas Llosa came to Berlin with Rosario Bedoya while I was writing the book. They were very generous to me.

My friend Iñigo García Bryce translated most of the first version during the summer of 1994. His translation became a draft that I rewrote several times as I added new sections in English. At various stages English drafts were read by Christopher Maurer, Roy Boland, Dain Borges, Enrico Mario Santí, Herbert Morris, and William Luis. The style and substance of the book has profited from their suggestions. Many others have helped me with the project: José Pascual Buxó, Richard Morse, Enrique Pupo-Walker, David Lagmanovich, Klaus Zimmerman, Karsten Garscha, Alexandra Weinstein de Bryce, Biruté Ciplijauskaité, Roland Greene, and Jean-François Fourny. I offer special gratitude to

Peter Johnson, who gave me access to the Mario Vargas Llosa papers at Princeton's Firestone Library. I would also like to express my appreciation to Dean Pauline Yu for providing a comfortable and supportive environment for my work at UCLA.

With the aid provided by UCLA faculty research grants, I enlisted Carmela Zanelli, Claudia Bautista, Susan Nichols, and Philip Walsh to find the published English versions of materials I had quoted from the Spanish, French, and German and to help in producing a bibliography in English. Philip Walsh was instrumental in transforming many footnotes from the Spanish version into an English draft that I could then edit. I am grateful to the director and editorial staff at Vanderbilt University Press for the care and good will with which they have worked on my book. Special thanks go to Maggy Shannon, Polly Law, and Bard Young, whose copy editing was exemplary, and to Sherrye Young for her sedulous preparation of the index. I also want to thank Romey Sutherland. She first read a version of this book in Melbourne in 1993, and I have relied on her encouragement, her patience, and her insights to finish the project over the last few months.

Finally, I wish to thank the editors of *Antipodas* and *The Review of Contemporary Fiction* for permission for substantive use of two of my artcles published in those journals: "A reading of Alejandro Mayta's Story in the Light of Joseph Conrad's *Under Western Eyes*" (*Antipodas* 7–9 [1996–1997]) and "*Captain Pantoja and the Special Service:* A Transitional Novel" (*The Review of Contemporary Fiction* 17, no. 1 [Spring 1997]).

INTRODUCTION

     Time of the Hero (1962), Mario Vargas Llosa's first novel, generated a considerable amount of interest and enthusiasm in Latin America and Spain. After the publication of *The Green House* (1965) his reputation as a world-class writer was firmly established. Vargas Llosa came into literary prominence when many Latin American writers believed that their literature had finally come of age and that it would play a significant role in the social and political transformation of the Western Hemisphere. Carlos Fuentes's criticism of the political plutocracy that had usurped the socialist ideals of the Mexican revolution was a major theme in his early novels; and Gabriel García Márquez's most celebrated novel, *One Hundred Years of Solitude,* expresses his socialist conviction that a people without solidarity is condemned to alienation. In the 1960s literary prestige gave clout to those writers who wished to diagnose the shortcomings of Latin America, especially if they expressed a measure of sympathy for the Cuban revolution. Like García Márquez and Fuentes—his most significant peers—Mario Vargas Llosa embraced the idea that literature had a political role to play. The young Peruvian believed that his novels were condemning capitalism in Latin America on the eve of a revolutionary period. He was eager to express his support for the Cuban revolution with the enthusiasm of a writer convinced that his new-found fame is emblematic of a momentous political change.

    In the four decades that followed, Vargas Llosa was determined to reconcile his passion for literature with his political convictions. Not content with registering his own novels' consistency with his personal views, he has felt the necessity to underscore the political significance of literature in general. In the 1960s he argued that any good work of literature is a boon to socialism because the main motivation for inventing alternative realities is a writer's dissatisfaction with the inequities of his own society. After his disenchantment with socialism in the 1970s, he has argued that literature can serve as an escape valve for the violent propensities of those who are dissatisfied with the inevitability of human limitations.

It was not enough for Vargas Llosa to claim that good literature has good political implications; he has argued that good literature is the product of absolute creative freedom. Vargas Llosa has respected writers who abandon their vocation to devote themselves to political causes, but he has not hidden his disdain for writers who sacrifice the literary integrity of their works in order to serve a political ideal. Aware that his views about creative freedom may be incompatible with his views about the political implications of literature, he has nevertheless insisted on both: in the 1960s he claimed that the freest and most spontaneous literary activity would have the greatest revolutionary force; and after his disenchantment with socialism he has made the more moderate claim that literature can appease human tendencies to incivility.

For the first time since he has been active as a writer, there are signs that politics may no longer be a central consideration in Vargas Llosa's views about artistic creation. In the play *Ojos Bonitos, Cuadros Feos* (1996) his three characters reflect on the connections between art and their lives: the philistine finds the artistic enterprise a useless nuisance, and the others, more artistically inclined, come to realize that the elusive compensations of artistic creation may be restricted to the very few.

Vargas Llosa's belief that art and literature necessarily serve a clear-cut political end could be on the wane for the first time since he has been an active writer, but politics continues to be a major source of inspiration for his own literary themes. He has often reflected about the significance of political ideas and situations in his creative process:

> I have never wanted to use my novels as mere vehicles to express political ideas; but I do think that political facts and experiences generate a whole host of situations, of characters, of psychologies, and of anecdotes that are very tempting, for me, from the creative point of view. There are also political problems in the case of my own country and Latin America, which are of such relevance, such drama, such gravity, that it is impossible for me to ignore these matters, to isolate them from my own concerns and ambitions as a writer.[1]

The political content of Vargas Llosa's novels has never betrayed his political convictions, but he has tried to avoid the temptation—fatal according to Flaubert—of the novelist who wishes to reproduce rather than to recreate reality. Vargas Llosa has had no qualms about transforming historical facts or biographical information to suit his literary purposes. His writing method involves the use of raw materials that he will modify in the creative process. He has always relied on but has never been faithful to his personal experience, research in specialized archives and libraries, other works of literature, the ideas of intellectuals he has admired, Latin American history, biographical information about people he has met, and so forth.

It is not necessary to command a thorough knowledge of these materials—Latin American history, for example—to enter into his literary world, because each of his novels is relatively self-contained. To understand how Vargas Llosa's novels were written, however, it is essential to study how he transformed and modified these raw materials. In addition, it is impossible to understand the origins of his literary themes if one ignores his political convictions and the vicissitudes of his political experiences: most notably his role as an intellectual spokesman for Latin American revolutionary movements in the 1960s; his unintended break with the Latin American Left after he was ostracized for criticizing the censorship and mistreatment of creative writers in Cuba in 1971; his period of activism for free-market democracy in Peru, which culminated in his failed bid for his country's presidency in 1990; and, more recently, his growing pessimism about political activity. Political ideas and experiences have inspired literary themes, anecdotes, characters, and situations that have also had a bearing on the development of his literary techniques. More importantly, his political convictions have had such an important place in his novels that the most relevant changes in his themes and literary techniques can be traced directly to them. It is, therefore, possible to divide his production as a novelist into distinct periods according to his changing political convictions.

Time of the Hero (1962), *The Green House* (1965), and *Conversation in The Cathedral* (1969) correspond to his socialist period. In these novels, upward mobility is unthinkable without moral degradation, and thoughtful individuals realize that their society is corrupt through and through. Vargas Llosa's literary themes were therefore in harmony with his conviction that capitalist society was too corrupt for reform. In his socialist period Vargas Llosa refined Faulknerian techniques; without sacrificing intrigue, strong emotions, or powerful action, he presents fictional events, thoughts, and dialogues by superimposing spatial and chronological planes.

Captain Pantoja and the Special Service (1973) and *Aunt Julia and the Scriptwriter* (1977) are works of transition from his socialist to his neoliberal (or neoconservative) period.[2] These novels were written while Vargas Llosa was repudiated by his former friends and associates from the Latin American Left but before he had reoriented his political views. He reiterates some of the themes from the novels of the 1960s with humor and irony. In *Aunt Julia* the historical period that precedes the Cuban revolution is explicitly portrayed as a time of lost innocence.

With *The War of the End of the World* (1981) Vargas Llosa abandoned his socialist illusions, and he first explored a new theme in line with the concerns of antiauthoritarian liberalism: the fragility of a civilized coexistence assailed by fanatics, political opportunists, and well-intentioned but misguided idealists. If in his socialist period Vargas Llosa believed that man's feelings of dissatisfaction with his social world resulted from the nature of capitalism itself, in his neoliberal period Vargas Llosa believes that dissatisfaction results from the human condition. The novels of this period underscore the significance of fantasy and eroticism as palliatives against human feelings of discontentment that can always unravel in political violence. After losing the Peruvian elections, the theme of man's inherent dissatisfaction with his world has taken a disturbing turn: in *Death in the Andes* (1993) violence takes place for no discernible reason.

This book is first and foremost about Vargas Llosa's novels. The heart of my study is the analysis of every one of his novels from *Time of the Hero* to *The Notebooks of Don Rigoberto* (1997).[3] To explain how Vargas Llosa approached writing each of them, I analyze many of the same sources he used, including the literary and philosophical works that he read and reread while writing them.

Before outlining the specific contents of my study, I would briefly like to set out my approach to literature. My methodology involves my background in hermeneutics and in analytic philosophy.[4] E. H. Gombrich once wrote that the more we know of an artist's palette, the more we are likely to appreciate his artistic choices.[5] Much of my work entails the cultural and aesthetic reconstruction of Vargas Llosa's novels taking as a starting point his palette, so to speak. I am interested in understanding Vargas Llosa's cultural options and constraints as a writer who had wanted to offer his literary prestige to revolutionary causes and who later became an outspoken critic of socialism. Yet I am not satisfied with abstract speculation. I take seriously the fact that writers read and respond to specific texts as they write their own literary works. I wish to avoid the abuses of contemporary literary theory and to write with as little technical jargon as possible. I refuse to force literary analysis into the service of agreement or disagreement with Vargas Llosa's political views. One of the troubling fallacies in Vargas Llosa literary criticism—practiced by tendentious critics and by eminent literary figures alike—is to confuse the merits of Vargas Llosa's novels with the merits of their political content.

I am interested in understanding how Vargas Llosa wrote his novels, and this necessarily involves an interest in his political context while writing and in the wide literary context informing his craft. I am not simply arguing that there are intertextual connections between Vargas Llosa's novels and those of Faulkner, Joanot Martorell, Tolstoy, and Hugo, among many others, but that Vargas Llosa must have taken notes and used these works actively in the creation of his own works. Much of my research into this fascinating matter involved reading or rereading literary works that could have been useful to Vargas Llosa in his own writing. After making some fruitful connections—such as the significance of Faulkner's *Light in August* for *Time of the Hero*—I systematically studied those literary works that we know Vargas Llosa has read because he has written about them in essays and books. I continued with works that I believe he might well have read. Rather than pointing out every connection I found between his novels and his sources, I decided to select the most relevant and representative, as a way of gaining insight not only into Vargas Llosa's own education but into the process of creative borrowing that Vargas Llosa has used to make his own contribution.

Many of my insights were confirmed and fine tuned in the Mario Vargas Llosa Collection at Princeton's Firestone Library, where I was able to read the rough drafts of the novels as well as the notebooks in which he sketched out his literary ideas. In reading the drafts of *The Green House*, for example, I could pinpoint when the story of the infamous Fushía (which was inspired by notes Vargas Llosa took on a trip to the Peruvian jungle in 1956) was rewritten according to themes and structures drawn from Joseph Conrad's *The Heart of Darkness*. I am also grateful to Mr. Vargas Llosa who graciously read a draft of this book. His most important correction involves *The Real Life of Alejandro Mayta*. I had the intuition that the novel had something to do with Joseph Conrad's depiction of the political fanatic in Conrad's *The Secret Agent*. Mr. Vargas Llosa told me that the links with that novel were circumstantial, and he suggested that I reread *Under Western Eyes*. The results of that hint appear in chapter 5.

Harold Bloom and George Steiner have both suggested that strong writers are strong critics when their fictional works respond in challenging ways to other fictional works.[6] Vargas Llosa, in this sense, is not always a strong critic when it comes to his sources. In *Time of the Hero,* for example, he simply borrows techniques from Faulkner's *Light in August* for his own purposes.[7] *The Real Life of Alejandro Mayta*, on the other hand, is a corrective to *Under Western Eyes* because Vargas Llosa transforms Conrad's conceits to undermine his notions about objectivity in literature.[8]

In this book I analyze all of Vargas Llosa's novels, and I believe that each analysis could be read on its own. When read as a whole, the individual analyses of the novels show that some features are common to all the novels while others are associated with specific periods in his literary development. This reading sheds light on how literary techniques, themes, and character types appear, recur, and are transformed. In turn, the literary criticism at the core of this book is enriched by attending analyses of the intellectual currents and of the political ideas and experiences that resurface in Vargas Llosa's works. I explore the Peruvian intellectual milieu in which he became a writer as well as the ideas of the thinkers who influenced his views about literature and politics. Even though the book is about Vargas Llosa's novels, I draw from the entire corpus of his writings, including his many books of literary and political essays and his plays. I also underscore an irrationalist streak in all of Vargas Llosa's writings because it has been a fundamental feature of his moral and literary vision. At bottom he believes that the ultimate explanations of human desire and action are beyond reason. That said, he has passionately held that certain types of human conduct and behavior are morally unacceptable. His changing political convictions have always been reoriented around his views that a great deal of human motivation is inscrutable and that peaceful social coexistence is the only justification for curtailing an individual's freedom of action.

To the extent that his political experience is also at the heart of his literary changes, I have organized the book accordingly. Chapter 1 is an analysis of Vargas Llosa's attempt to reconcile his socialist convictions with his view that literature is the product of irrational forces he has often called the "demons" of creation. I explore the significance of the writers whose ideas played an important role in shaping his literary and political vision. I give special attention to the ideas of Jean Paul Sartre and to three Peruvian writers that Vargas Llosa knew personally and who influenced his intellectual career: Sebastián Salazar Bondy, José María Arguedas, and César Moro.

Chapter 2 begins with a summary of Vargas Llosa's basic ideas about the craft of fiction. They were inspired by Flaubert, and he has not modified them over the years. It then gives a brief overview of the early short stories before offering detailed analysis of the novels he wrote in the 1960s.

Chapter 3 analyses Vargas Llosa's unintended break with the Latin American Left as well as the effects of this development in the opportunistic field of Latin American literary criticism. It also analyzes the two novels he wrote before his neoliberal period.

Chapter 4 explores the ideas of Albert Camus, Isaiah Berlin, and Karl Popper, who are chief among the thinkers Vargas Llosa studied as he reoriented his political views. This chapter also examines his attempts to reconcile the ideas of these thinkers with his long-held doctrine about the irrational elements of literary creation, reinforced by his devoted readings of Georges Bataille.

Chapter 5 offers detailed analysis of the novels of the neoliberal period from *The War of the End of the World* until *The Notebooks of Don Rigoberto*. The chapter is called "The novels of the 1980s," but it includes Vargas Llosa's most recent novel because it is the sequel to *In Praise of the Stepmother*. The sequel has affinities to its antecedent, but it also has subtle differences that will help to set the tone for the conclusion, where I make general observations about all of Vargas Llosa's novels. I postpone the analysis of *Death in the Andes* until the conclusion because I believe that this novel suggests an important change in Vargas Llosa's literary trajectory, which I suspect will be as significant as his transition from the socialist to the neoliberal period.

Throughout this study, I have tried to avoid the fallacy of that literary criticism that overemphasizes Vargas Llosa's realism while overlooking his own inventions, his dialogues with other literary works, and his transmutations of lived experiences, readings, and ideas into self-contained literary works.

TEMPTATION OF THE WORD

CHAPTER ONE

The Writer's Commitment

If human needs could be satisfied, there would be no reason to invent alternative realities, but life's imperfections beget "negative obsessions—individual, social and cultural—that put man so much at odds with his own reality as to give rise to the desire to subvert reality by verbally reshaping it."[1] This is Mario Vargas Llosa's main insight regarding literature's *raison d'être*. Vargas Llosa has always claimed that a writer's dissatisfaction with society, his traumas, failures, and humiliations produce unconscious obsessions that are the stuff of literary creation. "The demon" has been his favorite image of a writer's hidden motivations and impulses. "Demons" are the writer's obsessions, the often irrational desire, forces, or tendencies responsible for his literary themes.

Goethe, the first to secularize demonic metaphors to discuss the nature of literary creation, was an indirect influence on Vargas Llosa, who was more directly affected by the demonic in Victor Hugo, Gustave Flaubert, the *poètes maudits* such as Rimbaud and Baudelaire, and in César Moro and George Bataille, advocates of the so called "literature of evil." Although the influence was indirect, it is still worthwhile to review briefly Goethe's idea of "Das Dämonische" (the demonic). Vargas Llosa has made passing references to the German classic in essays defining his own literary ideas, and some of his most important views on literary creation were first expressed by Goethe.[2]

Goethe's concept of "the demonic" expressed the notion that artistic creation is the product of unconscious forces divorced from reason or understanding.[3] The demons not only stimulate an individual's imagination but also provide literary themes and modify those the writer has consciously decided to explore. Demons are to a writer what chance is to a gambler: they offer possibilities but do not ensure success. Not every writer is able to transform his obsessions into a good work of literature. For Goethe, the demonic also has social implications because it tends to agitate the creative imagination, especially in what he called those "dark" times when social life is in turmoil.

Like Goethe, Vargas Llosa sees literary creation as the product of irrational forces that determine or modify the subjects chosen by a writer. The raw material of literary creation is an unpredictable mixture of rational and irrational elements, and successful creation of a work of art from these elements depends on the writer's talent.[4] During his socialist period, which lasted until about 1975, Vargas Llosa also claimed that the demons of literary creation were most prevalent in times of social upheaval. In making this last claim Vargas Llosa was more in tune with the views of Victor Hugo, one of his favorite novelists, than with those of Goethe. Vargas Llosa believed, like Hugo, that literature is not just a barometer of turbulent times, for it has an important role to play in denouncing social injustices and in undermining the status quo.[5]

The satanic images of the Romantics were taken up by twentieth century writers such as César Moro and Georges Bataille, both of whom strongly influenced Vargas Llosa's views on literature. These writers took surrealism as a starting point to explore the darker side of human nature and to defend literature as an activity where the uncensored imagination is free to explore a writer's most disturbing obsessions. This approach to literature is called *la littérature du mal* (or "literature of evil"), alluding to Georges Bataille's best-known essay, because it suggests a strong link between literature and transgression. In *Literature and Evil*, one of the books that most influenced Vargas Llosa, Bataille summarizes the literary history of "the satanic" from its theological to its secular versions. He links the Romantic images of the demonic with freedom:

> [Liberty] is, as Blake said of Milton, "of the Devil's party without knowing it." Submission and obedience, on the other hand, are on the side of Good. Liberty is always open to revolt, while Good is as closed as a rule.[6]

Since the 1970s the name of Georges Bataille has often appeared in Vargas Llosa's essays. But long before, Vargas Llosa had been fascinated with writings and doctrines akin to those of Bataille. In 1960, two years before publishing *The*

Time of the Hero, Vargas Llosa had translated a scandalous anticlerical story by Rimbaud.[7]

Like the *poètes maudits*, Vargas Llosa could not conceive of a docile writer content with his own society or engaged in a serene dialogue with an inherited literary tradition. The writer is a "blind rebel," and his work a "coded testimony" of rebelliousness against his own society. The writer does not simply represent reality as it is but modifies it by adding his own resentment:

> [The writer's work is] a reconstruction of reality and a testimony of his dissent. . . . Every novel is a coded testimony: a portrayal of the world not as it is but as modified by the novelist who has *added* his resentment, his nostalgia, his critique. This *additional element* is what makes a novel a creative and not merely an informative work.[8]

The writer's own dissatisfaction—that "additional element" in a work of fiction—implies a rejection of the reality that tormented him in the first place. Unlike Flaubert, for whom a writer is to his work what God is to Creation, Vargas Llosa thinks of the writer as a "deicide" who rejects Creation by means of an alternative: the creation of a literary work.

Like other progressive writers in the 1960s, Vargas Llosa believed that the capitalist system had to be destroyed to establish socialism. Aware of and sometimes troubled by Stalinism, he nonetheless believed that the Soviet Union was the bulwark of political liberation for the entire world and that the Cuban revolution was the model for Latin Americans to follow. Social and political problems could not be peacefully resolved because it was inconceivable that the defenders of capitalism would voluntarily relinquish their privileges resulting from an uneven distribution of wealth. Vargas Llosa considered liberal democracy a scandalous farce because of its indifference to unemployment, extreme poverty, malnutrition, and other miseries that justify the violence of revolutionary movements.

From the 1950s when he first published his political views, until 1975 when he distanced himself from revolutionary socialism, Vargas Llosa sought to reconcile his conception of literature as a product of irrational forces with his commitment to pro-Soviet revolutionary movements. He wanted to show that the creative impulse is inherently at odds with capitalism, and that every authentic writer—even those who believe in art for art's sake—ought to sympathize with revolutionary movements. He felt that South American writers have a heightened propensity for rebellion because they live in an environment of acute misery, and he believed that this propensity is made more acute by mundane frustrations stemming from the primitive or practically nonexisting publishing industry and from rampant illiteracy greatly limiting a writer's potential reading public. Of course, the ultimate justification of a revolutionary movement is not society's indifference to literary creativity but poverty, corruption, and the injustice of any capitalist society.[9]

LITERATURE AND REVOLUTION

Although he acknowledged that liberal democracies respect the principles of freedom—specifically artistic freedom—Vargas Llosa thought, like other socialist intellectuals, that "freedom" under capitalism is not authentic because it is not founded on economic equality.[10] Vargas Llosa opposed censorship and believed that "only socialism, by laying the foundations of true social justice, can render expressions such as 'freedom of opinion' and 'creative freedom' truly meaningful."[11]

He first expressed his ideal of the intellectual who is faithful both to art and to the revolution in his 1956 essay on José Carlos Mariátegui (1894–1930), whom he considered a model for his own political and literary ideals. Vargas Llosa regarded Mariátegui as a pro-Soviet intellectual fully committed to the revolution and a defender of aesthetic freedom who had found a balance between literature and politics: "Mariátegui the artist and writer, who coexisted with Mariátegui the revolutionary, achieved that spiritual equilibrium that is undoubtedly the main reason for the lasting relevance of his work."[12]

Vargas Llosa's analysis of Mariátegui echoes the themes of his friend and mentor Sebastián Salazar Bondy's evaluation of Mao Zedong in *Literatura*, a short-lived literary journal for which both writers worked in 1958 (along with José Miguel Oviedo, who later became Vargas Llosa's most distinguished literary critic). Salazar Bondy claimed that the Chinese revolution was superior to the Soviet revolution because Mao was an authentic poet committed both to Communism and to freedom of artistic expression.[13] Salazar Bondy's naive but revealing appraisal, made a year prior to the Cuban revolution, was also Vargas Llosa's political ideal—a Communist revolution respectful of artistic freedom. In the 1960s, Vargas Llosa praised the triumph of the Cuban revolution precisely in those terms: "There are socialist countries—Cuba is the most advanced—where censorship barely operates, and state control of aesthetics is nonexistent."[14]

Vargas Llosa could not conceive of an ideal society where artists would be forced to work according to any preconceived political agendas. Nonetheless, he felt uncomfortable with the notion of apolitical art—literature ought to be both independent *and* revolutionary. He wanted to find a persuasive link between the demons of literary creation and socialism. To establish this link he needed to show that the revolt of a writer "who doesn't know the profound reason for his rebellion" is itself a symptom of a crisis within capitalist society.[15] To quote yet another of his favorite metaphors, he saw the novelist as a vulture who thrives on the established order's death throes: "[Novelists are] a bit like vultures: they feed on rotting organisms. Novels are ideally suited to depict societies on the verge of collapse."[16] Vargas Llosa claimed that his conception of literature was socialist, but he opposed "socialist realism," the official literary doctrine of international Communism, which demanded a literary portrayal of reality that would promote the ideological transformation of the proletariat. Although he insisted that all good literature somehow contributes to the revolution by denouncing social woes, Vargas Llosa did not believe that a writer ought to be *required* to write works for pedagogical or propagandistic purposes.

His best argument in favor of a simultaneously independent and revolutionary literature was speculative and somewhat muddled: it does not matter whether a writer is motivated consciously or unconsciously by the injustices of capitalism, for literature is inherently revolutionary: "All good literature is progressive, regardless of the author's intentions."[17] He was convinced that the misery and injustice deriving from capitalism were the main sources of literary creation in Latin American countries, whether or not the creative writers were truly aware of it.

Vargas Llosa defended the Marxist-Leninist thesis that only the destruction of the existing system could create the necessary conditions for establishing social justice. While men of action such as Lenin and Castro are required to lead the revolution, good literature contributes to the cause by denouncing the established order.[18] Literature's political task is not to identify those problems that can be resolved through reform, but to demonstrate that in capitalism justice is impossible because of its intrinsic hypocrisy and corruption. The most famous essay in which he put forward this argument was "La literatura es fuego" (Literature is Fire), a speech he read in 1967 when he was awarded the Rómulo Gallegos prize for *The Green House*. In this speech—arguably the most widely disseminated statement in support of politically committed literature in Latin America of the nineteen sixties—he stated that great Latin American literature denounces injustice and that the entire continent is destined to follow the Cuban model:

> The American reality, of course offers the writer a true surfeit of
> reasons to be rebellious and discontented. Societies where injustice
> is law, paradises of ignorance, exploitation, blinding inequalities,

poverty, economic, cultural and moral alienation, our tumultuous lands offer us exemplary material to reveal in fictions, in a direct or indirect way, through facts, dreams, testimonies, allegories, nightmares or visions that reality is imperfectly made, that life must change. But within ten, twenty or fifty years, the hour of social justice will arrive in our countries, as it has in Cuba, and the whole of Latin America will have freed itself from the order that despoils it, from the castes that exploit it, from the forces that now insult and repress it.[19]

Unlike other writers whose socialist convictions surfaced only with the triumph of the Cuban revolution, Vargas Llosa was a firm believer in socialism before he pledged his support to Fidel Castro. Years before the 1959 revolution, Vargas Llosa had expressed his commitment to the goals and ideals of José Carlos Mariátegui, the founder of the Peruvian Communist Party, widely considered the first Latin American Marxist thinker.

MARIÁTEGUI, ARGUEDAS AND SALAZAR BONDY

In one of his first literary essays, published in 1956, Vargas Llosa approvingly summarized the main thesis of Mariátegui's *Seven Interpretive Essays on Peruvian Reality* (1928), the first and most influential book to analyze Peruvian society in Marxist terms:

> The vision of Peru that emerges from the *Seven Interpretive Essays on Peruvian Reality* is based on an objective, direct observation of its problems. . . . On the one hand there is an authentic, native Peru originating directly in the pre-Hispanic epoch: the Indian Peru that flourished in the Andes. On the other, there is an inauthentic Peru that came into being with the arrival of the Spaniards who settled on the Pacific coast and whose ethnic, cultural, political and economic elements are foreign, and stand in contradiction to the Andean Peru. . . . The Indian problem has only one solution: the elimination of the *latifundio* [large landed estate that depends on an indigenous work force]. . . . The Indian has heroically resisted every effort to eliminate the custom of communal labor for which he has a natural propensity. Thus, to reclaim the rights of the indigenous class [in Peru], a collective and socialist system for working the land must be reestablished.[20]

According to Mariátegui the descendants of Europeans in Peru have ignored the country's true heritage and have produced a national history and literature that avoids the history of Indian exploitation and disregards the Indian's rights to recover the land usurped by the Spaniards during the conquest of America. Contemporary Peruvian writers, according to Mariátegui, have the duty to portray the Indians' problems. He coined the term *indigenismo* to describe a literature that attempts to depict Indian reality in order to help reclaim the Indian's political rights. Peruvian literature, in this view, must first and foremost explore the spiritual, political, and economic reality of the Indian.

The most influential figure of literary *indigenismo* was José María Arguedas (1911–1969) who, inspired by Mariátegui, attempted to document the social and spiritual reality of the Andean world. His literary works were also intended to contribute to the establishment of socialism in Peru by underscoring the connections between pre-Columbian collectivism and modern Communism, and by depicting the transition from Indian exploitation to Indian revolt and even to revolutionary action.

Vargas Llosa admired Arguedas and over the years has made important efforts in disseminating his work outside Peru. In a 1955 article, his first published journalistic essay on a Latin American novelist, Vargas Llosa praised Arguedas's project of revealing the true reality of the Indian for the first time in Peruvian literature, and he pointed to the "primarily constructive and social purpose behind his literary work."[21] Notwithstanding his lavish praise for Arguedas here and elsewhere, Vargas Llosa felt uneasy about Mariátegui's claim that Peruvian literature's most significant task was to explore Indian reality. He never felt comfortable with the project to which Arguedas dedicated his life: the reclaiming of Andean civilization as the main foundation for a future national culture.[22] Indeed, Vargas Llosa's main objection to the *Seven Interpretive Essays on Peruvian Reality* involves the point on which Arguedas most agreed with Mariátegui, that is, his insistence that Peruvian national literature must address the Indian question:

> [The paragraphs Mariátegui dedicated to] predict the future of Peruvian literature were unfortunate: he claimed that *indigenismo* was destined to improve and to become representative. Today we know that it was merely a frail and artificial experiment.[23]

Vargas Llosa reconciled his distaste for *indigenismo* with his admiration for Arguedas by stressing that *indigenismo* was a failed genre but that Arguedas was nonetheless a great writer able to portray the Andean world in his literary works.[24]

Without pressing the issue of the social and political significance of *indigenismo* as the literature most suitable for Peru, Vargas Llosa was committed to a different literary project: the denunciation of capitalism. Other literary critics made the connection between Vargas Llosa's and Arguedas's novels in ways he neither condoned nor criticized. In "Mario Vargas Llosa and José María Arguedas: Dos visiones de una sola América" (Mario Vargas Llosa and José María Arguedas: Two Visions of the Same America) an essay representative of the way Vargas Llosa's first novels were received by critics, Ariel Dorfman argues that the novels of Arguedas and Vargas Llosa are complementary: while the latter unmasks an unredeemable society, the former prophetically points toward the revolutionary path of Latin American liberation.[25]

Sebastián Salazar Bondy also saw his own literary project as complementary to Arguedas's *indigenismo*. In *Lima la horrible* (1964), his most important essay, Salazar Bondy accepts Mariátegui's thesis that contemporary Peru is a degraded continuation of the Spanish colonial system, and he attempts to reveal the stratagems by which Peruvian culture has invented national myths to evade the country's social injustices, particularly the exploitation of the indigenous people. Salazar Bondy claims that Peruvian culture invented the deceitful notion of a "Colonial Arcadia" in order to conceal historical injustices and to prevent present day injustices from being fully understood. His essay is an exhortation to condemn Peru's dominant culture and to understand Peruvian history as a struggle between a powerful class of European descent and an oppressed class that includes all Indians:

> The colonial period, idealized as Arcadia, has not yet been examined by an impartial judge, an incorruptible critic. The image of the colonial period found in works of fiction and nonfiction is one of alleged wealth and serenity. Nothing is said of the tensions between lords and serfs, foreigners and natives, the powerful and the impoverished: a tension that has permeated society.[26]

Salazar Bondy knew that his critique of Peru's upper classes would remain incomplete as long as socialists like himself did not find a way to unite their own political ideals with the aspirations of the Peruvian Indians. In a letter to Vargas Llosa he insisted that the revolution would not take place in Peru unless revolutionaries of European descent came to terms with indigenous culture: "The cultural divide between the Peruvian peasant and the revolutionary is an issue that worries me, and I fear that here lies the key to the failure of the Left in our country."[27] Salazar Bondy's observation was not meant as an admonition since he was convinced of the political value of Vargas Llosa's literature. After reading one of the final drafts of *Los impostores* (The Impostors), a provisional title of *The Time of the Hero*, he wrote a letter to Vargas Llosa exhorting him to publish his novel because of its timely revolutionary significance. This unpublished letter can be found in the Mario Vargas Llosa Collection at Princeton University's Firestone library:

> In your novel you depict the contradictions of the underdeveloped, dissonant and deformed world that we precariously inhabit. Things will explode, are already exploding. I think therefore that the publication of your novel ought not be too much delayed.[28]

By the early sixties, leftist literary critics were drawing links between the work of Salazar Bondy, Vargas Llosa, and Arguedas. In his review of *Lima la horrible,* where he praises the literary supremacy of José María Arguedas, Angel Rama, an influential critic, argued that both Salazar Bondy's essay and Vargas Llosa's first novel were symptomatic of an imminent revolution in Peru that would mark the end of exploitation in an indigenous nation after centuries "of domination by white foreigners."[29] Rama considers Salazar Bondy's book destructive in a positive sense, in the sense that it denounces a society that must be abolished. *Destruction* in Rama's usage is a prelude to *construction,* by which he means the establishment of socialism: "We humans are not here only to criticize, but, as Mariátegui said of himself, to construct and create. It is by performing these tasks that we will attain complete fulfillment."[30] Vargas Llosa also praised Salazar Bondy's essay for its denunciation of a political system that needed to be eliminated and replaced by socialism: "lucid, deeply grounded in reality, original, *Lima la horrible* is a book of constructive violence.[31]

Salazar Bondy felt proud of the links and parallels drawn by critics between his essay and Vargas Llosa's writing:

> It has filled me with pride that some reviews of *Lima la horrible,* particularly in Mexico, appeared at the same time as those of *The Time of the Hero,* and that someone wrote that the two books complement each another.[32]

This cycle of mutual praise among writers closes with the warm letters that Arguedas wrote to Vargas Llosa:

> You know well how encouraged I am by what you have said about

me, and also by your work and your conduct. To me you have become like one of those children who fulfill all their parents' expectations and truly give them new life.[33]

With gratitude and hope, I recognize in you the youth of Peru and of our indigenous America. In you lies the purifying fire, the purifying hatred, and an invincible and true rebelliousness because you are immersed in life and wisdom.[34]

CÉSAR MORO: A DECISIVE INFLUENCE

Even before reading Jean Paul Sartre in the 1960s, Vargas Llosa was convinced that literature ought to have political implications. He read Sartre's essays and manifestos on committed literature with enthusiasm. He was delighted with Sartre's claim that literature could fulfill a revolutionary role without submitting to the short-term pedagogical or propagandistic imperatives of Communist parties and governments. Sartre considered that truly politically committed literature was an aesthetic response to a historical situation and that the essay *and* the newspaper were better suited to didactic prose. Vargas Llosa passionately read Sartre and in *What is Literature?* ("a kind of handbook and guide of conduct for me at one time"[35]) found a host of arguments with which to defend his own notions of politically committed literature. He was particularly interested in one of Sartre's *idées maitreses*: "each book proposes a concrete liberation on the basis of a particular alienation,"[36] and he accepted a good part of the Sartrean literary doctrine: literature is an act of rebellion in the face of an unjust society and a denunciation of bourgeois society's false concept of freedom; literature need not reflect reality in order to criticize it; socialism would resolve the congenital injustices of capitalism; literature's denunciation of capitalist injustices would contribute to the inevitable transformation toward socialism to be guided by revolutionaries; and literature would eventually be able to play an altogether different role in a just society.

Vargas Llosa could not accept, however, the main thesis of *What is literature?* that a writer in an unjust society is *obliged* to write political literature. Sartre considered human beings to be products of both their actions and their choices. A writer is a writer because he chooses to be one. For Sartre an artist's rebellion is a conscious and premeditated act: a writer decides to denounce society through literature and his work counts as his decision. For Vargas Llosa, however, the writer is unaware of his artistic motives. A writer's political convictions may be reflected in his work, but that is not something he can control. During his socialist period, Vargas Llosa saw literature as a political phenomenon because a literary work was an *unconscious* expression of a writer's dissatisfaction with capitalism, not because the writer consciously *decided* to condemn his society through literature. It is not clear whether Vargas Llosa was explicitly aware of his differences with Sartre, as he did not point them out in his writings, but they were significant. He thought that the political content of a good work of literature was not due to a writer's conscious intentions, and thus his conception of politically committed literature in this regard is anti-Sartrean in spite of his use of Sartrean arguments and of other affinities he may have had with the French philosopher.

What sets Vargas Llosa strikingly apart from Sartre's main thesis on the nature of literary creation is his insistence on unconscious and irrational elements as the fundamental explanation of the literary drive. This view was grounded in surrealism, a movement Sartre rejected along with its romantic antecedents. Surrealism reached Vargas Llosa obliquely yet decisively through the influence of the Peruvian poet César Moro (1904–1956), whom Vargas Llosa has passionately praised: "few felt the demon of creation as totally and desperately as he did."[37] Vargas Llosa considered Moro "a man for whom poetry was neither an occasional exercise nor a profession, but a definite and desperate commitment, an implacable morality."[38] The figure and the work of Moro have been present in Vargas Llosa from his first literary essays in the 1950s and throughout his writing life. Moro's verses are used as the epigraph in his novel *In Praise of the Stepmother* (1988), an indication of the surrealist's continuing influence on the novelist.

Between 1923 and 1933, Moro lived in France. A one-time friend of André Breton, he contributed to surrealist journals, signed certain surrealist manifestos, and engaged in debates with the likes of Vicente Huidobro about the place of surrealism in the avant-garde. He spent some years in Mexico, where he wrote poetry and where with Breton he organized the 1940 international exhibition of surrealism.[39] Moro expressed his personal obsessions in poems with two recurrent and related themes: a disdain for the rational elements and social conventions that censure the imagination and an exploration of forbidden erotic experiences, in particular homosexual ones. Moro upheld sexual pleasure and repudiated the society that condemned it. As Julio Ortega and James Higgins have pointed out, the eroticism in his poetry is also a kind of allegory of the relation between the poet and his poetry.[40]

Moro defended a "literature of evil" and in his essays, written in an angry stylized way of his own, he reproached Peruvian intellectuals for their "bucolic-lyrical" ideas and respect for bourgeois values: "when it comes to love they are in favor of marriage, virginity, etc., and as for art . . . they dwell on its most superficial and derisive aspects."[41] Alberto Escobar has identified rebelliousness and subversion as the defining elements of César Moro's artistic activity.[42]

In the 1930s Moro sympathized with Breton's ideas on the political function of art. At the time, the founder of surrealism had established his friendship with Leon Trotsky, with whom he collaborated on a manifesto entitled "For an independent revolutionary art." The authors of the manifesto made the claim that totally free art would further the cause of political emancipation.[43] Moro, who had contributed in Paris to the journal Le surrealisme au service de la révolution, sympathized with the ideas of the Trotsky/Breton manifesto when all three were in Mexico.[44] In his political essays—written in a stylized, aggressive language— Moro criticized fascism, Stalinism, and liberal democracies in the name of an antibureaucratic socialism:

> And we confront the dark birds of obscurantism—fascist imperialism's somber crows with their decomposed brains hanging out, imperialistic democracies with the tongue of an aardvark and the tail of a mouse, Stalinist bureaucracy with a swarm of flies in each eye—by placing our trust in man's destiny and future liberation.[45]

In The Real Life of Alejandro Mayta Vargas Llosa mentions César Moro in connection with his fictionalized account of the arrival of Trotskyist ideas in Peru: "Trotsky's ideas were brought to Peru by a handful of surrealists who had come back from Paris—Westphalen, Abril de Vivero, and César Moro."[46] In the novel, Mayta belongs to a Trotskyist political group, and his personal utopia, like César Moro's, is a socialist system that solves economic problems and eliminates sexual prejudices:

> Social, moral and sexual prejudices would give way little by little, and it wouldn't matter to anyone, in that crucible of work and faith that Peru would be in the future, that he would be living with Anatolio [his homosexual lover]. By then, they would have gotten back together, and it would be more or less obvious that, alone, free of stares, with all due discretion, they could love each other and enjoy each other. He secretly touched his fly with the hand grip of his weapon. Beautiful, isn't it, Mayta? Very. But how far off it seemed. . . .[47]

As André Coyné has pointed out, Moro abandoned his revolutionary convictions in the 1940s when he concluded that socialist states have done more damage than good. He expressed this idea in his characteristically aggressive and laconic prose:

Today, more than ever—must we insist on this?—action has revealed its incompetence. It has aborted in its cruel efforts to resolve human problems. The fatuity, ineptitude, and, at times, the bloody bestiality of men of action has become abundantly clear: these features are the daily bread gone stale. And the solution does not lie in the despicable crusade of optimism taking place in some country or another.[48]

During his socialist period Vargas Llosa interpreted Moro's political change in terms of the effectiveness with which the bourgeoisie had defused surrealism's revolutionary charge. His explanation of the failure of Moro's political project heralds one of the main themes of Vargas Llosa's earliest short stories and novels, i.e., the ability of a corrupt society to neutralize rebellion:

> [Moro was] a rebel who translated his rebelliousness into action, who sought and accepted scandal when it could serve as a true weapon. Those were the heroic days of surrealism. Its adherents truly frightened the bourgeoisie with anarchic provocations; the press silenced them, official writers hated them. Moro took part in this battle with profound conviction. Later, after the bourgeoisie had appropriated, and thus destroyed the movement founded by Breton, Moro continued, alone and in silence, to fight the battle that would bring him solitude and death.[49]

Moro retreated from public life and returned definitively to Peru in 1946 after sojourns in France and Mexico. Shortly before his return, he wrote his last poem in Spanish. It includes the infamous phrase "Lima la horrible," borrowed later by Salazar Bondy as the title of his famous essay. In Lima, Moro continued to write poetry in French but chose not to publish it.[50] During his final years he led a quiet public life making a living as a French teacher at the Leoncio Prado military school where Vargas Llosa studied. He was Vargas Llosa's teacher in the school where his first novel *The Time of the Hero* is set. Moro is one of the most significant, yet least appreciated, literary influences on Vargas Llosa. Moro's conception of literature as a spontaneous and irrational activity expressing human freedom and his contempt for writers who put literature at the service of some political program left a lifelong mark on Vargas Llosa's essays and on his creative writing.

The reclaiming of César Moro for Peruvian literature occurred posthumously.

The first Peruvian homage to him occurred in a 1958 issue of *Literatura* two years after his death. In this issue, Sebastián Salazar Bondy and Vargas Llosa honored Moro and announced André Coyné's forthcoming editions of Moro's Spanish poems and essays, most of which had remained unpublished until then.[51]

In his contribution to the commemorative issue of *Literatura,* Vargas Llosa drew a profile of César Moro that he later incorporated with minor modifications in *The Time of the Hero* where Moro becomes the school teacher Mr. Fontana:

> I remember Moro imprecisely: I see him, in a fuzzy darkness, teaching his classes at the Leoncio Prado school, undisturbed by the savage hostility of the students. We used to take out on him all the bitterness we felt for the humiliation inflicted on us by our military instructors. Someone spread the word he was a homosexual and a poet. This made him the object of malicious curiosity and of an aggressive hatred that hounded him from the moment he stepped through the gates of the school.[52]

Vargas Llosa wrote several articles about Moro's work in the 1950s and 1960s. He translated some of Moro's essays from the French, including a polemical piece against Vicente Huidobro titled "La bazofia de los perros" (The scum of the dogs), which was published in *Los anteojos de azufre,* Coyné's edition of César Moro's prose works.[53] Vargas Llosa admired Moro's poetry as well as his views about literature. He considered Moro superior to writers who sacrificed the irrationality and spontaneity of literary creation in order to serve extraliterary causes, including political ones:

> He never commercialized art, never falsified his feelings, never posed as a prophet like the "revolutionaries" who demand that poetry become a cheerleader in rags. . . . He was a committed poet who did not betray his beliefs or his emotions. He undertook his commitment with the loyalty and transparency that casts ridicule on those poets who pretend they are committed because they rehearse a rhetoric and a number of political themes about which they ultimately have little care or understanding. These poets are as insincere as the "*indigenista*" painters, fabricators of pastiches who profit from a painful reality.[54]

Vargas Llosa praised Moro using the same kinds of images that Moro used to discuss poetry's subversive force: "Poetry has ceased to be a refuge because its fiery brilliance is a danger. It is a den of fierce beasts, and it represents the advent of the anthropophagous age."[55] According to Moro, poetry liberates both imagination and body from the moral conventions of bourgeois civilization. The poet celebrates the liberation of aesthetic desire in a society corrupted by moral conventions. The poet expresses "the ubiquitous fight of man against the conditions that rule and deform his life from birth until death."[56]

For Moro, as for Vargas Llosa, morality is conventional, and creative writing occupies a realm beyond good and evil. An artist need not concern himself with issues of moral responsibility because the very concept of responsibility is irrelevant to the creative drive. Insofar as it expresses human spontaneity, literature is a challenge to society, for spontaneity is always an affront to social conventions. A crucial antecedent to Vargas Llosa's image of the demons of artistic creation is the main image of Moro's poetry, the "equestrian turtle". As James Higgins has pointed out, this image represents "the forces of the subconscious that are the vehicle of the poetic adventure."[57] In this adventure, "Moro . . . saw the artist as a revolutionary waging a campaign of subversion aimed at undermining established values and liberating mankind from its spiritual shackles."[58] Higgins gives a good summary of Moro's symbolic insurrection in his commentary on one of Moro's central poems:

> Every poetic experience, every descent into the subconscious, effectively if only temporarily, abolishes the rational world and by undermining the values on which our civilization is based foreshadows and prepares for the eventual total extinction of the civilization.[59]

Poetry is a subversive activity that transforms the artist into an enemy of civilization. Not surprisingly, one of the recurring themes of Moro's poetry is the poet's challenge of moral conventions. Vargas Llosa used the following representative fragment from a poem by Moro as the epigraph to In Praise of the Stepmother:

> One must wear one's vices like a royal mantle, with poise.
> Like an aureole that one is unaware of, that one pretends not to perceive.
> It is only natures entirely given over to vice whose contours do not grow blurred in the hyaline mire of the atmosphere.
> Beauty is a—marvelous—vice of form.[60]

Moro's view on the writer's political convictions and on the creative process can be appreciated in his essay on the politics of Paul Eluard. Although Moro condemns Eluard's "bureaucratic activity, following Moscow's orders," he is equally disdainful of those whose anti-Communist prejudices lead them to scorn his poetry.[61] Vargas Llosa agreed with the criticism that Moro began to launch in 1939 against artistic movements like *indigenismo* that subjected art to the overt demands of socialism and nationalism.[62]

In his last years, Moro grew increasingly intolerant of political literature. Like Georges Bataille in *The Accursed Share*, Moro considered both capitalism and bureaucratic Communism to be repressive systems:

> How is one to emerge from the dangerous places where salvation is as impossible as turning back? And so much the worse if "reality" repeatedly triumphs, and succeeds in convincing the eternally con-vinced by displaying its spoils—iron and cement or the hammer and sickle—and using them as definitive arguments to justify the incredible bestialization of human life.[63]

As an admirer of the Soviet Union, the young Vargas Llosa did not share Moro's contention that Communism dehumanizes man. His only reservation to Moro—elliptically expressed—could refer to Moro's disenchantment with the Soviet Union: "without sharing many of his convictions, I feel profound respect and admiration for his work."[64]

In an article titled "¿Es útil el sacrificio de la poesía?" ("Is the sacrifice of poet-ry useful?") (1959) that appeared in another issue of *Literatura,* Vargas Llosa reveals the extent to which he had made Moro's ideas his own. Criticizing Ale-jandro Romualdo—a Peruvian poet whose socialist convictions he shared—he writes, "[Romualdo] wishes to convert poetry into a weapon, an instrument of war to be used effectively against the social injustice that exasperates him."[65] According to Vargas Llosa, poets like Romualdo sacrifice both the esthet-ic quality and the political force of their poems:

> The sacrifice of poetry furthers no cause. The reader who opens a book of poems expects foremost to find poetry, and feels cheated if under the guise of poetry an attempt has been made to impose an agenda. He may not be against the political content of the poetry ... but the consequences are the same: a refusal to accept the fraud.[66]

Although Vargas Llosa may have been taken aback at Moro's disappointment with the Soviet Union, he admired the poet who had remained faithful to his literary instincts. The opposite is true in Romualdo's case: he is disappointed that Romualdo sacrificed his art in order to serve a political cause Vargas

Llosa happens to support. Vargas Llosa never abandoned his conviction that the artist, when he creates, must be faithful to his calling rather than to his political ideas. This conviction led Vargas Llosa to formulate ambiguous and contradictory ideas in an attempt to reconcile Moro's views with those of Sartre.

Both Sartre and Moro considered literature a subversive activity, but each had a different notion of subversion. For Sartre the purpose of literature was to reveal the problems that socialism would eventually resolve. For Moro its purpose was to challenge repressive societies. Like Moro, Vargas Llosa is convinced that literary creation is not a rational process, but unlike the poet he has had no interest in liberating the human being's darker side anywhere other than in fiction. During his early period Vargas Llosa defended the liberation of irrational elements in fiction inasmuch as they would contribute to the establishment of socialism. When describing the creative process, he did so in the same terms as Moro. When insisting on literature's social function he used the rebellious language common to Moro and Sartre. And when pointing to the political consequences of a writer's rebelliousness, he adopted Sartre's socialist solution. Vargas Llosa sought to avoid the Scylla of premeditated creation and the Charybdis of antisocialism in order to reconcile creative freedom with his own political ideals. But he never managed to make a convincing argument to show that creative freedom would necessarily produce literary works that would be helpful in advancing his socialist ideals.

Vargas Llosa's proposal led him to the anti-Sartrean conclusion that writers do not determine the political content of their works of fiction and that good political literature is the result of a writer's irrational motivations. But even if Vargas Llosa had come up with better arguments linking literature and socialism, his desire to assign political significance to literature belies his own literary preferences for authors such as Gustave Flaubert, Alexandre Dumas, César Moro, and Jorge Luis Borges, none of whose works could be considered politically committed in the Sartrean sense.

FOR AN INDEPENDENT REVOLUTIONARY LITERATURE

The difficulty Vargas Llosa had in reconciling his arguments for politically committed literature with his defense of the autonomy of literature is most evident in his essay on Joanot Martorell's novel *Tirant lo Blanc*.[67] Vargas Llosa went to great lengths to have this Valencian novel translated into Spanish for the first time since the sixteenth century, and he wrote a substantive prologue for the 1969 Spanish edition. His enthusiasm for the novel led to translations into other languages, including English, and sparked growing interest in *Tirant lo Blanc* in the literary world. Vargas Llosa discovered this classic of Iberian literature in Lima while studying at San Marcos University. Later, after working on his doctorate in literature in Madrid, he read Dámaso Alonso's pioneering essay advocating that *Tirant lo Blanc* be reread as a modern novel.[68] In his own essays on Martorell, Vargas Llosa supported Alonso's thesis that *Tirant lo Blanc* is a modern novel because it breaks away from the medieval schemes of the romance of chivalry. During his socialist period, however, Vargas Llosa gave this thesis a twist by suggesting that the novel was politically subversive.

Although he tried to cast Joanot Martorell as a "rebel radical" and a "vulture feeding on historical waste" and passionately insisted that his literature heralded the fall of the Middle Ages, what Vargas Llosa most admired about Martorell was not the political implications of his work. Rather, he focused on the text's aesthetic qualities: the ease with which Martorell creates an autonomous literary world, his capacity to construct a story by linking events that occur at different times and in different places, his ability to interweave narratives within narratives, and his way of moving from an apparently objective, concrete reality to another clearly subjective, invented one. Vargas Llosa praises these purely literary elements for their artistic merits.[69]

Vargas Llosa's assessment of Martorell suggests a thesis that challenges his own notions about politically committed literature, namely, that art survives and transcends its social and historical motivations.

In evaluating Martorell, Vargas Llosa does not flesh out the issue of the political worth and possible usefulness of a novel of Chivalry to revolutionary causes, and he was probably wise not to press the issue. Instead, he focuses on the triumph of fantasy over reality: "The novel is so coherently put together that it gives the illusion of truth. The novel's persuasive power can deceive one into believing that the fantasy is a reality."[70] The specific instances of social denunciation that Vargas Llosa identified in the Iberian classic were minor and perhaps aleatoric. Consequently, after abandoning his socialist convictions, he continued to develop his ideas on the novel's literary aspects and stopped insisting on its political implications.[71]

By 1967 Vargas Llosa had become increasingly aware that he was on shaky grounds when he tried to prove that a writer's irrational motivations would necessarily produce works of literature that would contribute to socialist causes.[72] There were occasions on which, with a touch of humorous irony, he acknowledged the tensions between his political positions and aesthetic ideas: "Revolution and literature are two equally absorbing and exclusive lovers, and each is terribly jealous. Whoever goes to bed with both runs the risk of being torn to pieces at any moment by one or the other (or sometimes by both)."[73] At moments of more serious reflection he expressed the central ambiguity of his ideas on the socialist implications of art: "In a way, a creator faces a true duplicity, or, at least a great tension: he wants to be faithful to a certain political conception while remaining faithful to his calling."[74] This duplicity is also experienced by some of Vargas Llosa's characters sympathetic toward the revolutionary Left who are unable to accept the literary doctrines of Communism. For example, Santiago Zavala, in *Conversation in the Cathedral*, feels that his sensibilities conflict with the Marxist doctrines of his political group. Santiago despises social realist novels but admires writers like Kafka whom his comrades consider decadent and bourgeois.[75] Vargas Llosa himself expressed a similar uneasiness in a public dialogue with Gabriel García Márquez when he admitted that he tried in vain to show that the fictions of Jorge Luis Borges, the Spanish-language author he most admires, were of any value to socialist causes.[76]

Vargas Llosa also hesitated whenever he thought seriously about the role of literature in a socialist society. With trepidation he recognized that if literature's role is to denounce social injustices, it would lose its purpose in just societies. In the midst a polemic with the Uruguayan critic Angel Rama, he went so far as to claim that he would long for the disappearance of literature if socialism were established in Latin America: "Nothing would be more beautiful to me than a world without "demons". . . . For such a world I am prepared to welcome the disappearance of this calling which constitutes my life."[77] At other times he stated that under socialism the political power of literature would diminish, but it would not altogether disappear because no political system can do away with all injustices and all the causes of human discontent:

> Perfect societies do not and will not exist. Socialism knows better than anyone that man is infinitely perfectible. Literature contributes to human improvement by preventing spiritual recession, self-satisfaction, stagnation, paralysis, and intellectual and moral deterioration. Its mission is to agitate, to disturb, to alarm, and to keep men constantly dissatisfied with themselves.[78]

He also speculated that in a just society the role of fiction might have an extended future because a new type of erotic or mystic novel could arise.[79]

Vargas Llosa recognized that, in theory, the writer may feel torn between his literary calling and his political convictions. This tension, however, ought not affect the Latin American writer's role as intellectual or citizen in denouncing misery and in calling for the Socialist revolution. This was the main idea of a declaration he made in Cuba entitled "On the Role of the Intellectual in National Liberation Movements."[80] Vargas Llosa was optimistic that under the Cuban model, Latin American writers would no longer feel torn about their literary vocations because, he thought, the Cuban revolution had redressed social injustices while respecting freedom of expression.

While worried about the potential tension between a socialist intellectual's literary calling and his political convictions in capitalist states, Vargas Llosa remained cold and insensitive to another kind of personal dilemma: that of Albert Camus and others who could not reconcile their socialist ideals with the reality of Communist parties and Socialist states. In his postwar writings, Albert Camus exhorted Socialists troubled by the atrocities committed in Socialist states to consider the dilemma that led him to repudiate Communism. They can either tolerate Stalinist crimes in the name of Communist ideals or reject Marxist ideology because it serves to rationalize immoral behavior: "If they chose the former, their crisis of conscience will end, but if they admit the latter they would demonstrate that this era marks the end of ideologies."[81]

Vargas Llosa rejected Camus's moral dilemma. Although he conceded the existence of Stalinist atrocities, he considered them aberrations of socialism that would disappear as Communist states matured. Taking Sartre's side in his famous polemic with Camus, Vargas Llosa dismissed the writer of *The Rebel* as a confused intellectual and criticized him for repudiating the French Communist party, for his general disavowal of revolutionary activity and for his unwillingness to support the armed struggle to emancipate Algeria from France: "It is enough to read *The Rebel* to realize that [Camus's] thought is vague and superficial: banalities and empty formulas abound, problems always lead into the same blind alleys which he paces interminably like a prisoner in his tiny cell."[82]

The tension Vargas Llosa identified between a creative writer's vocation and his political convictions should not be confused with Camus's inability to be a Communist in the light of the inhumanity of revolutionary leaders and Socialist states. He had no patience for writers who condemned Communist regimes and revolutionary causes. In the 1970s Vargas Llosa did not question the supremacy of Soviet-style regimes and believed that only intellectuals and political leaders committed to Communism had the right to criticize their flaws. Nevertheless, he did worry about the possible discrepancy between a creative writer's political convictions and the political contents of his works.

In spite of this unease on an abstract or general level, on a personal level he felt untouched by possible dilemmas of the socialist writer because his support of Socialist regimes was solid and because he felt his own novels exemplified his doctrine of the demons of literary creation: he claimed to write them following his own irrational instincts, without making any artistic concessions, and they were in harmony with his socialist convictions. In a lecture on the genesis of *The Time of the Hero*, Vargas Llosa pointed out that his novel described "the tragedies of a broader reality, the reality of my country, Peruvian reality."[83] He added, however, that his personal achievement was not the result of premeditated intention:

> It was not my conscious intention, when writing the novel, to denounce the evils of my country, or even the evils of the Leoncio Prado school. I mainly wished to liberate myself from a kind of ghost, a kind of obsession that I had dragged around since my years as a cadet.[84]

Vargas Llosa insisted that his novels were about an intrinsically unjust society, laden with hypocrisy, criminality, and exploitation; but he was equally adamant in insisting that his literary motivations were personal rather than political: "The truth is that in writing that novel *The Time of the Hero*, in writing stories or anything else, I had never intended to address social, political or moral problems."[85]

Vargas Llosa was pleased with himself. He felt that his own novels confirmed his aesthetic ideas because he characterized them as unconscious acts of rebellion against a society whose injustices warranted a Socialist revolution. His own demons were apparently quite capable of producing politically valuable works of art, and he felt reassured about the political significance of his novels by his growing prestige among prominent leftist intellectuals around the world. He was especially gratified by the official recognition he had received from the Cuban government. He participated on editorial boards, on juries for literary prizes, and in other activities sponsored by the cultural organizations of the Cuban revolution. He was proud that many considered him to be an intellectual spokesman for the Cuban revolution ever since he denounced the Bay of Pigs invasion in the French press.[86]

In his socialist phase, Vargas Llosa sometimes conceded that literature's political effectiveness could be relative, but he never hesitated to criticize capitalism, to support Latin American revolutionary movements, and to defend what he considered to be two socialist ideals, both in theory and as embodied in the Cuban revolution: socialism and freedom of expression.[87]

Vargas Llosa zealously formulated a set of suggestive but irreconcilable propositions: he defended the irrational element in literary creation, the writer's absolute freedom of speech, the autonomy of literature, the moral and political superiority of socialism both in theory and practice, the inevitability of the advent of socialism, and the participation of independent literature in revolutionary movements. In the process he conceded that it is difficult to reconcile a literary calling with political militancy. Vargas Llosa was a socialist who defended the autonomy of art to the point of dissociating an artist's creative work from his political convictions, but his assumption that good literature would necessarily further socialist causes proved too optimistic. It led him to recognize an obvious dilemma he was not yet willing to resolve: if literature is autonomous it need not contribute to socialist causes, but if it has to contribute to socialist causes it is not autonomous. When he realized his own dilemma was impossible to resolve, he decided to live with the contradiction:

> The creative writer is pulled in two directions, or at least he experiences a terrible tension: he wants to be faithful to a given political conception and at the same time needs to be faithful to his calling. If both coincide, all is well; if they diverge, an inner tension emerges. This tension, however, must not be avoided. It must be faced head on, and the writer must use the contradiction to make literature, to create. It is a difficult option, tortured perhaps, yet inevitable.[88]

CHAPTER TWO

The Novels of the 1960s

Vargas Llosa eventually abandoned his ideas about the socialist implications of literature, but he has always defined his artistic aspirations in terms of Flaubert's concept of the novel as an aesthetic creation *in prose.*[1] He admired the artistic independence of Flaubert who did not write short stories and novels to make moral, historical, or religious points, even though he did use morality, history, and theology as inspiration for his literary themes.[2] Flaubert was not concerned with the accurate portrayal of reality or with a writer's moral or emotional attitude toward his characters. He was concerned with a novelist's ability to create a convincing work of art. Flaubert believed that any theme is suitable for literature. A novel should not be judged by the intrinsic significance of its theme but by the author's success in conceiving the literary devices most suitable for developing it into a work of art: "'*Everything depends on its conception.*' This axiom of the great Goethe is the simplest and most marvelous precept of all possible works of art."[3]

Flaubert was annoyed by novelists who interrupt their stories to express personal feelings, judgments, and opinions. He considered the narrator's interventions as irksome mediations and preferred the distance created between the writer and his fictional world when the narrator limits himself to describing the internal and external world of his characters. He preferred that a narrator be present in his work, to quote his well known apothegm, "like God in his creation—invisible and all-powerful: he must be everywhere felt, but never seen."[4] The Flaubertian narrator describes the feelings and thoughts of his characters, rather than those of the author. The writer silences his personal feelings and opinions and concentrates on the two elements that can turn a theme into a work of art: form and language. Vargas Llosa saw Flaubert as a turning point in the history of the novel: novels written before him are primitive and those written following his example are modern.[5] While the primitive novelist attempts to reflect or document realities, experiences, emotions, and values, the modern novelist draws on these to produce a work of art. The primitive novel is subservient to facts, feelings, and morals; the modern novel transmutes life into art.

Unlike the primitive novelist, the modern novelist knows that the narrator is a creation of the author, that every fact is colored by a perspective, and that the art of the novel entails the organization of narrative time while information is either presented or disguised. The vitality of narrative fiction does not depend on the story but on how it is told.[6] The modern novelist is not concerned with issues of sincerity, morality, originality, or fidelity to anything outside the text, but with the form suitable to whatever theme he has chosen, the development of a style and the care of language. After Flaubert, the modern novelist knows that one theme is ultimately as good as another and that in fiction "everything depends essentially on form, the deciding factor in determining whether a subject is beautiful or ugly, true or false . . . the novelist must be above all else an artist, a tireless and incorruptible craftsman of style."[7] Vargas Llosa has always held that the themes of literature are determined by a writer's personal obsessions, but the artistic value of a particular work depends on the writer's labor, on his "rational control of intuition."[8]

The greatest novelists before Flaubert were "intuitive geniuses," according to Vargas Llosa, because their novels are works of art even when their intentions were not primarily artistic.[9] The first intuitive genius was Joanot Martorell and the last one Victor Hugo. Vargas Llosa still considers *Les Misérables*, which he read as a cadet at the Leoncio Prado school, "one of the great creations of Western narrative fiction."[10]

For Vargas Llosa the writer who perfected the methods of the modern novel was William Faulkner, who used the achievement of James Joyce and Virginia Woolf—the interior monologue—to write novels where spatial and chronological planes are superimposed, where a single story can be narrated from various contradictory points of view, and where mystery and intrigue depend not only on the plot but also on intentional vagueness or ambiguity and on the fact that significant information may be hidden from the reader. In only two instances—in his first articles on José María Arguedas and in an essay on *A Day in the Life of Ivan Denisovich* by Alexander Solzhenitsyn—did Vargas Llosa praise literature for a faithful portrayal of a historical or political reality. These assessments, difficult to reconcile with his general ideas on literature as art, seem to be colored by strong personal sympathies, moral sentiments, and political convictions.[11]

VARGAS LLOSA'S LITERARY AMALGAM

Vargas Llosa has explained the development of the Latin American novel with the same criteria he used to define the modern novel. Until the first decades of the twentieth century (with the notable exception of Machado de Assis) the Latin American novel was primitive because, superficially imitating the European novel, it confused description with art. In Vargas Llosa's estimation no Spanish American novelist wrote a single work of literary merit in the nineteenth and early twentieth century:

> none of our romantic or realist narrators forged a literary world of universal value, a portrayal of reality—faithful or unfaithful— that was convincing.[12]

The only redeeming features of early twentieth century Latin American narrative are extraliterary. The primitive novel, at its best, attempts to represent Latin American realities and customs with "an impulse toward social critique."[13] Yet he insists that these novels can be dismissed because good political intentions do not compensate for poor literary results. His critique of *La vorágine* by José Eustasio Rivera is emblematic:

> The technique is rudimentary, pre-Flaubertian: the intrusive author interrupts the narrative to give his opinions, ignoring the notion of objectivity in fiction and the fact that his handling of the literary point of view is sloppy. Rather than showing he attempts to prove. Like a romantic novelist, he believes that what makes a novel interesting is the originality of the story rather than its treatment.[14]

For Vargas Llosa, the new Latin American novel has triumphed because its greatest practioners, including Carlos Fuentes, José Lezama Lima, and Gabriel García Márquez, are masters of narrative form.[15] In his view the Latin American novel reaches maturity when novelists no longer write to document the realities of their countries, when "the novel ceases to be 'Latin American,' and is thus freed from that burden."[16] Latin American novelists do not have to ignore their continent's reality, but they should not feel bound to it when writing fiction. Like all good novelists, good Latin American novelists make use of their experiences, readings, and imaginations as they see fit. The Latin American novel ceases to be primitive when it can be read like any other good novel, as a valid literary world.

Vargas Llosa has remained faithful to the Flaubertian principles with which he defined the modern novel. Like Flaubert, Conrad, and Faulkner—to cite three of his favorite novelists—Vargas Llosa has avoided the strategy of an omniscient narrator as spokesman for the author. The opinions and feelings in Vargas Llosa's works can always be attributed either to his characters or to his narrators, even when they appear to be autobiographical.

His definition of the modern novel expresses his own literary aspirations. He likes to fuse autobiographical, political, historical, and literary sources as he develops a self-contained literary world. His attitude toward originality in literature is well summarized in his statement—inspired perhaps by Hemingway— that the modern novelist engages in "a systematic plundering of everything within reach of his sensibility."[17] Part of the process of pillaging includes the appropriation of themes, characters and methods from other literary works:

> Imitation in literature is not a moral problem but an artistic one: all writers use, to varying degrees, forms that have been used before, but only those incapable of transforming these plagiarisms into something personal deserve to be called imitators.[18]

Like some of his characters who also write novels, Vargas Llosa borrows and modifies other writers' themes and methods.[19]

Each of his books makes use of the author's experience, his readings, or the anecdotes he has heard in conversation.[20] This does not imply, however, that his literature is autobiographical, political, or historical or that its intention is informative or documentary. To consider his works of fiction in this light would go against the grain of Vargas Llosa's adamant conviction that good literature ought to recreate reality, not reflect it. What differentiates a novel from a historical or biographical testimony is the element of fantasy.[21]

Vargas Llosa's literary sources are his raw materials. He has never hesitated to use or modify the characters, forms, and themes of the novels he has read, transform the facts of some personal anecdote, falsify the past of some well known personality, alter historical dates, or distort information from the geographic or anthropological publications he consulted while researching his literary themes.

One of Vargas Llosa's main sources of inspiration is undoubtedly his own experience: as a youth he attended the school that provides the main setting for *The Time of the Hero* (1963); his journeys to the Peruvian jungle helped him to create some of the key places and characters of *The Green House* (1965); his experience as an adolescent and as a university student during the 1950s inform the central situations of *Conversation in the Cathedral* (1969); and since *Aunt Julia and the Scriptwriter* (1977), first-person narrators whose experiences are deceptively similar to those of Vargas Llosa appear in his novels. In spite of the abundant autobiographical elements in his work, however, Vargas Llosa has never written short stories and novels to document his own life. As he has explained on numerous occasions in discussing the origins of his literary ideas, personal experiences are merely a point of departure. They are invariably transformed by fantasy and amalgamated with other elements that have little to do with his life.

Books, film, and painting are as crucial as his own personal experiences to the development of Vargas Llosa's literary works. In fact, his own fiction provides ideas for new novels, short stories, and plays. Over the years, his oeuvre is becoming a "human comedy" as his novels and plays are increasingly interconnected. The characters in *La señorita de Tacna* (*The Young Lady of Tacna*) (1981) avidly listen to the radio melodramas of Pedro Camacho from *Aunt Julia and the Scriptwriter* (1977). Santiago Zavala from *Conversation in the Cathedral* (1969) reappears in *Kathie y el hipopótamo* (Kathie and the hippopotamus) (1984). Saúl Zuratas's mother in *The Storyteller* (1987) is from Talara, the same town where a murder takes place in *Who Killed Palomino Molero?* (1986). The central anecdote of *La Chunga* (1986) is featured in at least two novels. Characters and anecdotes from *The Green House* (1966) reappear in *Aunt Julia and the Scriptwriter, La Chunga, Who Killed Palomino Molero?* and *The Storyteller*. *Los Cuadernos de don Rigoberto* (The Notebooks of Don Rigoberto) (1997) is a sequel to *In Praise of the Stepmother* (1988). Vargas Llosa's most recurrent character, Lituma, appears in at least seven fictional works: as criminal, as policeman, as soldier, and as unemployed person. These versions of Lituma represent different moments and pieces of a life story in different places spanning the coast, the sierra, and the jungle of Peru. In *Death in the Andes* (1993), his latest incarnation, Lituma is a criminal investigator in a region where the Shining Path guerrilla movement is active. Vargas Llosa has also expressed his desire to write a novel giving unity to Lituma's life.[22]

In sum, Vargas Llosa's novels can be read as a kind of amalgam of his own experiences, literary works, other genres including cinema, and the research he has done at libraries around the world. Vargas Llosa's fiction, from his first published short stories to his latest novel, contains echoes and parallels that can be traced to a greater or lesser degree back to literary and non-literary sources. Yet he has transmuted, modified, and combined them with his own inventions until the work of fiction develops its own self-contained character.

When Vargas Llosa writes a work of fiction, he always begins with an experience, reading, or observation that he transforms into a disorganized and often lengthy rough draft. He modifies the literary techniques of other writers or invents his own. Freely borrowing themes and characters from literature, he recasts them to fit with his own inventions. The literary world that emerges from this process gives the illusion of self-sufficiency and is undoubtedly his own. During his socialist period, his literary works were informed by the view that Peruvian society was too corrupt to be reformed. He fashioned a literary world where social respectability is a mask for corruption, where rebelliousness is crushed by institutions that defend the established order, and where failure is a precondition to morality because success is not possible without co-optation. His concern with a society too corrupt for reform is ubiquitous in all his narrative works from *Los jefes* (The leaders) (1959) to *Conversation in the Cathedral* (1969).

THE SHORT STORIES

In his first works of fiction, Mario Vargas Llosa created an environment of hypocrisy, criminality, and exploitation, a world of oppressors and oppressed, where vileness can be avoided only through failure and where rebelliousness is invariably neutralized. His first two books are about the integration, the rebelliousness, or the exclusion of the individual from the social milieu. In *Los jefes* (1959) and *The Time of the Hero* (1963), adolescents defy one another and rebel against authority.[23] Vargas Llosa's rebels are not anarchical; they establish and live by strict codes of behavior. As Luis Harss has pointed out, his "protagonists are hard boiled adolescents—or postadolescents—who live by a system of rugged priorities."[24] Vargas Llosa explores the mechanisms by which his adolescent characters are integrated into a corrupt society: they lose their innocence once they understand that morality is a mirage, a convenient veneer adopted by corrupt individuals and institutions.

With the exception of "The Grandfather," his first literary exploration of the "dark side" of humanity—the story of a perverse old man attracted by Satanism—each of the short stories in *Los jefes* establishes a tension between those who defend and those who defy the established order. In "The Leaders," the story that gives the collection its title, which is also the first fictional work Vargas Llosa ever published, two rivals become friends: they are the only rebel schoolboys who have not been intimidated by the school's unjust and arbitrary authorities. "On Sunday" (1957) is also about a friendship between two rivals.[25] But here the youths are brought together in their willingness to lie about each other in an environment where hypocrisy insures social success. While they can tolerate lies, Vargas Llosa's rebels do not accept betrayal or transgression of their tacit codes of honor, especially those that regulate the settling of scores. In "The Challenge," which is set in an underworld environment of hoodlums, a father allows his son to die rather than to violate the rituals of street fighting. These characters are indifferent to lying, cheating, and stealing, but they are firm in seeking vengeance when they feel betrayed or humiliated. In "The Younger Brother," Vargas Llosa's only *indigenista* story, two brothers ambush an Indian they believe has forced himself on their sister. The brothers find out that the purported rape was a capricious lie after they have already murdered the Indian. While the elder brother does not repent, the younger brother feels remorse for his crime. To compensate for the murder, he liberates a group of Indians detained at his *hacienda's* makeshift prison. This seemingly noble action only reaffirms the arbitrariness with which he and his brother exercise power on their landed estate.

The true marginal characters in Vargas Llosa's early stories are those who disregard the norms not only of the established order but also of the rebel groups. One such character is the protagonist of "A Visitor." In this story one criminal informs on another in exchange for freedom and is abandoned in the desert by the police officers—among them Lituma, future protagonist of *The Green House*—with whom he collaborated. The protagonist of the story is an outcast because he respects neither the law of the land nor the solidarity that thieves expect of one another and that the police tacitly respect. They know that in the desert, where they left him, he will be vulnerable to the deadly retaliation of the associates of the criminal he betrayed.

Los cachorros (The Cubs) (1967) was written some ten years after *Los jefes*. This novella whose theme is related to *Conversation in the Cathedral* (1969) is widely recognized by literary critics as artistically superior to the other stories.[26] As Guadalupe Fernández Ariza has shown, *The Cubs* includes some of the characters from the social world of Santiago Zavala, the young man of the 1969 novel who rejects his corrupt social class and refuses to participate in the rites of social integration. The protagonist of *The Cubs* is a relative of Santiago, and they belong to the same social milieu.[27] All the same, the publication of this novella in a volume with *Los jefes* is quite appropriate. While the earlier stories are about the co-optation of rebellion, *The Cubs* explores the exclusion of individuals useless to social reproduction. The protagonist of the tale, Pichula Cuéllar, is a youth who was emasculated by a dog in a freak accident. His physical defect renders him useless to a society whose main function is to reproduce itself. Pichula has been put in an impossible situation because he belongs to a society where inheritance and power fill the void made by the absence of morality. The indifference of his classmates, the "cubs" of Peruvian society, increases as Pichula's self-destructive behavior leads him to suicide. Skillfully manipulating both point of view and narrative time, Vargas Llosa concludes the novella by alternating between two grammatical voices: a second-person masculine collective voice that expresses the cold reaction of the protagonist's peers to his suicide, and a neutral third-person voice that accelerates narrative time to show how the classmates, as adults, have reproduced the world of their parents:

> Poor guy, we said at the funeral, how much he suffered, what a life he had, but this finish is something he had in store for him.
>
> They were mature and settled men by now and we all had a wife, car, children who studied at Champagnat, Immaculate Conception of St. Mary's, and they are building themselves a little summerhouse in Ancon, St. Rose or the beaches in the south, and we began to get fat and to have gray hair, pot-bellies, soft bodies, to wear reading glasses, to feel uneasy after eating and drinking and age spots already showed up on their skin as well as certain wrinkles.[28]

The destiny of Pichula Cuéllar, like that of all the characters in Vargas Llosa's early fiction from *Los jefes* to *Conversation in the Cathedral*, depends on his inclusion in or exclusion from the groups and social hierarchies that either defend the existing order or rebel against it in vain.

THE TIME OF THE HERO

In *Los jefes*, Vargas Llosa explored the theme of adolescent rebelliousness. In *The Time of the Hero* he drew further on this theme as he wrote what is arguably the most important Spanish American novel on adolescence. Vargas Llosa transformed his own experiences in the Leoncio Prado military school to create a corrupt social milieu: a pedagogical institution that prepares its students to function in Peruvian society because it makes a mockery of the values it is supposed to uphold, especailly those suggested by its motto, "obedience, courage, and hard work." The boarding school brings together Indians just arrived from the Andes, upper class boys sent there as punishment for their lack of discipline, young hoodlums rejected by their families, and adolescents from modest urban families proud to attend an institution that will prepare them for military careers.[29]

The boarders ruthlessly break the school's moral codes. Although they believe they are mocking the vigilance of their teachers while breaking the norms of their institutions, they are actually preparing themselves to function in Peruvian society where morality is a mirage that conceals a state of profound corruption. The Spanish title "La ciudad y los perros" (The city and the dogs) suggests a relation between the cadets of the academy (the first-year students are called "dogs" by their classmates), and the city of Lima where the school is located. The English version of the title was chosen by Vargas Llosa's editor even though the author would have preferred a direct translation of the original Spanish:

> My novel *La ciudad y los perros* was given the English title of *The Time of the Hero*. I must say I did not like it because *The Time of the Hero* does not give the same ideas as the original title. But the title was chosen by my publisher. When I suggested "The City and the Dogs," he said that that title was not at all catchy; and so we gave the novel a more catchy title. [30]

The plot structure of *The Time of the Hero* provides a kind of devastating mirror in which the corruption of school reflects the corruption of the larger society. Four Leoncio Prado cadets—Cava, Rulos, the Boa, and their leader, the Jaguar—belong to a secret group called "the circle." One night they meet to plan the robbery of a chemistry exam. By a game of dice, Cava (known as "the Peasant") is designated to steal the exam. During his shift as sentry, the cadet Ricardo Arana (known as "the Slave"), who knows about the circle's activities, sees Cava approaching the classrooms. The school's authorities discover the theft but are unable to identify the culprit. The cadets are not allowed to leave the school while the case is being investigated. Arana is unable to tolerate the punishment because he wants to visit his girl friend, Teresa. Because he feels compelled to name the thief but wants no trouble with the members of the circle, Arana secretly identifies Cava, who is then expelled from the school. Shortly afterwards, during military training games, the Slave is struck by a bullet that pierces his skull, perhaps an accident but perhaps a murder. On the basis of circumstantial evidence, cadet Alberto Fernández is certain that the Jaguar committed the crime. He is willing to make a formal accusation to their adult superior, Lieutenant Gamboa. In spite of the lieutenant's attempts to conduct a proper criminal investigation, the school authorities decide to protect the institution from any suspicion of foul play or negligence by claiming that Ricardo Arana killed himself accidentally. The reflection is complete.

The Time of the Hero impressed readers because of its vitality and because of its deft usage of sophisticated literary technique. Its formal scheme was unusual for a Latin American novel, but it was not original: the use of narrative time, the development of one of the main characters, and the vicissitudes of the plot can all be traced directly to *Light in August*, which Vargas Llosa still considers his favorite Faulkner novel. Vargas Llosa has given hints about Faulkner's significance for *The Time of the Hero*:

> [Faulkner] was the first novelist whom I wished to remake and rationally reconstruct by paying attention to how, in his novels, time was organized, how different spatial and chronological planes intersected, how sudden shifts occurred, and how it is possible to tell a story from different contradictory perspectives, in order to create ambiguity, mystery and depth.[31]

A brief review of *Light in August* will help provide insight into how Vargas Llosa wrote his first novel.

The core of *Light in August* relates an intense period in the lives of Lena Grove and Joe Christmas. Although these two characters do not know each other, crucial events in their lives take place in the same town in the month of August. The core events of the novel begin on the day the pregnant Lena, looking for her lover, arrives in the imaginary town of Jefferson, Mississippi, and Joe Christmas murders the spinster Joanne Burden. They conclude a month later, to the day, when Lena gives birth and Christmas dies as a fugitive killed by officer Percy Grimm.

The time-scheme of the novel is one of concentric circles: the last month of Joe Christmas's life is circumscribed by the longer three year period during which he lived in Jefferson, and Faulkner adds retrospective sections that explore the pasts of the three protagonists (Joe, Joanne Burden, and the reverend Gail Hightower, a character whose importance increases as the novel progresses).

Even though most people consider him to be a white man, Joe Christmas, the main character of the novel, is obsessed with the possibility of being black.[32] Christmas had been expelled from an orphanage for white children after the janitor, a character with evil intentions, raised questions about the child's race. That incident set Joe Christmas's life on a course of self-torment, violence, and criminality.

The vitality of Faulkner's fiction lies as much in his literary technique as in his plot. The most surprising moment in the novel does not depend on the action but on the fact that the narrator reveals a hidden fact at a particularly timely moment. This occurs toward the end of the novel, when it is revealed that Doc Hines—an angry and spiteful man who calls for Joe Christmas's death—is both Joe's maternal grandfather and the malicious janitor who schemed to have Joe expelled from his orphanage. Hines had murdered his daughter's lover (Joe's father) when he suspected the man might have black blood. For similar reasons he has pursued and slandered his grandson from childhood. Joe is a criminal, but the citizens of Jefferson do not despise him because he murdered Joanna Burden. The fury with which the citizens of Jefferson pursue Joe is a consequence of their perceptions that a black man has had sexual relations with a white woman. Faulkner is deliberately ambiguous about Joe's racial identity, which highlights the arbitrary cruelty of a racist society. The ambiguity about Joe's race leaves open various possibilities regarding a key fact in the action, but it does not sacrifice clarity. On the contrary, it elegantly brings the main theme of the novel into sharper focus, a Faulknerian procedure that Vargas Llosa uses so fruitfully in *The Time of the Hero* and onward.

In his first novel Vargas Llosa relied on *Light in August*. In both novels the central anecdote relates to a botched criminal investigation, and the main suspect was once an innocent child whose circumstances led him to a life of crime. In both novels, narrative time is organized on three levels: the main events of the plot occur in a matter of several weeks, the events are circumscribed in a three year period, and—to add depth—the past lives of three characters are also included.

In *The Time of the Hero,* the three levels of narrative time correspond to the main narrative threads of the novel. The first thread is also the main plot, beginning with the sequence of events that result from the theft of the chemistry exam and that culminate with Arana's death and with the successful efforts of the school's authority to preclude a criminal investigation. The main plot, therefore, takes place during the last couple of months before the protagonists were to graduate from the school. The second thread narrates, in an intermittent and fragmented way, the experiences of the protagonists during their three years of school. The third thread recounts the past of three of the cadets before they entered the Leoncio Prado school. Like Faulkner, Vargas Llosa uses two strategies to complicate his narrative: making a key fact ambiguous—the novel never reveals whether Ricardo Arana was actually murdered or killed accidentally—and concealing the identity of a central character in certain sections of the novel to achieve a surprising effect when he is later identified. In the last pages of the novel Vargas Llosa reveals that the nameless character appearing throughout the novel is the Jaguar, the same procedure Faulkner uses with Doc Hines.

The Time of the Hero is made up of elementary units, short narratives or "sequences," to use José Miguel Oviedo's useful terminology.[33] These sequences are organized into larger units: two books made up of chapters, and an epilogue. Book 1 narrates the incidents that lead to the death of Ricardo Arana;

and book 2 tells of the consequences of the death. The sequences pertaining to Ricardo's death alternate with those of the other two narrative threads in the novel: the lives of three boys before entering the school and the three years of their lives as cadets. Each of the three narrative threads follows a chronological order, but the novel complicates narrative time by moving fluidly among the three distinct threads. Thus, a sequence about the theft of the exam may be followed by a sequence about the childhood of one of the protagonists, and the next sequence may recount an event that occurred during one of the cadets' outings to the city months before the theft of the exam.

As in Faulkner's novels, the narrative strategies in *The Time of the Hero* are heterogeneous: the sequences pertaining to Ricardo Arana's death are narrated in the third-person preterite and imperfect. The story of the cadets' three years of schooling is mainly narrated in the third-person present. The first-person present interior monologue sections by the depraved "Boa"—a secondary character—provide information about the first two narrative series and offer an inside view of the cruelty at the military school.[34] The sequences on the lives of Alberto Fernández and Ricardo Arana prior to their admittance to the school are narrated in the third-person preterite, while those about a cadet (who is not identified as the Jaguar until the last few pages of the novel) are narrated in the first-person preterite. These sequences reveal an innocent youth who becomes a criminal molded by the violent environment in which he grew up.

Vargas Llosa drew on *Light in August* and on his personal experience to develop the main characters of *The Time of the Hero*, although it would be misleading to argue that these characters are strictly autobigraphically drawn. The Jaguar is clearly a transmutation of Faulkner's Joe Christmas, while both Ricardo (the Slave) and Alberto Fernández are inventions based on Vargas Llosa's personal experiences. The first rough draft of *The Time of the Hero*, which is at the Vargas Llosa Collection at Princeton University, offers illuminating clues to how Vargas Llosa transforms autobiographical information in the gestation of his literary characters.[35] In the draft, Alberto is a character from the world of *Los Jefes*. He was a student in the Salesian school in Piura, where Vargas Llosa also studied. His father is a violent and unfaithful man who separates from his wife. Years later, when the couple reconcile, he decides that his son has become effeminate in his absence and decides to send him to the military school. In the novel Vargas Llosa eliminated Alberto's Piura past. More significantly, he developed *two* distinct characters from the original Alberto: Alberto and Ricardo. Likewise, Alberto's father in the rough draft becomes two distinct characters in the novel: Alberto's father is an unfaithful husband who would lie to keep up the appearances of a happy marriage; Ricardo's is a violent and abusive man. In the novel Alberto's father is of a higher social class than Ricardo's.

Although *The Time of the Hero* is considerably indebted to Faulkner and particularly to *Light in August*, Vargas Llosa's literary world is not the same as Faulkner's, where the latent rancor of repressed or intolerant men erupts in acts of violence and racial hatred. Faulkner's introspective, tormented, and fanatical characters exercise their free will. By contrast, Vargas Llosa's characters are beholden to codes of behavior they cannot change. Jorge Luis Borges—who translated Faulkner into Spanish—once remarked that North American realism moves from sentimentalism to cruelty.[36] Vargas Llosa's realism can be said to move from cruelty to disenchantment. In his fiction, acts of aggression can harm individual victims but do not affect the immoral social order. Evoking a title Vargas Llosa considered for his novel, Alberto Escobar labels the youths and adults at the military school "impostors" because they lack moral values.[37]

In *Time of the Hero* the frustrations encouraged by the school's oppressive environment find an escape valve in romance, in sexuality, and in the alternative realities of fiction. These three themes come together in the character Alberto Fernández, also known as "the Poet." He writes love letters and pornographic stories and exchanges them for money, alcohol, tobacco, or for the exams stolen by "the circle." It is ironic that Alberto—sent to Leoncio Prado after the humiliating failure of his romance with a girl named Helena—should write love letters for his classmates to send to their girlfriends and equally ironic that he enthralls his fellow cadets with pornographic stories about the sexual adventures in local brothels: they, not he, have had sexual experiences. Alberto entered Leoncio Prado partly to comply with his father's wishes but also to escape the humiliation he felt after Helena's rejection. Both his failed adolescent romance and his sexual inexperience highlight the compensatory nature of Alberto's imagination:

> No one suspected that he knew about Huatica Street and its environs by hearsay, because he repeated anecdotes he had been told and invented all kinds of lurid stories. But he could not overcome a certain inner discontent. The more he talked about sexual adventures to his friends, who either laughed or shamelessly thrust their hands into their pockets, the more certain he was that he would never go to bed with a woman except in his dreams[38]

The novel's characters feed their fantasy not only on pornography but also on the world of the movies.[39] As one of the characters says, cinema is a way of forgetting daily life and a means for expressing feelings and desires.[40] Not a single character in the novel escapes the charm of cinema: from the Jaguar, who prefers North American Westerns, to Lieutenant Gamboa, who is fond of Mexican melodramas.

The compensatory nature of Alberto's writing is underscored when he stops writing love letters for his friends after he becomes involved with Teresa, the girl Ricardo Arana loves. Alberto meets her when Ricardo asks him to send her his apologies when he cannot keep a date with her. Teresa's aunt and guardian encourages the relationship: having noticed Alberto's uniform, she decides that he is a good prospect for her indigent niece.

The character of Teresa enables Vargas Llosa to explore class hierarchies and perceptions.[41] For Alberto, the Leoncio Prado school represents contact with adolescents of inferior social classes, but for Teresa and her aunt, the school is a prestigious institution. Alternatively, Teresa and her aunt belong to a world that is socially equivalent to Ricardo's but superior to the one in which the Jaguar grew up. In Vargas Llosa's narrative fiction, the affair with Teresa is the first of a series of romantic relationships in which female characters are attracted to men unable or unwilling to establish a relationship with women of their own social class.[42] In *Conversation in the Cathedral*, for instance, Santiago Zavala marries a woman who is his social inferior in order to reject his upper class family. In *The Time of the Hero*, Alberto takes Teresa as his girlfriend because he is intimidated by girls of his own social class. In so doing, he betrays his friend Ricardo, who was in love with the girl but who will never know that Alberto has become involved with her.

Teresa is instrumental, even though she does not realize it, in the unfolding of the core events of the novel's main plot. As long as the cadets are detained at the school while the exam theft is being investigated, Ricardo cannot visit Teresa. Under this romantic pressure, the lovelorn Ricardo secretly denounces Cava to the authorities. Alberto knows that Ricardo accused Cava and that the Jaguar hates informers. On the basis of this circumstantial evidence Alberto assumes that the Jaguar murdered Ricardo and makes the accusation to lieutenant Gamboa.

Alberto's motivations are ambiguous: it is never clear whether his action is a result of moral scruples or of guilt at having betrayed Ricardo with Teresa or a combination of both. What is clear is Alberto's belief that the Jaguar murdered Ricardo to avenge Arana's betrayal and Cava's expulsion. Since Gamboa is skeptical, Alberto makes his accusation more credible by informing the lieutenant about the unlawful activities that occur behind the backs of the school authorities: thefts of exams and uniforms, gambling, escapades to the city, violence among cadets, drinking, and other transgressions.

After Gamboa presents Alberto's accusation to the authorities, the cadets are punished for the thefts and illegal sales of alcohol and tobacco. But the school authorities do not wish to pursue the criminal investigation. To prevent Alberto from talking, they threaten him with expulsion from the school for having written the pornographic stories that were found together with the liquor and the tobacco in the cadets' lockers. Alberto withdraws his accusation but continues to believe that the Jaguar murdered Ricardo. When he confronts his fierce and violent classmate, the Jaguar appears truly surprised: "The Slave accused the peasant? . . . I didn't know he squealed on Cava. It's a good thing he's dead. All squealers ought to be dead"[43] Alberto then realizes that he could be mistaken: "If you really didn't know, I was wrong. Forgive me, Jaguar."[44]

When the Jaguar returns to his section, the cadets are convinced that he, rather than Alberto, has revealed their transgressions and clandestine activities. Together, the cadets confront and attack him. The Jaguar cannot believe that his classmates consider him an informer, but he is not willing to accuse Alberto, the real culprit. The Jaguar keeps quiet because he now feels disgusted with his classmates and because exposing Alberto would make him a squealer, and that would betray his own code of behavior.

Book 1 concludes with Ricardo Arana's shocking death; at the conclusion of book 2 not a single remaining character cares about the circumstances of that event, whether an accident or a murder. Impressed by the bravery of the Jaguar, Alberto offers him his friendship and volunteers to save his friend's reputation by confessing to the murder of Ricardo Arana. The Jaguar rebuffs him with contempt: "'I don't want to be your friend,' the Jaguar said. "You're a rotten squealer and you make me vomit. Get out.'"[45] Whether or not the Jaguar accepts Alberto's apologies, it is obvious that Alberto has become as indifferent as the school authorities are to justice. He may originally have accused the Jaguar out of moral indignation, but by the end of book 2 he has lost all moral scruples.

In the first sequence of the epilogue, where we get a glimpse of the characters' lives after leaving the school, Gamboa has received transfer orders to a degrading post as punishment for attempting to discover the truth. Gamboa is proud to be a soldier, but he prevaricates when he realizes that his superiors and his colleagues are more interested in their reputation than in the rules and regulations of the military institution he reveres:

> How could he maintain his blind faith in authority after what had happened? Perhaps it would be more sensible to go along with the rest. Capt. Garrido was surely right when he said that the regulations had to be interpreted according to the situation at hand, and that above all you had to keep an eye on your own security, your career.[46]

As a man committed to the values of military life and respectful of military authority, Gamboa is faced with a difficult dilemma: according to the regulations, he and his superiors are required to undertake a criminal investigation, but he has been ordered not to pursue the matter any further. Whether he obeys his superiors or upholds the regulations, he will betray the institution. He does not want to place the military school in a compromising situation, and so he chooses to obey his superiors, who were not pleased with his initiative to investigate the matter. When he finds out that he will be transferred to Juliaca, the most barren space of Vargas Llosa's entire literary geography, he willingly accepts the punishment even though he is given the opportunity to appeal. Gamboa would rather forego his own professional aspirations than to participate in the corruption of the institution to which he had dedicated his life.[47]

As Gamboa prepares to leave for his new post, the Jaguar—in a demonstration of his own distorted value system and naïveté—approaches to confess the crime. In all likelihood Gamboa believes him, but it is already too late for it to matter: Gamboa will neither compromise his institution nor accept the friendship of the school's leading hoodlum. From the Jaguar's point of view, as Gamboa must understand it, his confession is an act of solidarity. The Jaguar's confession is certainly not motivated by a sudden moral transformation but by a desire to sacrifice himself for the sake of Gamboa: "Then they won't send you to Juliaca, sir. Don't look so surprised. Do you think I don't know they've screwed you on account of this business? Take me to the colonel."[48] The confession does not mean that the Jaguar committed the murder. He may be willing to lie to establish a bond with the lieutenant.[49] Gamboa is as indifferent to the Jaguar's confession as the Jaguar was to Alberto's willingness to incriminate himself. Alberto had wanted to protect the Jaguar in the same way that the Jaguar wanted to protect Gamboa who was himself protecting the military institution. By the end of the novel the school authorities are not the only ones who have made a farce of justice.

The Jaguar sees Gamboa as the only member of the school who has been faithful to his own code of behavior, just as he himself has remained faithful to his code of loyalty and revenge. But the Jaguar is naive to think that the school authorities will accept his confession. He does not realize that they are as indifferent as he is to Arana's death.

Certain critics and shrewd readers of *The Time of the Hero* have claimed that it was the Jaguar who killed Ricardo Arana.[50] This possibility can be neither discarded nor confirmed. As in Faulkner, Vargas Llosa's deliberate ambiguity helps to underscore one of the novel's main themes: the indifference of a corrupt society toward crime. Whether Ricardo Arana was murdered or died accidentally is irrelevant for understanding the moral world of the Leoncio Prado school, a microcosm of Peruvian society. By the end of the novel no one is interested in finding out the truth: the school authorities care only about their reputation, Alberto is willing to confess to a crime he has not committed to win the Jaguar's friendship, Gamboa is unwilling to proceed with an investigation that might compromise his military institution, and the Jaguar is willing to confess to a crime in order to save Gamboa and thus remain faithful to his personal code of loyalty and revenge.

The novel's surprising disclosure that the Jaguar is the unnamed character in the first-person sequences serves also to recast the Jaguar, by virtue of the revelation of his childhood circumstances, as a poor and innocent child who became a criminal. He entered the military school thanks to the intervention of a relative interested in helping him to improve his situation. Vargas Llosa waits until the end of the novel to reveal that the mysterious suitor of Teresa, the same Teresa involved with Ricardo and Alberto, was the Jaguar.[51] With this information the reader is finally able to put together all the pieces of the Jaguar's life. The two crucial persons in his life are Teresa and Flaco Higueras, a criminal who gave him money and introduced him to a world of thieves and hoodlums. The decisive event in the Jaguar's life occurs when Higueras's gang is denounced to the police by another gang. This betrayal makes a permanent imprint on the Jaguar—from then onwards he hates informers. He is faithful to Flaco Higueras who protected him and showed him how to earn a living as a thief. While at the school, the Jaguar attempted to play a role with his fellow cadets that is similar to the one Higueras had played for him. He makes this point indirectly in his last interview with Gamboa: "I taught them how to be men. And now they've turned against me. Do you know what they are? They're a pack of traitors, that's what they are. All of them. I'm fed up. . . . It's their ingratitude that bothers me, that's all."[52]

The disclosure of the Jaguar's past reveals him to be a victim of his circumstances. He was an abused child who was offered a helping hand by Higueras, a hoodlum who taught him to become a thief. The boy took Higueras as a model, and their friendship continues even after the Jaguar graduates, reforms his ways, and lives as a law-abiding citizen. The Jaguar marries Teresa and gets a job at a bank, probably thanks to his affiliation with the military school.

Social success, however, is not for characters like the Jaguar but rather for ones like Alberto's father, a member of a prestigious family who can keep up appearances while getting away with many transgressions.[53] Before he entered the Leoncio Prado school, Alberto did not seem to be cast in the mold of his father. But the military school succeeded in transforming him as his father had expected. By the novel's end, Alberto has given up his literary inclinations, lost his moral scruples, and is determined to follow in his father's footsteps.[54]

While promising his new fiancée Marcela that he will be faithful to her, Alberto thinks:

> I'll work with my father, and I'll have a convertible and a big house with a swimming pool. I'll marry Marcela and be a Don Juan. I'll go to the Grill Bolívar every Saturday for the dancing, and I'll do a lot of traveling. After a few years I won't even remember I was in the Leoncio Prado.[55]

Like Helena, the girl who had previously rejected him, Marcela belongs to Alberto's social class. It is not coincidental that her name is an anagram of Carmela, the name of Alberto's mother. The school experience has turned Alberto into a replica of his father. Like his parents and grandparents, Alberto will probably occupy important positions in Peruvian society. In the end, the school served its purpose by making him insensitive to the immorality that keeps his family and others like it in power.

While the revelation of the Jaguar's childhood shows how a noble spirit has been trampled, the final transformation of Alberto into an individual indifferent to immorality clarifies the novel's central theme: how a corrupt institution contributes to the reproduction of an immoral society accustomed to concealing injustice, a society whose success depends on indifference toward transgression. The fate of Alberto in *The Time of the Hero* is consistent with Vargas Llosa's perception of the Peruvian bourgeoisie: "in a very indirect and insidious and hypocritical way, the Peruvian bourgeoisie is able to hide the fact that it is the primary beneficiary of violence in their society."[56] In the end, Vargas Llosa used, transformed, and modified literary and biographical sources to produce a novel whose political message was indentical with his political convictions.

THE GREEN HOUSE

Vargas Llosa often uses his autobiographical experiences to write novels but modifies his memories according to his literary intuitions and narrative strategies. The discrepancies between Vargas Llosa's biography and his successful autobiographical characters are significant. Alberto of *The Time of the Hero* is a character inspired by Vargas Llosa's experiences at the military academy, but he is not a strictly autobiographical character. Vargas Llosa's family was not as wealthy, he was not born or raised in Lima, and he did not complete his secondary school at Leoncio Prado. After two years as a cadet Vargas Llosa abandoned the military school to return to Piura. Back in Piura, a city surrounded by the desert sands, he understood that the mysterious green cabin that had fascinated him as a child was a house of prostitution. The cabin inspired the title of his second novel.

The Green House is set in the Piura desert and in the Amazon jungle (also known as *montaña* in Peru), two places that have little in common except that both are changing through contact with modern civilization. As in its most important literary forerunner, *La vorágine* (The Vortex) by José Eustasio Rivera, one of the main themes in *The Green House* is the wretchedness of human beings who live on the margins of civilization. Both novels explore the corruption of local authorities, the exploitation of indigenous populations by rubber traders, the internal divisions among traders, the establishment of private fiefdoms in remote regions, and the mystery of tropical plants, animals, and diseases. But while Rivera draws a literary portrait of the rubber boom epoch, Vargas Llosa sets his novel during a period of bust when the brutality of traders toward indigenous populations is increasing as the business becomes less lucrative.[57]

There are also some coincidences in the ways these two novels were written. Both writers traveled to the Amazon jungle: Rivera as a member of a commission investigating border problems between Colombia and Peru, and Vargas Llosa, in 1958, as part of a scientific expedition organized for Juan Comas, a Mexican anthropologist, by Protestant missionaries of the Summer Institute of Linguistics. Vargas Llosa published a long chronicle of this journey.[58] Rivera and Vargas Llosa were both struck by the human wretchedness of the jungle. Each author incorporated his impressions of the jungle into a novel he was currently writing and whose theme was organically unrelated to the jungle. Rivera's novel was about the troubles of a poet, and Vargas Llosa's novel was about a brothel in the desert of Piura. Both writers made a second trip to the jungle before finishing their respective novels, and in both novels, as Neale-Silva has pointed out in the case of Rivera, an association is made between "the barbarism of the jungle and the indifference of the city."[59]

Both novels are set on the margins of civilization. For Rivera, the jungle is the locus of barbarism. For Vargas Llosa this is also the case but, in an aesthetic *tour de force*, he combines elements from the lush jungle vegetation and the arid desert sands to create a symbol that unifies those marginalized areas of Peru that are beginning to confront the civilized world. The opposition suggested by a character who knows the jungle and the desert ("In the jungle everything is green, and here everything is yellow"[60]) is resolved in the central image of the novel: a green house whose color evokes the jungle in the midst of the desert's yellow sands.

According to popular legend, within the context of the novel, Don Anselmo, the house's founder, was a mysterious and inscrutable entrepreneur. He resembles the mysterious foreigners in Knut Hamsun's novels who, like the protagonists of Hamsun's *Mysteries,* transform the towns they arrive in without the narrators' ever revealing their feelings or motivations. Anselmo, who is from the jungle—although this is not revealed until the novel's last pages—establishes Piura's first brothel in a solitary house in the desert outside the city. The illicit activities at this establishment draw the attention of the town's inhabitants and enrage Father García, who eventually sets fire to the brothel. Years later, Anselmo's daughter known as La Chunga will set up a second brothel also called "The Green House." By then, the original Green House has become the source of many local legends.

Luis Loayza has pointed out that in the novel the original Green House takes on a mythical dimension because of the point of view from which Vargas Llosa narrates its history: a third-person narrator summarizes what was said and thought, but not what actually happened. Loayza defines this as "a voice with a mythical resonance that represents the collective memory of Piurans."[61] Once the desert has been taken over by the city and the house no longer exists, its image becomes myth and its history becomes legend.[62] The narrator refers to an original or primitive Green House because of the second one, established later by La Chunga, Don Anselmo's daughter. In the new house, Don Anselmo plays his green harp and denies the existence of the brothel that he himself founded, according to the legend: "'There never was any fire, any Green House,' the harp player declared. 'People made it all up. . . . Just a tale.'"[63] Whether real or imaginary, the original Green House is a complex image that heralds the appropriation of the barren sands of Piura deserts by the civilized world. This complex and fluid image, however, cannot be reduced simply to any of its connotations. Depending on one's point of view it represents modernization and the corruption of the modern world, social depravation, or a product of popular imagination.

Vargas Llosa based his novel on five idea-provoking experiences in Piura and from his trips to the Amazon jungle: (1) the green cabin in the desert outside the city of Piura, a brothel where an old man played the harp in a musical trio; (2) the Manganchería, a Piura neighborhood of "vagabonds, beggars and artists"; (3) his visit to the Santa María de Nieva convent in the Peruvian jungle where Spanish nuns forcefully abducted jungle girls in order to educate them; (4) the story of Jum, a jungle chieftain tortured by the Governor of Santa María de Nieva for attempting to bypass the local middlemen and sell rubber on his own; and (5) the story of Tushía—named Fushía in the novel—a man who formed an army of Indians to attack and rob other Indians who collect rubber and hunt. As Vargas Llosa has pointed out, these five anecdotes are the "raw material" from which he wrote the novel.[64]

Each of these recollections is associated with one of the novel's protagonists: Jum, the Urakusa chieftain; Fushía, the jungle pirate; Don Anselmo, the harpist who founded the Green House; Bonifacia, the servant of the missionaries; and Lituma, the Piuran sergeant. The first four protagonists developed from anecdotes Vargas Llosa heard during his trips through the Peruvian jungle. Lituma is derived from his own story "A Visitor" from *Los Jefes*.

The earliest version of the jungle anecdotes of *The Green House* are in the chronicle Vargas Llosa wrote in Brazil (on his way to Europe) about his first trip to the Amazonian jungle in 1958. In these impressions written days after the expedition, he recalls a story he heard about someone called "Tushía" whom he refers to as the "blue beard of the jungle":

> He could be a character taken from a macabre novel. His name is Tushía—he is of Japanese origin—and he lives on the Santiago river on an island. In that inaccessible region, Tushía rules like a feudal lord. He has a personal harem made up of many women.[65]

Vargas Llosa also found out how indigenous girls were kidnapped and taken as servants. He was moved by a story about some Aguaruna Indians who were robbed of their rubber and supplies by a corporal named Roberto Delgado Campos. The Indians captured the corporal and brought him to Jum, the community leader. Fearing reprisals from the authorities Jum released the prisoner. A few days later Julio Reátegui, the governor of Santa María de Nieva, arrived with a military expedition. Jum and other Aguaruna Indians

> were whipped and kicked by the soldiers who came with the governor. The two indigenous women captured were raped. . . . The following day [Jum] was strung up and whipped until he lost consciousness. His armpits were gruesomely burnt with hot eggs. . . . The reason for the sadism of the authorities of Nieva seems to have been a punishment for the Aguaruna plan to organize a cooperative to escape exploitation by the overlords.[66]

The next step toward the creation of the novel was the writing of a series of unpublished short stories set in Piura and in the Peruvian jungle. The Mario Vargas Llosa Collection at Princeton contains several drafts of the short stories that Vargas Llosa wrote after his trip to the jungle but years before publishing *The Time of the Hero*: "La aventura," the story of Lituma; "Jum, Alcalde de Urakusa," the story of the chieftain; "Los manganches," a Piuran story about a group of friends in a bar; and "Taito," a primitive version of the Fushía story.

The amalgamation of the original stories into the novel was a gradual process. In the story "Los manganches," for example, a character called La Chunga owns a bar where Don Casimiro, an old man, plays the flute. In *The Green House* Don Casimiro will become the harp player Don Anselmo. "Los manganches" is about a man, Jerónimo, who returns from jail to find that during his absence his friends have forced themselves on his girlfriend, La Tula. In later versions, Vargas Llosa rewrites "La aventura" and "Los manganches" into a single plot. He changes the name Jerónimo to Lituma and La Tula becomes Lituma's wife, a woman from the Peruvian jungle.

Like the green and yellow of the book's central image, all the anecdotes and stories are fused: Lituma marries Jum's daughter Bonifacia, who works for Fushía and ends up as a prostitute at the second Green House, where she discovers that Don Anselmo, like herself, is from the jungle. Each protagonist's experience relates to that of other secondary characters whose experiences in turn are also linked. Five main plots emerged from the process of piecing together the early texts. These do not correspond exactly to the five anecdotes that inspired Vargas Llosa in the first place nor to the primitive stories: (1) The story of Bonifacia, the servant of the jungle missionaries, and her expulsion from the house and subsequent marriage to sergeant Lituma who takes her to Piura where she ends up as a prostitute in the second Green House; (2) The story of Lituma, who after being jailed in Lima returns to Piura to take revenge on the man who seduced his wife and made her a prostitute. Eventually Lituma will become his wife's pimp as he enjoys a life of drinking and gambling with his Manganchería chums the "champs," who frequent the second Green House; (3) the story of Fushía, the cruel and bloody Japanese trader who comes to Peru from Brazil; (4) The story of Don Anselmo the harpist, who establishes the first Green House, and his relationship with Antonia, the mute and blind orphan girl whom he abducts; and (5) the stories about Jum, the Aguaruna Indian from Urakusa who is brutally tortured by the national military authorities on the pretext that his tribe mistreated a corporal Delgado (the man who had stolen the tribe's property). As Vargas Llosa records, the real reason for the violence against Jum was his initiative to form a cooperative against the wishes of Julio Reátegui, the main rubber trader, who will not tolerate any competition from Indians. Jum ends up as a demented hoodlum after becoming Fushía's servant.

Vargas Llosa also drew on literary models to develop the five stories. The plot of Bonifacia's story resembles a Mexican cinematic melodrama; the love affair between Anselmo and Toñita is reminiscent of the relationship between the man with the grotesque smile and the blind girl who loves him in Victor Hugo's *The Man Who Laughs*; the environment of "the champs" is inspired as much by Dumas's novels as by Vargas Llosa's memories of Piura[67]; and the strategy adopted by Vargas Llosa to narrate the story of Fushía is derived from Joseph Conrad's *The Heart of Darkness*. Vargas Llosa also conducted research at specialized libraries to study the jungle's natural environment, tropical diseases, and other aspects of the Amazon region.

In writing his books, Vargas Llosa is no more faithful to the research of specialists than he is to any of his literary sources. His craft as a writer can be summarized by an enlightening observation José Emilio Pacheco made in reference to *The Green House:*

> *The Green House* demonstrates that originality also means knowing how to join and relate, because the only thing that remains alien to the Latin American writer is that which he has been unable to appropriate and use for his fictions.[68]

THE FORM

The Green House is a complex novel with many plots and sub-plots. The novel consists of four books and an epilogue. Each book is composed of sequences that make up chapters with numbered headings, and each book begins with an independent introductory sequence that takes place in the Amazon jungle. The five sequences that compose each of the chapters in books 1 and 2 form a repeating pattern: the first sequence of each chapter occurs in the Santa María de Nieva Mission; the second narrates the story of Fushía; the third narrates the events relating to the story of Jum; the fourth narrates the establishment of the Green House; and the fifth narrates the adventures of the champs who are awaiting the return of their buddy Lituma. After book 3, each chapter is composed of four repeating sequences: the first is the story of Lituma and Bonifacia that takes place in the jungle and in Piura; the second is the story of Fushía; the third is the story of Don Anselmo; and the fourth is a continuation of the adventures of the champs. Books 3 and 4 have no sequences on the story of Jum.

The story of Bonifacia in the jungle is narrated in the first sequence of each chapter in each book. The story that narrates the return of Lituma to Piura after his imprisonment in Lima begins in the last sequence of each chapter of each book. The story of Fushía is narrated in the second sequence of each chapter, and the story of Don Anselmo is narrated in the third. The story of Jum is narrated in the fourth sequence of the chapters of books 1 and 2 and is mentioned intermittently in all of the jungle sections of the novel. The epilogue is constitued of a prologue and four chapters that have numbered headings and are not subdivided into sections. It narrates the outcomes of the stories of Anselmo and Fushía.

Like the poems of Góngora, his favorite poet, Vargas Llosa's more ambitious novels, such as *The Green House*, are complex but not obscure: most of the apparent contradictions and deliberate ambiguities can be figured out. Even if they are not, the main plots are easy to follow, for the most part, even on first reading. One of the pleasures of reading Vargas Llosa, however, is to reread him to disentangle the intricacies of intermingled narrative threads, none of which are narrated in a strict chronological order. Another is to recognize the importance of hidden facts that are revealed as the novel progresses.[69] The most important hidden facts in *The Green House* are the identities of the sergeant who appears in the jungle sections and of the woman from the jungle who appears in the Piuran sections: the reader gradually discovers that the sergeant is Lituma and that the woman from the jungle is Bonifacia, his wife. Even more surprising, although less relevant to the main thread of the plot, are the facts that Bonifacia's father could have been Jum, the Aguaruna chieftain, and that the person who rescued her and took her to the nuns' mission was the man responsible for punishing Jum, the merchant Julio Reátegui. Also surprising are the facts that Anselmo, the founder of the Green House, originally came from the jungle and that La Chunga, the administrator of the second Green House, is his daughter, born of the unusual relationship he had with Antonia, the blind and mute girl.[70] Together with Bonifacia and Lituma, Anselmo is the third protagonist who is familiar with both the jungle and the desert. Although the reader knows nothing about Anselmo's past or about his life in the jungle, his jungle origin clarifies a few mysteries: his predilection for the color green, the color he used in painting the brothel and his harp; and his Spanish accent, which sounds unusual to the characters from the Peruvian coast.

The complexity of the novel stems not only from the organization of its narrative sequences but also from the construction of each sequence. The initial sequence that serves as a prologue to book 1, illustrates the intricacy of the novel's narrative units. This exemplary sequence deserves special study because it contains in embryonic form the connections to be established later between the jungle and the desert. It also serves as the point of departure for the main plot, which unifies two narrative threads that initially seem independent of each other: the stories of Lituma and Bonifacia.

On first reading, the initial sequence of *The Green House* cannot be fully intelligible. It begins with the abduction of two girls from an Aguaruna tribe by two missionary nuns assisted by a sergeant, his four subordinates, and Nieves, the guide and pilot of the river boat that takes the crew to the heart of the Peruvian jungle. The boat journey takes the group along a river in a desolate and lush jungle, but only indirect clues later allow the reader to guess the journey's purpose. In this sequence, Vargas Llosa makes remarkable use of the method of "delayed decoding"—a term used by Ian Watt in his studies on Joseph Conrad's fiction.[71] This literary technique entails the description of actions and events before the reader is given information about the motivations of the characters.

The first pages of *The Green House* produce a verbal vertigo resulting from the use of the delayed decoding technique in a narrative that links, without transitions, the thoughts and conversations of various characters while describing the exotic atmosphere of the steamy Amazon jungle with the thick smells and uncanny sounds of insects, animals, vegetation and the river. The characters are identified as if the reader was familiar with them, and they express themselves laconically. The clue that reveals the purpose of the journey is a difficult one: "Shorty and Blondy were to take care of the kids [*churres* in the original Spanish]."[72] We know that Shorty and Blondy are the nicknames of the subordinates of the sergeant in charge of the expedition. However, the regional expression *churres* first used to identify the Aguaruna girls may be misleading even to those who know what it means: it is not a linguistic expression from the jungle, but from Piura. *Churres* is not the only hidden reference to the city of Piura. In the sergeant's thoughts—"the Manganches were right"[73] and "that pair of buzzards!"[74]—are references, in a regional slang, to the inhabitants of two Piura neighborhoods, or slums, that will appear later in the novel: "the Manganchería" and "the Gallinacería." But because these neighborhoods have not been mentioned yet, the allusions remain obscure in a first reading of the novel, even for readers familiar with Piuran regionalisms.

In "La ciudad y el forastero" (billed as a fragment of *The Green House* and appeared in the journal *Casa de las Américas* a few months before the novel was published), Vargas Llosa had carefully explained the Piuran regional expressions:

> [An outsider becomes acquainted with] the formulas of the local language with its warm and lazy tones: in a few weeks he was already saying 'Gua' to show surprise, was calling children '*churres*', donkeys '*piajenos*,' was adding superlatives to superlatives . . . and dancing the *tondero* like an old *manganche*.[75]

In the novel, Vargas Llosa rewrote this fragment, and he also scrapped all definitions and easy clues for recognizing the regionalisms that reveal Lituma's Piuran origin. Only in retrospect will the reader be able to identify these regionalisms when he reads the Piuran sections that shed light on their meanings and contexts.

The retrospective clarification of hidden facts is a pattern throughout the novel. In book 1, the first sequence of every chapter offers an increasing number of clues that the nuns of the Santa María de Nieva Mission kidnap jungle girls to "civilize" them and that the girls who were captured during the prologue of book 1 are the same ones who later flee with the help of Bonifacia, a servant who arrived at the mission as a small child. Like many other subplots in the novel, the story of the two abducted girls will be dropped. In contrast, the story of Bonifacia gradually becomes one of the novel's central plots. Bonifacia's boldness on behalf of the captured girls sets off a series of events that will connect the world of Piura with the world of the jungle; as punishment for her role in the escape of the two girls, she is expelled from the mission. Bonifacia will eventually meet and marry Lituma, who will take her to Piura.

In *The Green House* complex references and hidden facts are combined with a simple plot. The novel's plot *does not depend* on the complexities of the episode in which the two jungle girls are captured nor on the details of their escape from the mission. The continuity of the story does not depend on whether the girls will ever return to the mission because these characters will not reappear in the novel. In fact, the reader need not even realize that the girls captured in the prologue are the same ones whom Bonifacia liberates. The facts necessary to follow the novel's main plot are narrated clearly and precisely. The expulsion of Bonifacia from the mission initiates a chain of events that will take her to the brothel in Piura.[76]

The main events in Bonifacia's life after her expulsion are narrated in chronological order. She works first as a servant and then marries Sergeant Lituma who takes her to Piura. After Lituma is sent to a Lima jail for his part in a bar squabble, Josefino, a pimp who is supposedly Lituma's friend, seduces Bonifacia who becomes a prostitute in the second Green House. When Lituma eventually returns, he rejoins Bonifacia as a pimp at the Green House. As Carlos Fuentes has pointed out, *The Green House* could be summarized as "a pilgrimage from convent to brothel,"[77] a master plot of the Mexican cinematic melodrama popular throughout Latin America in the 1940s and 1950s.[78] Vargas Llosa has not hidden the fact that he has been attracted by the melodramatic content of the Mexican cinema:

> and despite the fact that I cannot bear literary melodrama in its pure
> state (though I am a devotee of melodramatic movies, and it may
> well be that this weakness of mine stems from the Mexican films to
> which I was addicted in the forties and fifties and for which I still
> feel a keen nostalgia), when a novel is capable of using melodra-

matic materials within a broader context and with artistic talent, as is the case of *Madame Bovary*, my joy knows no bounds.[79]

One of Vargas Llosa's achievements is his capacity to combine the complexity of Faulknerian structures and the Joycean interior monologue with the plots of melodrama and the adventure story. Vargas Llosa's genius as a narrator lies in his ability to bring together complexity and simplicity and to make use of other works of literature in that process.

LITERARY FUSIONS

In conceiving of *The Green House*, Vargas Llosa was probably inspired by his interest in the gestation of *Les Misérables*. Hugo's novel originated as a fusion of two separate stories: a short story about injustice in French prisons and a novel about an extraordinary bishop. The characters in these two texts "strangely abandoned their fictional and independent worlds, developed a relationship and became the pillars of a new more ambitious and vast project that combined the previous two."[80] Vargas Llosa also admired Faulkner's radical experiment in *The Wild Palms*, a novel whose chapters alternate between the story of two fugitives escaping from jail and the story of two desperate lovers. The plots of the two stories are independent of one another, but there are resonances and dissonances between their themes.

In *The Green House* Vargas Llosa interweaves five stories. Like Hugo he fuses some originally independent plots into a single story, and like Faulkner he produces a major novel where some of the most important plot lines are completely autonomous. The stories about the jungle mission and the stories about the desert and its brothels are fused by tinkering with the characters of Lituma and Bonifacia, while the story of Fushía and the story of Anselmo have completely independent plots, like the stories of the fugitives and the lovers in *The Wild Palms*.

The story of Anselmo, and in particular his relationship with the blind and mute girl Antonia, resulted from a complex fusion of themes from Vargas Llosa's readings and characters from his imagination. According to Vargas Llosa, a memory from his reading of Paul Bowles's *The Sheltering Sky* inspired him to write a love story about a blind woman.[81] A more important source is probably Victor Hugo's *The Man Who Laughs*. There are significant resemblances between Hugo's novel and *The Green House*, and they are apparent from the outset. Both begin with children being kidnapped. In Hugo's novel the children, too young to remember their family origins, become hoodlums called "les comparachines." One of them is Gwynplaine, an abandoned boy whose disfigured face gives the impression of a permanent smile. The boy finds a blind girl cowering in the arms of a dead woman. Gwynplaine calls her Dea; no one knows her real name. Gwynplaine and Dea find a protector in Ursus, a juggler who mounts plays and travels from city to city in "The Green Box" a wagon that can turn into a theater stage. When Gwynplaine's identity as a nobleman is revealed, he abandons Dea to marry a beautiful duchess, as he was destined to do. Disillusioned with court life, he is anxious to return to Dea—his true love. When he finds her it is too late: Dea dies in his arms and he commits suicide.

As with its Romantic forerunner, the plot of *The Green House* turns on an unconventional protagonist who falls in love with a blind girl. In Hugo's story Gwynplaine is considered a freak because of his physical malformation, and in Vargas Llosa's novel Don Anselmo is considered an eccentric and even a moral deviant. In both cases the protagonist falls in love with a blind girl whom he shelters in a disreputable place: the ambulatory theater called "the Green Box" in one case, the brothel called "the Green House" in the other. Finally, in both cases, the protagonist loses his desire to live when the girl dies.

Vargas Llosa used elements from Hugo's novel to develop the theme of an unusual love that transgresses conventional morality. Vargas Llosa also had Faulkner in mind when he developed the form of the Antonia/Anselmo sequences.[82] He created a subtle narrative point of view to present this unusual relationship: a present-tense second-person monologue, a voice that speaks to Don Anselmo or to his conscience and asks him questions and sometimes even gives him commands. This voice is sometimes impersonal, and at other times it suggests either Don Anselmo's conscience or the voices of characters who at some point speak to or about Don Anselmo. As in a Faulknerian novel, the Antonia/Anselmo sequences include lyrical and quasi-philosophical reflections and oblique commentaries on experiences the characters are not in a position to understand fully. Compare Faulkner's narrative voice in *Light in August,* when Joe Christmas loses his childhood innocence, with Vargas Llosa's, as it displays tensions between Don Anselmo's sexual desires, guilt feelings, and fantasies:

> *Faulkner:* Memory believes before knowing remembers. Believes longer than recollects, longer than knowing even wonders.[83]
>
> . . . .
>
> Perhaps memory knowing, knowing beginning to remember; perhaps even desire, since five is still too young to have learned enough despair to hope.[84]

Vargas Llosa: Things are the way they are, reality and desire become mingled.[85]

. . . .

Ask yourself if it was better or worse, whether life should be like that, and what would have happened if she no, if you and she, if it was a dream or if things are always different from dreams . . . and if it's because she died or because you're old that you accept the idea of dying yourself.[86]

The Faulknerian technique permits Vargas Llosa to introduce the theme of sexual transgression surreptitiously. In these dreamy passages, Don Anselmo treats Antonia tenderly, and their sexual relationship is narrated without any moral comments. The narrative voice is not judgmental and provides no clues as to whether Don Anselmo feels, or will ever feel, guilt or remorse over his sexual involvement with a defenseless child. Don Anselmo's morality is finally discussed in the novel's epilogue set some thirty years after Antonia's death, when doctor Zevallos and Father García take opposing views on the liaison. In a conversation at La Chunga's bar, father García insists that Don Anselmo's sexual relations with Antonia were sinful. Doctor Zevallos disagrees:

one would have to know whether he really deserved to be punished. And what if Antonia hadn't been his victim but his accomplice? If she had fallen in love with him? . . . Antonia didn't know right from wrong and after all, thanks to Anselmo, she became a whole woman.[87]

Zevallo's value judgment is consistent with the description of Don Anselmo's and Antonia's tenderness in their intimate moments. This relationship is Vargas Llosa's first literary exploration of a theme that had captivated him in the writings of César Moro and Georges Bataille: literature as a privileged genre to explore the connection between eroticism and transgression.

The stories of Anselmo and Fushía are independent of one another; there is no personal contact between the two characters, and the fate of one does not affect the fate of the other. Fushía's story unfolds in many of the novel's sequences. In book 3, Fushía's story is told by a third-person narrator and by the intermingled voices of other characters. In books 1, 2 and 4 it is told using a technique Jose Miguel Oviedo has named "telescopic dialogues."[88] By means of this technique, Vargas Llosa weaves a conversation that takes place between Fushía and his friend Aquilino during a boat trip along the Marañón river, with many other conversations from the past. In addition to these crisscrossing, "telescopic" dialogues there are narrative sections that shed light on the present and past dialogues. These sequences foreshadow the form of *Conversation in the Cathedral* where a conversation constitutes the backbone of the novel while other conversations, monologues, and descriptive narratives are organized around it.

In *The Green House*, the backbone of Fushía's story consists of conversations that take place from the moment Fushía and his old friend Aquilino enter the Marañón river in a boat navigated by the latter, until they arrive at their destination, the town of San Pablo, where Aquilino will probably leave his dying friend at a leper colony.[89] The narration of Fushía's story begins with the river journey. Through the series of conversations and narratives interwoven with those of the journey, Vargas Llosa takes the reader back to Fushía's childhood in a Brazilian town where he went to school and worked at a store. The owner of the store, a Turkish merchant, unjustly accused Fushía of theft and had him sent to prison. Fushía's life as a criminal began when he attacked a prison guard and fled thinking he had killed the man.

Until his dying days Fushía felt bitter anger for his unjust imprisonment: "No one would believe that he was honest, and they put him in a cell with two crooks. It was damned unfair, wasn't it old man?"[90] Like Jean Valjean in *Les Misérables*, Joe Christmas in *Light in August,* and the Jaguar in *The Time of the Hero*, Fushía hates society because of the injustice he has suffered. His hate is rooted in the indignation he feels for the abuse he endured as a child and in his ensuing conviction that "justice" is merely an instrument of exploitation. Fushía has no misgivings about his criminal schemes for making money ("all business is dirty, old man"),[91] and he has no qualms about the ruthlessness with which he treats other people.

After escaping from prison he flees from Brazil to the Peruvian jungle, where he begins his life of crime. He makes an alliance with Reátegui, the caucho merchant, who later betrays him. After his falling-out with Reátegui, Fushía takes Lalita, his wife, to an island in the heart of the Amazon jungle where he forms a gang of pirates and keeps a harem. He becomes skillful at manipulating ethnic rivalries in the jungle, where he persuades the Huambisa Indians to terrorize the Aguaruna Indians in order to steal the rubber they collect. He abandons his enterprises only when his body begins to deteriorate as a result of leprosy.

In writing Fushía's tale, Vargas Llosa borrowed directly from Joseph Conrad's *The Heart of Darkness*.[92] In both works the evil instincts of a character from the civilized world emerge in the context of the jungle, and the events are revealed during a boat trip. Fushía, like Conrad's protagonist, Kurtz, creates a fiefdom in the most remote and barbaric spaces. In both cases, a barbaric setting unleashes the evil element of their personalities. Kurtz, a merchant who manages a commercial company in the Belgian Congo, had the intention of civilizing the natives.

Instead, he himself becomes a savage who is convinced that the human soul is moved by evil. Kurtz's enemy, the district manager, is an exploiter who is in the Congo searching for ivory but who is more sanguine and less obsessed about the human condition. Like Kurtz, Fushía has learned that human beings are intrinsically evil. Fushía's only regret is not having had the necessary capital to compete with and eventually eliminate Reátegui—the character equivalent to Kurtz's rival, the district manager. In both novels, a navigator on a journey feels sympathy for the sick and dying man whom he transports from a savage world to civilization: Marlow tries to save Kurtz, and Adrián decides to help Fushía. Kurtz and Fushía both ally with an ethnic minority, learn its rituals, and dominate and use it to terrorize other ethnic groups. Kurtz, who obtained ivory from the natives at a very low price, eventually steals their ivory with the help of another tribe. When Marlow asks an acquaintance of Kurtz how he managed to persuade one tribe to attack another, the answer is short but clear: "They adored him."[93] Similar feelings are expressed about Fushía in *The Green House*: "he's a god to the Huambisas."[94]

Vargas Llosa's fusing of Conrad's plot materials with his own was clearly a conscious, overt procedure. Materials at the Mario Vargas Llosa Collection at Princeton demonstrate that important aspects of *The Green House* developed from Vargas Llosa's study of *The Heart of Darkness:* early drafts, written prior to the author's study of Conrad, are narrated purely in the third person, without the intermingling of other voices, and do not contain the theme of ethnic rivalries in the jungle or the river journey with the dying protagonist and the companion who comes for him.[95] It is certain that by immersing himself in Conrad's novel, Vargas Llosa fused a number of that novelist's procedures with his own.

In similar fashion, Vargas Llosa fused Faulkner's forms with his own. Like Faulkner's stories of the lovers and of the convicts in *The Wild Palms*, the stories of Fushía and Don Anselmo in *The Green House* have completely separate plots. Like Faulkner, as well, Vargas Llosa makes the themes of the two stories complement one another: in *The Wild Palms* both the lovers and the fugitives attempt to abandon the violence of an infamous and unjust world; in *The Green House* both Anselmo with his Green House and Fushía with his island of pirates achieve the triumph of a short-lived personal dream before suffering a humiliating decline.

José Emilio Pacheco has suggested that *The Green House* is comparable to the novels of James Joyce in its literary conception: "Its relationship to the poetical and didactic novels of the jungle is not very different from the relationship of *Ulysses* to the Naturalist novel."[96] With *The Green House*, Vargas Llosa has contributed to the modern novel by using and inventing complex literary structures and also by fusing the formal exuberance of the Joycean or Faulknerian novel with vigorous action and melodramatic plots.

Edmund Wilson could not have expressed the same reservation about Vargas Llosa that he did about Joyce, that the unprecedented vitality of Joycean narrative is developed at the expense of the action. Vargas Llosa's originality lies in his capacity to combine the bold techniques of twentieth century narrative with a heightened sense of action and intrigue.[97]

CONVERSATION IN THE CATHEDRAL

The Green House is a display of Vargas Llosa's narrative virtuosity: the novel brings together the Peruvian jungle and desert; combines five different stories to create a balance between the Faulknerian novel, the adventure story, and the melodrama; and explores the theme of precarious illusions sometimes fulfilled but invariably lost. *Conversation in the Cathedral* (1969), the novel that closes the cycle of his first literary period, uses the methods of *The Green House* to narrate a set of stories that gravitate around Santiago Zavala, Vargas Llosa's most complex and best developed character. Santiago is a young man who chooses social failure rather than success. Like Alberto Fernández's father in *The Time of the Hero*, Santiago's father is a respected member of Peruvian society, and like Alberto, Santiago is expected to follow in his father's footsteps. Instead, Santiago associates with people of a lower social milieu to distance himself from his father and from the productive activities of a class that he considers corrupt.

To establish and develop this theme, Vargas Llosa has stressed his character's moral dimension:

> Let us say that in his case failure is a choice accompanied by a certain dignity and by a secret grandeur. He is a frustrated individual because, in his world, people are either frustrated or vile.[98]

Santiago is convinced that social success depends on corruption, and he refuses to seek personal gain in a society that thrives on exploitation. Santiago does not regret his choice, even though he admits his life has been a failure: "In this country either you screw someone over, or you get screwed."[99] The phrase used by Santiago is the same one used by the Jaguar in *The Time of the Hero,* as both characters inhabit the same moral world. But while the cadet wants to dominate in order to avoid being dominated, Santiago renounces his dominant position to avoid harming others.

The events in *Conversation in the Cathedral* are inspired by a period of Peruvian history when Vargas Llosa was a university student: the political transition from the dictatorship of Odría to the election of Fernando Belaúnde Terry. During the Odría dictatorship, Santiago despises his society. When democracy is reestablished in Peru, he is not optimistic because he sees the new regime merely as one more chapter in the vicissitudes of a corrupt society. This view coincides with Vargas Llosa's own political position and with that of his friend Sebastián Salazar Bondy, who had analyzed the Peruvian situation on the eve of the elections in which Belaúnde was elected to his first presidential term. Salazar Bondy's analysis could also be read as a commentary on the political message of *Conversation in the Cathedral:*

> I write these lines on the eve of Peru's new electoral experience after years of dictatorship. I certainly do not think that the elections will bring about the radical solutions that can address Peru's most pressing problems. Whatever the result of the elections—even if they are not frustrated by some kind of military intervention—the Peruvian crisis will continue. A small and powerful export and financial oligarchy owns the means of production, and will continue to run things in this country as it has done for over a century and a half. . . . On a slightly more hopeful note, true resistance is beginning to mount from below even though it is sometimes repressed by brute force, or neutralized by other means. The violent potential of the popular sectors is often diffused by vague or useless objectives. Take for example the student movement. University students express their contempt for the false values of the bourgeoisie by protest alone, but that is not enough. More disappointing is the fact that some students become conformists and fall prey to the pursuit of personal success, to a thirst for money, and to corruption.[100]

Like Malraux's *The Human Condition, Conversation in the Cathedral* is a moral novel set in a political context. In Malraux's novel, moral purity is impossible in an environment where the tactics for obtaining power corrupt all forms of political idealism. Consider the main events of the novel: Chang-Kai-Chek makes a military alliance with the Communists to unify China; the Communists accept the alliance for tactical reasons but plan to eliminate Chang at the appropriate time; meanwhile, the Soviet Union makes a tactical alliance with Chang, who then dismantles the Communist party. In this context, idealists necessarily experience a tension between their political effectiveness and the moral justification for their actions. The political climate in *Conversation in the Cathedral* is comparable. For tactical reasons, Marxist groups are willing to collaborate with APRA, a populist opposition party. APRA, in turn, is willing to make a pact with the dictator.[101] When elections are called, the APRA party and Odría are in collusion to oppose a new party that is attracting the support of the bourgeoisie. Santiago's family, who had previously supported Odría, now supports Belaúnde, the new political leader.

The political environment of *Conversation in the Cathedral* bears similarities to that in Malraux's novel because of the frustration felt by Santiago Zavala. Santiago is incensed by the corruption of his society and is supportive of revolutionary solutions, but he has doubts about the ideologies and tactics of the leftist groups he knows:

> The worse, was having doubts. . . . He realized he sometimes cheated. . . . He would say I believe or I agree but he was really doubting. . . . Clench your fists, bite your teeth . . . say that the APRA is the solution, that religion is the solution, that Communism is the solution, and believe it. Life would straighten herself out and you would no longer feel empty.[102]

Santiago laments his own doubts, but cannot avoid them: "'I knew that if everybody set himself to being intelligent and having his doubts, Peru would go on being screwed up forever,' Santiago said. 'I knew there was a need for dogmatic people, Carlitos.'"[103] Santiago is frustated because he does not feel comfortable with any of the political groups that share his hate for his father's social world: "'But I hated those people, I still hate them,' Santiago said. 'That's the only thing I am sure of. . . .'"[104]

While Vargas Llosa used his own experiences as a student during the Odría epoch to develop the main characters and Peruvian settings in *Conversation in the Cathedral*, he also used the themes and methods of a novel by William Faulkner to create them. Mary E. Davis has pointed out that in *Conversation in the Cathedral*

> the multiple conversations within the conversation make remarkable use of the multiple narrators to be found in the long conversations that form the narrative core of *Absalom*.[105]

One could add that the main theme of *Absalom, Absalom!* has significant links to Vargas Llosa's novel. The title of Faulkner's novel evokes the biblical story of Absalom, King David's son who rebelled against his father. The conflict between son and father is central to Faulkner's novel: Henry Sutpen is the son of Thomas Sutpen a man who has amassed a great fortune: "There was Henry who had father and security and contentment and all."[106] The young man decides to repudiate both his father and his inheritance.

In a dormitory at Harvard University, Quentin Comptson discusses Henry's rejection of his father as the core of his response to Shreve MacCannon's questions: "Tell me about the South. What is it like there? Why do they live there.? Why do they live at all?"[107] The answer to MacCannon's questions initiates a long conversation but also a process of introspection that Faulkner takes up again in *The Sound and the Fury*, where Quentin commits suicide. The conversation between the students (that begins in the sixth chapter of *Absalom, Absalom!*) is interspersed with the voices of other characters who had participated in the saga of the Sutpen family. The family story, in which voices contradict one another because the same experiences are remembered and understood in different ways, becomes a kind of window on the a society founded on slavery. Thomas Sutpen, Henry's father, appears to be the patriarch of a well-established family. But toward the middle of the novel, Faulkner reveals that Sutpen was actually a poor farmer who won fame and fortune through guile in the corrupt world of the South. Likewise, Vargas Llosa will reveal that Santiago's father, who seems to be from a good family, is actually a man of humble origins who attained his present position through cunning and dubious means.

In *Conversation in the Cathedral* and *Absalom, Absalom!* the rejection of a father who has succeeded through corruption becomes the center of an exploration that reveals the corruption of an entire social world. In both novels, a dialogue between two characters that takes place years after the events forms the narrative core that incorporates other voices, intermingled with one another, that add complexity and social pathos. In both novels, the story of a young man who has repudiated his father sheds light on the failure of an entire society.

The experience of Santiago Zavala and his family forms part of a web of human relations that includes numerous characters from a wide range of social settings and situations: servants, journalists, union laborers; small and bigtime criminals, including the henchmen of President Odría; members of the bourgeoisie and of the petit bourgeoisie; people who live in and frequent the brothels, shanty towns, bourgeois homes, jails, universities, bars, and elegant clubs. The trials and tribulations of a frustrated young rebel are the vehicle for an unprecedented literary exploration of Peruvian urban life.

Santiago's rebellion begins with his decision to study at San Marcos, the public university, rather than at the private or foreign universities where upper class children are usually sent. His rebellion intensifies when he participates in the subversive activities of leftist groups, and as a result, he lands in jail as a member of a seditious group. When he allows his father to use his government contacts to release him from jail, Santiago effectively breaks from the organized Left who consider him a sellout to the dominant class. Santiago becomes isolated from his leftist friends, but he does not reconcile himself with his father, whom he shuns. Rather than accepting an important position with his father, he looks for work at the sensationalist tabloid newspaper where his uncle Clodomiro works as a journalist.

The appearance of the uncle offers an important but unexpected clue about Don Fermín's social background: Santiago's father was not of upper class origin. He was an ambitious young man from a poor family who achieved social success through amoral craftiness. Yet Clodomiro does not find fault with his brother. On the contrary, he respects Fermín's ambition to overcome their family's low social status: "He always wanted to be somebody. Well, he got to be and you can't reproach anyone for that."[108] Santiago's parents tolerate their son's newspaper job as a passing fancy. But Santiago confirms the rupture with his family and social class when he drops out of school and marries a woman of an inferior social class. The marriage with an unpresentable woman is equivalent to Pichula Cuéllar's castration in "The Cubs" where Vargas Llosa had already explored the fall from grace of an upper class individual gradually excluded and eventually forgotten by the members of his own coterie.

Conversation in the Cathedral explores the dissatisfaction and growing self-awareness of a disillusioned young man who rejects his father's world long before he understands it. Fermín Zavala's reality is more sordid and more complicated than Santiago realizes when he first repudiates him. Santiago assumes that his father is a man devoted to his family, but he feels that his family's social position and respectability is shameful because Don Fermín's wealth and social position depend on his prominence in a society that excludes and exploites the masses—the type of corruption exemplified in the novel when, with an eye to later favors, Don Fermín proposes a shady but lucrative business deal to the Peruvian head of national security. Santiago is correct about Don Fermín's corrupt political and business deals, but he does not suspect that his father, who feels sincere affection toward his son, is leading a tormented double life.

While working as a journalist, Santiago is astonished to discover many details of his father's private life: he is a homosexual and is well known in criminal circles. Santiago's discovery of his father's hidden side evokes the Mexican film melodramas in which an upper-class youth discovers the sordid side of his parents, whom he had considered irreproachable because of their apparent morality and propriety.[109] Santiago learns about his father's anguished private life as his colleagues investigate a murky crime whose details are also melodramatic: Hortensia, who was used and abandoned by an airplane pilot, her only love, becomes a drug addict and a prostitute whose clients include politicians; desperate for money she blackmails Don Fermín, but Ambrosio his chauffeur and homosexual lover, murders her before she can embarrass him. When Santiago discovers the details of his father's private life, his anger toward him dissipates. He now sees his father as another victim of the system against which he had rebelled. The father's double life sheds light on the title of the novel. Although at first glance the title suggests a conversation in a house of worship, in reality the conversation takes place in a seedy bar called The Cathedral. In the novel, the Cathedral of Lima intermittently appears as a sad witness of Peru's social degradation. For Santiago, religious piety in his country is a pathetic illusion: "you're closer to reality in a whorehouse than in a convent."[110]

The bare bones structure of the novel is a conversation between Santiago Zavala and Ambrosio, his father's chauffeur. Ambrosio, too, had abandoned the milieu into which he was born in order to seek a better life. His father was a criminal who robbed and assaulted his own children. This was also the social world of Cayo Bermúdez, Ambrosio's childhood friend (now the head of Odría's secret police) who is ruthless, astute, ambitious, and corrupt. Cayo offers Ambrosio a job as a chauffeur, which is how he becomes familiar with the brutal world of the police state. When given the opportunity, Ambrosio is delighted to offer his services to Don Fermín. In comparison to the environments he knew as a child and as an employee for Don Cayo, Don Fermín's world strikes him as a breath of fresh air. Ironically, from Ambrosio's perspective the real world of Don Fermín is the epitome of decency, whereas Santiago considers it to be a horrid existence worthy of his pity. Ambrosio feels such admiration for Don Fermín that he is willing to become his homosexual lover and to assassinate the woman who wanted to blackmail him.

The encounter between Santiago and Ambrosio, which provides the structural vehicle for the novel, is accidental and ironic. Santiago, who writes editorials calling for the eradication of rabies in Lima, goes to the city kennel to recover his healthy pup taken by kennel workers whose salary depends on the number of dogs they put to sleep. The individual who stole his dog happens to be Ambrosio, whom Santiago had not seen for twelve years. The narrative backbone of the novel is the long conversation between Santiago and Ambrosio in The Cathedral bar. As they talk, Vargas Llosa adds many conversations and the voices of many other people who, directly or indirectly, have touched the lives of Ambrosio and Santiago.

Like *The Green House*, the space of *Conversation in the Cathedral* is defined by two poles: the bourgeois home of Don Fermín and the house set up by Cayo Bermúdez for his orgies and corrupt business deals. The first space symbolizes the family world rejected by Santiago while, at first sight, the second space represents a considerably more corrupt and degraded social world. As in the novel about the jungle and the desert, some characters gravitate around one of the two spaces, while others move between the two. Such is the case with Amalia, who worked as a domestic servant at different times in both houses, and Ambrosio, who worked as chauffeur for both men. As in *The Green House*, two apparently opposite spaces are amalgamated as the novel progresses and the reader discovers Don Fermín's double life. At the beginning of the novel the apparently stable world of the bourgeois home stands in opposition to the sordid world of Cayo Bermúdez's house where criminal and even bestial acts occur, ranging from prostitution to castration. When the novel begins, Don Fermín and Don Cayo appear to be opposites. The first is respectable and seems to come from a proper family, while the second is of lower-class origin—Don Cayo's social background is the same as Ambrosio's—and has succeeded through brutal corruption. But as the hidden facts about Santiago's father are gradually revealed, Vargas Llosa dissolves the polarity he has created. Don Fermín's reality is as sordid and corrupt as Don Cayo's. Don Fermín has participated in crime and blackmail and is even known in low-life environments by the *nomme de guerre* "Gold Ball." The novel's structure is complex, but it basically tells two stories. The first story, narrated chronologically, is about the young Santiago who rejects his father's world; the second, narrated obliquely, is the story of his father's double life.

A secondary structural vehicle in the novel pulls the reader, along with Santiago, toward greater awarenes. From the initial chapters, an unidentified and intermittent voice asks a series of questions with the same idea: "You did it for me?"[111] By the end of the novel it is clear that these questions are fragments of a conversation in which Don Fermín finds out that Ambrosio murdered Hortensia to protect him from blackmail. Hortensia's murder is narrated in the second part of the novel, but only at the end of the novel does it become clear that Don Fermín did not order her execution. Vargas Llosa complicates the disclosure of this surprising fact by providing false clues, such as the statement by Queta, Hortensia's friend: "'Gold Ball had her killed,' Queta said. 'The killer was his pratboy. His name is Ambrosio.'"[112]

The reader of the novel becomes Santiago's traveling companion on his journey of self-awareness while overhearing the monologue in which Santiago reflects on his own and his country's predicaments. The reader discovers the salient facts in the life of Santiago's father in the same order as the character does. By the end of the novel, the reader is able to appreciate Santiago's situation as clearly as the character does when he begins talking to Ambrosio. The encounter is accidental (Ambrosio has returned to Lima after many years in hiding for Hortensia's murder), but the conversation is important for both characters. Santiago wants to understand why Ambrosio was willing to kill someone for his father, and Ambrosio wants to understand why Santiago would rebel against Don Fermín. The conversation between the two characters, however, does not lead to any mutual understanding. Santiago is unable to comprehend why Ambrosio was his father's lover or why he murdered to protect him from Hortensia's black-mail, and Ambrosio is unable to understand why Santiago rejected the man whom he loved. Ambrosio tries to explain, but does not know how to express himself: "'Because he was, son,' Ambrosio says. 'so intelligent and such a gentleman and so everything else.'"[113] Although Ambrosio cannot explain his submission to Don Fermín, he does not hide the contempt he feels toward Santiago: "I want you to know that you don't deserve the father you had, I want you to know that. You can go straight to shit hell, boy."[114] Ambrosio's differences with Santiago are irreconcilable. Santiago is complacent about his mediocre life in which his conscience feels free of responsibility for the injustices of Peruvian society. He has also reconciled himself to the memory of his late father whom he came to see as another victim of the social and political system he despises. Ambrosio cannot see the connection between Santiago's political views and his personal life. For Ambrosio the political abstractions with which Santiago rationalizes his repudiation of Don Fermín are nothing but an insolent rant.

Santiago Zavala's muted tragedy—a rejection of family and nation that justifies his decision to live a mediocre life—evinces a corrupt society that may be understood but cannot be changed. In *Absalom, Absalom!* Quentin is able to understand himself through a conversation in which Shrevlin asks him about the South. Likewise, in *Conversation in the Cathedral*, Santiago asks the rhetorical question, "At what precise moment had Peru screwed itself over? . . . He was like Peru, Zavalita was, he'd screwed up somewhere along the line. He thinks: when? . . . He thinks: there's no solution."[115] The same futility is more poignantly expressed, through a combination of direct and indirect speech, when Ambrosio—alone and abandoned on the verge of destitute poverty—tells Santiago about his future plans: "He would work here and there . . . and after that here and there, and then, well, after that he would have died, wasn't that so, son?"[116]

THE MORAL VISION

Each of the characters in Vargas Llosa's first novels of the 1960s responds in his or her own way to an unjust and hypocritical society of exploiters and exploited where success is incompatible with morality. This vision coincides with the opinion Vargas Llosa then had of Peruvian reality: "Peru is a country whose social structures are based entirely on a kind of total injustice that encompasses all areas of life."[117] Vargas Llosa's moral vision during his socialist period is compatible with the Marxist-Leninist justification for revolution, as the Peruvian novelist understood it. Yet his literary expression of this vision has important connections with other literary works that explore ostensibly sound but clearly corrupted social institutions. Vargas Llosa's indictment evokes *Les Misérables*, Victor Hugo's exploration of the theme of judicial institutions as instruments of evil. Comparison of some of the elements of Hugo's novel and Vargas Llosa's early novels sheds light on how deeply Vargas Llosa was influenced by the French writer.

Hugo develops the theme of social exploitation and entrenched injustice by contrasting two characters: Jean Valjean and inspector Jauvert, the law breaker and his prosecutor. Valjean is a good man who steals a loaf of bread to feed hungry children. Valjean's theft is discovered because of a pane of glass is accidentally broken during the robbery (also, in homage to *Les Misérables,* how the school authorities discover the theft of the exam in *The Time of the Hero*). For his crime, Valjean is unjustly imprisoned for years. While in jail he concludes that life is a constant struggle among men, that the world is divided into victors and vanquished, and that justice is simply an instrument of the victors. According to the narrator, Valjean's long sentence is an immoral situation that can only be corrected by escaping from prison, that is, by once again breaking the law. Although kindness is Valjean's most spontaneous instinct, his jail experiences lead him to believe that true justice does not exist:

> Jean Valjean was not naturally evil; he was still good when he entered the galleys. He condemned society, and felt that he was growing wicked; he condemned Providence, and felt that he was growing impious . . . society had never done him aught but harm; he had only seen its wrathful face, which is called its justice, and which it shows to those whom it strikes.

> From suffering after suffering, he gradually attained to the conviction that life was war, and that in this war he was the vanquished. As he had no weapon but his hatred, he resolved to sharpen it in the galleys and to take it with him when he left.[118]

Valjean is reflecting on his own situation when he says:

> The galleys make the convict what he is, and this is something that you must bear in mind. Before going to prison I was a peasant with very little intelligence, almost an idiot. It was prison that changed me. I had been stupid but I became wicked. I was a log, I became a firebrand.[119]

Jauvert, Valjean's prosecutor, is a man who believes that respect for the law is the only morality, that which differentiates honest men from criminals. Jauvert is incapable of seeing Valjean's inherent goodness. Valjean has broken the law and must be punished for his transgression. Nothing he does to compensate for his crimes can change the facts. He must be arrested and punished severely.

According to the narrator of *Les Misérables*, a corrupt society turns honest men into criminals. In Hugo's novel there are plenty of evil men. They are respected individuals in positions of power who take advantage of their fellow men. The main opposition in *Les Misérables* is not that between the honest man and the criminal, but between the official morality of a corrupt society and real morality found in the spontaneous behavior of a good man whose instincts clash with the injustices that are underwritten by the legal system.

Like Hugo's, Vargas Llosa's literary world portrays a supposedly moral society that is, in fact, corrupt. Vargas Llosa's criminals are not intrinsically bad once they are understood in the light of their circumstances. Like Jean Valjean they have been exposed only to injustices and grow convinced that the world functions according to the law of the jungle. Their feelings about society are summarize by one of Hugos's characters: "A man must either eat or be eaten; and so I eat, for it is better to be the tooth than the grass. That is my wisdom."[120] Variations on this theme abound in *Les Misérables* and apply easily to the moral world of Vargas Llosa's first three novels: "He must conquer or be vanquished."[121]

Like Jean Valjean, the most ferocious characters in Vargas Llosa's first three novels—the Jaguar in *The Time of the Hero*, Fushía in *The Green House*, and Cayo Bermúdez in *Conversation in the Cathedral*—are all well meaning individuals who develop mechanisms to cope with their sense that justice is simply an instrument of the victors and that life is a struggle in which the strong win and the weak lose. The words the Jaguar uses to describe his philosophy could have been adapted directly from *Les Misérables*: "Screw them first before they screw you. There isn't any other way. I don't like to be screwed."[122]

In *The Time of the Hero*, Gamboa, like inspector Jauvert, is unable to distinguish between morality and order. He believes that the armed forces are a source of morality that can benefit a society in need of order and discipline. The difference between Jauvert and Gamboa is not their temperament but their circumstances. Jauvert can continue to live with the illusion that legality is equivalent to morality because the legal procedures to which he is accustomed are more or less respected. Gamboa, on the other hand, is forced to give up the illusion. The fact that the criminal investigation was aborted by the school authorities makes him recognize the immoral nature of the institution he had considered irreproachable. In an interview, Vargas Llosa has analyzed the change in his character: "The system in which he blindly believed—like the natural order of things—is not as intrinsically just as he thought."[123] Unlike his forerunner Jauvert, Gamboa is forced to recognize that the legal system is a sham. Vargas Llosa's narrative fiction is ultimately in tune with his socialist conviction that capitalist society is inherently beyond reform, whereas for Hugo there may be room for reform. This difference notwithstanding, Hugo and Vargas Llosa share the view that crime is more likely a symptom of a social evil rather than the responsibility of the perpetrator. In Vargas Llosa's novels individuals are never wholly responsible for their faults. The moral dilemmas of his characters, therefore, depend on their involvement with the social order, which is the ultimate source of immorality.

In Vargas Llosa's novels of the 1960s, there is a certain regularity in the functioning of an unjust society. Four rules of order seem to apply consistently: (1) the people who rise to the top do so as a result of personal sacrifice and destroy the lives of the people at the bottom; (2) someone will always be willing to accept corruption to occupy a position of power; (3) the exploiters live their official lives as though they were moral individuals; (4) and those at the bottom are forced to adapt to the false morality of the people at the top—although sometimes their ignorance or naïveté leads them to believe in the goodness of the powerful. Vargas Llosa's novels also rely on four types of characters: (1) the immoral who destroy the lives of others to obtain positions of power; (2) the moral who could occupy positions of power but choose not to; (3) characters who are victims of the first group; and (4) those able to live on the margins of power. In this literary world, regardless of whether a character understands or ignores the surrounding corruption, accepts or rejects the role society offers, benefits or is harmed by circumstances, that character does not know how to change the rules of the game.

The moral choices available to Vargas Llosa's characters underscore the oppression of a corrupt society. Some of the most memorable characters in his first novels—like Santiago Zavala in *Conversation in the Cathedral*, or Gamboa in *The Time of the Hero*—are the ones who discover a contradiction between their ethical code and an unjust society they are able to understand but unable to change. When faced with the opportunity to acquire power, these characters prefer to evade corruption by destroying their own personal aspirations while relinquishing the privileges offered by society. Gamboa's dilemma is not the result of abstract reflection on the nature of the school or on his position in it. His dilemma results from his involvement in the investigation of a crime. Gamboa's choice helps neither to resolve the crime nor to mitigate the corruption of the military institution. Yet it evinces more than a modicum of integrity: he would rather accept personal failure than to submit to the corruption of his institution. Gamboa is a victim of corruption, but, like Santiago Zavala, he becomes more conscious of his social reality than do innocent characters like Ricardo Arana in *The Time of the Hero* or Ambrosio in *Conversation in the Cathedral*, who do not realize that their failures are due to social corruption.

The main theme of Vargas Llosa's narrative fiction in the 1960s is the brutality of a corrupt, unjust, hypocritical, and frivolous society.[124] His novels were compatible with his socialist convictions because they portrayed an unredeemable society where every act of rebellion is gratuitous and every attempt at reform is useless. His view of society is summarized in Sebastián Salazar Bondy's contention that democracy could not solve the problems of a nation as corrupt as Peru. And it is no coincidence that Salazar Bondy set the tone for the political reception of Vargas Llosa's literary work. In his 1959 article on *Los jefes*, the first article published about his compatriot, he argued that Vargas Llosa portrays Peru as an unjust and corrupt society that cannot be reformed. He considers Vargas Llosa's literature revolutionary in spite of the fact that his characters— including the rebels—lack a socialist consciousness:

> Although Vargas Llosa does not explicitly say so—indeed there is no reason to do so—his characters are destined to build a better world through justice, education and solidarity. . . .[125]

Salazar Bondy expressed similar ideas in a letter to Vargas Llosa after reading a manuscript of *The Time of the Hero*:

> There is no crisis of youth—as we all know—but there is a youth of the crisis. In your novel I see the contradictions in the under-developed, dissonant and deformed world that we precariously inhabit.[126]

Some leftist literary critics were concerned that Vargas Llosa's novels did not make explicit claims about the inevitability of socialism in Latin America. In an essay on *The Time of the Hero* and *The Green House*, Mario Benedetti acknowledges that Vargas Llosa portrays Peru's society as corrupt and that some of his rebel characters contain the seeds of revolutionary action. But because the novels simply identify problems without expressing a true revolutionary consciousness, Benedetti considers Vargas Llosa's literature to be "committed but not militant."[127] However, Benedetti did not doubt the implicit socialist message and spoke of a "clear correspondence" between Vargas Llosa's novels and his "adhesion to the Cuban Revolution."[128]

In her reading of *Conversation in the Cathedral,* Jean Franco sees the portrait "of a society that neutralizes rebellion and turns young people into either failures or conformists."[129] The world of the novel

> lacks a dialectical process which would provide an escape. The regime and the powerful are constantly threatened by treachery and blackmail, but the revolution never breaks out. . . . The stability of the dominant class is always guaranteed [and] individual fulfillment loses all meaning in such a completely corrupt environment.[130]

The characters may all be failures and conformists. Yet together they offer a view of Peruvian society with its irreconcilable tensions. The novel suggests a social critique that is not explicitly spelled out: "The novel is a model that allows for criticism of Peru and simultaneously opens the way for improvement."[131]

Ariel Dorfman considered Vargas Llosa's literature to be valuable because it portrayed and denounced the fatalistic ideology of the Latin American bourgeoisie. Unlike Jean Franco, Dorfman did not believe that Vargas Llosa's novels contained all the necessary components to overcome the problems that were presented from a socialist perspective. He thus proposed that they be read as a complementary vision to the political novels of José María Arguedas that herald a Socialist revolution for Latin America.[132]

Without denying Vargas Llosa's intent to denounce corruption in Peruvian society, some critics claimed that his first novels lack a true Marxist revolutionary consciousness. Washington Delgado considered that *The Time of the Hero* expresses a secret admiration for the military authoritarianism it intends to criticize.[133] Jorge Lafforgue took Delgado's thesis a step further by claiming that Vargas Llosa's novels are contradictory and deceitful. In Lafforgue's view Vargas Llosa shares the ideology of the society he is denouncing because fatalism and skepticism of his characters are the very elements of bourgeois ideology that hinder revolutionary action: "He does not accept the lie and he fearlessly denounces it. Yet the principles he uses to evaluate the lie are the very same ones that produced it in the first place."[134] Lafforgue announced that he would reconsider his minority view by citing Mario Benedetti, Angel Rama, and others who considered Vargas Llosa's first novel an omen of Latin American revolution.[135]

CHAPTER THREE

The Transition

In *The Real Life of Alejandro Mayta*, a novelist meets with the man who had inspired him to work on the novel he is currently writing about the origins of political violence in Peru. Twenty-five years have elapsed since Mayta participated in Peru's first act of leftist insurrection. He has lost touch with his old comrades, some of whom now hold prominent positions in Peruvian intellectual and political life. The novelist wonders why the former revolutionary seems to have lost interest in politics. Mayta recalls wistfully that he did not abandon subversive activity willingly: "It wasn't a decision I made consciously. It just happened, the force of events. . . . It isn't that I gave up politics. You might say that politics gave me up."[1]

Although in the 1960s Vargas Llosa often expressed his solidarity with Peruvian revolutionary movements, Mayta is not an autobiographical character. Vargas Llosa never participated in the armed struggle he advocated. All the same, he could have uttered Mayta's words to describe his own estrangement from the Latin American Left. Years before he distanced himself from Fidel Castro's revolution and other Latin American movements, Vargas Llosa was ostracized and repudiated by leftist circles and organizations in which he had been an active participant.

Although some of his literary ideas and political positions were incompatible with official Communist doctrines, Vargas Llosa was not initially repudiated for them. His views on the autonomy of literary activity, on literature as a "permanent insurrection," and on the right to dissent within a socialist society had been either ignored or tolerated by his leftist associates, perhaps for tactical reasons. After all, he was a prestigious and useful ally: an outspoken critic of capitalism and an energetic defender of the Soviet model, the Cuban Revolution, and Latin American movements of armed struggle. When Vargas Llosa was repudiated by leftist intellectuals, his heterodox views about the political role of the writer were brought to bear; yet he was not repudiated for ideas he had been expounding for years. Rather, he was rebuked for his protest against the Soviet invasion of Czechoslovakia and for denouncing specific cases of intellectual censorship in Communist countries.

Retrospectively, Vargas Llosa dates the beginning of his estrangement with the Left to 1967, when Alejo Carpentier, in his diplomatic capacity, informed him that if he would publicly donate the value of the Rómulo Gallegos literary prize to Che Guevara, the Cuban government would discreetly reimburse him for the amount.[2] Vargas Llosa was not willing to go along with the proposition, but he sought to make a conciliatory gesture to his Cuban friends. In "Literature is Fire," the speech he read at the award ceremony, Vargas Llosa expressed his conviction that every Latin American nation would soon follow Cuba's revolutionary path.[3] Notwithstanding the praise he received for his speech from prominent revolutionary leaders and sympathizers, he felt his relations with Cuban officials remained somewhat strained.

His first public deviation from the politics of Communist countries was his protest in 1967 against literary censorship in the Soviet Union. Vargas Llosa reproached Soviet authorities for their "presumption that the State should direct and plan artistic creation." He insisted that socialism is compatible with artistic freedom and that its repression is disconcerting to leftist writers:

> [Artistic censorship in the Soviet Union] can only alarm and sadden any writer, and especially writers like ourselves who are convinced of the gigantic benefits that the revolution brought to the Russian people, and who hope for a Socialist solution to the problems of our own countries.[4]

His second public disagreement with the Left was his vehement criticism of the invasion of Czechoslovakia and of Fidel Castro's support of a Soviet action that "constitutes an embarrassment for Lenin's fatherland and a political stupidity of enormous dimension, and irreparable harm for the cause of Socialism in the world."[5] He made this criticism in *Caretas,* a weekly magazine published in Lima, but he wrote it in the United States during a visit to an American university.

Vargas Llosa's article had negative repercussions in leftist circles and provoked immediate expressions of skepticism about his role as a prominent ally of the Cuban Revolution. Oscar Collazos wrote an influential article in which he accused Vargas Llosa of arrogantly daring to give "Fidel Castro lessons on international politics and common sense from the pages of a reactionary publication, regarding the occupation or 'invasion' of Czechoslovakia."[6] Collazos interprets Vargas Llosa's outrage as a symptom of ideological prevarication and diagnoses "a process of intellectual mystification, and of theoretical contradictions that are evident in his reasoning."[7] Collazos probably took his cue from a brief statement made by Roberto Fernández Retamar—arguably the chief literary ideologue of the Cuban Revolution—in a 1969 Havana round-table discussion concerning the intellectual's role in the Socialist revolution. Fernández Retamar made a guarded criticism of Vargas Llosa's article about the invasion of Czechoslovakia. He did not think it proper for an article written in the United States to express a position with counterrevolutionary implications. Fernández Retamar added that Vargas Llosa's doctrine of "permanent insurrection," according to which literature can be an instrument of criticism even from within the socialist system, is counterrevolutionary because the work of the intellectual within the socialist society is not to criticize but to reinforce the political system.[8] The reproaches that Vargas Llosa received for protesting the invasion of Czechoslovakia were the prelude to his definitive repudiation by the Left, which developed from the Padilla case.

THE PADILLA CASE

In the spring of 1971, when he had moved from London to Barcelona, Vargas Llosa learned that the Cuban government had imprisoned his friend, the poet Heberto Padilla. He helped to organize an international protest with other prominent leftist writers and intellectuals who signed an open letter demanding Padilla's freedom.[9] Padilla was released from prison, but he signed a long confession recognizing moral and political shortcomings: "under the veil of a rebellious writer," he wrote, "the only thing I was doing was hiding my contempt for the Revolution. . . . That is my truth. . . . I am the man who was objectively working against the revolution."[10] Padilla denounced his own literary works as counterrevolutionary and criticized those intellectuals who had protested his imprisonment as enemies of Cuba. Vargas Llosa led a second act of protest.

With Carlos Barral, his editor, he drafted a letter to Fidel Castro, affirming the unequivocal allegiance to Cuban socialism by the signatories but also communicating their anger regarding Padilla's confession as an unnecessary and deplorable Stalinist practice on the part of the Cuban government.[11]

Vargas Llosa's second letter, cosigned by many prominent intellectuals sympathetic to the Cuban Revolution including Simone de Beauvoir, Italo Calvino, Hans Magnus Enzensberger, Carlos Fuentes, Carlos Monsivais, Juan Rulfo, Jean-Paul Sartre, and Susan Sontag. The letter precipitated his definitive fall from grace from the Latin American Left. At first he was condemned for counter-revolutionary behavior. Soon after he was scorned for his literary ideas, and finally he was criticized for the "reactionary" content of his novels. Vargas Llosa was condemned with the same criteria with which he previously had been praised: the ways in which his conduct, his literary ideas, and his works of fiction had contributed to the cause of the Revolution or confirmed socialist doctrines concerning the role of literature in the advent of socialism.

During the First National Congress of Education and Culture, held on April 23–30, 1971, in Havana, Vargas Llosa was chastised by Fidel Castro himself. Even though he was not mentioned by name (Castro rarely uses names in these contexts), it was patently clear that he was considered to be a prominent (if not the most prominent) figure of a group of

> shameless Latin Americans who live far away from the trenches of combat in the bourgeois salons, ten thousand miles from where the problems really are, profiting from the fame they gained when in an early stage they were able to express something about Latin America's problems. But as far as Cuba is concerned, they will never use Cuba again. Never! Not even in her defense. When they defend us, we will tell them: "do not defend us, *compadres*. Please. Do not defend us. It is not in our best interest that you defend us!" . . . for you already know, you bourgeois intellectuals and liberal intellectuals, and agents of the CIA and of other secret services of imperialism, that is to say, of the intelligence and spy services of imperialism: in Cuba you will have no entry. No entry! Just as we allow no entry to UPI and AP. Entry to Cuba is barred to you indefinitely, for an indefinite and infinite period of time![12]

When Castro gave this speech Vargas Llosa had been preparing an extended visit to Cuba to give a creative writing course and to participate in other cultural and editorial activities of the "Casa de las Américas," Cuba's official cultural organization, which published an influential journal of the same name. Under the circumstances his visit became impossible, even though the invitation was not officially withdrawn.

In response to Castro's speech, Vargas Llosa wrote a letter to Haydée Santamaría, editor of the journal *Casa de las Américas*, resigning his position on the editorial board of a publication with which he had been associated since 1964:

> You understand that this is the only course of action open to me after Fidel's speech upbraiding "Latin American writers who live in Europe," to whom he has forbidden entry to Cuba "for an indefinite and infinite period of time." Was he so irritated by our letter asking him to clarify the situation of Heberto Padilla? How times have changed. I remember very clearly the night we spent with him four years ago when he listened willingly to the observations and criticisms which a group of "foreign intellectuals," which he now calls "swine," made to him."[13]

In her response, published as an open letter in *Casa de las Americas*, Santamaría calls him one of the "worst slanderers" of the Cuban Revolution, citing his participation in the protests regarding Heberto Padilla as well as other differences with the Cuban Revolution, among them his rejection of the Cuban proposal to donate the Rómulo Gallegos prize to Che Guevara and his "ridiculous opinions" on the invasion of Czechoslovakia. Santamaría brands his affirmations of solidarity with the Cuban Revolution as grotesque. She calls him

> the living image of the colonized writer who despises our peoples; a vain and self-assured individual. Because he writes well he thinks he will be forgiven for acting poorly, and will even be allowed to pass judgment on a magnificent process like that of the Cuban revolution. Despite human errors, it is still the greatest attempt to date to establish in our lands a regime of justice. Men like you, who put your wretched personal interests ahead of the urgent needs of "our suffering republics," as Martí called them, have nothing to do in this process.[14]

Vargas Llosa's condemnation by his old Cuban friends and leftist associates was swift: within weeks he was repudiated as a credible spokesman for leftist causes, and within a year his ideas about socialism and literature were rebuked. The reconsideration of the socialist value of his novels took somewhat longer, but it came in due time as many critics downplayed and reconsidered their admiration of his literary qualities.

Casa de las Americas published Fidel's condemning speech in its issue of March–June, 1971. In subsequent issues the magazine included dozens of articles and declarations, with hundreds of signatures, written against Vargas Llosa and others who protested the Padilla case. Writers of all Latin American nationalities distanced themselves from Vargas Llosa, including a group of his compatriots who wanted to make clear "to public opinion that Vargas Llosa's line, and that of other 'voluntary exiles,' is not now, nor has it ever been, our line of combat."[15] Monotonously and invariably, these declarations dwelled on the counterrevolutionary complicity of Vargas Llosa. The judgment of Juan Marinello is representative: "The novelist from Lima expresses the criteria and the intention of the majority of his accomplices in his attacks against the Cuban revolution." [16]

The political condemnations of Vargas Llosa were accompanied by essays written by poets and novelists who repudiated Vargas Llosa's ideas about the political role of literature. In the fall of 1971, Mario Benedetti joined his voice with those of Collazos and Fernández Retamar to criticize Vargas Llosa's ideas on literature and politics and on the responsibilities of a socialist writer:

> Vargas Llosa . . . has maintained that the role of literature is always to be subversive. . . . The majority of those who write subversive literature in the capitalist world take it for granted that once that order is subverted, their subversive mission will be accomplished.[17]

Academics added their voices to the wave of criticism in order to discredit Vargas Llosa's intellectual credentials. Carlos Rincón, today a professor of Latin American literature in the Free University of Berlin, wrote an essay in which he discussed Vargas Llosa's views on Joanot Martorell's *Tirant lo Blanc* in order to repudiate the novelist's literary ideas and to suggest that his shortcomings as a literary critic are equally applicable to his work as a creative writer. Rincón complains of the "opportunistic eclecticism," "unhistoricized subjectivism," "anachronistic denominations," and "vulgar reductionism" that he finds in Vargas Llosa's "bourgeois reading" of Martorell's novel. All of this, he writes, reflects an understanding not of the novel but of "his own concerns as a novelist."[18] After rejecting Vargas Llosa's reading of the Valencian classic, Rincón formulates "a query regarding the ideological conjuncture in which he aligns himself with theses like the ones here reviewed."[19] He reproaches Vargas Llosa for his sympathy for the Flaubertian concept according to which "art should be in the work like God in the universe," because the novel, from this perspective, is an absolutely bourgeois product that corresponds fully to the ideological needs of that class.[20] Through and through, and not only in isolated clauses, something is affirmed as if programmed by a precise matrix: the bourgeois esthetic of representation.[21]

According to Rincón, the dichotomy that Vargas Llosa had set forth between the literary vocation and the political commitment of a writer is "an idealist recourse" that leads to

a blockade in establishing the differences and correlations between political activity and literary practice. The fabricated antinomy and the attempt to overcome it lead him to the cliché of "feeling torn apart" (surely cruel) and to an exhibitionism of the "tortured option."[22]

For Rincón, Vargas Llosa's ideas belong to a family of "bourgeois" conceptions: the doctrines of Roland Barthes, the French nouveau roman, Lucien Goldmann, and George Lukács.[23] Invoking "the materialist conception of writing as scientifically valid,"[24] Rincón includes in it the contributions of Karl Marx, Friedrich Engels, Ernst Fischer, Jacques Lacan, Michel Foucault, Walter Benjamin, Mikhail Bakhtin, Louis Althusser, and Bertold Brecht. Rincón affirms that Vargas Llosa's "theoretical deficiencies" apply to his works of fiction as well: "The study of historical-literary theses, of critical theses, and of the poetics of a novelist, defined in relation with that system, also serve in the final analysis to determine his character, not as a theorist, but precisely as a novelist."[25] The skeptisism cast on Vargas Llosa's novels became increasingly common among the very critics who had once praised them.

Some of the writers who participated in the political and intellectual repudiation of Vargas Llosa were old enemies with axes to grind. Most, however, had earlier praised Vargas Llosa's ideas, essays, and novels as contributions to leftist causes; and some even recycled old publications while substituting their original praise with negative value judgments. Carlos Rincón, for instance, had published an essay with Gisela Leber in 1968 in which he formulated a thesis diametrically opposed to that of his 1971 essay. In the earlier piece, Rincón argued that the influence of Flaubert, among other authors, had helped Vargas Llosa to write a devastating denunciation of Peruvian society:

It did not surprise the author that dominant groups in Peru would try to discredit his novel [*Time of the Hero*] with a public scandal. With his novel Vargas Llosa had eliminated every false image of Peruvian reality and had set forth the representation of Peru as a strong hierarchy of classes, a military mythology, and the moral decadence of the Leoncio Prado school; from a consistent antioligarchical perspective. Vargas Llosa whose readings of Flaubert, Tolstoy, and Sartre are among his decisive formative experiences, has utilized in this narrative appropriate experiences of his own youth.[26]

Underscoring the success with which Vargas Llosa had used the Flaubertian technique, Rincón and Leber praised *The Green House* as both a literary and a political triumph:

> Vargas Llosa has attempted to transmit to the reader the full force of the matter at hand by means of a variety of techniques in his book. Vargas Llosa has looked for and found the national weight of Peruvian popular classes and the force of destiny of modest individuals. He has taken their anonymity away and has integrated them into universal literature. The question of the prospects of that society is fully resolved in his novel *The Green House*.[27]

Citing the authority of Lukács (who would also lose his good standing in Rincón's 1971 essay), the authors underscored the importance of Vargas Llosa's novels among those of other Latin American writers such as Alejo Carpentier, Juan Rulfo, and Carlos Fuentes:

> Whereas the socially critical novel of the thirties convinced us above all through its political and social pathos; writers such as Carpentier, Fuentes, Rulfo, or Vargas Llosa succeed in their novels in a deeper portrayal of society that is upheld by analysis of collective social and moral norms in their historical process. But one would not apply to this sort of novel, which progressively advances an ever deepening comprehension of reality, the antipodes of narration and description that Lukács established to differentiate the realist from the naturalist novel.[28]

In his 1971 essay Rincón does not seem to recall his ostensibly erroneous reading of 1968, perhaps because the criterion by which he had earlier rated Vargas Llosa as progressive (the use of Flaubertian techniques to achieve a representation of Latin American reality) is brought to bear in 1971 to brand him as a "bourgeois" writer. Any reference to his earlier essay would have begged explanation beyond the scope of the task at hand and raised the thorny issue of intellectual integrity. But for Rincón, intellectual integrity was probably beside the point. Like others who contributed to *Casa de las Américas* in the several issues that followed the publication of Santamaría's open letter to Vargas Llosa, he was responding to an official call—summarized in Fidel's speech—to repudiate the intellectuals protesting the Padilla case. By 1971, Vargas Llosa's high regard in leftist circles as an intellectual and a writer was deflated, and his dissent was dismissed as groundless enemy propaganda.

Vargas Llosa knew of the criticism directed at him, but he continued to affirm his support for the Cuban Revolution. In May of 1971 he lamented that the controversy could harm the revolutionary cause:

> Some journalists are using my resignation from the editorial committee of the journal *Casa de las Américas* to attack the Cuban Revolution. I want to meet this dirty maneuver head-on and to remove my name from any campaign against Cuban socialism and against the Latin American revolution.[29]

His repeated expressions of solidarity with the Cuban Revolution were discredited as intellectual posturing and opportunist hypocrisy from the beginning: "The least that we, Che's real comrades, can ask of you today," wrote Haydée Santamaría in her letter, "is that you no longer write or even utter that name that belongs to all the revolutionaries of the world, and not to men like you."[30] Vargas Llosa ultimately declared that "nothing would make me happier, than that this episode were only a passing one."[31] But his hopes were not to be realized.

His efforts to express solidarity with the broad Latin American revolution following the Padilla case did not persuade his critics. On the contrary, the rejection of his literary ideas spilled over into the academic institutions of Europe and the United States, where his reputation as an intellectual and a novelist was soon to diminish. Following the publication of his book *García Márquez: Historia de un deicidio* (1971), Vargas Llosa participated in a polemic with Angel Rama. His old friend dismissed Vargas Llosa's ideas about literary creation as an "unthinkable" Romantic anachronism for practitioners of "the methodology of our time (which includes such heterogeneous things as structuralism's reconstruction of rhetoric, post-Jungian psychoanalysis, Western neo-Marxism, and transformational linguistics.)"[32] Rama finds Vargas Llosa's literary criteria useless as critical tools, and harmful to younger writers who might take him as a role-model: "I feel that the application of [his thesis about literary creation] will not yield good results in young admiring writers."[33] The central theme of Rama's two essays refuting Vargas Llosa's literary conception argues that literary creation that embraces unconscious or irrational elements is incompatible with Marxism: "Contradicting the idea of art as human and social work, a contribution of Marxism, Vargas Llosa dwells on the idealist thesis of the irrational (if not divine, at least demonic) origins of the literary work."[34] José Miguel Oviedo, the most authoritative critic of Vargas Llosa's work, did not contradict Rama's main contentions. Oviedo argued that Vargas Llosa's literary ideas are generally invalid, but that Rama had gone too far in his categorical dismissal of ideas that illuminate Vargas Llosa's own literary works: "There is only one sense in which the 'theory' is totally valid: as a justification of his personal case. [But his thesis] cannot be elevated, as Vargas Llosa would wish, to a universal category that would explain the craft of the novel."[35]

Following the repudiation of Vargas Llosa's literary ideas came the repudiation of the political content of his novels. This resusitated Jorge Lafforgue's once-retracted thesis, according to which Vargas Llosa's novels are a boon to the bourgeois society they purportedly denounce. Antonio Cornejo Polar wrote that Vargas Llosa's novels are "a variant of commodity fetishism."[36] Cornejo Polar argues that although Vargas Llosa's early novels "offer the image of national society as an inevitable space of human degradation,"[37] in the final analysis they generate a skepticism in the reader that is incompatible with a Marxist analysis.[38]

In Latin America a great deal of the intellectual and academic critical reception of Vargas Llosa's works has continued to echo the claims made by leftist critics in the aftermath of the Padilla case. In a representative essay published in 1989, Mirko Lauer gives an account of Vargas Llosa's rift with the Left in which he also explains why progressive literary critics changed their views about novels they once considered significant contributions to socialist causes. Lauer portrays Vargas Llosa as a liberal in leftist clothing who used the Cuban Revolution to gain literary prestige. After he became successful selling his books in the imperialist markets of Europe and the U.S., it was no longer necessary to pretend he was supportive of leftist causes and his political activity became an "indiscriminate exercise of conservatism."[39] Comparing Vargas Llosa to José de la Riva Agüero, a turn-of-the-century Peruvian intellectual he labels "profascist," Lauer declares that Vargas Llosa "is not yet there, but his passion for one very specific liberty, i.e., liberty of the press, may well evolve into its formal opposite: a passion for authority in the name of the defense of individual liberty; authority which fears the threat of collectivism."[40] Lauer regrets that literary critics had once considered Vargas Llosa's early novels to be progressive, and he celebrates the newer estimates of their political worth: "As consensus builds regarding the fickle social content of his works, political criticism begins to breathe easier."[41] According to Lauer, the "methodological errors" of the literary critics who first explained the novels of Vargas Llosa can be attributed to the writer himself, because he "deceived" them about his solidarity with leftist causes:

> Thus *Time of the Hero* was received exclusively as an antimilitary and antiauthoritarian statement. No one in the seventies was interested in seeing that novel as the advent of a literary technique that blurs reality, that posits and inaugurates the apogee of ambiguity, which is something different from denunciation. In the twenty years since *Time of the Hero* it has gradually been revealed that the apparent coherence was no such thing. What was called a technical revolution in narrative evolved into a notable capacity for a consumer literature. . . . A liberalism which was taken as Leftist evolved into an authoritarianism of the Right that some still consider liberal.[42]

Lauer's position reveals the cynicism of many who reassessed their interpretations of Vargas Llosa's novels. In short, the same critics regarded the same novels as great contributions to literature when their author was in good standing with the Cuban regime but products of bourgeois ideology when he had fallen from grace.

During his condemnation by the Left, Vargas Llosa's most important ally was the Chilean novelist Jorge Edwards, who described the "farce" of intellectuals whose literary judgments and cutting-edge critical theories are mere window-dressing for opportunistic political complacency:

> Whoever is in a position of authority and inhaling the incense burnt on the altar of the heroes will always have right on his side. And those who do not think like him will be crushed beneath the wheels of the ongoing Revolution, to the applause of the writer-bureaucrats from their corners, who will happily wheel out the latest fashionable sophistries without any scruples at all, and with all their pseudo-intellectual paraphernalia, will further blacken the misdeeds and finish making mincemeat of those who have already been singled out as propitiatory victims by the Number One Writer. [43]

To explain Vargas Llosa's repudiation, Edwards reflects on the Padilla case: "It is another matter that these intellectuals may, at some stage, be useful for a particular policy, as Mario Vargas Llosa or Jean-Paul Sartre were useful at one time for Fidel's policies, and later ceased to be."[44]

Although Edwards also considered himself a leftist intellectual, his ideas were not given any more credence than Vargas Llosa's in progressive circles. After all,

Persona Non Grata: An Envoy in Castro's Cuba, in which Edwards expresses these views about intellectuals and the Cuban Revolution, is the chronicle of his disenchantment with the Castro regime during his stay in Havana as a Chilean diplomat. In this book, Edwards sides with Vargas Llosa in criticizing the imprisonment of Padilla as a disgusting political maneuver.

Vargas Llosa praised Edwards' book as "a serious criticism of important aspects of the revolution made from a leftist perspective. . . . *Persona Non Grata* breaks a sacred taboo in Latin America for a leftist intellectual—that the Cuban Revolution is untouchable, and cannot be criticized in public without one's automatically becoming an accomplice of reactionary forces."[45] Rather than denounce or condemn the strategy of the revolutionary Left, however, Vargas Llosa used his review of Edwards's book to explain the circumstances that precipitated his own ostracism from Cuba. He justified the authoritarian measures taken by Fidel Castro as a pragmatic response to protect the Cuban Revolution from the kind of economic blockade that contributed to the military coup that toppled Salvador Allende (whom Edwards had served as diplomat):

> The harsh dominion of economic realities, the scarce resources of a tiny underdeveloped island, and the gigantic and savage blockade imposed by Imperialism to drown it could not allow that "socialism in freedom" to prosper from the very beginning. Given the dilemma of maintaining an open Socialism, but devoid of international support which could spell the demise of the revolution and the return of the old neo-colonial system, or to save the revolution by linking its fate—that is to say its economy and its policies— to the Soviet model, Fidel, in his famous pragmatic spirit, chose the lesser of the two evils. Who could reproach him, especially after the death of Allende and the fall of Unidad Popular [Allende's political movement]. . . . This is why, notwithstanding the horror that I have for police states and for the dogmatism of systems that believe in single truths, if I have to chose between one and the other, I bite my tongue and continue to say "on with Socialism."[46]

Four years after the Padilla case, Vargas Llosa continued to defend the moral and political superiority of Communist governments and parties, whose leaders and ideologues continued to consider him a traitor to the Cuban Revolution for his literary ideas. These ideas were considered either the sinister defense of counterrevolutionary ideology or anachronisms useful for understanding his work as a creative writer. Within months of the day he drafted the letter protesting Heberto Padilla's confession, Vargas Llosa's image changed from the novelist committed to leftist causes to the bourgeois defender of reactionary thinking. And ironically, Vargas Llosa continued for years to justify the moral and political superiority of the political regime that had humiliated him.

THE PERPETUAL ORGY

When the dust from the Padilla case began to settle, Vargas Llosa reconsidered his ideas on the political function of literature. He could not easily continue to express views about the socialist relevance of the unconstrained creative drive, when his literary ideas had been universally repudiated by the literary Left, from Cuban cultural organizations to North American universities. For years Vargas Llosa had tried to demonstrate that spontaneous literary activity would have socialist implications. In the aftermath of the Padilla case he gave up.

Although he still identified himself as a socialist, in 1975 he finally abandoned his conviction that literature is, in essence, revolutionary in a political sense. *The Perpetual Orgy: Flaubert and Madame Bovary* (1975) is, therefore, a transitional book; Vargas Llosa continues to affirm his socialist convictions, but for the first time he rejects the doctrines of engaged literature: "[Sartre's] pronouncements concerning literature and the role of the writer, which at one time I regarded as articles of faith, seem to me today to be unpersuasive."[47]

In *The Perpetual Orgy* Vargas Llosa claims, as he had ever since his 1958 essay on César Moro, that literature is an act of rebellion that expresses the dark side of man, but he abandons his views that literary transgression is necessarily good for socialism. Instead he embraces Georges Bataille's idea that good literature expresses transgression purely and simply. With this idea Vargas Llosa interprets Flaubert's general views on literature, as well as the main theme of Madame Bovary:

> Emma wants sexual pleasure. . . . Emma wants to know other worlds, other people . . . and she also wants her existence to be different and exciting, to ensure that adventure and risk, the magnificent gestures of generosity and sacrifice, will play a role in it. Emma's rebellion is born of one conviction, the root of all her acts: I am not resigned to my lot, the dubious compensation of the beyond doesn't matter to me, I want my life to be wholly and completely fulfilled here and now. A chimera no doubt lies at the heart of the destiny to which Emma aspires, above all if it becomes a collective

pattern, a common human goal. No society can offer all its members such an existence; it is evident, moreover, that in order for communal life to be possible man must resign himself to keeping a close rein on his desires, to limiting the will to transgress that Georges Bataille called Evil.[48]

In Vargas Llosa's book on Flaubert, the leitmotifs of his essays on the political commitment of the writer reappear without socialist implications: the metaphor of the vulture eating the carrion no longer represents the affronts of the revolutionary writer against capitalist society. It now refers to the process whereby a writer transforms his experiences and observations to create a work of fiction.[49] The theme of the duplicity of the writer reappears, but it no longer signals the ambivalence of an artist who may feel torn between his political convictions and his literary vocation. It is now "this dual nature of the novelist, this living and sharing of human experience and at the same time being a cold and avaricious exploiter of one's own life and that of others. . . ."[50] The "added element" no longer suggests dissatisfaction with social injustice: it now refers to any fictional manipulation of the real.[51] He repeats his thesis regarding the intentions of an author: "A frequent result of Flaubert's artistic strategy is that the author's intentions go astray in the course of creation and come to be replaced by a moral, political, or philosophical intention generated by the fiction itself, which may well conflict with the conscious ideology of the creator."[52] But he no longer uses this argument to explain why good literature is always progressive even though the author may be reactionary. On the contrary, Vargas Llosa affirms that, as much as he still admires socialist ideals, socialist literature tends to be authoritarian. To make his point he analyses the case of Bertold Brecht.

> Brecht was a man with generous social ideas, sensitive to the injustice of which the majority of humanity is the victim, and an optimist as well: he believed that this situation could change through revolution and that literature would contribute to this change by opening people's eyes and awakening their consciousness to the "truth.". . . [Brecht's] literature thus becomes, like dictatorships, something that leaves no other alternative to total acceptance or total rejection. Proselytizing, paternalistic, doctrinaire, it is an art that is, in a profound sense of the word, religious, not only because it is addressed to men who are already believers or catechumens, but because it demands of them—despite its apparent dogged appeal to reason—from the outset, and before all else, an act of faith: the acceptance of a single truth that exists prior to the work of art.[53]

If in 1965 Vargas Llosa had admired Flaubert for his testimony of a "reality doomed to disappear,"[54] in 1975 he asserts that

> The ever-contemptuous Flaubert, by contrast, brought into being a body of work which in practice presupposes (since it requires them) the maturity and the freedom of the reader: if there is *one* truth in the work of literature (because it is possible that there are several and they are contradictory), it is hidden, woven into the very pattern of the elements constituting the fiction, and it is up to the reader to discover it, to draw, by and for himself and at his own risk and peril, the ethical, social, and philosophical conclusions of the story that the author has set before him.[55]

Vargas Llosa's propositions concerning the social implications of literature in *The Perpetual Orgy* are somewhat confused. He oscillates between a doctrine that understands literature as a protest against the status quo and a new position that regards literature as a compensation for an inherent human need to fabricate illusions:

> Like Don Quixote or Hamlet, [Emma Bovary] sums up in her tormented personality and her less than glorious life story a certain permanent attitude toward life, capable of appearing in the most diverse guises in different places and different eras. And while it is a universal and enduring story, it is at the same time one of the most personal attempts to define the limits of the human, that quest from which all the heroic feats and all the cataclysms of mankind have derived: the capacity to fabricate illusions and the mad determination to make them real.[56]

The idea that literature's raison d'etre is linked to the fact that man's possibilities are always inferior to man's desires can be gleaned from Flaubert's letter that inspired the title of Vargas Llosa's book: "For want of the real, one tries to console oneself by way of fiction. . . . The one way of tolerating existence is to lose oneself in literature as in a perpetual orgy."[57]

In *The Perpetual Orgy* Vargas Llosa recalls that in the sixties he was uncompromising in his enthusiasm for the Cuban Revolution and in his passion for Flaubert. In 1974, "Fourteen years later, I am more tolerant of criticism of the Cuban revolution; I am as intransigent as ever, on the other hand, when the subject under discussion is Flaubert."[58]

CAPTAIN PANTOJA AND THE SPECIAL SERVICE

By 1975 Vargas Llosa had reconsidered his ideas on the social implications of literature. The first half of the seventies was also a period of artistic transition, during which he gradually abandoned the character type most prevalent in his first novels: tragic and innocent victims of a corrupt society the likes of Ricardo Arana, Gamboa, Santiago Zavala, Jum, and Ambrosio. Vargas Llosa's artistic transition becomes apparent in *Captain Pantoja and the Special Service* (1973), where he explores, with humor and irony, two themes he had earlier treated with the utmost seriousness and pathos: the corruption of military institutions and prostitution in a society "with a corrupt heart but with a puritan façade."[59] Although this novel is not a reflection of the author's completed artistic and political transition, its ingredients indicate in an incipient way the path that leads to *The War of the End of the World*.

Captain Pantaleón Pantoja has received a special mission from the general headquarters of the Peruvian armed forces—to establish a secret prostitution service to placate the sexual appetite of soldiers who are molesting women at the outskirts of their jungle garrisons. In order to carry out his duties in secret, Pantaleón is ordered to live as an ordinary citizen. He is forbidden regular contact with other soldiers, and he is not allowed to reveal the nature of his clandestine activities to anyone, including the women with whom he lives: his wife Pochita and his mother Leonor. The novel's main story line traces Pantaleón's adventures and misadventures from the fateful day he receives his orders until his failure and transfer to a humiliating post.

The novel has two types of chapters. Four of them consist of dialogues in which conversations that took place in distinct times and places are juxtaposed, a literary technique José Miguel Oviedo has called "telescoping dialogues."[60] Vargas Llosa gives this technique a twist with a formal adjustment summarized in his book *A Writer's Reality*. He eliminates the *verba decendi* (e.g.: "he said," "she affirmed with sincerity," and such interpolations) and replaces them with the descriptions by an observing third-person narrator.[61] Thus, for example, instead of including a simple annotation identifying Pantaleón as the speaker, Vargas Llosa interjects description into his character's transcribed speech:

> "Because the first time you name me or speak about the Service, I'll throw all fifty specialists on top of you, and let me warn you, they all have long fingernails," Pantaleón Pantoja opens a desk drawer, takes out a revolver, loads and unloads it, spins the cylinder, takes aim at the backboard, the telephone, the rafters. "And if they don't

put an end to you, I'll finish you off myself, with one shot in the head. Understood?"[62]

The other six chapters *Captain Pantoja and the Special Service* are composed of letters, notes, and reports from the military, articles from local papers, clips from radio programs, and accounts of Pantaleón's dreams.

The contrast between Pantaleón's keen sense of professionalism and the outrageous nature of his operation create many comic situations in the novel. Determined to carry out his orders and accomplish his secret mission according to strict military protocol, Pantaleón resorts to a series of euphemisms. He refers to his prostitutes as "visitors," and he uses the word "service" to designate intercourse.

With scientific rigor Pantaleón reads books and articles on male sexuality to determine the number and the duration of the "services" each soldier requires per month to placate his sexual appetite. For the sake of thrift and efficiency he distributes pornographic materials among the soldiers to reduce the length of each "servicing." The comedy in the novel arises not only from the unusual nature of the service but also from the way in which the matter is presented to the reader. The activities of the service are never narrated from the point of view of an omniscient narrator or a character but by indirect means, such as letters and documents. Panta's official reports use dry bureaucratic language to describe his struggles against unexpected follies: the fury of a soldier who discovers his sister is the prostitute waiting to serve him; the cunning of a homosexual who dresses as a woman "to practice his vice with the troops"; the connivances of a soldier who escapes with the prostitute he wishes to marry.[63]

The local authorities are aware of, and displeased with, Pantaleón's service. Father Godofredo Beltrán Calila, commander and chaplain of the Peruvian Amazon region, resigns his position as a discreet protest. Also, Scavino, the general in overall charge of the region, distances himself from Pantaleón and his activities. Closer to home, Pochita feels uneasy about her husband's mysterious activities. She eventually learns of Pantaleón's relationship with "the Brazilian," a prostitute he takes as a lover. Pochita finds out about her husband's secret service and his infidelity in a letter she receives from Maclovia, a prostitute who has been expelled from the service and who hopes to regain her job by ingratiating herself with the wife of her former boss, whom she assumes is privy to the whole thing. After reading the letter, Pochita leaves Pantaleón.

In the first rough draft of *Captain Pantoja and the Special Service*, Vargas Llosa had created an opposition between Pantaleón and "el Sinchi," an announcer for the local radio station who takes to the air-waves to judge the morality of the local citizens.[64] He is a farcical character unlike any in Vargas Llosa's previous novels, an opportunist who utilizes his radio show to ruin the reputations of those who refuse to surrender to his blackmail. The first rough draft of the novel does not contain the complete development of the novel's plot, but it is evident that "el Sinchi" represented the main threat to Pantaleón's success: he figures out the nature of the secret service and threatens to expose it if Pantaleón does not pay him off.[65]

In the second draft, Vargas Llosa began to elaborate a new counterpoint, more important and decisive to the plot of the novel in its final form: that of Pantaleón and Brother Francisco, the leader of "The Brothers of the Ark," a religious cult that expresses its spirituality in weird rites that include the crucifixion of insects and small animals. In the novel:

> [Brother Francisco] goes everywhere on foot and wherever he goes he hangs up an enormous cross and dedicates Arks that are his churches. He has a lot of followers, especially among the working people, and it seems the priests are furious about the competition he's giving them but until now there hasn't been one peep out of them.[66]

The men and women of the brotherhood must remain celibate. They can "live together, but only as 'brother' and 'sister'; the apostles have to be pure."[67] As their numbers grow, the brotherhood's religious practices degenerate into criminal acts: the members begin to crucify children and adults. Brother Francisco and his followers are prototypes of new characters and situations that will become commonplace in Vargas Llosa's fiction.

THE FANATIC

After completing the first draft of *Captain Pantoja and the Special Service*, but before writing the second one in which Brother Francisco appears, Vargas Llosa read a book that would have a great impact upon his literary career: *Rebellion in the Backlands* by Euclides da Cunha. The influence of this book on Vargas Llosa is a clear indication of his artistic transition. He read *Rebellion in the Backlands* on the recommendation of the Brazilian film maker Rui Guerra, who had asked him to write a screen play (the movie was never shot) based on some of the historical events that had inspired da Cunha. The principal event for da Cunha was the Canudos rebellion of 1896, in which a community of humble devotees of Antonio the Counselor—a messianic leader—were massacred by the army of the recently constituted Republic of Brazil. Vargas Llosa went beyond da Cunha's book and studied other works on the history of Brazil and on religious messianism that helped him to develop the theme of fanaticism in other literary projects, including *The War of the End of the World*. The atmosphere of popular exaltation for a charismatic, messianic leader is elaborated in both the drafts of the screenplay Vargas Llosa wrote for Rui Guerra. It is the same kind of atmosphere that Vargas Llosa transposes with black humor into the second and subsequent drafts of *Captain Pantoja and the Special Service*. It is no coincidence that Brother Francisco is Brazilian.

In his first novels there were characters such as Gamboa of *Time of the Hero*, or Pantaleón himself, obsessed by the rules of the institution to which they belong. Brother Francisco, however, is a new kind of character in Vargas Llosa's narrative: the fanatic, ready to challenge anything or anyone who presents obstacles to his heartfelt beliefs. The model for his religious fanatic in *Captain Pantoja and the Special Service* was clearly Antonio the Counselor from da Cunha's *Rebellion in the Backlands*. But the development of this character-type in Vargas Llosa's narratives also owes something to William Faulkner. In essays and works of fiction, Vargas Llosa has expressed his fascination with the fanatic in Faulkner's literary world. In *The Storyteller*, for example, Vargas Llosa recalls "a character out of Faulkner—single-minded, fearlessly stubborn, and frighteningly heroic."[68] Beginning with *Captain Pantoja and the Special Service*, Vargas Llosa's fanatics recall Faulknerian characters of unbending convictions, such as Percy Grimm of *Light in August*:

> He seemed to be served by certitude, the blind and untroubled faith in the rightness and infallibility of his actions.[69]

> He was indefatigable, restrained yet forceful; there was something about him irresistible and prophetlike.[70]

> Somehow the very sound of the two words with their evocation secret and irrevocable and something of a hidden and unsleeping and omnipotent eye watching the doings of men, began to reassure Grimm's men in their own make-believe.[71]

The importance Vargas Llosa grants Brother Francisco and his brotherhood as the main counterpoint to Pantaleón and his service led him to downplay el Sinchi's role as the character who, in the first draft of the novel, was to precipitate the failure of the Special Service. Vargas Llosa decided to water down Sinchi's significance and turn him into a burlesque character with which he projects onto the Peruvian jungle the amusing epistolary quarrels of medieval knights who don a fierce façade only to hide their cowardice.

One of the ways in which Sinchi attempts to blackmail Pantaleón is through a threatening letter; and here Vargas Llosa is alluding to the letters Joanot Martorell wrote to challenge knights he had no intention of confronting. Vargas Llosa and Martín de Riquer edited Martorell's letters in a book entitled *The Imaginary Combat*, published shortly before *Captain Pantoja and the Special Service*.[72] According to an introductory note by Riquer, Martorell would scrupulously follow the epistolary protocol with which medieval knights accused other knights of an offense and demanded satisfaction. If the addressee denied the charges he should expect a challenge to a duel. Sinchi's epistolary threat fits the pattern:

From *The Imaginary Combat:*

> So that your wrongdoing and disloyalty do not go unpunished, I request—unless of course you admit your errors—a fight to the finish.[73]

From *Captain Pantoja and the Special Service:*

> . . . if you persist in your lack of understanding and obstinacy, and if, before the end of the month, what is due me is not in my hands, there will be for your enterprise, as well as for its boss and the brains behind it, nothing less than a fight to the finish with neither piety nor compassion, and both of you will suffer the fatal consequences.[74]

Eventually Sinchi decides to make peace with Pantaleón; he has made enough enemies with his attacks on Brother Francisco, whose influence in the jungle region has overshadowed his own. In the course of the novel Francisco's Brotherhood of the Ark becomes overwhelmingly popular. Several prostitutes abandon the Service in order to become chaste members of the brotherhood, and even Pantaleón's mother becomes a follower of Francisco, until she finds out that they have crucified a child. The military, which had been indifferent to the activities of the brotherhood, decides to repress the movement when it begins to crucify people. Brother Francisco is captured but escapes with the help of his converts, some of whom are soldiers and officers. He dies a martyr when he orders his devotees to crucify him.

Pantaleón's mission fails after the crucifixion of "the Brazilian." The story of the Brazilian, like that of Bonifacia of *The Green House,* or that of Hortensia of *Conversation in the Cathedral,* evokes the standard plot of a Mexican cinematic melodrama. She was a poor child forced into a life of prostitution because of her unusual beauty. Her life as a prostitute leads her to a bloody death (the kind worthy of tabloid journalism), attended by strange and mysterious circumstances. It is suspected at first that the Brotherhood of the Ark was behind her death because she was crucified in their customary style. After other suppositions and conjectures, the case is finally clarified: she was murdered by Teófilo Morey, the ex-mayor of a jungle town, and his accomplices, who had plotted to attack a ship of the Service to force themselves on the prostitutes on their way to a military outpost. They had decided to commandeer the ship because Pantaleón had denied them, as he had many other civilian requests, the use of his Service. The Brazilian's murder was not premeditated, but the criminals had crucified her to implicate the Brotherhood of the Ark.

Pantaleón decides to give a eulogy at the Brazilian's burial dressed in full military regalia. He does it (as he explains to his superiors) to raise the morale of his female "visitors" following the assault of the ship and threats of further violence. Pantaleón is unable to convince his superiors of the propriety of his action and the Service is subsequently dissolved. Like Gamboa in *Time of the Hero*, Pantaleón is punished with a humiliating transfer before his actions jeopardize the reputation of the military. His story and the novel end with an attenuating irony. Pantaleón and Pochita have reconciled and are living together in a remote and barren military outpost. Pantaleón is as obsessed as ever with his military duties, but he is still in love with the deceased Brazilian, and he has become a devotee of the cult of Brother Francisco: "Poor little specialist, oh, how awful, my little crucified girl, my pretty little 'sister' from the Ark."[75]

Although treated with humor and irony, the theme of *Captain Pantoja*—the downfall of a well-meaning military man who fails precisely because he has tried to be faithful to a hypocritical military institution—has an antecedent in Gamboa's predicament in *Time of the Hero*. But the contrast between Pantaleón Pantoja, as a man obsessed with military discipline, and Brother Francisco, as a religious fanatic ("some guy crucified himself to announce the end of the world"[76]), would reemerge years later as Vargas Llosa developed the theme of his most important novel. In *The War of the End of the World*, he juxtaposes Moreira César, an obsessive general, and Antonio the Counselor, a messianic leader, to explore the nature of violence aroused by fanaticism, be it religious, military, or ideological. In 1973, when he published *Captain Pantoja and the Special Service*, he was not yet fully prepared to explore a theme that would have clashed with his conviction that capitalist society should be liquidated in order to establish socialism.

In short, the historical figure of Antonio the Counselor inspired the creation of Brother Francisco; and the opposition between Francisco and Pantaleón anticipates that of Moreira César and Antonio the Counselor in *The War of the End of the World*. Brother Francisco is not, however, the only literary antecedent to the Counselor. He is the first fanatic in Vargas Llosa's narrative, but several others appear in *Aunt Julia and the Scriptwriter*.

AUNT JULIA AND THE SCRIPTWRITER

Aunt Julia and the Scriptwriter (1977) is what Umberto Eco would call an "open novel" because it deliberately leaves many loose ends. It is not necessary to tie them all up in order to follow its main plot. The principal relationships in the novel involve Varguitas, a young Peruvian writer, two Bolivians who have recently arrived in Lima, Varguitas's aunt Julia, with whom he falls in love, and Pedro Camacho, the scriptwriter and director of radio-plays for a local radio station. Varguitas, aunt Julia, and Pedro Camacho are the three protagonists of a novel whose main theme is the relationship between life and art. With *Aunt Julia and the Scriptwriter* Vargas Llosa abandons the fatalism of his first novels in order to explore, with humor and irony, the vicissitudes of literary creation. With this novel, the theme of the unsalvageable capitalist society disappears from Vargas Llosa's narrative.

Vargas Llosa had begun to work on the novel before he began his book on Flaubert and finished it after the latter had been published. In *Aunt Julia and the Scriptwriter* the Flaubertian echoes are evident and clear. There are connections, for example, with *The Sentimental Education*. In both novels a young, aspiring novelist (both Varguitas and Fréderic write stories inspired by their own emotional experiences) falls in love with an older woman. Greater perhaps is the influence of Flaubert's *The Temptation of Saint Anthony*. In this novel Flaubert creates an opposition between the austere and solitary life of the hermit saint and sections in which the demons tempt him with illusions that alleviate his misery and his loneliness: "O Fantasy, carry me off on your wings to distract me from my sadness!"[77] Flaubert never considered *The Temptation of Saint Anthony* to be a theological exploration of temptation, although he did study treatises of moral theology to aid in his elaboration of the inner worlds of his character. Rather, he understood his novel as an allegory about the consoling powers of fiction.[78]

Aunt Julia and the Scriptwriter is also a novel about the human need to fabricate illusions. Vargas Llosa intertwines two alternating series of narratives: Varguitas's episodes, narrated in the first person, in which he explores the daily life of his protagonists, and Pedro Camacho's radio-plays, written in narrative form, through which the imaginary world of the scriptwriter is explored. This Flaubertian formula of alternating the mediocrity of an individual's life with the intensity of his or her imagination is something Vargas Llosa developed years after he had originally begun to work on the story of a radio scriptwriter.

The origins of *Aunt Julia and the Scriptwriter* can be traced to Vargas Llosa's notes of 1971 or 1972 that appear in the first pages of the same notebook in which he wrote the first draft of *Captain Pantoja and the Special Service*. The annotations are brief, but they contain the germ of the novel, which was clearly inspired after he met Raúl Salomón in 1953. Salomón could write several radio-plays at the same time. Vargas Llosa's note read:

Raúl Salomón
Radioplays=

A young woman faints during her wedding
ceremony
A black stowaway is discovered in a warehouse in
the port of Callao
The beating of a strict and puritan father by
his family.[79]

In later drafts Vargas Llosa worked on narrative sections devoted to the life of Raúl Salomón, whose name would become Pedro Camacho, and on the plots of his radio-plays. In time, Vargas Llosa also decided to draw on material from his own life: the romance between eighteen year-old Varguitas and his thirty year-old aunt is based on Vargas Llosa's own relationship with Julia Urquidiz Illanes, his first wife, to whom he dedicates the book.[80] In the final versions of the novel, the everyday-life sections are Varguitas's first person narratives. Varguitas writes about his romance with a woman who has recently divorced his uncle and about his fascination with Pedro Camacho. Varguitas's episodes are not strict autobiographical narrations, as Vargas Llosa has explained:

At first I wanted to write all of Varguitas's episodes with absolute objectivity, that is to say, to tell the truth of my personal experience. In practice, however, I realized this was absolutely impossible. My own experiences were modified in order to become literature. Literature is always more of a contradiction of the real than a representation of the real. In literature reality is invariably modified and transformed.[81]

After writing *Aunt Julia and the Scriptwriter,* Vargas Llosa published an essay on Victor Hugo in which he argued that the narrator in a work of fiction who purports to speak for himself and to write in an autobiographical mode has more than likely modified his personal experience in order to create a convincing literary world:

> [Hugo's narrator] interrupts his narrative to state opinions, sometimes in the first person, always in a loud and rhythmical voice, with a name he would like us to believe corresponds to the real Victor Hugo. He often assures us that he is just the obedient writer of a story that took place before he wrote the novel. He would like us to believe that his story is as true as life itself, as truth itself, that it transcends him as a mere intermediary, a reporter of the real. What a fairy-tale! In fact he is the cunning creator and the super-star of this grandiose lie. His creative work is full of life not because it resembles a pre-existing reality, but rather because it is a product of his fantasy, of the power of his inspiration and of the convincing strength of his words, of the tricks and magic of his art.[82]

Vargas Llosa's observations about the autobiographical narrator can also be read as a commentary on the narrator of *Aunt Julia and the Scriptwriter*. In the novel he modified certain events of his own life, and he changed the order in which biographical events took place. For instance, the main action of the novel takes place between 1958 and 1959 (when the real Vargas Llosa was working on his doctorate in Madrid), but his romance and marriage to Julia Urquidi actually took place in Peru five years earlier, between 1953 and 1954.

Vargas Llosa modified the facts of his existence by adapting and fusing them with the themes and literary motives of his favorite readings. The romance between a younger man and an older woman has a long literary tradition that includes works Vargas Llosa has cherished, not only Flaubert's *Sentimental Education* but also *Tirant lo Blanc*, a novel which may have aided Vargas Llosa in his elaboration of the feelings and even the words of the older woman as she is being wooed by a young man. In the Valencian classic, the older woman, who is afraid of violating social conventions, responds to the advances of the young man with bittersweet retorts that mingle pleasant surprise and cautious incredulity. She is a mature woman who has not lost the illusions of her youth. There are tender passages in *Aunt Julia and the Scriptwriter* that suggest Vargas Llosa's possible debt to Martorell's classic:

> From *Aunt Julia:*—Your amusing words require an answer, and not as you would like, for you have troubled and preoccupied my heart. I am trying to think what could have been the cause that has given you hopes about myself, since my age is so unequal to yours; and if

such a thing were known, what would be said of me? That I have fallen in love with my grandson.[83]

From *Tirant:*—I've been doing a lot of thinking and I don't like this situation, Varguitas. Don't you realize it's absurd? I'm thirty-two years old, I'm a divorcée—can you tell me what I'm doing with a kid eighteen years old? That's a typical perversion of women in their fifties, and I'm not old enough yet for that.[84]

Aunt Julia and the Scriptwriter consists of twenty chapters. In the odd-numbered ones, from 1 to 19, the adult Varguitas remembers the events of a single year: his frustrated attempts to write serious literature, which he contrasts to the extraordinary ability of Pedro Camacho to write and direct nine different radio-plays each day at the station where they both work. These odd-numbered chapters, which we will call the "Varguitas episodes," also narrate the romance between Varguitas and his aunt Julia from their first meeting—occurring on the same day that Camacho joins the staff of the radio station—until they marry. The narrator recalls Pedro Camacho's eccentricities, the impact of his radio-plays on the Peruvian public, and how his scripts become increasingly incoherent as he goes mad. In the last chapter, Varguitas, several years after his divorce from Julia and returning to Peru after a long stay in Europe, encounters Pedro Camacho. Varguitas has become a successful novelist while the impoverished and mentally unstable scriptwriter has long since abandoned his writing craft.

The even-numbered chapters—with the exception of chapter 20—are stylized narrations based on Pedro Camacho's radio-plays and represent Camacho's point of view. Vargas Llosa adopts a melodramatic tone in these stories that reveal the idiosyncrasies and obsessions of the scriptwriter. In each there is a sympathetic fifty-year-old character ("in the prime of life"), which is Pedro Camacho's age. In each there is also a pejorative reference to the Argentinians whom Pedro Camacho constantly and obsessively criticizes. These chapters are not Pedro Camacho's scripts; they are narrations whose main plots coincide with those that are attributed to Pedro Camacho in Varguitas's episodes. Vargas Llosa has explained that he neither listened to nor studied radio-plays to come up with Pedro Camacho's stories. Instead he utilized sketches and drafts of unpublished work.[85] Some of the sources of Pedro Camacho's radio-plays could also be, as Marie-Madeleine Gladieu has pointed out, anecdotes taken from the scandalous Peruvian press of the fifties; in particular, articles from the newspaper *La Crónica*.[86]

The most melodramatic of the even-numbered chapters is about the bride who faints at her wedding. Eliana, one of Lima's most beautiful young women, is to marry Antúnez, a good but unsophisticated young man unaware that his bride loves someone else. The story is narrated in the third person, but the perspective is that of a perceptive and discreet gentleman: doctor Alberto Quinteros, Eliana's uncle, who discovers both that his niece fainted because she is pregnant and that her lover is not her fiancée but her brother, with whom she is having an incestuous relationship.

Vargas Llosa utilizes Lituma, the most recurrent character in his narrative, for another radio-play. He is a policeman who receives orders to kill an African stowaway in the port of Callao, near Lima. Lituma knows that the order is immoral and is repulsed by it but feels reluctant to disobey his superiors.

The main characters of the even chapters 6 through 16 are all fanatics who resemble Brother Francisco of *Captain Pantoja and the Special Service*: Gumercindo Tello, the Jehovah's witness who attempts to castrate himself in order to demonstrate his innocence in response to accusations of rape; Don Federico Télez Unzátegui, a zealously dedicated exterminator of rats in Peru who is motivated by the death of his sister, a baby devoured by rodents in the Peruvian jungle; Lucho Abril Marroquín, the man who loses all his moral scruples after psychoanalytic treatment relieves his feelings of guilt about a death he caused in an automobile accident; Ezequiel Delfín, the timid murderer of landlord and would-be father-in-law; and Seferino Huanca Leyva, the orphan who becomes a crazed priest obsessed with masturbation as a religious practice.

The first five even-numbered chapters are independent, open-ended stories. Beginning with chapter 12, the sixth even-numbered chapter, Pedro Camacho's stories lose coherence: the characters of one story appear in another, proper names become confused within a story, plots of different radio-series become entangled, and dead characters come back to life. When these inconsistencies first occur, the listening public believes they are the brilliant and intentional tricks of Pedro Camacho, but this is not the case. They reflect the growing and uncontrollable insanity of the scriptwriter who will suffer a nervous break down and wind up in a mental hospital.

PEDRO CAMACHO'S FANATICISM

Like most of his own protagonists, Pedro Camacho is an obsessive fanatic: "not the slightest shadow of a doubt ever appeared in his fanatic, bulging little eyes." [87] His main obsession is his self-definition as an artist:

> And naturally it was the words "art" and "artistic" that were repeated most frequently in this feverish discourse, like some sort of magic

formula that revealed and explained everything. But even more surprising than the Bolivian scriptwriter's words was the fervor with which he uttered them, and perhaps more surprising still, the effect that they caused. Gesturing furiously and standing on tiptoe as he talked, he spoke in the fanatical voice of a man in possession of an urgent truth that he must disseminate, share, drive home.[88]

Pedro Camacho insists that his fictions are true, objective depictions of reality: "I work from life; my writings are firmly rooted in reality, as the grapevine is rooted in the vine stock."[89] He is adamant about his artistic views and will not tolerate dissent. He is, according to the narrator, "a man of unshakable convictions."[90]

The origin of Pedro Camacho's convictions, which explain why he became a writer, is revealed in the last chapter. Vargas Llosa surreptitiously prepares his reader for this revelation by introducing a series of characters that are fascinating from afar and keenly disappointing up close. The first of them is a medium of séances whose magic perplexes the ingenuous Varguitas until he bumps into him in the bank where he works as a common notary. The encounter destroys Varguitas's fascination with spiritualism:

> the beyond had lost its poetry and mystery for me. . . . I had incontrovertible proof that dead people became stupid idiots, that . . . I could no longer be an agnostic and would hence forth have to live with the certainty that in the next life, which beyond a doubt existed, an eternity of imbecility and boredom awaited me.[91]

Varguitas is also disenchanted with other characters, including a Chilean singer who is idolized by Latin American women. From afar he is a charismatic figure who inspires passionate admiration in his fans. Up close, however, Varguitas discovers him to be an unattractive boor:

> the celebrated artist . . . was a short little man, livid and filled with hatred toward his female admirers. . . . "I know their kind all too well," he said, half terrified and half enraged. "They begin by asking for an autograph and end up scratching and biting."[92]

Varguitas's disenchantment with both spiritualism and the singer sets the tone for his disenchantment with Pedro Camacho. This is the novel's greatest moment of pathos, which Vargas Llosa wrote with care and which justifies a narrative strategy akin in nature and effect to that of Flaubert's *Sentimental*

Education. In both novels the time span between the act of narration and the main action remains undefined until the last chapter, when they become almost simultaneous as the narrator begins to use the present tense. The famous seventh chapter of Flaubert's novel begins with a reference to the present because it tells the events of "this winter."[93] And in *Aunt Julia and the Scriptwriter* the narrator says "and now that I've returned to Peru to live."[94] Both novels begin by describing the first meeting of the young man and the older woman, and both utilize a long temporal gap between the penultimate and the final chapter. In both novels the last chapter recalls events that occurred during the gap in the narrative but owes its impact to the surprising revelation of something that took place before the events of the first chapter, and that calls for a reconsideration of the whole novel. Flaubert's revelation, that the happiest moment of Frédéric's life was his visit to Madame Nogent's brothel before he met Madame Arnoux, has the same impact as Vargas Llosa's revelation, that Pedro Camacho's wife, a prostitute, had left him but returned to care for him after he went mad. In both novels, the reader is confronted with the unexpected mediocrity of a character's past. In Vargas Llosa's novel the reader is also confronted with Varguitas's insensitivity. He regrets his encounter with his old friend because Camacho's pathetic situation—which he narrates with a measure of indifference—makes him feel uneasy and distinctly disenchanted.

These various disenchantments prepare for the revelation of Camacho's past. The writer of countless stories—the innocuous fanatic, who believed he was a true artist, who had gained success and fame throughout Lima for a short while—reappears in the epilogue of the novel, forgotten by his public and humiliated by his peers, after leaving the insane asylum where he had been confined. He now works menial odd jobs at a newspaper while his wife has affairs with the journalists. He is embarrassed to encounter Varguitas after many years.

The revelations concerning Pedro Camacho's past show that his fanaticism and creativity were the consequences of a great personal humiliation. His compulsion to write fiction and to lie about his personal life was a way to hide his shame and sorrow. Varguitas comes to understand that Pedro lied to him about his past and that his artistic theories were rationalizations he used to cope with his broken marriage. Pedro Camacho had told Varguitas that he abstained from sex to enrich his imagination and that his love life was very rich, "but I have never loved a flesh-and-blood woman."[95] In the last pages of the novel Varguitas realizes that Pedro Camacho had a wife whom he loved and continued to love even after she left him, apparently "to go off whoring around somewhere back there. They got together again when he was put in the mental asylum. That's why he goes around saying that she's such a self-sacrificing woman. Because she went back to him when he was crazy."[96] As Varguitas looks at Pedro, he no longer recognizes the features of a fanatic: "The bulging eyes were the same, though they had lost their fanaticism, their obsessive gleam."[97] His reconciliation with his wife rid him of his fanaticism, the essence and raison d'être of his works of fiction; but he also lost his sense of personal dignity he had when he lived the illusion he was an artist who was immune from the frailties of men and women.

Pedro Camacho's personal history is most closely reflected in his radio-play about Crisanto Maravillas, the "bard of Lima," a deformed orphan who as a child fell in love with an orphan girl. When the girl is enclosed in a convent, Crisanto becomes Peru's most famous composer of popular music. Many believe he became a songwriter to compensate for his physical defect. It is his person-al secret, however, that the beauty of his compositions comes from the love he feels for his muse. The scriptwriter's sentimentalism is underwritten by the delu-sions that fuel his creative drive. As Varguitas comes to terms with Camacho's predicaments, he becomes a novelist who has gained insights about the com-pensatory nature of fiction precisely because his illusions about the mysteri-ous motivations underlying the creative process have dissipated. Unlike Camacho, Varguitas is able to write with the knowledge that literature is a sublimation of personal obsessions.

THE POLITICAL DIMENSION

Aunt Julia and the Scriptwriter is, at first glance, an apolitical novel, but, in fact, the novel makes a subtle political point akin to Vargas Llosa's disen-chantment with the Cuban Revolution. Although the main events that inspired the plot took place between 1953 and 1958, Vargas Llosa situates the novel in a shorter, one-year time frame that condenses the events of the Cuban Revo-lution. The management of radio station, where, through most of the novel, Varguitas works, buy Cuban radio plays but instruct their editors to remove the Cubanisms before broadcasting.[98] They hire Pedro Camacho as a convenient and cost-effective way to satisfy the need for a director to direct their own productions and for a scriptwriter who writes in a language more accessible to Peruvians.

It is also due to events in Cuba that the owners of the radio station find them-selves in a bind when Camacho goes mad; they can no longer buy the radio-plays from their previous source, the CMQ company that dissolves with the Cuban Revolution: "Cuba was in a mess, . . . with the terrorism and the guer-rillas, CMQ has been turned topsy-turvy, with people arrested and all kinds of troubles."[99] Because of the confusion, Varguitas finds work that gives him the financial means to marry Julia: he is hired to edit and Peruvianize old CMQ scripts until they find a company or a writer who can provide new ones.

With *Aunt Julia and the Scriptwriter* the fifties is no longer, as in Vargas Llosa's previous narrative, a period of hopeless corruption. The fifties in Peru becomes a period that evokes nostalgia because its problems seem innocent and unimportant in comparison to those that the Cuban Revolution would bring.

Aunt Julia and the Scriptwriter and *Captain Pantoja and the Special Service* are novels of transition toward a new period in Vargas Llosa's fictional writing. With them he elaborates the theme of the fanatic of unbending convictions, but he has yet to develop the main theme of his novels of the 1980s: the consequences of fanaticism on a social and historical level. Vargas Llosa developed this new theme as he began to investigate more seriously an intellectual tradition of pluralist thinkers who had written about the violent propensities of the fanatic and the utopian. In the 1970s, however, he left the political issues in his novels vague and humorous. He was confused about his own political convictions and was therefore not prepared to make a decisive connection between fanaticism and utopias or to explore themes that would have clashed with his waning belief that capitalist society should be eradicated in order to establish socialism.

CHAPTER FOUR

Against Wind and Tide

Vargas Llosa's political disenchantment with the Left occurred in stages. From 1959 until 1974 he was an outspoken advocate of socialism, the Soviet Union, and the Cuban revolution. His first public misgivings about the politics of socialist states were his criticisms of the Soviet invasion of Czechoslovakia in 1968 and his protests against the censorship and intimidation of writers in Cuba in 1971. In 1975 he declared, for the first time, that Cuba and the Soviet bloc did not represent the socialist ideal in which he still believed. In 1979 he finally disavowed his socialist convictions and began to regard Marxism as a utopia incompatible with justice and liberty.

When he first denounced cases of intellectual censorship in the Soviet Union, the invasion of Czechoslovakia, and the imprisonment of Heberto Padilla, Vargas Llosa did not withdraw his support for the socialist states. As late as 1974 he was still willing to rationalize those unfortunate events from the Communist perspective. Although he viewed the incidents he had criticized as errors of judgment by the Communist governments, he still maintained his belief in those governments and even justified Fidel Castro's hard line against independent Socialist intellectuals, like himself, as a pragmatic step to ensure the survival of Cuban socialism besieged by American imperialism.[1] Later, in 1989, he interpreted the Padilla case as the opportunity Fidel Castro used to rid himself of undesirable allies while consolidating an authoritarian regime aligned with the Soviet bloc.[2]

Until 1975 Vargas Llosa still approved of Sartre's contention that only committed Socialists were entitled to criticize Marxist doctrines or Communist regimes.[3] His support of the Soviet bloc was therefore not altogether naive: he was aware of Stalinist atrocities, and he knew Sartre supported the Soviet Union in spite of the German-Soviet pact, the revelations of Solzhenitsyn and others about the Gulag, and the invasion of Hungary.

Vargas Llosa did not distance himself from the Left because he had agonized about the atrocities of the socialist states or because he had forebodings about his socialist ideals. He was forced to reconsider his position within the Latin American Left because he had been repudiated by the Cuban government and by many of his former leftist friends who considered him a counterrevolutionary for his role in the Padilla case. His break with the Left was due initially to his realization that freedom of expression, which he cherished above his revolutionary commitments, was not a priority either for the socialist regimes he supported or for the leftist intellectuals with whom he had associated.

Vargas Llosa's circumstances prepared him to reconsider and to appreciate Albert Camus's rejection of the French Communist party, of revolution, and of armed struggle against French colonialism in his native Algeria. For his views Camus was admonished and spurned by prominent French leftist intellectuals, beginning with Sartre. Vargas Llosa himself had echoed Sartre's views deploring Camus's critiques of revolution as the "paralyzing pessimism" of a moralist incapable of "facing the contradictions of a critical epoch."[4] By 1975, however, Vargas Llosa was beginning to reconsider his political views, and he came to appreciate Camus as an intellectual who was compelled to repudiate Communist regimes after coming to terms with the magnitude of Stalinist crimes and the true nature of Communist ideology. The origins of Vargas Llosa's new political position can be traced to his reassessment of *The Rebel* (1951) and other political essays by Camus. It is ironic that Sartre—who ostracized Camus from the leftist intellectual milieu in France—was himself flouted by Fidel Castro and by Latin American leftist intellectuals for signing the letters Vargas Llosa drafted to protest the incarceration and forced confession of Heberto Padilla.

CAMUS RECONSIDERED

In the essay "Albert Camus and the Morality of Limits" (1975), a turning-point in his intellectual biography, Vargas Llosa expresses remorse about the articles he had written about Camus in the 1960s and about his own support for

Communist regimes. Although he still considered himself a socialist, he began to criticize Communism and the revolution and thus to agree with Camus's views on socialism: "On my own, after a number of lapses, I came to exactly the same conclusions as Camus."[5]

Vargas Llosa was impressed by Camus's proposition that ideologies—understood as abstract conceptions of an ideal society—lead inevitably to violence:

> The entire political tragedy of humanity originated when it became acceptable to kill a person in the name of an idea—in other words, when the following abominable notion became acceptable: that certain abstract concepts could be worth more than real beings of flesh and blood.[6]

Camus argues that Communism must be rejected because it is a utopia that leads to unjustified violence and because Marxism-Leninism is a philosophy that has promoted intellectual conformism and opportunism.[7] He finds Leninism toxic because it sacrifices morality, justifies any means to achieve its ends, and hopes to establish a society run by social engineers.[8] Camus attacks not only the aberrations of revolutionaries but the very idea of revolution. He defines revolution as the violence perpetrated by people who are willing to hate the man of the present because they are committed to a spurious abstraction: the man of the future.[9]

Camus did not claim that his views on the fanaticism and opportunism of Marxist-Leninist intellectuals were original. These ideas had been disseminated from the time of the Russian revolution by dissidents and social critics such as Arthur Koestler and George Orwell. Disillusioned with Communism, Camus incorporated their thoughts with his doctrine of the absurd man in an attempt to reject the nihilism and political opportunism of the Communist intellectuals with whom he had previously collaborated. His morality and politics were still grounded on the same existentialist position he once thought was compatible with Marxism: that the search for meaning can only be resolved when man—like Sisyphus in Camus's well-known essay on the Greek myth—decides to act knowing that life has no intrinsic purpose.

Camus' critique of ideologies and his distrust of abstract systems and comprehensive social theories were also framed as a lament over modern man's alienation from nature:

> When one tries to subsume the whole world under a theory, the world becomes as bare, blind, and deaf as the theory itself, and now is disconnected from his roots to life and to nature.[10]

In his notebooks, the *Carnets*, published posthumously in 1962, Camus had sketched an idea for a story summarizing his ideas about the redeeming force of nature: "To write a story about a contemporary man who is cured of his torment by the sole and prolonged contemplation of nature."[11]

Vargas Llosa was not interested in Camus's thoughts on the absurdity of human existence or on man's alienation from nature.[12] He was taken by Camus' ideas about Communism and revolution, and he soon came to realize that they were not original. Karl Popper and others had made the link between utopias and violence while Camus was still a member of the French Communist party.[13] Vargas Llosa became a great admirer of Popper in the 1980s after he realized he had been espousing his ideas before he read him. But he came to Popper in the late 1980s by way of Isaiah Berlin and Jean-François Revel, whom he read in 1979 when he was writing *The War of the End of the World.*

BERLIN, REVEL, AND POPPER

During his period of political transition, Vargas Llosa published in Spanish the book *Entre Sartre y Camus* (Between Sartre and Camus) (1981). These essays reappear in *Contra viento y marea* (Against wind and tide) (1983) with others in which he expresses his break with socialism. The definitive Spanish title of his collected essays alludes to *Against the Current* by Isaiah Berlin, whom Vargas Llosa has acknowledged as a source of inspiration and whom he has called a hero of our times:

> Some years ago I lost my taste for political utopias, the apocalypses that promise to bring heaven down to earth. I now know that in fact they tend to cause iniquities as terrible as the ones they purport to remedy. I now believe that common sense is the most valuable of political virtues. My reading of Isaiah Berlin clarified something about which I had previously a vague intuition. True progress of the kind that pushed back or eliminated barbarous customs and institutions that were a source of unending human suffering, and which replaced them with more civilized ways and styles of life, has only been possible as a result of a partial, heterodox, and deformed application of social theories.[14]

Vargas Llosa admired Berlin for some of the same reasons he had sympathize with Camus: he appreciated their mistrust of dogmatic revolutionaries and social theorists who propose final solutions to human problems. In *Against the Current* Berlin mentions his own affinities with Camus's views on the propensity of revolutionaries to become oppressive tyrants.[15]

For Berlin and Camus pluralism is a means of avoiding the potential ravages of ideology. But they had different reasons to mistrust ideologies. Camus was suspicious of them because he believed that humans are fallible when expressing their political ideals. One should not trust abstraction because of the human tendency to make mistakes and then to permit self-delusion that masks or dismisses error, even to the point of countenancing abuse of those with different views:

> I am in favor of a plurality of positions. Is it possible to form a political party among those who are not sure they are right? If so it would be mine. In any case I do not insult those who are not with me. That is my only originality.[16]

Camus's main justification for pluralism is the human propensity to err. He advocates tolerance because human's are fallible, but he admits, at least in theory, that an ideal society is conceivable. Berlin's justification of pluralism is not based on man's fallibility but on the view that the classical concept of an ideal man or an ideal society is incoherent:

> [Pluralism is] the belief, not merely in the multiplicity, but in the incommensurability of the values of different cultures and societies and, in addition, in the incompatibility of equally valid ideas, together with the implied revolutionary corollary that the classical notions of an ideal man and of an ideal society are intrinsically incoherent and meaningless.[17]

Berlin recognizes the relative importance of theories but does not see an intrinsic value in any one of them: they are useful insofar as they contribute to the practical needs of human beings.

The touchstone of Berlin's pluralism—a concept that Vargas Llosa has referred to as "the contradictory truths"—comes from the realization that cultures and individuals live by principles that are incompatible. Berlin singles out Machiavelli as the first theorist who understood the political dilemma implicit in the recognition that human values can rarely be reconciled:

> Machiavelli's cardinal achievement is . . . his uncovering of an insoluble dilemma, the planting of a permanent question mark in the path of posterity. It stems from his *de facto* recognition that ends

equally ultimate, equally sacred, may contradict each other, that entire systems of values may come into collision without possibility of rational arbitration, and that not merely in exceptional circumstances, as a result of abnormality or accident or error . . . but (this was surely new) as part of the normal human situation.[18]

If human values are incommensurable, then human coexistence can be assured only by pragmatic attention to the concrete needs of individuals rather than by application of abstract theories designed to resolve social problems.

Berlin recognizes that it may be comforting to believe that society is perfectible according to some preconceived blueprint. Humans may well have a metaphysical need for immutable beliefs. But only fanatics are willing to impose their ideal vision of man or society on others. For Berlin, a serious commitment to a utopia is a dangerous symptom of political immaturity:

It is surely a sign of immaturity (even though it may be evidence of a noble and disinterested nature) to stake everything on any one final solution to social problems. When to such immaturity there is added a ruthless will, and a genius for organization which enables its possessor to force human beings into patterns unrelated to their nature and their own wishes, then what starts as pure and disinterested idealism, inevitably ends in oppression, cruelty, and blood.[19]

Vargas Llosa had already decided to repudiate socialist ideals when he read Berlin, but after reading his essays in the late 1970s the novelist found a compelling justification for his decision: utopias are impossible ideals that lead to needless violence:

Every social utopia—from Plato to Marx—has begun with an act of faith: the belief that human ideals, the great aspirations of individual and community, can be harmonized, that the satisfaction of one or many of these ends is not an obstacle for bringing about the others. Perhaps nothing conveys this optimism better than the rhythmic motto of the French revolution: "Liberty, equality, fraternity." That well-intentioned attempt to establish a government of reason upon earth, and to put these simple and unquestionable ideals into practice, demonstrated to the world, through a succession of carnages and frustrations, that social reality is more tumultuous and unpredictable than the impeccable abstractions of the philosophers who had prescribed recipes for human happiness.[20]

From 1958 until around 1975, Vargas Llosa believed that socialist states brought about by revolutionary movements would offer humanity liberty and equality. From 1975 until 1979 he was less willing to make strong pronouncements in support of socialism. After reading Berlin he began to argue that the kind of absolute equality promised by Marx can only be achieved by sacrificing liberty. He therefore concluded that the socialist ideal is unattainable. Berlin's ideas gave Vargas Llosa a new framework for understanding political reality, for reconsidering the significance of his own socialist experience, and even for reinterpreting some of the human situations that had inspired his own literary works. Among those experiences was his 1958 trip to the Peruvian jungle, which had been crucial in the creation of *The Green House*. In his visit to the Amazon he had observed a school where nuns educated girls they had abducted from the jungle. Vargas Llosa had surmised that these girls would eventually become servants or prostitutes. In his socialist period he had interpreted this situation as an instance of capitalism extending its tentacles into the farthest reaches of civilization. But he revised his analysis of the same situation in accordance with his reading of Berlin:

> On that journey I got my first intuition of what Isaiah Berlin calls "contradictory truths." . . . That with the best intentions in the world, and at a cost of limitless sacrifice, they could cause so much damage is a lesson that I have never forgotten. It has taught me how vague is the line that separates good from evil and how prudent one must be in judging human actions and deciding on the answers to social problems if one is to avoid the cure being worse than the illness.[21]

Berlin's essays on the history of political ideas gave Vargas Llosa a framework to criticize socialism, but he needed to look elsewhere for guidance in analyzing current events from a pluralist perspective. He found such a guide in Jean-François Revel to whom he dedicated the third volume of *Contra viento y marea*.[22]

Vargas Llosa was impressed by Jean-François Revel's essays on the fragility of Western democracies threatened from within by intellectuals who embrace totalitarian ideologies and regimes.[23] Revel labeled the Soviet bloc as a totalitarian and repressive system that generates extreme poverty. He has also criticized the dogmatic nationalism of third world intellectuals who rely on conspiracy theories rather than self-criticism to account for underdevelopment. For Revel—and Vargas Llosa agrees—national liberation movements and military dictatorships bear equal responsibility for the lack of economic progress in the third world.[24] The solution Revel proposes to the problems of the third world is the same as the one he proposes for the first world: a purge of totalitarian elements from social life, respect for democracy, the defense of the rights of the minorities, and freedom of speech:

> A society in which nobody is listening is an oligarchy. . . . When a citizen cannot criticize a worthless political or economic policy without being sent to prison, then the whole of that society is in danger—not only because one of its members has been subjected to "an intolerable violation of the rights of the individual," but also because a workable alternate policy may have been lost and buried forever.[25]

OPEN SOCIETY AND ITS ENEMIES

The title of one of Vargas Llosa's essays on Revel, "*La sociedad abierta y sus enemigos*" (The open society and its enemies), is an allusion to an influential book by Karl Popper, the philosopher whose political ideas have most influenced Vargas Llosa's debunking of socialist doctrines.[26] Popper developed his fundamental philosophical views in Vienna—in opposition to the theories of Sigmund Freud and Karl Marx—as early as the second decade of the twentieth century. He wanted to show that the success of Marxism and psychoanalysis was due to a fallacy: both theories are irrefutable, but irrefutable theories can be false and do not advance knowledge. It is impossible to find a psychological phenomenon (a dream, a behavior, a confession, etc.) that can unequivocally refute the diagnosis of a Freudian analyst, who will never be at a loss for explanations. A patient's resistance to the analyst's diagnosis can always be interpreted as a state of denial that confirms the diagnosis. It is likewise impossible to refute the Marxist thesis according to which the exploited classes are generally unaware of their status as exploited classes: either they become aware of their exploitation, in which case they can begin to organize against the ruling class, or they continue to be unaware of their situation and the ruling classes will continue to exploit them. The psychoanalytic view that every neurosis or psychosis reflects an abnormality in the psychosexual development of the patient is irrefutable, and so is the Marxist claim that every historical event can be explained by an analysis of the class struggle. The basic premises of psychoanalysis or of Marxism are not susceptible to serious criticism: the psychoanalyst can always claim that a critic's resistance to the psychoanalytic evinces an inability to recognize the workings of the unconscious; and the Marxist can always charge that the critic is defending the interests of the ruling class.

Popper argued that a verifiable and irrefutable theory can be false, and that the progress of human knowledge does not depend on the verification but on the refutability of hypothesis. If a hypothesis can be refuted in principle, then it is possible to come up with an even better hypothesis. This is how knowledge advances. Progress in human knowledge depends on the critical approach that subjects every hypothesis to the test: "Criticism always consists of pointing out contradiction either within the theory to be criticized; or between it and some facts of experience."[27] Popper considers that his main contribution to epistemology is the concept of "demarcation," the criterion for distinguishing pseudosciences from sciences: irrefutable and universally valid theories are pseudosciences where knowledge stagnates; refutable and falsifiable theories allow knowledge to advance.[28]

Popper does not believe in absolute truths. He believes in relative truths that change as our theories get better. In science there is progress because good hypotheses are replaced by better ones. Truth is relative to the state of our knowledge that increases through a process of conjectures and refutations.

His conception of science is the touchstone of his social theory. Popper identifies two types of societies: those able and those unable to differentiate the natural from the social order. He calls tribal or closed those societies unable to tell the difference between a human convention and a regularity of nature, and he calls open or civilized those who can make that distinction. In *The Poverty of Historicism* and in *The Open Society and Its Enemies*, Popper demonstrates the pitfalls of any social theory that confuses human conventions and individual passions, on the one hand, with the laws of nature, on the other.

Tribal life is dominated by what he refers to as a magical attitude toward social customs:

> It is one of the characteristics of the magical attitude of a primitive tribal or 'closed' society that it lives in a charmed circle of unchanging taboos, of laws and customs which are felt to be as inevitable as the rising of the sun, or the cycle of the seasons, or similar obvious regularities of nature. And it is only after this magical "closed society" has actually broken down that a theoretical understanding of the difference between "nature" and "society" can develop.[29]

The closed society does not belong to a particular stage of human prehistory. It designates any human association founded on dogma and does not tolerate change or dissent. In open societies, on the other hand, ideas can always be refuted, and they can outlast their usefulness.

Popper claims that the concept of an ideal society is a utopia that has seduced philosophers from antiquity to the present. For many of these thinkers history would fulfill its ultimate purpose if their notion of an ideal society were ever realized. Popper uses the term "historicism" to refer to the way of thinking peculiar to a closed society and its most influential twentieth century proponents, meaning the ideologues of Fascism and Communism. Historicists believe that they can either predict or determine the course of human events. In *The Poverty of Historicism*, Popper aims to refute these possibilities:

> The belief in historical destiny is sheer superstition, and there can be no prediction on the course of human history by scientific or any other rational methods.[30]

Popper claims that historicism is as seductive as it is pernicious. Instead of reducing human misery by direct means, historicists point to the imperfections of their societies as a justification for imposing their grand schemes on others. Their philosophical and political ideas are at odds with liberty when they serve as rationalizations for either political movements or regimes that promise to establish an ideal social order. These views are not harmless: when intellectuals justify the imposition of their views by force, they augment, rather than decrease human misery.

In "Utopia and Violence," an essay published in 1948, years before Camus presented a similar argument in *The Rebel*, Popper claims that utopias lead inevitably to violence.[31] Popper argues that "rationalism is linked up with the recognition of the necessity of social institutions to protect freedom of criticism, freedom of thought, and thus the freedom of men."[32] The freedom defended by Popper is based on the principle of equality under laws that offer everybody the same rights and opportunities:

> I continue to appreciate the humanitarian ideals of socialism. The important aspect of equality is that every human being should be equal under the law. If one tries to establish other kinds of equalities, take for instance equality of color, then that can only be realized through violence. If one wants to establish the equality of income, that can only be accomplished through a great strengthening of the State and through a great control of the private lives of citizens by bureaucrats.[33] Each increase of equality is paid for by a decrease in liberty.[34]

Equality before the law, rationality, and social institutions to protect freedom are, for Popper, the pillars on which open societies and human progress must be based: "Ultimately, progress depends very largely on political factors; on political institutions that safeguard the freedom of thought."[35]

The final step in Vargas Llosa's political reorientation away from socialism was his reading of Fernand Braudel. The French historian convinced him that the free market was the historical event that established the conditions for individual liberty and that it is the best mechanism available for safeguarding it in the present:

> In his monumental work *Civilisation materielle, Economie et Capitalisme XVe-XVIII Siécle*, [Fernand Braudel] masterfully reveals the extraordinary change that took place in the development of society with the emergence of free trade. . . . The foundations of civilization were transformed by the appearance of an independent and sovereign space where human activity could be unleashed according to the individual's will and interest to buy or sell, to produce or consume.[36]

In the 1970s Vargas Llosa distanced himself from his socialist ideals, but he had not yet reoriented his political position. In the 1980s, as a result of assessing his own experience coupled with his wide reading in the works of Berlin, Popper, Braudel, Revel, and others whose views challenged the authoritarian structures implicit in socialism, his new political position became clarified. He came to deplore any kind of authoritarian regime and became an outspoken advocate of free market democracy. The label used in Latin America to refer to his political position is *neoliberal*, which has some of the same connotations as *neoconservative* in the United States. In the 1980s, therefore, Vargas Llosa espoused ideas that would have been anathema to him in his youth. Socialism, authoritarian in essence, became odious to him, and democracy, anchored in the notion of a free market, became his political framework: "Without economic freedom, any political freedom is limited."[37]

THE NEW LATIN AMERICAN LIBERALISM

Vargas Llosa's political conversion coincides with that of other Latin American writers such as Jorge Edwards and Octavio Paz. While they appreciated Marxism's humanist ideals, all three writers grew disappointed with Communist regimes and socialist doctrines. Vargas Llosa's change also coincides with the advent of an antiauthoritarian movement among intellectuals and politicians who disapprove of government intervention in private initiative and fear that Communist nations and revolutionary intellectuals can undermine the already weak foundations of democracy and the free market in Latin America.

One of the most important books associated with the new liberalism is Hernando de Soto's *The Other Path: The Invisible Revolution in the Third World* (1986), for which Vargas Llosa wrote the prologue. In his book, which offers the results of years of research by his team of sociologists and economists, de Soto explores the informal sector of the Peruvian economy and argues that the Indians and the poor of Peru have laid the foundations for an economy that could overcome the obstacles of a corrupt and inefficient government bureaucracy. According to de Soto, the market in Peru is not truly free because it is controlled and manipulated by powerful elites.

In Peru all economic initiatives are subject to the will of those who hold political power and control economic activity. In this context good relations with powerful elites are the necessary condition for private enterprise to succeed. This economic system, which exists throughout Latin America according to de Soto, produces monopolies and corruption. In the prologue to de Soto's book, Vargas Llosa affirms that states like Peru are "mercantilist" (the label that de Soto uses to describe his country's economic system):

> The term is confusing, since it defines a historical period, an economic school, and a moral attitude. Here, "mercantilism" means a bureaucratized and a law-ridden state that regards the redistribution of national wealth as more important than the production of wealth. And "redistribution," as used here, means the concession of monopolies or favored status to a small elite that depends on the state and on which the state is itself dependent.
>
> The state, in our world, has never been the expression of the people. The state is whatever government happens to be in power—liberal or conservative, democratic or tyrannical—and the government usually acts in accordance with the mercantilist model.[38]

Latin American neoliberals, like Vargas Llosa and de Soto, criticize the ineffectiveness of bureaucratic governments in the West (and sometimes compare them to the inefficient regimes of the former Soviet bloc). As a residue from their own youthful sympathies to leftist doctrines and arguments, the social diagnoses offered by de Soto and Vargas Llosa echo some socialist claims: they speak in the name of the poor and accuse the state and misguided intellectuals for the underdevelopment and extreme poverty that persists over much of the American continent. De Soto and Vargas Llosa accept the social diagnosis proposed by José Carlos Mariátegui, the intellectual who laid the foundations of Peruvian Marxism, but reject his political solution. Like Mariátegui, they equate their own economic solutions for Peru's most important problems with the wishes of the oppressed masses.

In his *Seven Interpretive Essays on Peruvian Reality*, Mariátegui argues that the Indian must free himself from the defects of the existing political and economic system to reaffirm his authentic culture, and at the same time he states that Peru must become a Communist country. To avoid contradictions, Mariátegui claims that Communism is a modern philosophy that corresponds to the nature of the Peruvian Indian.[39]

According to Mariátegui, Communism in Peru has a special significance because the Incas were primitive communists. In Mariátegui's view the Spanish conquest of the Andean region was a regression from ancient communist economic practices to feudalism. Resistance to the Communist economic model must be overcome through a revolution that would undermine the feudal system whose laws have legitimized the usurpation of Indian lands by Europeans and their descendants. Another obstacle to revolution in Peru is the activity of intellectuals, writers, and educators who maintain the status quo.

Mariátegui believes that Communists will ultimately triumph in Peru. His optimism is based not only on the creation of socialist movements like the one he himself founded but also on his conviction that the Indians themselves have begun to participate in such movements. Hernando de Soto and Vargas Llosa express some of their ideas with arguments and a vocabulary similar to Mariátegui's: they establish correspondences between the nature of the Indian and their own political ideals; they claim that Indians and poor people in Peru must free themselves from the defects of the prevailing political and economic system to find an authentic path; and they simultaneously claim that social progress is naturally based on the free market because Indians spontaneously develop private-initiative projects. In the prologue to *The Other Path*, Vargas Llosa discredits the utopian revolution of the Left as he hails the "revolution" of the victims of the status quo:

> But the revolution this study analyzes and defends is in no way utopian. It is already under way, made a reality by an army of the current system's victims, who have revolted out of a desire to work and have a place to live and who, in doing so, have discovered the benefits of freedom[40]

Using the same rhetoric with which Marxist intellectuals defended the illegality of their militant revolutionaries, the new Latin American liberals justify the illegality of the informal sector that is laying the foundations for the free market:

> "Legality" became a privilege which those in power granted at a cost that frequently made it inaccessible to the poor. The answer to this situation has been the emergence of the informal sector, or the capitalism of the poor who were expelled from legal life by the discriminatory and antidemocratic practices of the patron-State.[41]

Like Mariátegui, Vargas Llosa and de Soto propose their economic solutions in the name of the poor and for the benefit of all society. Long after having rejected his socialist convictions, Vargas Llosa continues to admire Mariátegui. He even sounds like that first Marxist intellectual in Latin America when he calls for a revolutionary change in the Peruvian political and economic system and when he criticizes the negative influence of many intellectuals who "undermine or destroy the possibilities for political democracy to work [in society]."[42] However, now that he has ceased to believe that freedom can be reconciled with Marxism-Leninism, Vargas Llosa offers a political solution different from Mariátegui's: "Marxist-Leninist regimes do not tolerate ideological neutrality, and to prevent it they have established censorship methods that are both perfect and ridiculous."[43]

Vargas Llosa has not offered penetrating insights into his own dogmatic adherence to the Soviet Bloc and to revolutionary movements in Latin American, nor has he fully explained his rationale for his role as an intellectual spokesman for the Cuban revolution for over a decade. His inability to come to terms fully with his own socialist past is clear in his memoir *A Fish in the Water* (1993), where he presents his political life by alternating chapters of his youth with chapters about his campaign for the Peruvian presidency in 1990. Devoting little attention to the socialist convictions of his youth, he completely avoids the period when he was most active in socialist politics. Vargas Llosa has engaged in polemics with leftist intellectuals with the same self-assurance with which he once attacked capitalism in his socialist period.

CRITICISM OF THE LEFTIST WRITER

Mario Benedetti, Günther Grass, Regis Debray, and others have criticized Vargas Llosa for his political turn to the right. In lively and sometimes heated polemics with these writers, Vargas Llosa has deepened his own criticism of leftist intellectuals in general and of Latin American writers in particular. While he admires the literary works of Gabriel García Márquez, Pablo Neruda, and Alejo Carpentier, he has criticized them for supporting authoritarian governments or for ignoring the injustices and atrocities of Communist regimes.[44]

According to Vargas Llosa, Pablo Neruda's "view of the world, as a politician and a writer (when writing about politics) was Manichean and dogmatic."[45] Carpentier, on the other hand, "entirely abandoned his ability to criticize and even to think politically. From 1959 on, all his political actions and writings in this regard were not so much the expression of an opinion [but the] pious repetition of the dictates of the government he served."[46] Vargas Llosa has directed his harshest criticism at García Márquez:

> I cannot understand why a writer like García Márquez behaves as he does toward the Cuban regime. His support goes beyond ideological solidarity and frequently takes the forms of religious piety or adulation. . . . By unconditionally placing his prestige at the service of Fidel Castro, García Márquez misleads many people in Latin America as to the true nature of the regime.[47]

To counteract the influence of leftist writers, Vargas Llosa has become as outspoken an advocate of private initiative as he had been of collectivist economic policies in the 1960s. In keeping with his antiauthoritarian convictions, Vargas Llosa does not believe that a government intended to protect the free market should be imposed without prior consensus. Because he feels he cannot and ought not force anyone to adopt his political position but should convince others through democratic means, he decided to participate actively in Peruvian politics when he felt indignation at the measures taken by President Alan García to nationalize the financial system in Peru. Vargas Llosa was the main speaker in several large demonstrations that strongly condemned García's policies. The success of these demonstrations gave him considerable political clout and set the stage for his presidential candidacy for the 1990 elections in Peru. He lost the elections and has blamed his defeat on his inability to gain the trust of the lower classes and on his failure to convince the majority of Peruvians of the benefits of a designed political program of which he is still proud.[48]

THE INTELLECTUAL BACKGROUND OF THE POLITICAL PROGRAM

In his government program, *Acción para el cambio* (action for change) (1989), Vargas Llosa announces his intention to dismantle the mercantilist state: "After being a passive spectator, incapable of performing its function, our State dwelled on its administrative apparatus and participated abusively in business activities."[49] His proposal to reorganize the state is consistent with a series of measures he proposes to "establish a free and competitive economy as the basis for an open society."[50]

Vargas Llosa developed his political program with the advice of specialists and technocrats. But the program's intellectual background clearly bears the mark of his most important political readings, which helped to move him to reject Marxist solutions. In the article "A Fish Out of Water," Vargas Llosa indicates that he read Karl Popper's *The Open Society and Its Enemies* every morning during his political campaign.[51] Popper's ideas appeared in his political program and in other essays he published to disseminate his political positions. In a speech published by "Libertad," his political movement, Vargas Llosa refers to Popper's book as a "masterpiece of libertarian thought"[52] and cites Popperian arguments to claim that one of the triumphs of the culture of freedom is the sovereign individual:

> in modern times the individual becomes differentiated and emancipated from the gregarious placenta to which he had been attached since the remote times of the horde, and acquires an individual face and a space of his own. This process occurs in an epoch when the proliferation of unrestrained economic, social, and artistic activities allowed and called for the spontaneity and creativity of individuals, and stimulated the evolution of philosophical and political thought which produced a groundbreaking notion in the history of humanity: the sovereignty of the individual.[53]

In interviews and political speeches, in which he often alluded to Popper, Berlin, Braudel and Revel, Vargas Llosa reiterated his main political message: "Liberty is an option that has never truly been exercised in our country." In speeches and written material destined for his activists and volunteers he underscored the importance of getting his message across "if we want not only to win the elections but also to profoundly transform our country."[54] During the campaign his political speeches and essays outlined the practical measures that he and his advisers considered necessary for solving specific problems while laying the foundations for a free market in Peru.

In his speeches, Vargas Llosa insisted that the political change he hoped for Peru could only take place through democratic means, and he saluted President Alan García for respecting "freedom of speech and pluralism in the media."[55] But García drew harsh criticism for his economic policy. Vargas Llosa attacked his "so-called heterodox policy of subsidizing consumption and imports to the detriment of production and exports. This model, borrowed from the realm of Marxist socialism, denies basic economic laws and dangerously increases the size and influence of the state."[56]

THE ACCURSED SHARE

During his socialist period, Vargas Llosa had attempted to reconcile his political convictions with his doctrine about the demons of literary creation. Since rejecting Marxism-Leninism, he has attempted to reconcile the pluralist theses of Karl Popper and Isaiah Berlin with the doctrines of Georges Bataille who underscores the importance of the irrational side of human experience. It is significant that Vargas Llosa's only objection to Isaiah Berlin is that he has ignored the insights of Bataille:

> Few people in our time have seen in such a penetrating way what life is—the life of the individual in society, the life of societies in their time, the impact of ideas on daily experience—there is a whole other dimension of man that does not appear in his vision, or does so in a furtive way: the dimension that George Bataille has described better than anyone else. This is the world of unreason, the world of the unconscious which, in ways that are always unverifiable and very difficult to detect, impregnates, directs and sometimes enslaves consciousness; the world of those obscure instincts that, in unexpected ways, suddenly emerge to compete with ideas and often replace them as a form of action and can even destroy what these ideas have built up. Nothing could be further from the pure, serene, harmonious, lucid and healthy view of man held by Isaiah Berlin than this sombre, confused, sickly and fiery conception of Bataille. And yet I suspect that life is probably something that embraces and mixes these two enemies into a single truth, in all their powerful incongruity.[57]

Since 1958, when he wrote his first essay on César Moro, Vargas Llosa has insisted on the importance of affirming man's irrational side against the pressures of bourgeois morality. After reading Bataille in the sixties, he became increasingly fascinated by a stronger claim, namely, that pleasure is not possible without transgression. As a kind of axiom obvious for those who have eyes to see, Bataille insisted on a paradox: human beings will be unhappy and will not experience true pleasure unless they transgress those very norms and taboos that make collective life possible.[58] The transgression of prohibitions is, to use one of Bataille's favorite terms, an affirmation of individual *sovereignty*. If traditional morality seeks to restrain human drives for the sake of collective existence, Bataille seeks a morality that liberates human drives while avoiding collective destruction. Bataille's ideas about sovereignty are in harmony with the Nietzschean assumption that suppressing the Dionysian is not a good thing for the human spirit.

Bataille considers the need to transgress (Evil with a capital E) is an ambiguous necessity: to affirm life one needs to risk it, one needs to imagine and sometimes to expose oneself to danger: "Since death is the condition of life, Evil, which is essentially cognate with death, is also, in a somewhat ambiguous manner, a basis of existence."[59] It is important, for Bataille, to find activities and practices with which individuals can express their "sovereignty" without undermining social stability. Literature, for example, is an activity where transgressions can be imagined, and the erotic is a realm where they can be experienced. Vargas Llosa has toyed with these ideas:

> Eroticism ([Bataille] defines it gloomily as "the approval of life even in death"), a sexual practice freed from reproduction, an activity which is essentially sterile, gratuitous, profuse, wasteful, is one of those "tumultuous", "excessive" movements which is opposed to reason, to Good, to the activity of work. That is, it is one of those privileged areas of "Evil and the diabolical", through which man, by approaching death, can exercise his freedom, rebel and reach fullness.[60]

The transgressions with which human beings affirm their sovereignty are acts that need to be considered immoral, not merely by an observer but by the very individual who transgresses a norm or a prohibition. An awareness of one's own depravity is a condition for Bataille's brand of pleasure.[61] The literature of Evil that Bataille practiced and about which he theorized is not innocent: it is meant to expresses man's darkest side. For Bataille the need to transgress is essential in literature. Literature, therefore, has moral implications that supersede conventional morality:

> Literature is either the essential or nothing. I believe that the Evil— an acute form of Evil—which it expresses, has a sovereign value for us. But this concept does not exclude morality: on the contrary, it demands a "hypermorality."[62]

Vargas Llosa seems to agree fully:

> The transgression of restrictions and taboos, especially when risk is involved, significantly increases pleasure and produces spiritual as well as intellectual enrichment. On this I am very much in agreement with Bataille.[63]

Vargas Llosa's attempt to reconcile Bataille's "hypermorality" with Karl Popper's sociological ideas are evinced in his essay "The Truth of Lies" where he argues that the transgressions of literature can be useful to the health of an open society if the boundaries between the historical and the fictional are clearly demarcated:

> Well-defined boundaries between literature and history—between literary truths and historical truths—are prerogatives of open societies. In these societies, both coexist, independent and sovereign, although complementing each other in their utopian desire to include all of society. Perhaps the greatest demonstration that a society is open, in the meaning that Karl Popper gave to this term, is that fiction and history coexist, autonomous and different, without invading or usurping each other's domains and functions.[64]

POPPER AND IRRATIONALISM

It is possible, from an irrationalist perspective such as Bataille's, to espouse some of Karl Popper's main ideas including his defense of liberty and his critique of historicism. From Karl Popper's perspective, however, doctrines such as Georges Bataille's should be as unacceptable as Marxism or psychoanalysis because they are irrefutable and therefore useless. The contention that man needs to transgress social norms in order to find fulfillment cannot be refuted. Any human behavior will confirm Bataille's contentions: the individual who transgresses is affirming his sovereignty; the individual who does not transgress is repressing it. An individual who does not transgress and who thinks he has experienced true pleasure is deluding himself, because true pleasure cannot take place without transgression, and so forth.

Vargas Llosa is willing to deploy Popperian arguments against socialist doctrines, but the same arguments apply to irrationalist positions like Bataille's. Popper himself has taken great care to refute them in essays that Vargas Llosa has not chosen to discuss. Popper shows no tolerance for irrationalist doctrines claiming that any aspect of knowledge depends on unconscious, subconscious, or irrational elements:

> Irrationalists are dangerously mistaken when they suggest that there is any knowledge, of whatever kind, or source, or origin, which is above or exempt from rational criticism. I make no concessions to irrationalism, but insist, on the contrary, that any theory or belief may, and should, be made subject to severe and searching rational criticism, and that we should search for reasons—for rational arguments—which might refute it.[65]

Popper dedicates a chapter of *The Open Society and Its Enemies* to doctrines that rely on irrationalist sources to explain the actions of human beings. He concludes that irrationalist positions are irreconcilable with his moral conviction that "the authority of objective truth is indispensable for a free society based on mutual respect."[66] Popper claims that irrationalist explanations of human behavior are assaults on the critical spirit of open societies:

> It is my firm conviction that this irrational emphasis upon emotion and passion leads ultimately to what I can only describe as crime.[67] The stress upon "deeper" layers of human nature . . . must lead to the view that thought is merely a somewhat superficial manifestation of what lies within these irrational depths.[68]

Popper concedes that irrationalists are not inconsistent in their defense of humanist doctrines. Yet, even in these cases he rejects them: an irrationalist can always justify any deviation from morality by appealing to the "deeper" levels of human experience.[69] At best, irrationalism can be viewed as an intellectual misunderstanding that occurs when an individual confuses reason with dogmatism and authoritarianism. Thus, Popper considers that the most humanistic of irrationalisms is still immoral and irresponsible:

> Irrationalism, which is not bound by any rules of consistency, may be combined with any kind of belief, including the belief in the brotherhood of man.[70] Irrationalism will use reason too, but without any feeling of obligation; it will use it or discard it as it pleases.[71]

Vargas Llosa has accepted some of Popper's main theses (for instance, his critique of historicism, his optimism about science in a democratic society, and his ideas about utopia and violence), but not his main thesis, that the only valid methods for understanding nature and society are rational ones. Vargas Llosa's attempt to reconcile the critique of historicism and of utopias with Bataille's irrationalist doctrines may be as tenuous as his attempt to reconcile socialism and the demons of creation during his socialist period.

But Vargas Llosa is not one to be discouraged by contradictions, and his attempt to reconcile a critique of fanaticism with Bataille's doctrines has inspired many of his literary themes. *In Praise of the Stepmother*, for example, focuses on a businessman's attempts to tame his dark side with innocuous activities. Bataille was also in the offing when Vargas Llosa worked on his most ambitious and successful literary work. In an interview with José Miguel Oviedo before he finished writing *The War of the End of the World*, Vargas Llosa stated that he had developed some of the main sections of his novel while thinking about the relation between fanaticism and transgression:

> The characters of the novel move between two opposite poles, and I believe that as human beings we all do. I think that our condition is a struggle between two sorts of inevitable needs at war with one another: the need for freedom and the need for survival. At the level of the individual, the family, or the collectivity the need for survival can thwart our most destructive inclinations but it can also restrict our freedom. How does one combat those inclinations? One does so by creating the kind of order embodied mainly in institutions such as the military and religion, both of which curb our natural tendencies and are therefore the worst enemies of freedom. I believe those to be the main issues of the novel.[72]

Vargas Llosa's attempt to reconcile the doctrines of Bataille with pluralist currents of thought had a direct impact on his ideas about the nature of literary creation. He continues to insist on the irrational elements of literary creation, an idea that is consistent with sympathies for Georges Bataille and César Moro; but he has completely discarded his views that irrational forces produce a literature with socialist implications. Since around 1980 he has been writing that the irrational forces responsible for literary creation offer a kind of escape valve for our most dangerous drives. Literature, for Vargas Llosa, is no longer a way to diagnose the evils of social injustice as he vehemently argued in the 1960s. It is a compensation for the imperfections inherent to the human condition. It is a controlled way for writers and readers to explore and perhaps exorcise those darker aspects of themselves that can endanger open societies. To summarize, Vargas Llosa's views about the irrationalist nature of literary creation have remained the same for three decades. What has changed is his attempt to link them to a political vision. In the 1960s he tried to show the socialist implications of literature, and in the 1980s he has argued that literature can contribute to the social vision of thinkers like Popper and Berlin. His desire that literature contribute to the well-being of the open society is the motivation of his new literary doctrine that he sometimes calls "la verdad de las mentiras" whose direct translation into English ("the truth in falsehoods") may miss the intended connotation of "the literal truths in the lies of literature."

Vargas Llosa's attempt to reconcile the demons of literary creation with his political convictions of the 1980s was first expressed in the prologue of his play *Kathy and the Hippopotamus* (1983). Vargas Llosa's new conception of literature reflects his need to find a connection between his critique of political utopias and the doctrines of Bataille on the human need to transgress social norms:

> The inevitable abyss between the concrete reality of an individual and the desires he will never be able to satisfy is the origin of human unhappiness, dissatisfaction and rebelliousness. It is also the raison d'être of fiction, that falsehood thanks to which we can deceptively compensate for the insufficiencies of life.[73]

Stripped of their socialist connotations, the demons continue to be, for Vargas Llosa, the driving force behind literary creation. Vargas Llosa proposes a new and complementary metaphor to refer to the conscious forces that struggle against the demons when these jeopardize social life. These he figures as the "angels" that "bridle the individual's desires and passions so that specific appetites, roused by the imagination, do not endanger the social body. This is the very definition of the idea of civilization."[74] But, according to Vargas Llosa, human desires will never be truly satisfied: "the angel that inhabits man is never able to totally defeat the demon with whom he shares the human condition, even though in advanced societies it may seem that this victory has been achieved."[75] The best that can be expected is the establishment of

> a modus vivendi between the angels whom the community would ideally like to have as its only members and the demons that these angels cannot help simultaneously being, regardless of how elevated the culture or how powerful the religion of the society in which they are born.[76]

Uncensored literary activity is, for Vargas Llosa, a most sensible way to encourage the modus vivendi between demons and angels because the transformations of lived experience by the workings of fantasy can serve as palliatives to the desires and inclinations that can threaten social coexistence. The transformation of lived experience into fantasy can take on many guises. Writers can purport to represent reality accurately, or they can make it patent that their fictional world is distinct from their lived experience. To illustrate Vargas Llosa's views of literature in the light of his new conceptions it might be instructive to review his essays on Jorge Luis Borges and Victor Hugo two of his favorite authors who represent, for him, the two extremes when it comes to exploring the relationship between literature and lived experience.

During his socialist period, Vargas Llosa was unable to justify his admiration for Borges. But in recent years the Argentine master has received the highest praise Vargas Llosa has bestowed on any modern writer in the Spanish language: "[Borges is] the most important thing to happen to imaginative writing in the Spanish language in modern times."[77] Vargas Llosa believes that Borges abhors the physical aspects of human experience and that these feelings have a decisive effect in Borges's fictional world, where "the intellectual always devours and destroys the mere physical."[78] Vargas Llosa thinks that Borges did not write novels because he wanted to avoid the most realistic of literary genres:

> His attitude toward the novel was one of scorn. Predictably its realistic tendencies would trouble him because, with the exception of Henry James and a few other illustrious practitioners, the novel is a genre that resists being bound to what is purely speculative and artistic and so it is condemned to melt into the sum total of human experience, ideas and instincts, the individual and society, reality and fantasy. The novel's congenital imperfection and dependence on human clay Borges found intolerable.[79]

Borges does not pretend to invent alternative realities that one could confuse with lived experience. Instead, his writing, according to Vargas Llosa, is an affirmation of the autonomy of the fictional world:

> What lends greatness and originality to Borges's stories is not the materials he uses but what he turns those materials into. A small imaginary world populated by tigers and highly educated readers, full of violence and strange sects, acts of cowardice and uncompromising heroism in which language and imagination replace objective reality and the intellectual task of reasoning out fantasies outshines every other form of human activity.[80]

If Borges represents, for Vargas Llosa, one extreme of the range of literary activity, Victor Hugo is at the other extreme, because he insisted that his books were true to life. Few texts could be further from the aesthetics of Borges than Victor Hugo's *Les Misérables*, an enormous novel whose narrator claims to be a spokesman for his age and an advocate for the downtrodden. Vargas Llosa has called this novel

> a luxuriant jungle: the central story has other independent or parasitical stories appended to it, as well as numerous philosophical, social and religious digressions. This growth is sometimes disproportionate and anarchical, with so many comings and goings that the thread of the plot is sometimes lost and the reader's attention diluted. However, it is because of this quantitative factor—its torrential nature emulates the vertigo of life—that *Les Misérables* with all its ingenuities and excessive sentimentalities, its effects of the period and its unskillfullnesses characteristic of serial stories, continues to strike readers as one of the most memorable works of fiction ever written.[81]

Vargas Llosa considers the novel to be realistic in its intention and its effect. One must not confuse, however, the effect of realism with reality itself:

> Its pretensions are extraordinary; thanks to them this beehive of adventures has become so vast that it seems "real." Yet it is not. On the contrary. Everything in it is fictional, starting with that which the narrator is determined to present to us as "history," or "slice of life," and ending with the narrator himself, the most impetuous invention in the novel, the most complex and versatile character.[82]

Applying his aesthetic of the truth of falsehoods to *Les Misérables*, Vargas Llosa says:

> It is not . . . a testimony about French society between 1815 and 1833 but a beautiful fiction, inspired by that reality and by the ideals, dreams, traumas, anxieties, obsessions—the demons—of France's first romantic. The documentary aspects of the book are not precise and have grown stale. What retains its freshness and charm is everything that Victor Hugo stylized by beautifying or darkening it

to the rhythm of his fantasy which expresses a profound truth that corresponds to the dreams with which he brought that fiction into being.[83]

Vargas Llosa has written that historians who try to be objective can only offer imperfect interpretations of reality, but novelists who transform lived experiences and distort historical events can give a satisfactory coherence to human events.[84] From this point of view, historians and bad novelists have much in common. His most impressive attempt to give coherence to a historical event is also his most important novel: *The War of the End of the World*.

CHAPTER FIVE

The Novels of the 1980s

T*he War of the End of the World* (1981), Vargas Llosa's greatest work of literature, is a historical novel of epic grandeur intended for the era of the end of ideologies. Its main anecdote—around which hundreds of characters and situations are crafted with a mastery unprecedented in Latin American literature—was inspired by a tragic historical episode in Brazilian history. Vargas Llosa transforms the historical events in order to develop his most ambitious and accomplished theme—a human cataclysm unleashed by the unexpected consequences of fanaticism and, nevertheless, the affirmation, without pathos, of life in situations of adversity. *The War of the End of the World* is a contribution to a literary tradition, including masterpieces by Stendhal and Tolstoy, about the propensity of humanity to idealize violence, either with the visions of the idealist or with the abstractions of the intellectual who fails to comprehend war—the most devastating collective experience of all. For José Miguel Oviedo this novel's greatest merit is its power to evoke "the huge variety of the human happening. It exercises a relentless hypnotic force upon the reader despite the sheer length of the narrative."[1]

The rebellion took place in Canudos, the backlands of the state of Bahia, a few years after the fall of the monarchy and the establishment of the new Brazilian republic in 1889. It was documented by journalists, chroniclers, and novelists who witnessed the events and has been analyzed by historians and sociologists. The most important work about Canudos, rightly considered a classic of Latin American literature, is *Rebellion in the Backlands* (1902) by Euclides da Cunha. Vargas Llosa was impressed when he read it in 1972 on the recommendation of Rui Guerra, a Brazilian film-maker who hoped to persuade him to write a screenplay based on the Canudos rebellion. Vargas Llosa agreed to work on the project, and he read many other fictional and historical accounts to help him conceive a historical setting for the characters he wanted to invent. The treatment (or prose text with the plot of the first screenplay) and the two screenplays Vargas Llosa wrote for Rui Guerra are embryonic versions of *The War of the End of the World*. They contain two of its main story-lines: the Galileo Gall, Rufino, and Jurema triangle and the political intrigues that led to the repression of the Canudos rebels.

In the first screenplay, entitled "The War of Canudos" (1972), a sexual intrigue is entangled with a political one. Galileo Gall, an Irish anarchist (in the final version he will be Scottish) and an enthusiast of the Canudos rebellion, meets and forces himself on a local woman named Jurema. Jurema's husband, Rufino, a local tracker and pathfinder, kills Gall to regain his honor. Gall's cadaver serves as the pretext to repress the rebels in Canudos. The dead foreigner is taken as an agent in an international conspiracy to assist the old Brazilian monarchy in regaining political power. The mastermind of the malicious hoax is Epaminondas Gonçalves, who takes advantage of the rebellion to settle old scores. He expects to ruin his political enemy, Luis Vianna, the governor of Bahia, by imputing to him complicity with the enemies of the new republic.

In the second screenplay entitled "War Dogs" (1974), Vargas Llosa develops Epaminondas Gonçalves in greater detail. He now appears as the owner of the farming-estate where Rufino is employed. In this version Gonçalves's scheme is more diabolical: he meets anarchist Gall and offers him weapons for the rebels in Canudos. He tells Gall, with apparent candor, that he wants the rebellion to succeed in order to ruin Vianna, his political enemy. Gall accepts Gonçalves's proposition, thinking that he can contribute to a rebellion that will eventually dwarf the petty squabbles of local politicians as it unleashes a revolution worldwide. But Epaminondas's false intimations are a trap. He needs the body of a dead British subject to lend credence to his hoax about the presence of foreign agents in Bahia. Gonçalves tries to murder Gall, but the anarchist survives the attempt and rushes to Canudos to warn the rebels they may become scapegoats in a loathsome political ploy. But before he reaches Canudos, he is killed by Rufino who has been tracking him to avenge the rape of his wife. Epaminondas is delighted to learn of Gall's death, which he will publicize as undeniable proof of the collusion between Britain, the old Brazilian monarchy, and the rebels.

In the spring of 1976 Vargas Llosa taught a course on Latin American literature at Columbia University that included *Rebellion in the Backlands*. His lecture notes on the Brazilian classic can be read as a link between the screenplays and *The War of the End of the World*. To explain the historical significance of da Cunha's book, he chose an approach akin to his own literary treatment of the war in his novel. Rather than following da Cunha in explaining the geographical and anthropological phenomena of the region as the keys for understanding the war, Vargas Llosa explains the conflict from the points of view of two warring camps, each led by a fanatic: Antonio the Counselor, the "mystical idealist," and general Moreira César the "nationalistic military man."[2]

In the novel's final form, Vargas Llosa integrates the Gall-Jurema-Rufino triangle in the context of a larger story of war whose protagonists are Antonio the Counselor, the messianic leader of the backland rebels, and Moreira César, the general of the Brazilian republic. Vargas Llosa also invented an unnamed character—an opportunistic journalist—based on the biography of Euclides da Cunha. Vargas Llosa's challenge was to integrate into a single novel a number of elements he had conceived independently: the Jurema, Gall, Rufino-triangle; Epaminondas Gonçalves's hoax; the war between rebels and soldiers; and the story of the journalist. To fuse these elements, Vargas Llosa made some important changes to the plot of the film scripts. He transformed Epaminondas Gonçalves into two distinct characters. The first, as in the two film scripts, is the inventor of the hoax, a powerful political boss who runs an influential newspaper. The second is the Baron of Cañabrava, the owner of the ranch where Rufino works.[3] In the novel, Galileo Gall does not find out, as he does in the second film script, that he is a pawn in Epaminondas's schemes, and he sets out for Canudos eager to participate in the rebellion.

Vargas Llosa's research on the Canudos rebellion went well beyond *Rebellion in the Backlands*. As a fellow of the Wilson Center in Washington D.C. and in the library of the British Museum, he found a wealth of relevant information in works of history and folklore. When Vargas Llosa visited the Brazilian backlands in the company of the novelist Nélida Piñon, he also interviewed individuals who knew legends, poems, and songs about the rebellion. Early on in the writing of the novel, he invented many characters inspired by his research and by other literary works that have little to do with Brazil, most notably Tolstoy's *War and Peace*.

Literary and historical works about Canudos had hitherto presented the uprising from the perspective of the victorious republicans. Vargas Llosa drew on these sources, but he felt free to transform them. He was especially keen on presenting the perspective of the rebels, which he was obliged to invent because it was unavailable from Brazilian historiography at the time:

The vision of the vanquished is totally unknown. Not a single individual from the backlands who participated or witnessed the events wrote about them, and the versions offered by others are totally subjective and distorted. Some details of their story are only now beginning to surface. That leaves one with a great margin for the imagination.[4]

Vargas Llosa's great invention in *The War of the End of the World* is the private lives of the men and women of Canudos who rejected the sovereignty of the new Brazilian republic. Galvanized by their messianic leader, they defeated the modern army of the Brazilian republic in two battles before losing a final clash in which not a single male rebel survived.

In his book about *The War of the End of the World*, Leopoldo Bernucci has shown in great detail that Vargas Llosa drew facts and even imitated phrases and turns of phrases from *Rebellion in the Backlands*. Bernucci strongly suggests that Vargas Llosa also borrowed from other historical, literary, journalistic, political, and sociological texts related to the Canudos rebellion.[5] Bernucci's book is required reading for anyone who wishes to compare *The War of the End of the World* with *Rebellion in the Backlands*. But in his valuable study he makes an error common to most of the literary criticism on the novel: he reads it as a rewriting of da Cunha's work or as a novel that presupposes previous knowledge of its illustrious antecedent.[6]

Vargas Llosa did not rewrite da Cunha's book with different literary techniques, and he did not make his own book intelligible only to those who can decipher allusions to Brazilian history and literature. He wrote a novel based on the same historical incident as *Rebellion in the Backlands*, a work of fiction based on a historical event and not a literary version of historical facts. As Angel Rama aptly puts it, *The War of the End of the World* is a novel "that anyone can read without previous knowledge of its antecedents. It is purely a product of Vargas Llosa's writing."[7]

Vargas Llosa obviously admired da Cunha's work. In fact, he dedicated the novel to his memory. But he was no more faithful to the spirit of *Rebellion in the Backlands* than he was to da Cunha's biography in developing the feeling and thought of the opportunistic journalist. Vargas Llosa's intellectual concerns are strikingly different from those of his illustrious antecedent. There are no traces at all in *The War of the End of the World* of the numerous philosophical, sociological, and psychological theories that da Cunha used to justify the organization of his work and to substantiate his judgments, opinions, condemnations, and diagnosis of Brazilian reality. In *The War of the End of the World* only Galileo Gall, a pathetic character with a remarkable incapacity for fine judgment, believes that human history has a meaning and a finality that can be determined with sociological theories.

DA CUNHA'S HISTORICISM

Da Cunha was a historicist: he believed there is a pattern to human history. Human evolution takes a definite course with steps and phases. Individuals, societies, and nations may be left out of history; some may become players in accelerating or retarding the course of human events; but no one can alter the inevitable progress of humanity. In the first lines of *Rebellion in the Backlands* he declares his adherence to Ludwig Gumplowics's sociology according to which the struggle of the races is the motor of human progress:

> Civilization is destined to continue its advance in the backlands, impelled by that implacable "motive force of history" which Gumplowicz, better than Hobbes, with a stroke of genius, described in the inevitable crushing of weak races by the strong.[8]

Da Cunha interpreted the Canudos uprising as a war that hindered rather than furthered the cause of human progress in a part of the world that may eventually be left out of history. Dain Borges has shown that Da Cunha believed that the racial composition in Canudos was weak and prone to degeneration because the different races of the Brazilian had not cohered into a solid unit.[9]

Da Cunha studied the geography and the climate of the Brazilian backlands as well as the racial and psychological constitution of the inhabitants (the sertaneros) of the region in order to explain the madness of the Republican government of Brazil, which committed an act of genocide against a population whose only offense was the defense of their land and property. Da Cunha's book is simultaneously the condemnation of a crime and a diagnosis of the sick society that perpetrated it. He concludes that the cause of the genocide was the republicans' lack of knowledge and understanding of the geographic and racial reality of their own nation. In order to rectify this negligence, he devotes about a third of his book to the study of the land and of the sertaneros. According to da Cunha the messianic inclinations of the sertaneros makes them incomprehensible to anyone who ignores the geographical and climactic peculiarities of the region: the unpredictability of an unfriendly climate explains the sertanero's oscillation between fatalism and excitation.

Da Cunha relies on current sociological theories to explain the character of the sertanero, and he draws on psychological constructs to explain the mental pathologies of Antonio the Counselor, the leader of the rebel community, and Moreira César, the general in charge of their repression. For da Cunha both are individuals on the verge of madness.[10] He calls the Counselor an insane clown blinded by an apocalyptic vision; and he thinks Moreira César is a grotesque man physically and spiritually ill-suited for military life. In da Cunha's view, both César's patriotism and the Counselor's religiosity are fraught with criminal propensities. If their pathologies have been unrecognized, it is because their social milieu is pathological.[11]

Da Cunha wrote his book in a polemical tone to refute other interpretations of the rebellion. He was particularly incensed with the prevalent assumption that the sertaneros had participated in a political conspiracy against the Brazilian republic: "To attribute the backlands crisis to a political conspiracy of any kind is to reveal a glaring ignorance of the natural conditions surrounding our race."[12] Da Cunha denounces the military campaign as a macabre criminal act akin to a collective suicide: it is a racial genocide committed by soldiers whose ethnic constitution is identical to that of the individuals they massacred.[13]

In *The War of the End of the World*, as in *Rebellion in the Backlands*, Antonio the Counselor and Moreira César are main characters, and the monarchic conspiracy is a woeful lie. But the differences are greater than the similarities. In da Cunha's version the war takes place because Brazilians lack a scientific understanding of their own reality. In Vargas Llosa's novel the war occurs as a result of misunderstandings and incomprehension on both sides, self-serving scheming by opportunists, and, above all, fanaticism. Da Cunha's book is a sociological treatise written with literary insight and sensibility, but its intentions are sociological.[14] Vargas Llosa's novel is a literary work inspired by sociological, historical, and literary sources. Vargas Llosa utilized *Rebellion in the Backlands* and other sources in crafting a work of fiction but with no intention to be faithful to Brazilian history or to any of his research materials. He modified and altered at will. An instructive example is his transmutation of the sections in *Rebellion in the Backlands* in which da Cunha mentions the "Jurema," a plant the natives of the backlands use as a narcotic to relieve fatigue. Da Cunha describes the plant as "yielding but impenetrable."[15] Its thickets slow the movement of people through the backlands. Vargas Llosa used the name of the plant and transforms the botanical description into a female character: the woman of golden skin for whom the circumlocution "yielding but impenetrable" is aptly suited for Vargas Llosa's purposes. Jurema's involvement with several men in the novel (she is Rufino's wife, Galileo Gall's reluctant companion, and she becomes the myopic journalist's lover during the war) reminds one of Teresa in *The Time of the Hero* and of Lalita from *The Green House*. The romantic and sexual relationships of these female characters illuminates the personal dramas of the male protagonists.

Christina Arkistall makes a valid point when she argues that Jurema is but one of many women character's in Vargas Llosa's fiction who behaves according to the sexist assumptions of a society where female obedience and submission to a male protector is a given.[16] Vargas Llosa is unable to transcend the stereotypes of a sexist society and must flatten the psychology of characters such as Jurema, Teresa, and Lalita to make credible their apparent vitality and resilience after suffering untold humiliation and abuse. Female characters in Vargas Llosa are often primarily the allies of men or the object of their desire. *The War of the End of the World*, as Arkinstall has shown, is no exception.

Jurema's story is interwoven with many other equally elaborated stories. In *The War of the End of the World* Vargas Llosa explores a wide array of human experience. He masterfully moves from the culminating moments of combat to the most private moments of self-reflection of a fighter, from vast expanses to enclosed spaces, from the ceremonies of public display to the rites and tensions of personal encounters.

THE WAR OF THE END OF THE WORLD

Vargas Llosa's novel was conceived with precision and elegance and is composed of four books. Books 1, 3, and 4 are divided into chapters and subdivided into narrative sequences, while book 2 is made up of three short chapters. With each narrative sequence the plot advances, and each book introduces new perspectives adding unexpected dimensions to a novel that is complex in its organization and focused in its execution. The impressive network of major and minor story lines—that advance with a myriad of hidden elements and deliberate ambiguities—increases the intensity of the main plot, which tells the story of the war from the origins of the seditious community until the Republican army's decisive victory.

Book 1 sets up a contrast between two characters, Antonio the Counselor and Galileo Gall. The Counselor is the charismatic spiritual leader of the rebels. His messianic vision strikes a chord with those who suffer the hardships of the backlands: drought and poverty are signs of the impending apocalypse. He establishes a religious community with hundreds of followers and sympathizers who await for the end of the world. Vargas Llosa devotes many narrative sequences to the stories of more than a dozen of the members, from birth to first contact with the Counselor. They are marginal figures in a poor and inhospitable region: Antonio el Beatito, a cobbler's bastard son, who always wanted to become a priest; João Grande, who was born of the eugenic experiments of a landowner and is the brutal murderer of the woman who raised him; María Quadrado, the self-taught artist who paints Christ's passion; João Abado, a rugged man fascinated by wandering troubadours; Leon of Natuba, a dwarf with short legs, long arms, and an oversized head who becomes the secretary and chronicler of the Counselor; Alejnandrihna Correa, a soothsayer who had been sexually abused by Don Joaquim, her parish priest.

When the Brazilian republic is established, the Counselor interprets the secularization of political life as conclusive evidence that the end of the world is approaching. He is equally certain the republicans wish to reinstate slavery, which the monarchy had abolished. When the laws and edicts of the new Republican government arrive in Canudos, the Counselor organizes a public gathering and bonfire in which he proclaims that "the Antichrist was abroad in the world; his name was Republic."[17] His public repudiation of the Republican laws is an act of defiance marking the beginning of the Canudos rebellion.

The other main character of book 1 (Vargas Llosa devotes as many narrative sequences to him as he does to the Counselor and his supporters in Canudos) is Galileo Gall, a phrenologist by training and an anarchist by conviction. He "had grown up hearing that property is the origin of all social evils and that the poor will succeed in shattering the chains of exploitation and obscurantism only through the use of violence."[18] Gall is in Brazil by accident, but when he learns about the Canudos rebellion he convinces himself that the defiance of the backland population is an ingenious application of anarchist political theories by a benevolent leader who knows how to help the oppressed by manipulating their superstitious beliefs: "It is as though he were putting our ideas into practice, hiding them behind the façade of religion for a tactical reason, namely the need to take into account the cultural level of his humble followers."[19] With a shipment of British rifles, Gall travels to Canudos to participate in what he believes is an anarchist rebellion whose repercussions may be felt around the world.

In every chapter of book 1 the Counselor gains an ever-increasing number of followers and sympathizers, but Galileo Gall does not manage to convince a single soul. The only character of the backlands who responds in any way to his exhortations is a circus-freak, a bearded woman disgusted by his political preaching:

"Your sickness is called injustice, abuse, exploitation. Do not resign yourselves, my brothers. From the depths of your misery, rebel, as your brothers in Canudos have done. Occupy the lands, the houses, take possession of the goods of those who have stolen your youth, who have stolen your health, your humanity. . . ."

The Bearded Lady did not allow him to go on. Her face congested with rage, she shook him and screamed at him: "You stupid fool! You stupid fool! Nobody's listening to you! You're making them sad, you're boring them, they won't give us money to eat on! Free their heads, predict the future—do something that'll make them happy!"[20]

For all his proselytizing, Galileo Gall does not gain a single convert to his cause. His only close contact with the people of the backlands is despicable: he rapes Jurema, the wife of Rufino, a tracker and pathfinder whom Gall hired to guide him through the uncharted regions of Canudos. As Christine Arkinstall has shown, Jurema has no choice but to run off with Gall. The fact that she has been forced upon does not make her any less guilty of dishonoring her husband in a society where women are considered property.[21] Gall's grandiose political ideals are belied by his pathetic behavior. His projects come to an abrupt end when the dishonored husband tracks him down and confronts him in a bloody brawl, the details of which are not revealed until book 3. Gall starts out as a picturesque odd-ball and ends up as a grotesquely repellent fool. He embodies Vargas Llosa's ideas about the dangers and pitfalls of political fanatics who do more harm than good to the people they purport to help.

Book 2 is brief but significant: it is set in Rio de Janeiro where the Brazilian legislative assembly votes to repress the Canudos rebels. The legislators are ultimately swayed by a hoax concocted by Epaminondas Gonçalves, a cynic indifferent to the human cost of his schemes. He presides over the Progressive Republican Party and is the editor-in-chief of a newspaper, the *Jornal de Noticias*. Epaminondas wishes to take advantage of the rebellion to smear his political enemies of the Autonomous Party who govern the state of Bahia. In his journal and in the legislative assembly where he is a representative, Epaminondas charges that the Canudos rebellion is a conspiracy by the old monarchy supported by the British empire in order to reestablish imperial power in Brazil. He incriminates the Autonomous Party in the conspiracy by suggesting that government officials in Bahia conspired with British agents to arm the rebels. To back his accusations, Empaminondas cites as "irrefutable evidence" the discovery of British rifles in Canudos and the death of Galileo Gall, whom he identifies as a British spy. His claims are diabolical fabrications.

Epaminondas Gonçalves meets Gall when he arrives in Brazil. He knows his new Scottish acquaintance is a fanatic who can be easily manipulated. Epaminondas provides Gall with British rifles to distribute among the rebels who had humiliated a small military expedition dispatched to the backlands to punish them for repudiating the laws of the Republic.

Gonçalves's newspaper reports the events as follows:

> The Progressivist Republicans reminded the Assembly that two weeks have now passed since the defeat of the Brito expedition by rebels vastly superior in number and better armed, and that despite this fact, and despite the discovery in the hamlet of Ipupiará of a shipment of English rifles being delivered to Canudos and the corpse of the English agent Galileo Gall, the State authorities, beginning with His Excellency Governor Dom Luiz Viana, have demonstrated a suspect apathy and passivity by not having immediately called for the intervention of the Federal Army, as the patriots of Bahia are demanding, in order to put down this conspiracy that is threatening the very existence of the Brazilian nation.[22]

The writer of the newspaper article is skeptical about the story he has written with such an air of certainty and conviction. For him, however, truth and falsehood are all the same, as long as he pleases his superiors and follows their instructions. He is an opportunistic unnamed journalist who is willing to change his political allegiances on whim. He once worked for a newspaper that had sympathized with the old monarchy and is presently employed in Goncalves's *Journal de Noticias*. He is the nearsighted, ugly, unkempt journalist with a squeaky voice and a wry expression who loves adventure and wishes to accompany general Moreira César in his expedition to repress the rebels of Canudos: "I don't have any political convictions and politics don't interest me."[23]

The narrative of book 3 is considerably more complex than that of book 2. Although Gall's death is revealed in book 2, his adventures on the road to Canudos until his death are narrated in book 3, as pathetic events in the light of the genocide he inadvertently helped to unleash. In a recursive pattern each chapter in book 3 includes a sequence devoted to the baron of Cañabrava and another sequence devoted to Gen. Moreira César. The baron's movements belie Goncalves's cynical scheme. Although he is accused of being one of the protagonists of a conspiracy with the British empire, the baron had in fact been abroad during the Canudos events. He is as surprised by the events as anyone when he returns to his ranch. The other main character in book 3, Antonio the Counselor's true rival, is Gen. Moreira César, a man with dictatorial tendencies in charge of repressing the Canudos rebels. The defender of the republic does not believe in democracy. He feels no need to justify his actions, even when he kills his detractors, including journalists who write about him unfavorably. His dogmatism leads him to believe Epaminondas Gonçalves's hoax:

> The Seventh Regiment is here to put down a monarchist conspiracy. For behind the brigands and fanatical madmen of Canudos is a plot against the Republic. Those poor devils are a mere tool of aristocrats who are unable to resign themselves to the loss of their privileges, who do not want Brazil to be a modern country.[24]

The opposition established in book 1 between the rebel community of Antonio the Counselor and the political ideal of Galileo Gall dissolves in book 3, giving way to a new and more significant contrast between the religious fanaticism of the Counselor and the military fanaticism of Gen. Moreira César.

Book 4 narrates the denouement of the war: the death of the leaders and the continuation of the combat until its bloody conclusion with the massacre of the entire male population of Canudos. Each chapter has two new sets of sequences. The first set narrates the adventures of the nearsighted journalist whose glasses have broken and who therefore witnesses a war he cannot see. The second set of sequences take place after the conclusion of the war. In them the journalist and the baron of Cañabrava interpret and evaluate the nature and the significance of the war. They conclude that the conflicts arose from misunderstandings and that the war was unjustified on both sides. In their discussions they come to comprehend the fanaticism of the pious men and women of Canudos:

> Everything was crystal-clear. . . . The Dog or the Father, the Antichrist or the Blessed Jesus. They knew immediately which of the two was responsible for any given event, whether it was a blessing or a curse. . . . Everything becomes easy if one is capable of identifying the good or the evil behind each and every thing that happens.[25]

They also come to an understanding about the fanaticism of a military establishment intoxicated with nationalist propaganda. As the journalist who reported Epaminondas Gonçalves's hoax, and as a witness of the war, the manipulative journalist knows what he is talking about when he says that newspapers were used as cynical means to manipulate public opinion and that "The lies that have been harped on night and day have turned into truths."[26] In Canudos he saw that the military, against all evidence to the contrary, continued to believe in accusations against the rebels:

They could see and yet they didn't see. All they saw was what they'd come to see. Even if there was no such thing there. It wasn't just one or two of them. They all found glaring proof of a British-monarchist conspiracy. . . . People's credulity, their hunger for fantasy, for illusion. . . . There had to be some explanation for the inconceivable fact that bands of peasants and vagabonds routed three army expeditions, that they resisted the armed forces of this country for months on end. The conspiracy had to exist: that's why they invented it and why they believed it.[27]

THE LITERARY TRADITION

The theme of the discrepancy between the realities of war and the abstractions of human ideals has important forerunners in literature. In Stendhal's *The Charterhouse of Parma*, Fabrizio del Dongho, a young Italian, sets out to enlist in Napoleon's army, but his journey ends in frustration. He thinks he has observed the trivial comings and goings of soldiers and perhaps a few minor skirmishes, but he does not believe he came near any major battlefield or any important military post where he could offer his services. He never realizes that he was present at the battle of Waterloo in 1815 and that he was a bystander at the fall of Napoleon. Fabrizio's idealism blinded him to the reality of war.

Leo Tolstoy gave a universal dimension to Stendahl's theme about the discrepancies between the reality and the idealization of war. In *The Charterhouse of Parma* an individual is unable to see war for what it is. In *War and Peace* there is an abyss between real warfare and the abstractions of intellectuals, politicians, and military strategists. They fail to make war comprehensible to anyone who is willing to take their ideas to task. Tolstoy sets up a contrast between the military leaders of the two sides: Napoleon Bonaparte, regarded as Europe's military genius even by his enemies, and Kutuzov, the modest Russian general incapable of conceiving a single strategy that will impress Russian intellectuals and nobles.

Tolstoy is relentless in mocking the frivolity of Moscow and Saint Petersburg high society, whose opinions about war are a pretext to display personal sophistication or family connections.[28] His most interesting characters, on and off the battlefield, are those who, like Prince Andrei, give up their categorical opinions as they humbly recognize that it may be beyond the human intellect to understand fully a social phenomenon as complex as war.[29] Andrei is a Fabrizio del Dongho who has gained wisdom. Like Fabrizio, he once had an idealized vision of war and a deep admiration for Napoleon Bonaparte. But Andrei is able to acknowledge that his experiences on the battlefield have undermined his preconceptions and idealized notions about heroic action and war. He can no longer admire Napoleon when he realizes that the general's military triumphs were produced by the unpredictable vicissitudes of battle, rather than by any preconceived design. Andrei eventually comes to understand that the chaos of war is more atrocious and less predictable than he believed when he was under the illusion that Napoleon could determine the course of a battle by the sheer genius of his military mind.[30]

As Isaiah Berlin has pointed out, the wise characters in Tolstoy's works are not those who know more than others but those who recognize human limitations:

> These great men are wiser, not more knowledgeable; it is not their deductive or inductive reasoning that makes them masters; their vision is 'profounder,' they see something that others fail to see; they see the way the world goes, what goes with what, and what never will be brought together; they see what can be and what cannot; how men live and to what ends, what they do and suffer, and how and why they act, and should act, thus and not otherwise. This 'seeing' purveys, in a sense, no fresh information about the universe; it is an awareness . . . which . . . cannot be deduced from, or even formulated in terms of, the laws of nature demanded by scientific determinism.[31]

> Kutuzov does not defeat Napoleon because he is a better strategist but because he has understood the uselessness of strategies and has grasped that in war a military leader must respect and be attentive to the needs and limitations of his own people. He has understood "that ideas and the words which serve to express them are not what move men into action. . . . This extraordinary power of insight into the significance of contemporary events sprang from the purity and fervor of his identification with the people."[32]

To explain Tolstoy's intellectual position, Berlin developed the metaphorical dichotomy of the hedgehog and the fox. The hedgehog is the intellectual who understands, thinks, and feels on the basis of a central vision or universal principle, while the fox pursues various potentially contradictory ends at once. Berlin concludes that Tolstoy was "a fox bitterly intent upon seeing in the manner of a hedgehog."[33]

According to Berlin, Tolstoy's realism had a corroding effect on the theories he had studied and on the ones he tried to formulate. As a result, the Russian literary genius lived a tormented life, for which Berlin considers him the most tragic of all the great novelists:

> Tolstoy's sense of reality was until the end too devastating to be compatible with any moral ideal which he was able to construct out of the fragments into which his intellect shivered the world, and he dedicated all of his vast strength of mind and will to the life long denial of this fact.[34]

Vargas Llosa was mindful of Berlin's essay about Tolstoy when he conceived the main theme of *The War of the End of the World*: the discrepancy between historical reality and human abstractions about reality. As in *War and Peace*, in *The War of the End of the World* the significance of the great historical events is beyond the grasp of most participants, eyewitnesses, and bystanders. Interpreters of historical events must not underestimate human ignorance, gullibility, prejudice, duplicity, and the effects of disinformation. Those who offer unwavering explanations of historical events are either rueful victims of their misguided convictions or dishonest charlatans.

Like Tolstoy, Vargas Llosa believes that humans long for the comfort of absolute principles or a comprehensive vision of their place in the world. But unlike Tolstoy, Vargas Llosa is not interested in the search. He admires Tolstoy's attention to human detail and his skepticism of intellectual abstractions, but he criticizes the Russian master's desire to seek a unitary vision of life:

> The brilliant novelist of the "particular," the prodigious describer of human diversity and of the protoplasmic differentiation between the individual cases that constitute daily reality, the fierce challenger of all the abstractions of those historians and philosophers who attempted to explain human development by means of a rational framework . . . lived hypnotically tempted by the desire to attain a unitary vision of life.[35]

The absence of a unitary vision of life does not trouble Vargas Llosa. His own vision is not riddled with intellectual or spiritual dilemmas. Tolstoy doubts that human beings can grasp the meaning of history, yet he is convinced that such meaning exists. Vargas Llosa distrusts theories that attempt to explain the meaning of history because he does not believe that history has any hidden meaning or purpose. Thomas M. Scheerer correctly points out that *The War of the End of the World* is not written to challenge any particular philosophy of history because the novel exemplifies Vargas Llosa's skepticism about all philosophies of history.[36]

Tolstoy establishes a contrast between Napoleon, the general who wishes to change the course of history through his brilliant strategies, and Kutuzov, the prudent general who goes along with its flow. Vargas Llosa sets up a counterpoint between Antonio the Counselor and Moreira César, both of whom epitomize equally mistaken and pernicious views. He is interested in exploring the attitude shared by the two protagonists: their willingness to fight for their fixed ideas, their inability to view the world in any other way, their rigidity of thought, their indifference to human life because their ideals are worth more to them that the lives of those who stand in their way. The cause of the conflict is not illuminated by the differences between the military man and the religious leader but by that which the two share: fanaticism.

Leftist critics have assailed *The War of the End of the World* because its view of history is not teleological. Angel Rama expresses moral and political reservations about the historical vision in the book, although he considers the novel to be the finest achievement in Latin American literature from an artistic point of view. According to Rama, the violence in the novel "stems from fanaticism and fanaticism is provoked by idealism which in turn has no apparent legitimation in reality." He follows this remark with an accusation of political disingenuity and bad faith on the part of Vargas Llosa, for he claims that novel's condemnation of violence is part of "a discourse widely cultivated by those sectors of society who prefer to forget that the power they now hold was achieved through violence."[37] Rama criticizes Vargas Llosa' novel because he cannot reconcile its view of history with his own socialist convictions. His question-begging turns into a tendentious attack when he claims that Vargas Llosa's implied rejection of violence as a legitimate means to achieve political goals makes him an accomplice of those who have conquered power through violence.

The Canudos rebellion in Vargas Llosa's novel is not caused, as Rama has argued, by the resistance of the dispossessed to an unjust and exploitative regime. Nor is it caused by the cynicism of the leaders on either side. Moreira César would be justified in subduing the Canudos uprising if it had been an attempt by the old monarchy to recover power, and Antonio the Counselor would be a true popular hero if he were organizing the resistance of a people threatened by the opprobrium of slavery. The reasons both protagonists justify their turn to violence would be legitimate if their assumptions about their foes were warranted. But their assumptions are wrong, and they are no more able to recognize their misconceptions as misconceptions than Don Quixote can recognize windmills as windmills. The only character in the novel who has a clear view of the Canudos events from the beginning is the cynical Epaminondas Gonçalves, a man without scruples willing to lie, cheat, deceive, and murder to achieve his aims. He is indifferent to the massive loss of life that results from his scheme to ruin his political enemy.

Moreira César, Antonio the Counselor, and Galileo Gall cause needless misery and death, but they die as dogmatic and self-assured about their fanatical views as ever. Moreira César and the Counselor—more than Gall, who is ultimately a bystander—die ignoring the enormity of their personal responsibility in a totally unjustified war. At some level Vargas Llosa seems to be making the disturbing suggestion that the delusions of the leaders are not very different from those of the common person who resorts to fantasy at moments of adversity. Take for example a poignant moment at the end of the novel when an old woman prisoner is interrogated about the whereabouts of a rebel leader: "Archangels took him up to heaven," she says, clacking her tongue. "I saw them."[38]

Euclides da Cunha concludes *Rebellion in the Backlands* with an impassioned indictment of the Brazilian people's madness. He is outraged that his countrymen lack the knowledge that would oblige them to take individual and collective responsibility for the worst tragedy in his nation's history. The issue of personal responsibility is left ambiguous in Vargas Llosa's novel. In *The War of the End of the World* the author insists on human irrationality and inclination toward fanaticism, but he offers little or no insight into the motivations of his characters because he is ultimately convinced that there is nothing to explain, that no explanation can shed light on their dark internal world. The motivations of his protagonists are impenetrable, but their actions spark and fuel a human cataclysm. In the novel, some characters, like Gonçalves, manipulate historical events to their own ends, and others, like the unscrupulous journalist and the baron of Cañabrava, come to realize how the misunderstandings of fanatics can lead to violence. But no character feels any personal responsibility for the tragedy.

The novel's supreme moments offer glimpses of the effect of war on the lives of those secondary and minor characters who appear intermittently to grapple with suffering, abomination, and humiliation. The novel reaches its heights when the absurd dimension of the war emerges with the same intensity as the affirmation of human dignity, as when a badly wounded Republican soldier begs a friend to help him end his life:

> "Death may be worse than what has happened to you already," Teotônio says. "You'll be evacuated. You'll recover, you'll come to love life again."

"With no eyes and no hands?" he asks quietly. Teotônio feels ashamed. The lieutenant's mouth is half open. "That isn't the worst part, Teotônio. It's the flies. I've always hated them, I've always been revolted by them. And now I'm at their mercy. They walk all over my face, they get in my mouth, they crawl in under the bandages to my wounds.". . .

"Would you like some water?" Teotônio says gently.

"It's not easy to kill yourself when you have no hands and no eyes," Pires Ferreira goes on. "I've tried hitting my head against the rock. It didn't work. Nor does licking the ground, because there aren't any stones the right size to swallow, and . . ."

"Be quiet, Manuel da Silva," Teotônio says, putting his hand on his shoulder. But he finds it absurd to be calming someone who seems to be the calmest man in the world, who never raises his voice, whose words are never hurried, who speaks of himself as though he were another person.

"Are you going to help me? I beg you in the name of our friendship. A friendship born here is something sacred. Are you going to help me?

"Yes," Teotônio Leal Cavalcanti whispers. "I'm going to help you. . . ."[39]

ALEJANDRO MAYTA'S STORY

If *The War of the End of the World* (1981) is Vargas Llosa's first incursion into the genre of the historical novel, *The Real Life of Alejandro Mayta* (1984) is his first novel about revolutionary activity. Its main anecdote is based on an incident that took place in the Andean city of Jauja on May 29, 1962, the first attempt at leftist insurrection in Peru. According to the newspaper articles that Vargas Llosa consulted to reconstruct the events, a young military officer, Francisco Guillermo Vallejos Vidal, stole armaments from the local police and broke into the city jail to liberate a prisoner named Vicente Mayta Mercado. With the assistance of twelve schoolboys they proceeded to rob a bank.[40] Several hours later Vallejos and Mayta were killed in a bloody confrontation with the police, and the schoolboys were captured. A jailed adult accomplice made declarations to the national press about the revolutionary intentions of his comrades. Some of the newspaper reports treated the incidents as the acts of common criminals. Others suggested links with pro-Cuban revolutionary movements as can be surmised from the following headline: "The operation fits into Fidel's scheme."[41]

In a preliminary sketch for the novel, preserved at the Princeton archives, Vargas Llosa had developed three characters who participated in the foiled revolutionary attempt: Vallejos and Mayta, who die convinced of their revolutionary ideals, and Condori, a man who recants his commitment to the pro-Cuban Left after the failure of the subversive attempt. In the final version of the novel Vargas Llosa decides to roll back the date of the historical events to 1958, so that they precede the Cuban revolution; he eliminates Condori as a protagonist; and Mayta survives the police repression.

It is possible to read *The Real Life of Alejandro Mayta* as a political treatise in the form of a novel as José Miguel Oviedo and Antonio Cornejo Polar have done.[42] Vargas Llosa does not believe in violence as a legitimate means to effect political change, and he is convinced that political utopias, in particular Marxist-Leninist ones, create greater harm than good. Indeed, *The Real Life of Alejandro Mayta* narrates a tragic and absurd attempt to initiate the socialist revolution in Peru.

The reading by Latin American literary critics of *The Real Life of Alejandro Mayta* as a political reflection—and even as a reactionary novel—influenced the international reception of the novel. Salman Rushdie remembers that his Spanish-speaking friends warned him the novel was a right-wing political treatise and that he reluctantly concurred:

> I came to Mayta entirely prepared to disagree with all those, in Spain and in Central America, who had told me, sadly, that Vargas Llosa had written his first overtly right-wing tract. Having read it, I can't disagree with them after all.[43]

Interpretations of *The Real Life of Alejandro Mayta* as a political treatise in narrative form abound. According to Antonio Cornejo Polar, who does not hide his contempt for it, *The Real Life of Alejandro Mayta* is a defective novel because it does not represent revolutionary activity as the result of Peruvian society's misery and economic injustice:

> According to *The Real Life of Alejandro Mayta* revolution takes place in a vacuum, produced by the delirium or the irresponsibility of certain somewhat messianic individuals, with no relation to the social and economic conditions of the nation. To be sure, when the narrator evokes the year 1958 (that is to say 1962) he hardly alludes to the extremely grave problems of Peruvian society, except when he remembers that young Mayta would deprive himself of some meals to share the destiny of the poor. This is why misery invades

the narrative only in the representation of the contemporary period, and it is purported to be the effect and not the cause of the
revolutionary process previously misrepresented. In other words:
if "Peru is finished" (p. 239) it is the work of crazy individuals. This
truncated causality (according to which in the origin there is revolution and not the injustice of the social system) has political connotations that are so dramatically contemporary that it is not necessary
to make them explicit.[44]

One need not discuss Cornejo Polar's interpretation of Peru's political situation, or the accuracy of the political vision he attributes to Vargas Llosa, to notice
the deficiency of his explanation of the novel. The primary criterion with which
he evaluates its literary merits is Vargas Llosa's ability to express political positions he can agree with.

The Real Life of Alejandro Mayta is not a political novel like those of José
María Arguedas or Alexander Solzhenitsyn who denounce the injustice and the
oppression of man against man. It is a political novel in the tradition of Joseph
Conrad and André Malraux, for it explores the social environments and the
psychological states of individuals who are prepared to legitimize violence as a
political tool or who are willing to kill for their ideals.[45] As in *Man's Fate* Vargas Llosa explores the emotional intensity of revolutionaries as they prepare
and carry out subversive acts; and as in *Under Western Eyes*, its most important antecedent, it explores the environments where revolutionary fervor is
generated.

THE STRATAGEM OF THE PERPLEXED

The narrator of Conrad's *Under Western Eyes* (1911), an English teacher, pretends to document a world he has come to know as a distant observer: that of
Russian conspirators and revolutionaries. He harbors no illusions about Russian autocracy and absolutism, which he brands as horrific and grotesque. To
him, revolutionary fervor expresses "the invincible nature of human error."[46]
Despite his skepticism about the Russian revolutionaries, he feels esteem for the
noble nature of some of them. This is not the case with Razumov, the protagonist of his story, who considers revolutionary activity the product of the criminal idealism of men and women so intoxicated with the utopias in which they
believe that they lose the ability to see things as they are and to appreciate the
true character of men: "Visionaries work everlasting evil on earth. Their Utopias

inspire in the mass of mediocre minds a disgust of reality and a contempt for the secular logic of human development."[47]

The English teacher intermittently interrupts his narrative in order to remind the reader that his intention is to document, in a novel, the social environment and the emotional and psychological state of those Russian conspirators with whom he has become acquainted. By reference to a remarkable private diary, he also acquaints the reader with Razumov, the university student who unwillingly became entangled in a web of people and events he despises: the revolutionaries, their crimes, intrigues, and conspiracies. The narrator insists that he is incapable of inventing what he is narrating, and he excuses his errors of literary composition with the disclaimer that his intentions are not literary but documentary. He dwells on his inability to understand the Russian character and the true motivations of the revolutionaries. His perplexity about the motivations of revolutionary activity, however, is not due to his ignorance of the world he describes nor to doubts he may have about political affairs. His description of the emotions of those who sympathize with subversion is masterful, and his opinions about Russia's political situation and about revolutionary activity are clear. The narrator's warnings about the limitations of his literary imagination and about his inability to illumine the motivations of his characters is a stratagem. Through it Conrad creates the illusion of an objective presentation of an all but impenetrable world.

If Conrad's stratagem is to create a novelist who expresses his *inability to invent* the characters and situations of a reality he wishes to describe objectively, Vargas Llosa's stratagem is to create a novelist who needs to invent characters and situations because of his *inability to understand* a reality that concerns him. In both novels the narrators feel incapable of explaining or judging the motivations of their characters. But whereas Conrad's novel presents itself as an objective portrayal of a human environment, Vargas Llosa's presents itself as the subjective invention of an individual. While *Under Western Eyes* reads like a documentary in the form of a novel, *The Real Life of Alejandro Mayta* reads like the chronicle of an author preparing to write a novel.

MAYTA'S SUBVERSION

Vargas Llosa's novelist is preoccupied with a foiled revolutionary act whose main protagonist was Alejandro Mayta. Never identified with a proper name, but certainly inspired by Vargas Llosa's own biography, the novelist explores the events of the revolutionary attempt, interviews those who knew its participants, and makes observations about the political situation in Peru and about the nature of literary creation. He speculates about why he feels compelled to write a novel about Mayta while recognizing that he does not know why he is so obsessed by that story.[48]

Like the first-person narrator of the Varguitas episodes in *Aunt Julia and the Scriptwriter*, *Mayta's* narrator is a novelist whose personal experiences are intertwined with those of a character he is obsessed with. What is new in *Mayta* are the narrator's reflections on the nature of fiction and the paradoxes he uses in the confines of a work of fiction, as when he insists that "in my novels I always try to lie knowing why I do it."[49] *Mayta* is a novel full of contradictions, mysteries, and incompatibilities. In a first reading, all the facts that the narrator gathers are doubtful. In a second reading, however, one can discern a small but significant core of consistent facts around which the narrative is organized: (1) the revolutionary Alejandro Mayta was one of the protagonists in a failed insurrection that took place in Jauja in 1958; (2) it began when a group of four adults and seven school-boys seized the city jail and assaulted two banks; (3) it lasted only twelve hours, until all the principals were either killed or detained by the authorities. In 1983, twenty-five years after the events, a writer interviews a group of individuals to gather information that will help him write a novel about Alejandro Mayta, the has-been revolutionary.

The narrator is not concerned withthe obvious inconsistencies nor with the difficulties of getting at the truth, because he is not interested in getting at the truth. He is interested in writing a novel, not history, but a novel inspired by the historical events which led to the rise of revolutionary groups in Peru. He investigates the historical event involving Mayta "so I could lie and know what I'm lying about."[50] The narrator is willing to transform his informants' accounts to the extent that his literary intuitions require it, but the tone he adopts is neither cynical nor frivolous: he is interested in Mayta in order to recover aspects of his own past, to reconstruct a human trajectory that could well have been his own. The narrator recalls the events of 1958 as a more naive period than that of the one he is living as he writes his novel in 1983. The events of the earlier period seem to him even innocent in the light of future revolutionary movements in Peru, and of their atrocities. The narrator remembers with bittersweet nostalgia that the events in which Mayta was involved occurred before the Cuban revolution but that they have been mostly forgotten: "Today no one remembers who took part in it."[51]

When Vargas Llosa was making preliminary sketches for the novel, he made lists of important revolutionary acts that took place in Peru from 1962 until the rise of the Shining Path guerrilla movement. In writing the novel, Vargas Llosa wanted to draw on Peru's recent history, but he also wanted to imagine the origins of subversive activity at a time when leftist revolutionary ideas had not yet been put into practice Latin America, or at least in Peru. He chose to draw upon the events in Jauja in 1962 while turning back the calendar to 1958 so that the events of the novel would precede the Cuban revolution and the guerrilla movements in the Andean region inspired by it. The narrator does not specifically point out that the fictional events of 1958 were inspired by actual events of 1962, but he spells-out the procedure: "Of course I've changed dates, places, characters, I've created complications, added and taken away thousands of things."[52]

CHAPTERS 1–9 AND CHAPTER 10

In the first nine chapters the novelist interviews a number of individuals who had something to do with Mayta's life or with the subversive act in which he was involved. Each chapter consists of the juxtaposition of the interviews with informants to the narrative sequences that either confirm or contradict their statements. The first seven chapters deal extensively with the events that lead to the insurrection. Chapter 8 is devoted to the insurrection itself and 9 to its repression at the hands of lieutenant Silva and corporal Lituma, recurring characters in Vargas Llosa's literary world. These last two are the chapters that most evoke Malraux's *Man's Fate,* in as much as it explores the strong emotions and heart-felt danger of individuals engaged in subversive acts. Chapter 10, which José Miguel Oviedo rightly considers "one of the most noteworthy moments in the author's narrative,"[53] sets out the encounter between the novelist and Mayta. This chapter transforms the first nine into a fiction within a fiction, as the narrator tells Mayta that he has been writing a novel about him with many inventions and distortions about his life and times.

Peruvian society in the first nine chapters is a degraded version of the same society as it appears in the final chapter. Unlike the historical period it ostensibly represents, Peru in the first nine chapters is run by a "Military Junta of National Restoration" in the context of a civil war. The chaos of the war fuels extreme and mutually destructive left- and right-wing death-squads and only grows worse with the intervention of Cuban, Bolivian, Soviet, and U.S. military forces. Vargas Llosa describes well-known neighborhoods of Lima and other Peruvian cities while grafting onto them an increasing sense of political terror with invented elements: police patrols with portable communication equipment, machine-gun nests that spring up from sand-bag trenches in city avenues, the visible presence of armed revolutionaries, as well as right-wing death-squads that decapitate, mutilate, and disfigure those whom they suspect sympathize with the leftist insurrection.[54] With force, but also with irony for readers who recall the vulture metaphor Vargas Llosa would often use in his socialist period to express his optimism about the demise of capitalism, *Mayta*'s narrator paints a bleak picture of subversion and of its dramatic consequences in the heart of Peru. The vulture feeding upon the decaying society that the revolutionary would help dissolve has now become the accidental beneficiary of an irrational vortex of violence:

> And those little black spots that flew, innumerable, from all four points of the compass toward Cuzco—they weren't ashes but vultures. Spurred on by hunger, braving smoke and flames, they dove on toward their desirable prey. From the heights, the survivors, parents, wounded, the fighters, the internationalists, all of them, with a minimum of fantasy, could hear the anxious tearing, the febrile pecking, the abject beating of wings, and smell the horrifying stench.[55]

In the novel Mayta's subversive attempt is presented as the starting point of a whirlpool of violence that has brought Peru to the edge of disintegration. Mayta's motivations are the subject of much speculation but are never clarified. And, yet, the various and contradictory opinions expressed by the informants who knew Mayta or who knew of him do much to illumine the context in which his subversive ideas were generated. Among the motley crew of characters that offer opinions are Moises Barbi Leyva, the progressive intellectual who directs a research institute; senator Campos who is working to establish a united front of leftist parties to participate in Peru's political process; Blacquer the narrator's Marxist mentor; Ubilluz, the arrogant school-teacher, ideologue of Jauja's high-school revolutionaries; Adelaida, the nun converted to liberation theology and admirer of Ernesto Cardenal, the poet-priest and former minister of Culture of Sandinista Nicaragua.

In the first nine chapters the significant events of Mayta's life can be ascertained early by the novelist: he was a pious young boy who was moved by Peru's poverty and who abandoned his religious faith in order to participate in revolutionary groups. He was a member of a tiny Trotskyite cell in Lima, was homosexual, married, and was present and involved in a revolutionary act that took place in Jauja in 1958. There are contradictions, however, in the interpretation of this information and about Mayta's true motivations. According to his aunt, Doña Josefa Arrisueño, Mayta was induced into revolutionary activity by his chance encounter with Vallejos, the young soldier with Marxist sympathies. According to Moises Barbi Leyva, Mayta was a naive idealist who undertook a Quixotic quest. Juanita, Vallejos's sister, is convinced that

Mayta was a seductive character who managed to sway his brother to participate in a foolish act. According to senator Campos, Mayta was a man who sold himself to American imperialism, which organized a bogus revolutionary event in order to give the Peruvian right an excuse to repress authentic leftist groups. According to Ubiluz, the high school teacher, Mayta was and remains a compulsive liar who conned him into believing he was a link to leftist groups in Lima who would support the revolutionary attempt that Ubilluz himself was preparing with Vallejos, his disciple. Blacquer, the Stalinist, thinks that the revolutionary project was sincere but stupid, because it lacked the necessary infrastructure and outside support to carry it out successfully. Adelaida, Mayta's first wife, is more concerned about the homosexuality of her husband than about his revolutionary activity, about which she seems to be largely ignorant. At times, the narrator can see no way to determine whether some event reported by an informant truly occurred. At others, all the versions agree on some point. At times he is sure he has confirmed a fact, and at other times he is sure an informant has lied to him. The difficulties he undergoes to reconstruct Mayta's story are not presented as a special case but as an example of the difficulties inherent in interpreting historical experiences.[56]

At the end of the novel the reader cannot determine Mayta's true motivations. The bits of information the narrator has gathered are contradictory, not only because reconstructing historical facts is inherently difficult at best—because of the partial knowledge of informants and their memory lapses—but also because the informants have lied and contradicted each other on purpose to hide their own misdeeds and weaknesses. Thus, for example, Senator Campos contradicts Leyva's thesis that Mayta was an idealist and explains that the director of the research institute had been wise to lie in order to hide his own questionable past. All three—Campos, Leyva, and Mayta—had been members of a Trotskyite cell. Even though Campos had accused Mayta of being an infiltrator serving Peruvian governmental and U.S. masters, he pretends that Leyva, and not himself, took the actions that led to Mayta's expulsion from the Trotskyite group. According to Campos, Mayta was an opportunist who had sold out: "Mayta collaborated with Army Intelligence and probably with the CIA."[57] He explains his old comrade's treason on account of his weak character and brings Mayta's homosexuality to bear as a proof of his frailty. Campos's accusations are dubious because, in his youth, he had been Mayta's homosexual lover.

The narrator also expresses the impossibility of reconstructing Mayta's real story, sometimes with metaphors: "Mayta: his face appears and reappears, it is a will of the wisp."[58] But whenever an image of the character is shaped in the novelist's imagination, it is invariably that of a fanatic:

In that exhausted and tense countenance, there glows as well, somehow, that secret, intact integrity in the face of setbacks which it always
thrilled me to find in him over the years, that juvenile purity, capable or reacting with the same indignation to any injustice, in Peru
or at the ends of the earth, and that honest belief that the most urgent
task, the one that could not be shirked, was to change the world.[59]

Mayta's utopia, as represented by the novelist in the first nine chapters, is a
vision of Communism where sexual prejudice would also be eliminated.[60] He
is certain that his convictions are irrefutable truths. From the perspective of
1983, his unshakable views turn from ironic to pathetic because all of his main
convictions were wrong: he believed that Fidel Castro's revolution was petit
bourgeois rather than socialist; that the shanty-towns would never become a
true base of support for Peruvian revolutionary groups; and that the catholic
religion is incompatible with socialism.[61]

Mayta's ideas about Fidel Castro also reflect the confusion and the disagree-
ments among fragmented and discordant leftist groups whose members do not
always respect party discipline. Mayta himself decides to participate in the Jauja
insurrection with his buddy Vallejos even though his own leftist collaborators
consider it to be "a petit-bourgeois adventure."[62] When it fails, Mayta bitterly
imagines his colleagues

> asserting that reality had confirmed the scientific, Marxist, Trot-
> skyist analysis the party had made, and completely justified its
> distrust and its refusal to participate in a petit-bourgeois adventure
> destined to fail.[63]

Vargas Llosa does not need to reconstruct Mayta's motivations in order to
suggest that subversive activity is harmful to an individual's life and contributes
to a country's social and political undoing. Jean-François Revel is right in reading *Mayta* as the novel of a moralist because of its "superb and suffocating representation of the birth and growth of terrorist ideology in the heart of a group."[64]
However, it can also be read as a novel about the seduction of revolutionary
activity, for the novelist is not a distant observer who sees Mayta as someone
whose sensibilities are different from his own and simply condemns him. Rather,
he remembers Mayta as the incarnation of his own youthful ideals, his own
enthusiasm for revolutionary movements. For the novelist, Mayta embodies
the origin of what had been his own political hope. He had studied Marxism
with Blacquer, the Stalinist, and was thrilled when he first heard of Mayta's revolutionary attempt.[65] The novelist recalls his own enthusiasm and excitement

when he read an article in Paris that he immediately discussed with other sympathizers of revolutionary causes: "'Is this the beginning?' we asked ourselves, openmouthed and euphoric. 'Is the volcano finally reawakening?'"[66] Twenty-five years later Mayta's story moves the novelist because in it he hears the strain of his own ideological siren song. He knows that Mayta's subversive attempt was once for him the illusion of his own ideals materializing.

In the surprising chapter 10, the novelist interviews Mayta and tells him he has been writing a novel about his life and his involvement in the Jauja insurrection. In his conversation he reveals the novel's fictionalized deterioration of Peruvian society. He also reveals that he has invented much about Mayta's life that is not true, such as their being classmates in elementary school and Mayta's being a homosexual. He also affirms that he has invented the insinuations that Mayta had participated in the revolutionary adventure as a kind of a suicide, thus dissolving the association Vargas Llosa had established between Mayta and Tchen from *Man's Fate*.

In the early part of the interview, the novelist feels disenchanted because he thinks he knows Mayta's story in more detail than this frail, beaten, abandoned man who was repudiated and betrayed by his old collaborators. Mayta's reticence at the novelist's questions is reminiscent of Don Anselmo's reticence in *The Green House* to discuss the origin of the bordello burned some fifteen years before and that he had ostensibly founded. Mayta talks about his revolutionary period as though it were a closed and forgotten chapter of his life. But the novelist discovers, late in the interview, that Mayta's reticence is a posture, that his fanaticism has not cooled, that he is still ready and willing to participate in subversive acts, and that he still believes in the ideals that inspired the failed insurrection of 1958. In the tenth chapter Mayta expresses a telling view of Fidel Castro that is different from the view his persona expresses in the first nine chapters—the view that the Cuban leader was petit bourgeois. In chapter 10, Mayta says that the only difference between Castro's revolution and his own revolutionary attempt is that Castro was luckier:

> "Those things seem impossible when they fail," he reflects. "If they succeed, they seem perfect and well planned to everyone. For example, the Cuban Revolution. How many landed with Fidel on the Gramma? A handful. Maybe even fewer than we had that day in Jauja. They were lucky and we weren't."[67]

Twenty-five years after the Jauja events, Mayta still believes that he was right and that he was simply a victim of his circumstances. Mayta's reflection about his revolutionary failure reveals the depth of his fanaticism, as well as Vargas

Llosa's cunning in setting the Jauja subversion three years before the events actually took place. In the world of the novel, Fidel Castro's triumph cannot provide justification for Mayta's revolutionary optimism, Thus, one can more fully appreciate Mayta's stubborn fanaticism in all its pathetic tenacity.

Mayta has failed but is not a beaten man because his experiences have not led him to abandon his fanaticism. He is not a tragic figure like Gisors, the Marxist professor of *Man's Fate*, who admits, "Marxism has ceased to live in me," after the failure of the Shanghai insurrection in which several young Communist militants died, including his own son and some of his disciples.[68]

The Real Story of Alejandro Mayta is a close relative of Conrad's *Under Western Eyes*: the narrator of Vargas Llosa's novel, like the language teacher in Conrad's, is penetrating in his description of the inner states of those who support and carry out subversive activity, and he ends up equally perplexed about the motivations of those willing to kill for an idea. The perplexity in *Mayta*, however, is not, as in *Under Western Eyes*, that of foreigners who gaze at curious individuals. It is rather the perplexity of one who looks at himself in the mirror. This is why Vargas Llosa does not invent, as Conrad did, a narrator who pretends to give an objective account of a world he does not understand, but one who gives up the objective representation of reality. *Mayta* is not simply a fictionalized account of a revolutionary attempt and its antecedents. It is a fictionalized obsession of a writer who has found in literature perhaps a palliative to the same obscure motivations that led his protagonist to believe that ideas are worth more than human lives.

The Real Life of Alejandro Mayta scratches the surface of a dimension of human experience Vargas Llosa has not explored in depth in his novels: the individual who confronts, without illusion or fantasy, the consequences of his own weaknesses and crimes. No one in the novel assumes responsibility for the debacles for which they are responsible. At the end of the novel Mayta is as fanatic as he ever was; and the narrator who used to believe that violence was a legitimate means to accomplish political gains has channeled his own fanaticism to a work of fiction where no one can attribute moral responsibility to the products of his imagination.

UCHURACCAY

After writing of *The Real Life of Alejandro Mayta* but before *Who Killed Palomino Molero?* (1986), Vargas Llosa agreed to become a member of the "Investigatory Commission" that inquired into the brutal murder of eight journalists by the villagers of Uchuraccay in January 1983. The commission was summoned by Fernando Belaúnde Terry, then president of Peru, to investigate events that had shocked the public. The commission included anthropologists, jurists, psychoanalysts, linguists, and other distinguished Peruvian citizens. It was not intended as a body convened to conduct a criminal investigation:

> The main purpose of the Commission was to provide information in the same way as a newspaper, magazine, radio or television station trying to determine the truth and make it known to the public.[69]

In a detailed report, the commission concluded that the eight journalists were murdered by villagers from Uchuraccay who mistook them for Shining Path terrorists. It also highlighted the fact that the villagers lived in a sordid environment resulting not only from terrorist activities but also from the abuses of government supported military operations. [70]

From the time of the announcement of his participation in the commission, Vargas Llosa was vilified by sectors of the Peruvian press. These slanderous reports were taken up abroad in newspapers such as *The Times* of London and *Dagens Nyheter* of Stockholm, where articles appeared stating that the eight journalists were murdered to prevent them from reporting the presence of Peruvian government paramilitary forces and that Vargas Llosa had participated in the commission to support the Peruvian government's cover-up of the affair.[71] The facts revealed by the commission have not been disproved. Violence in the region increased and led to more bloodshed and greater tragedies than those of Uchuraccay. Vargas Llosa's participation in the investigation continues to be the cause of defamations, polemics, and specialized studies by academics.

WHO KILLED PALOMINO MOLERO

Vargas Llosa began writing *Who Killed Palomino Molero?* (1986) a few months after publishing his last article in response to the slander he had been subjected to as a result of his participation in the "Investigatory Commission." His novel is by no means an attempt to reconstruct the Uchuraccay incidents. It can be read, as Roy Boland has shown, as a literary exorcism of his own experiences on the commission.[72] It narrates how two police officers investigating a savage murder manage to determine who committed the crime, how it was committed, and why. Yet they are rewarded for their efforts only by the incredulity of their fellow citizens.

The investigators of the atrocious crime in *Who Killed Palomino Molero?* are Vargas Llosa's two most recurrent characters, Lituma and Silva. Their first appearance together may be in the short story "A Visitor" in *Los jefes* where Lituma and his superior are searching for bandits on the sandy plains outside the city of Piura. They later reappear in *The Real Life of Alejandro Mayta* as the officers in charge of repressing Mayta's subversive uprising in Jauja, which occurs—following the imaginary chronology of Vargas Llosa's "human comedy"—four years after the murder of Palomino Molero. In *Who Killed Palomino Molero?* as well as in *The Green House* and *La Chunga*, Lituma was one of the "champs" who used to frequent Chunga's bar but has since distanced himself from this place's negative influences to start a new life as a member of the *Guarda Civil* in a precinct of Talara, a city not far from Piura. In *Lituma en los Andes* (1993) Lituma reappears to investigate murders and disappearances attributed to the Shining Path guerrilla movement.

Who Killed Palomino Molero? begins when Lituma, guided by a shepherd boy, finds the brutally tortured body of Palomino Molero. It ends when Lituma and Silva are punished by transferral to remote posts because their investigation displeased their superiors. In *The Time of the Hero* and *Captain Pantoja and the Secret Service* Vargas Llosa had already explored the dilemmas of individuals who cannot uphold morality or justice without denouncing the authorities and institutions supposedly upholding these values. This similarity makes clear that more than mere coincidence lies behind the similar punishments imposed on Silva and Lituma in *Who Killed Palomino Molero?* and on Gamboa and Pantaleón in the earlier novels. In *Who Killed Palomino Molero?* however, the theme of *The Time of the Hero* is ingeniously inverted. In his first novel, Vargas Llosa made the cause of Ricardo Arana's death deliberately obscure to highlight the indifference of the military school's authorities who aborted Gamboa's criminal investigation to avoid jeopardizing the institution's reputation. In *Who Killed Palomino Molero?* the investigators are certain that Palomino was murdered, and they are confident they have identified the murderer as well as his motive. What remains mysterious is the reason for the displeasure of Silva and Lituma's superiors, an issue that hinders the investigation and renders it only partially successful.

The process by which Silva and Lituma reach conclusions that are tentative but about which they can be pleased is another important component, one that develops from Vargas Llosa's readings of Karl Popper, specifically Popper's doctrine of "conjectures and refutations." According to Popper, conjectures must be tested by refutations that allow better conjectures to be developed. According to this doctrine, false hypotheses may contain information that brings an investigator closer to the truth as long as he is willing to reconsider them with an open mind.[73]

It is not necessary to debate the philosophical or epistemological validity of Popper's ideas or to discuss Vargas Llosa's interpretation of these ideas to understand that the doctrine of conjectures and refutations as a means of determining the truth is used as literary inspiration by Vargas Llosa in *Who Killed Palomino Molero?* Silva and Lituma investigate the murder of Palomino Molero by developing conjectures that collapse like a castle of cards—to quote an image Vargas Llosa has used to explain Popper's ideas—when the facts that refute them allow the two police officers to develop new conjectures.[74]

POPPERIAN DETECTIVES

The chief investigator of the crime is lieutenant Silva, an honest police officer who performs his duties with integrity. Silva's only weakness is his sexual fixation with Doña Adriana, an obese woman old enough to be his mother who owns an inn and is married to an old fisherman. Vargas Llosa uses the lieutenant's salaciousness to develop humorous interludes that lighten the sordid atmosphere of the story. On duty, Silva is able to check his lust, and his approach is decidedly Popperian: "The truths that seem most truthful, when given many turns and examined closely, are only half truths or cease to be truths at all."[75] Silva proceeds slowly and with composure, never risks making a definitive judgment unrelated to the facts, and does not propose definitive assertions until he is sure of having resolved the case.

As in the stories of Sir Arthur Conan Doyle, the reader discovers the detective's intellectual process through the observations and reflections of his assistant. *Who Killed Palomino Molero?* is not narrated in the first but in the third person. The narrator, however, confines himself mainly to Lituma's experiences, observations, feelings, and thoughts.

As an impulsive sentimentalist, Lituma has a more emotional response toward the crime than Silva, whose approach seems cold and intellectual. Lituma is moved by the case because he identifies with Palomino Molero: both came to Talara from their home town of Piura, and both abandoned the bohemian life of bars and brothels to bear arms—Lituma in the police force, Palomino in the military. Lituma is also moved to find that Palomino Molero may be the broken-hearted melancholic guitarist and songwriter whose sad boleros he sometimes heard at La Chunga's bar. Palomino Molero is a likely incarnation of "the Kid," a character of *The Green House* who believes that one's destiny is determined by one's sorrows:

"That's why I believe that the troubles a person carries around inside of himself explain everything," the Kid said. "That's why some people end up as drunkards, others as priests, others as murderers."[76]

Lituma's personal identification with Palomino explains his eagerness to work on the investigation. Anxious to get to the bottom of the case, he makes precipitous conjectures based on limited information. As the investigation proceeds, he is forced to reconsider most of his hasty conclusions.

The evidence collected by Lituma and Silva is verbal rather than material, based mainly on casual conversations and formal interviews. Obtaining some information through accidental encounters, anonymous messages, and unsolicited confessions, they find out that Palomino was a soldier stationed at an airforce base he had deserted shortly before his death. Because the authorities at the base are unwilling to cooperate with Silva's investigation, Lituma, finding their impolite reluctance to cooperate unusual, develops his first conjecture: Palomino's conscription was forced, he could not bear the military life, and he was murdered by someone from the base when he attempted to desert. This initial conjecture is refuted by Palomino's mother, who tells Lituma that her son had enlisted voluntarily: "the impression he had of the bolero singer was completely false."[77] Lituma picks up two additional clues while talking to Moisés, a bartender who knew Palomino before he enlisted. Moises tells Lituma that the guitarist had confided to him that he was painfully in love and that he had to leave Piura as a matter of life or death. On the basis of these clues, Lituma concludes that Palomino joined the air force because he had been threatened in Piura, or else he left Piura to be near a woman he loved.

Silva and Lituma request an appointment with Mindreau, the colonel in charge of the base. During the interview Mindreau treats them with scornful arrogance and Lituma prevaricates. He now supposes that the colonel's despotism is reason enough for a soft-hearted man like Palomino to desert. After the interview, Lituma is as confused as the reader and feels the investigation is going nowhere. Silva, on the other hand, feels optimistic: "Now I'm sure that he knows a lot, maybe everything that happened."[78]

The investigation proceeds not because Silva and Lituma themselves move it along but because of two fortuitous events. The first is an accidental encounter with Lieutenant Dufó, the fiancé of Alicia Mindreau, the colonel's daughter. Dufó hints that he knows why Palomino was murdered: "he asked for it and he got it."[79] The second is an anonymous message: "Palomino Molero's killers kidnapped him from Doña Lupe's house in Amotape. She knows what happened. Ask her."[80] Silva and Lituma visit this Doña Lupe in Amotape, a run down little town. Silva manages to extract important information from the begrudging woman. According to her, a couple came to the town looking for a priest to marry them, but the marriage did not take place because some men in uniform detained and took the couple away. She remembers that the young woman was not intimidated by her abductors. In an insolent and defiant voice she threatened to reveal some disgusting secret about the man in charge and to commit suicide, as if she knew that the men in uniform were responsible for her life. In his interrogation of Doña Lupe, Silva would like to determine whether those involved are Colonel Mindreau and Lieutenant Dufó, and whether the young woman is Mindrau's daughter, Alicia. At this point, Lituma believes the case is cut and dry. But Silva teaches him a Popperian lesson: "'I'm not even completely convinced that it was Colonel Mindreau and Lieutenant Dufó who killed him.' There was no irony in his voice. 'The only thing I'm sure of is that they were the two men who came here and took them away.'"[81] Lituma then proposes another conjecture with which Silva agrees: Palomino enlisted in the army to be close to Alicia Mindreau.

The next step in the investigation is also fortuitous: out of the blue Alicia comes to Silva and Lituma and reveals intimate confidences. She tells the two policemen that in spite of the fact that he was poor, Palomino Molero was more worthy of her love than any of her wealthier suitors. They met in Piura and saw each other often until her father was transferred to the Talara base. Alicia's confession seems to confirm a prior suspicion of Lituma's, that colonel Mindreau and lieutenant Dufó, the father and the fiancé, murdered Palomino to put an end to a romance they would not tolerate. Alicia accuses her father of the murder ("What's going to happen to my father? . . . Will they shoot him?"[82]) and makes another bizarre confession, apparently speaking of Dufó: "Once he went and got his revolver. He said to me, 'Just pull the trigger like this. Now take it. If you really hate me so much, I deserve to die. Do it, kill me.'"[83] Her confession seems to implicate Dufó, but she makes a surprising clarification: "The one who brought me the revolver and told me to kill him was Daddy."[84] Alicia accuses her father of sexual abuse and demands his arrest: "when he does those things, when he cries and asks me to forgive him, I hate him. I only wish the worst things would happen to him."[85]

To solve the murder case, Silva does not feel obliged to understand Alicia's motivations or to determine whether Mindreau actually molested his daughter: "Some details are still unclear, but I think the three key questions have been answered. Who killed Palomino Molero. How he was killed. Why he was killed."[86] Vargas Llosa does not offer the reader all the facts necessary to understand Silva's final deduction, but the lieutenant is sure that Mindreau is responsible for committing the crime. Silva's certainty about what he knows and his acknowledgment about what he does not know in connection with the case are expressed in the same language with which Vargas Llosa wrote about the results of the Uchuraccay investigation: "If the essential facts of the death of the journalists have been clarified—who killed them, how and why—there are some that still remain obscure."[87] And just as with his personal experience with the investigation, the events that follow the resolution of the crime in the novel are bizarre and disconcerting for the investigator.

When confronted with the accusation, the colonel willingly confesses that he ordered Palomino's murder and that he feels no remorse for his act: "Have you ever heard of an airman who could kidnap and rape the daughter of a base commander and get away with it?"[88]

Silva and Lituma do not arrest Colonel Mindreau, who murders his daughter and commits suicide before his case is brought to trial. There are reasons to believe that his superiors had intended to cover up the matter even before Mindreau's suicide. The people of Talara are incredulous about the results of the investigation and rumors spread wildly: the case involved contraband, espionage, or a homosexual intrigue. In the end, Silva and Lituma's investigation was futile, and the cause of justice is not served to anyone's satisfaction. Their investigation unearthed for them and for the reader a dark environment of ill will, malicious gossip, corruption, and foul-play. Silva and Lituma are convinced that they have solved the case, but they ignore the reasons why their investigation has upset important people, including their own superiors who reward their efforts with humiliating transfers to remote posts.

Who Killed Palomino Molero? is disappointing. The reader lacks the necessary information to confirm the solution that has convinced the detectives, and has little reason to care. The voluntary confessions of the colonel and his daughter are bizarre, their motivations are unexplored, and the significance of the crime is unclear. The novel succeeds, however, in conveying a deep sense of irritation and bewilderment like the one Vargas Llosa must have felt when he was personally maligned and slandered by journalists and academics after he participated in the investigation of the Uchuraccay tragedy.

THE STORYTELLER

Vargas Llosa has written about the lack of communication between two cultures that coexist in Peru—one modern, Western, and dominant; the other he often refers to as archaic, especially in connection with the indigenous populations of the Peruvian Amazon region. He has conjectured that the preservation of the cultural integrity of autochthonous populations may be a utopian project. To overcome the shame of exploitation and abuse, the indigenous populations may have to pay the price of integration into the modern world:

> Perhaps there is no realistic way of integrating our societies other than by asking the Indians to pay this high price. Perhaps the ideal, that is, the preservation of America's primitive peoples, is a utopia incompatible with a more urgent goal: the establishment of modern societies where social and economic differences are reduced to reasonable proportions and all can attain, at the very least, a free and decent life.[89]

Vargas Llosa's concern with the problem of the survival of indigenous cultures dates back to 1958 when he first traveled to the Amazon jungle and was moved by the precarious lifestyle of the Machiguengas:

> The Machiguenga Indian is obsessed with death. The diseases and tragic conditions of life he must endure have given him a fatalistic conception of life. As a result, his actions are always ephemeral and momentary. A Machiguenga never makes plans because he believes that death will overtake him before they can be put into practice. Even the smallest aspects of daily activity are surrounded by a sense of imminent catastrophe.[90]

During the weeks of the Uchuraccay investigation, Vargas Llosa once again came face to face with "a different Peru from the one in which I live my life, an ancient and archaic Peru, which has survived among these sacred mountains despite centuries of isolation and adversity."[91] The commission concluded that the villagers of Uchuraccay murdered the journalists. Vargas Llosa considered that the villagers in turn were victims of the tremendous violence resulting from the clashes between the Shining Path terrorists and the Peruvian army's counterinsurgency troops:

> The fact is that the war between the guerrillas and the armed forces is a settling of accounts between "privileged" sectors of society, in which the peasant masses are used with cynicism and brutality by those who say they wish to "liberate" them.[92]

Vargas Llosa has not resolved his own dilemmas about the preservation or eventual modernization of indigenous cultures. But his reflections undoubtedly run counter to the dominant intellectual currents in Peru that consider socialism as the political system most suited to the Indian's race and culture.

During his socialist period, Vargas Llosa expressed admiration for José Carlos Mariátegui and José María Arguedas, who were both convinced that modern socialism harmonized with pre-Columbian forms of social organization. Yet his admiration did not mean that he shared the agenda of the epigones of Peruvian *indigenismo*. He never defended Arguedas's notion of an Indoamerican national culture nor did he support Mariátegui's claim that socialism was suited to Peru because of autochthonous society's collectivist tendencies. But he did not criticize these justifications for socialism in Peru until he became disenchanted with Marxism. It was then that he reconsidered his judgments on Mariátegui's political solution and began to describe Arguedas as a writer caught between two utopias, an archaic and a socialist one. Vargas Llosa has claimed that Arguedas's passion for Andean culture inspired his best works of fiction but that the pressure he felt to express a socialist political position spoiled his literature.[93]

The Storyteller can be read as a literary expression of Vargas Llosa's concerns about Peru's autochthonous cultures after he ceased to believe in Marxist solutions. His protagonist is disenchanted with socialist *indigenismo* and decides to write a novel about an old university classmate devoted to the preservation of the Machiguengas and their culture. In his novel Vargas Llosa creates two parallel worlds, one modern and the other archaic, which are secretly linked.

The novel is not, nor does it pretend to be, an accurate portrayal of the Machiguengas or of the Western characters, some of whom were inspired by well-known Peruvian intellectuals. Vargas Llosa transmutes information about the Machiguengas and the Peruvian academic scene in order to establish a counterpoint between two groups of people who are culturally isolated from each other. *The Storyteller* is not an *indigenista* novel because it does not purport to document the complex historical, political, or anthropological reality of the Peruvian Indians. Literary *indigenismo* pretended to document Indian reality from a perspective committed to political change. But the novel does address the issue of *indigenismo* through the narrator, a man who had sympathized with *indigenismo* in his youth but who became disenchanted with it as he grew older.

THE LITERARY CONCEPTION

The first chapter of *The Storyteller* presents an enigma that animates the entire novel and is not resolved until the last chapter. These two chapters can be read as the prologue and epilogue of the novel. A Peruvian writer vacationing in Florence yearns to take a rest from his otherwise relentless obsession with his own country and to devote a few weeks to enjoy the art and literature of the Italian Renaissance. One day he accidentally wanders into an art gallery that is exhibiting photographs of the Peruvian Amazon jungle. He is astonished by one of the photographs: a group of men and women from the jungle are seated around a man standing upright whom the novelist identifies as a "storyteller." The reason for his astonishment is not fully cleared up until the last pages of the novel when the individual in the photograph is unequivocally identified as Saúl Zuratas, the narrator's university classmate. The identification of Saúl has the impact of a revelation because it clarifies points that had until then remained obscure for the reader—for example, the fact that Zuratas's old acquaintances had completely lost track of him after their university years. But this "revelation" is in fact a literary decision. The narrator chooses to identify the individual in the photograph as Mascarita (Zuratas is also known by this nickname), but because he only does so in the last pages of the novel the resolution of the mystery coincides with the reader's retrospective realization that the novelist's recollections are intertwined with his fictional inventions. The novel is a Borgesian game of Chinese boxes: the story of Mascarita's integration into the world of the Machiguenga is a fiction of the unnamed novelist whose obsession with Mascarita is a fiction of Vargas Llosa's.

The photograph in the Florentine chapters of *The Storyteller* is an image that brings together the story's main themes in much the same way as the Green House does in his first jungle novel. The individuals in the photograph are Machiguengas, the figure of the storyteller is an invention of Vargas Llosa, and the fact that the narrator identifies him as an old university classmate is an ingenious device that allows an archaic and a modern world to be juxtaposed in a work of fiction.

In the six central chapters of *The Storyteller*, as in *Aunt Julia and the Scriptwriter*, two literary registers alternate. In the even chapters, henceforth referred to as "the novelist's episodes," a novelist disenchanted with socialist *indigenismo* narrates his personal obsession with Saúl Zuratas and his desire to write a novel about him. The odd chapters, containing fictionalized anthropological material, suggest a world of myths, legends, anecdotes, and other features of an Amazon jungle culture.

In the novelist's episodes, Vargas Llosa's literary work is similar to equivalent episodes in other novels where he has used personal experiences to create an unnamed novelist who narrates his obsession with another individual about whom he would like to write a novel. In *Aunt Julia and the Scriptwriter* the narrator would like to write a novel about a writer of radio-plays, and in *The Real Life of Alejandro Mayta* the narrator is intrigued by a revolutionary.

In *The Storyteller* Vargas Llosa the narrator is obsessed with a friend from his years as a university student.

THE NARRATOR AND THE STORYTELLER

Counterpoints and oppositions between the modern and archaic worlds are the core of the novel. The novelist's episodes alternate with chapters written in a stylized language where a Machiguenga personage, "the storyteller," tells myths, legends, and anecdotes. The two sorts of chapters are related in ways that are surreptitiously revealed. At the outset the reader knows that Saúl Zuratas of the novelist's episodes is interested in the Amazon Indians, but he is not aware that the narrator's friend has become a Machiguenga storyteller.[94]

Saúl is a red-haired anthropology student, nicknamed Mascarita (a Spanish diminutive for mask) because of a birthmark that covers his entire face. His mother is Christian, his father Jewish. Saúl is from Talara, the region near Piura where *Who Killed Palomino Molero?* is set. Saúl's literary forerunner is Efraín Lerner, the protagonist of *The Fragmented Life of Jacob Lerner* by Isaac Goldemberg. Efraín is torn between the Christian world of his mother and the Jewish world of a father who abandons him while a small child and removes him from his mother's care when the boy was old enough to sense the complications of his upbringing.

In *The Storyteller* Vargas Llosa does not explore, as Goldemberg does, the experience of an innocent victim of religious tensions and class hatred. Saúl's Jewish origin, and his physical defect, establish him as a character on the margins of his society.[95] He is not troubled by his religious identity and does not exhibit emotional scars from guilt or hate. He would prefer to go unnoticed, and he keeps a low profile concealing his feelings and thoughts. His interests are limited but seem to absorb him. He cares passionately for Kafka's *Metamorphosis*, the great contemporary parable about the exclusion of the individual from his own community, and for the Machiguenga Indians with whom he established a connection during his fieldwork as an anthropology student. The two passions are apposite: The Machigengua are a society excluded among societies, as Gregor Samsa is an individual excluded from his own society. The apposition is poignant because Saúl knows the Machiguenga would have killed him at birth on account of his birthmark:

"I wouldn't have passed the test pal. They'd have liquidated me," he whispered. "They say the Spartans did the same thing, right? That little monsters, Gregor Samsas, were hurled down from the top of Mount Taygetus, right"[96]

Vargas Llosa crafted a character so marginal that even the fragile, helpless, and isolated Machiguenga community would have excluded him. The narrator refers to him as "a marginal among marginals."[97]

The novelist recalls his acquaintance and friendship with Mascarita when they studied at San Marcos University in Lima. The novelist studied Peruvian history under Raul Porras Barrenechea, and Saúl studied anthropology under Jose Matos Mar. Vargas Llosa made a bit of a caricature of these two well-known Peruvian scholars to establish a sharp dualism: Porras as the inveterate defender of the European heritage in Hispanic America, and Matos Mar as a socialist devoted to a new nationalism based on the indigenous culture. The novelist recalls that in his youth he shared the political position of his friend's professor:

[Socialism] by substituting for the obsession with profit—individual gain—the idea of service to the community as the incentive to work, and reintroducing an attitude of solidarity and humanity into social relations, socialism would make possible that coexistence between modern and primitive Peru. . . . In the new Peru, infused with the science of Marx and Mariátegui, the Amazonian tribes would, at one and the same time, be able to adopt modern ways and to preserve their essential traditions and customs within the mosaic of cultures that would go to make up the future civilization of Peru.[98]

Saúl, on the other hand, is neither a socialist nor a defender of Western values. He wants the modern world to leave archaic cultures alone:

No, I'm not an indigenist like the ones of the thirties. . . . I know very well that there's no turning back for the descendants of the Incas. The only course left them is integration. The sooner they can be Westernized, the better: it's a process that's bogged down halfway and should be speeded up. For them, it's the lesser evil now. So you see I'm not being utopian. But in Amazonia it's different. The great trauma that turned the Incas into a people of sleepwalkers and vassals hasn't yet occurred there. We've attacked them ferociously but they're not beaten. We know now what an atrocity bringing progress, trying to modernize a primitive people, is. Quite simply, it wipes them out. Let's not commit this crime. Let's leave them with their arrows, their feathers, their loincloths.[99]

With hindsight, the narrator criticizes his old ideas as well as Mascarita's: "Thinking it over—in the light of the years that have since gone by . . . we were as unrealistic and romantic as Mascarita with his archaic, anti-historical utopia."[100]

Saúl does not show interest in anthropology for the intellectual challenge of understanding cultures different from the ones he knows. He probably studied anthropology to gain understanding about himself, and in the process he stumbled upon the Machiguenga and decided to adopt their way of thinking and being as his own. He was introduced to the world of the Machiguenga by Fidel Pereira, the son of a white man from Cuzco and a Machiguenga woman. Pereira is also the real life informant of father Andrés Ferrero, the Dominican missionary who wrote one of the few books available on the Machiguenga.[101] Pereira's actions evoke characters from José Eustasio Rivera's *The Vortex* (a classic of Colombian literature) whose knowledge of both the modern and aboriginal worlds enables them to become a cross between a feudal lord and an aboriginal chieftain.

After the novelist beats up a drunk for making fun of Mascarita's birth-mark, he receives a letter from his friend suggesting that Saúl's experience in the jungle has led to a kind of religious conversion. In the letter Saúl expresses gratitude for the friendly intentions but dismisses the gesture as unnecessary and inauspicious. He states that insults do not bother him and that violence disturbs the natural order of things. In the letter that mentions the Machiguenga's main deities, Saúl exhorts his friend to control his hatred: "You wouldn't want life, through your fault, to fall apart and men to return to the original chaos."[102]

Mascarita's affinity with the Machiguengas is as much a mystery in *The Storyteller* as Mayta's revolutionary motivations in *The Real Life of Alejandro Mayta*. The narrator asks himself: "what was it that Mascarita was defending?"[103] and offers various conjectures involving his friend's physical deformity and his Judaism. Saúl himself also considers the issue of his Judaism: "Well, a Jew is better prepared than most people to defend the rights of minority cultures. . . . And, after all, as my old man says, the problem of the Boras, of the Shapras, of the Piros, has been our problem for three thousand years."[104] But the narrator finds none of these answers convincing and resigns himself to his bewilderment: "I have thought about it a lot these last years, and of course I'll never know."[105] His inability to comprehend Mascarita's motivations, however, gives birth to a literary project: "I must invent, since I have given in to the cursed temptation of writing about him."[106]

The novelist's inventions involve his relationship with Mascarita, his speculations about his friend's life after they lost touch at the end of their university studies, and his own trips to the jungle where he invariably remembers their friendship, and where he gains insights that will allow him to invent the connection between Mascarita and the story-teller of the picture gallery in Florence. The unnamed novelist learns about the Machiguengá in conversations with the Protestant missionaries that have been in the background of Vargas Llosa's other jungle novels and plays, all of whom share many common themes and characters. In *Captain Pantoja's Secret Service* there are references to the missionaries who had "come from so far away to this lonely place and all this heat to civilize the wild jungle Indians."[107] In *The Storyteller* the missionaries are known as Edwin Schneil and his wife. They are based on Wayne Snell and Betty Elkins-Snell, a married couple whom Vargas Llosa met during his first trip to the Amazon jungle in 1958 and "who work with the Machiguengas in the region between the Urubamba, Paucartambo and Misagua rivers."[108] The Snells lived among the Machiguengas and studied them for years. Wayne Snell has written about Machiguenga kinship structures and shamanism. Betty Elkins-Snell has published a Machiguenga language handbook, and translated a collection of Machiguenga folk stories.[109]

In *The Storyteller*, the Schneils are the novelist's main informants concerning the Machiguenga. They show him a Machiguenga song that had been translated by "a Dominican missionary in the thirties." The novelist copies the song and always carries it with him "folded in four in a corner of my billfold, as a charm."[110] Vargas Llosa transcribes the Machiguenga poem:

> Sadness is looking at me
> sadness is looking at me
> sadness is looking hard at me
> sadness is looking hard at me
> sadness troubles me very much
> sadness troubles me very much
> air, wind has brought me
> air has borne me away
> sadness troubles me very much
> sadness troubles me very much
> air, wind has brought me
> sadness troubles me very much
> sadness
> the little worm. the little worm has brought me
> air, wind, air.[111]

The poem is not a literary recasting but a transcription of a Machiguenga song as collected by Father Joaquín Barriales and translated into Spanish in his book *Matsigenka*.[112] Vargas Llosa used Barriales's works to develop both his own descriptions of the Machiguengas and the novelist's dialogues with the Schneils. Note, for example, the similarity between the text that follows the poem in the novel and the text that precedes it in Barriales' book. Both insist on the language's expressiveness:

> Novel: It was an archaic tongue, vibrantly resonant and agglutinative, in which a single word made up of many others could express a great overarching thought.[113]

> Barriales: The Matsigenka language, like all languages, is properly structured and its codification is no mystery. It is a language that allows a man to express everything he may wish to express by means of signs. [Its] extraordinary agglutination gives deep meaning to its words.[114]

FICTIONALIZED ANTHROPOLOGY

The presence of an indigenous people's mythological world is unprecedented in Vargas Llosa's fiction. In some of his earlier works he had included myths about the jungle but never myths by the native inhabitants of the jungle. The literary work in the sections of fictionalized anthropology is also new in Vargas Llosa. He develops a stylized language and narrative mode that reads like a translation from a native language whose form and content suggest a non-Western perception of time and space. Vargas Llosa drew from anthropological and linguistic works on the Machiguenga but did not follow them strictly. In some cases, as in the poem quoted above, he simply transcribed. More often than not, however, he transmuted the specialized works to invent his own myths, categories, and kinship patterns. He also transfigured stories from Western literature in his own invented Machiguenga style.

Some elements of the Machiguenga cosmology and cosmogony in *The Storyteller* seem to come from the pages of anthropological literature: Tasurinchi, the benevolent god whose breath created humanity; Kientibakori, the wicked god who has created the forces of evil such as the Kamgarinis, or Machiguenga imps. The Machiguenga universe is divided into parallel worlds that can come into contact with each another. Each world has a river. The sun is the male child of the moon and the *seripigari* is the Machiguenga priest or shaman. In the novel Vargas Llosa gives but slight importance to topics such as shamanism that are stressed in anthropological literature. According to anthropologists, the *seripigaris* participate in secret rites and are entitled to use certain drugs, forbidden to other Machiguengas, that allow them to communicate with the parallel worlds of their cosmos. If some of these myths have Christian resonances, that is probably the result of the religious presuppositions of the missionaries who are primarily responsible for the anthropological works available on the Machiguenga. But this is an issue for anthropologists to resolve. Vargas Llosa was content to pick and choose from the literature to fit his literature purposes.

Vargas Llosa's main invention is "the storyteller" as an anthropological type. Anthropological handbooks on the Machiguenga stress the significance of priests and shamans. But the figure of a storyteller who walks through the jungle to meet the various communities to share stories and gossip does not exist in anthropological literature about the Machiguenga. This itinerant storyteller who knows the myths and legends of the Machiguenga and who moves freely about the Amazon jungle is Vargas Llosa's own invention.

Another invention is the stylized language that suggests an indigenous way of speaking and thinking. These narrative sequences, based to some extent on Machiguenga linguistic handbooks, give the impression of a translation by someone who is trying to give the feel of a non–Western worldview imbedded in the indigenous language. The most salient feature of this stylized language for the reader is a recursive pattern of ungrammatical conventions suggestive of a different way of thinking. Take for example a construction that joins a verb in the imperfect with the gerund of a reflexive verb to create expressions such as "parecía burlándose." The Spanish has more of an ungrammatical feel than the English "seemed to be making mock of us" because the Spanish gerund never follows a verb conjugated in the imperfect.[115]

The three "storyteller's storytelling" chapters (as Vargas Llosa likes to call them) are composed of myths, legends, and anecdotes. In the first of these chapters, Vargas Llosa develops a narrative voice for whom the notions of an autonomous individual is a foreign concept. The narrative voice does not attribute acts or thoughts to individuals, and listeners do not expect the narrator to do so. This is consistent with the anthropological literature that claims that the Machiguenga lack the concept of individuality and believe that human bodies can be inhabited by living forces, possessed by the powers of good and evil, and metamorphose into animals.

Proper names do not exist and life does not cease with the decay of a human body. The Machiguenga conceive of death as the moment when life ceases to pass from one body to another, when the cycle of reincarnations, metamor-phoses, and transmutations ceases. Although they lack the concept of the individual, the Machiguenga are well aware that they belong to a distinct group with its own language, dress, and customs that are different from other com-munities. The circumlocutions "the men who walk" ("los hombres que andan") or "those who walk" (los que andan) refer to the Machiguenga. Once a human being abandons such identifying attributes, he or she ceases to belong to a group. A human body is Machiguenga as long as it exhibits Machiguenga ways. If the body ceases to dress, speak, and behave in the way of the community, if it trans-gresses certain taboos, then it becomes a foreign entity rather than an entity inhabited by a Machiguenga spirit. The Machiguenga know of the existence of other human groups whom they fear. Among these are Amazon Indians like the Maschco, Andean Indians, and whites also known as "viracochas." Recent history has surreptitiously crept into Machiguenga consciousness. They per-ceive events such as the period of caucho exploitation in the Peruvian jungle (a theme of *The Green House*) as a catastrophe and refer to it as the "bleeding of the trees."

The Machiguenga cosmogony in the novel is an inversion of the anthropo-logical information. A comparison between the fundamental Machiguenga myths in *The Storyteller* and some of their sources such as the collection of Machiguenga legends compiled by Betty Elkins-Snell will illuminate the novel-ist's technique. The most remarkable and moving myth of her collection is called "When the Sun Goes Out or The End of the World (Intsivakera poreatsiri)." It expresses overwhelming feelings of abandonment:

> When the Sun goes out, everything will suddenly change. Many of the animals in the jungle will come to us. They will talk to us and say:
> —Where shall we go?—
> The dogs will despise us, and will remind us of all the times we beat them. They will hit us and give us bones to eat. Things will all rise up (straw mats, arrows, chairs etc.) and begin to speak to us, saying:
> —Father—to men and—Mother—to women and asking—Where shall we go?[116]

In Vargas Llosa's version the theme of the end of the world does not have the fairy-tale flavor that characterizes Elkins-Snell's compilation. Vargas Llosa bor-rows the disappearance of the sun motif as the ominous sign of the end of the world, but he inverts the story and transforms the Machiguenga's central myth to suit his anthropological fiction. Vargas Llosa's Machiguenga are a nomadic people who live in scattered communities in the amazon jungle. According to the anthropological literature the Machiguenga are a stationary people. In myths and legends wayfaring seems to be a taboo. In "A trip around the world," another story in Elkins-Snell's compilation, a Machiguenga community's departure from their normal habitat brings about cosmic retribution and general disarray among the people.[117] In their confusion they hunt and eat forbidden animals, and their transgressions intensify their suffering. In Vargas Llosa's version they also fear cosmic punishment for transgressing the most important taboos. But in the novel the taboo has been inverted, because the Machiguenga believe the sun will disappear and the world will come to an end if they *cease* their nomadic existence. The storyteller recalls a catastrophic time when the sun began to disappear because the Machiguengas tried to settle down in a region of the jungle:

> Then why, if they were so pure, did the men of earth begin walking? Because one day the sun started falling. They walked so that it wouldn't fall any farther, to help it rise. . . . It began blinking, moving, its light dimmed, and you could hardly see it. . . . Then, in the half darkness, confused, frightened, men fell into their own traps, they ate deer meat thinking it was tapir, they could not find the path from the cassava patch to their own house. . . . Rivers changed course, rafts broke up on the dams, ponds turned into rivers. Souls lost their serenity. That was no longer going. It was dying. Something must be done, they said. Looking left and right, what? What shall we do? they said. "Start walking," Tasurinchi ordered.[118]

In the second "storyteller storytelling" chapter, Vargas Llosa invents another linguistic convention not found in the anthropological literature. According to anthropologists Tasurinchi is a deity. But in *The Storyteller* the name *Tasurinchi* also designates the Machiguenga. The storyteller refers to all adult males and to each one individually as *Tasurinchi*. To distinguish his anecdotes from one another, the storyteller adds epithets and periphrasis to the name *Tasurinchi*, such as, "Tasurinchi, the blind," or "Tasurinchi the one who lives at the bend of the stream." While some of the anecdotes are based on anthropological sources others are based on literary ones. For example, the storyteller offers a Machiguenga version of the rape of Lucretia when he tells the story of a woman who plunges "a chambira thorn into herself" after a man forces himself upon her against the sexual taboos of the community.[119]

In the third "storyteller storytelling" chapter, the storyteller becomes progressively identifiable as Mascarita. One of the most obvious clues is the Machiguenga adaptation of his favorite book, Kafka's *Metamorphosis*: "I was people. I had a family. I was asleep. Then I woke up. I'd barely opened my eyes when I understood. Alas, poor Tasurinchi! I'd changed into an insect, that's what. A buzz-buzz bug, perhaps. A Gregor-Tasurinchi."[120]

THE ETHNOGRAPHER

Saúl Zuratas and the narrator lead parallel lives, both obsessed with the problem of archaic cultures. But while Saúl enacts his obsession by joining an indigenous community, the narrator transforms his obsession into a novel. Yet the counterpoint is not entirely symmetrical because Mascarita's success in enacting his archaic utopia is a fantasy of the narrator. At the end of the novel the narrator acknowledges that Mascarita's conversion first into a Machiguenga and then into a Machiguenga-storyteller "was adding what appeared impossible to what was merely improbable."[121] The narrator's remark is an obvious allusion to "Pierre Menard, Author of Don Quixote," Jorge Luis Borges's masterpiece where the narrator insists on the literary value of searching for interesting ways to carry out impossible tasks.[122]

The Storyteller's most relevant literary antecedent is "The Ethnographer" from Borges's *In Praise of Darkness*. In the story a young student of anthropology and indigenous languages conducts field work and is accepted by a tribe of North American Indians as one of their own. He, in turn, "came to dream in a language that was not the language of his fathers. His palate became accustomed to new tastes, he dressed in strange clothes, he forgot his friends and the city."[123] After returning to the city, the student refuses to do the work expected of him by his advisor at the university because he has ceased to believe in Western sciences: "Science—our science—seems frivolous to me."[124]

Like Borges's story, *The Storyteller* explores the dilemmas of a young anthropology student who becomes skeptical about his discipline. Saúl Zuratas is convinced that any contact with Western culture can be detrimental to the Machiguenga. As with his Borgesian antecedent the process of understanding a new culture becomes a conversion. But the radical integration into another culture has its price. The experiences and knowledge gained, whether profound or superficial, cannot and ought not be revealed, except perhaps, in a work of fiction.

IN PRAISE OF THE STEPMOTHER

In Praise of the Stepmother, Vargas Llosa's last novel of the 1980s, is strongly influenced by his conviction that George Bataille's ideas cannot be overlooked by individuals who are commited to the health of open societies. Vargas Llosa invents a character who has thought about Bataille's claim that pleasure can only take place as a transgression and who thinks he has found the means to live a fulfilling life while respecting the most conventional social codes of his society. The novel tells the story of his failure to maintain the balance between his private transgressions and his personal sense of right and wrong. Don Rigoberto, a widowed businessman, marries a woman who becomes her stepchild's lover. Like *Aunt Julia and the Scriptwriter* and *The Storyteller*, *In Praise of the Stepmother* has two alternating narrative series. Both *Aunt Julia* and *The Storyteller* develop from a first-person realistic mode and another more stylized narrative mode that evokes a world of fantasy. In *In Praise of the Stepmother* Vargas Llosa alternates between third-person episodes that take place in the home of Don Rigoberto and first-person narratives inspired by paintings of famous artists. These passages are not so much descriptions of those paintings (whose reproductions are included in the novel) as they are characters of the narratives inspired by the erotic fantasies of the characters of the realistic chapters offering insights into their intimate desires.

Don Rigoberto, the manager of an insurance company, leads a conventional and routine public life. His private life, however, is devoted to solitary practices and to little perversions he considers "sufficient compensation for his normalcy."[125] Rigoberto has found a balance between a conventional life that he finds pleasing and a set of controlled deviances limited to his private and marital life. Rigoberto expects his forty-year-old wife (they have been married for four months when the novel begins) to be a faithful spouse, an honorable mother, and a cohort in acting out his sexual fantasies inspired by his contemplation of erotic art.

Like Santiago Zavala and Mayta, Rigoberto had been a young militant in religious or political groups because he thought he could help to change the world. As he grew older he reached the conclusion that collective ideals are doomed to failure and "that, as an ideal, perfection was perhaps possible for the isolated individual, if restricted to a limited sphere in space."[126] Elaborate personal hygiene and sexual activities stimulated by his contemplation of erotic art "constituted his particular religion and his personal way of bringing about a utopia."[127] With his body, he believes, he can do what would be impossible in the social world:

"My body is that impossibility: an egalitarian society."[128] Rigoberto feels happy and fulfilled from the pleasure he derives from his body and from the fantasies he indulges in with his wife after examining his collection of erotic prints and artistic reproductions.

LUCRECIA'S INCUBUS

Alfonsito, Rigoberto's son, is the most impenetrable character in the novel. It is impossible to determine whether Alfonsito's seduction of his stepmother is spontaneous or premeditated. It is clear, however, that Alfonsito takes the initiative and behaves like a natural seducer.

All the characters who judge him say Alfonso is innocent and angelic, but his behavior belies this characterization. He caresses Lucrecia with determination in a manner resembling the adolescent cupid touching Venus in the detail of the Bronzino's painting "The Allegory of Love," reproduced on the cover of the book: "Then his little hands grasped her by the temples and thrust her head back. . . . [His lips] alighted on hers for an instant, hungrily pressing down to them."[129] Alfonsito's kiss is nothing short of a sexual provocation reminiscent of Varguitas's first step in the willful seduction of his aunt.[130] And Lucrecia from *Stepmother* is no less disconcerted than was Aunt Julia by the unexpected embrace. Nonetheless, she insists on seeing him merely as an innocent child: "Could a child's unthinking caress have put her in such a state? You're becoming depraved, woman. Could this be the first symptom of old age? Because there was no question about it: she was all aflame and her thighs were wet."[131]

Justiniana, the house maid, also insists on Alfonso's naiveté when she reveals to her mistress that the young boy spies on her while she undresses: "Fonchito doesn't have the least idea he's doing something bad. I give you my word he doesn't. He's like a little angel; he doesn't know good from evil."[132] Lucrecia does not confront her stepson, but withdraws her affection. Alfonsito, like other seducers in Vargas Llosa's fiction who use the same melodramatic tactic to manipulate the emotions of the women they want to seduce, responds to his stepmother's calculated coldness by threatening to commit suicide.[133]

After his sexual exploit, Alfonsito behaves like Tirso de Molina's Don Juan who dishonors the women whom he has enjoyed by boasting of his triumphs.[134] Alfonsito shows his father a school composition titled "In Praise of the Stepmother," where he narrates his sexual adventure in detail. Outraged by the content of his son's text, Rigoberto casts Lucrecia from his life. Like Pantaleón after his sexual adventures, Don Rigoberto has a religious conversion as he loses his sexual desire: "all of a sudden, his ruined fantasy desired, desperately, to be transmuted: he was a solitary being, chaste, freed of appetites, safe from all the demons of the flesh and sex."[135]

Alfonso shows no remorse about his role in his stepmother's undoing and remains indifferent about her misfortune. He takes advantage of the servant's curiosity about his feelings to initiate another seduction: "I did it for you, Justita."[136] When the servant flees, Alfonso reacts with uncontrolled laughter. His laugh does not enable the reader to decide whether Alfonso's Machiavellian behavior has been spontaneous or premeditated: "she heard Fonchito laugh once more. Not sarcastically, not making mock of her flushed cheeks and brimming indignation. With genuine delight, as though enjoying a splendid joke."[137]

THE ART COLLECTION

In contrast to the straightforward third-person narrations of the episodes set at the home of Don Rigoberto, the alternating chapters, which include the reproduction of a famous painting, are brief narrative sequences in which a first-person narrator tells a story inspired in the imagination of one or more of the protagonists of the novel. While the descriptions of the Jordaens and Titian paintings would disconcert art historians who might not appreciate the vulgarity of the free associations based on these masterpieces, the sections on Bacon and Szyszlo include penetrating observations and original artistic aperçus.[138]

The first-person narrator of these chapters does not fully assume the identity of a character represented in the painting. Rather, the narrator is seeking to play a role as much inspired by the painting as by his or her own desires. It is even possible to interpret the first-person narrator as the alter ego of the fictional and impersonal narrator of the chapters that take place in Don Rigoberto's home. But whether the chapters based on the paintings are stories inspired by the fantasies of the characters or by the fantasies of the narrator, it is clear that each of these chapters reveals a fantasy inspired by a painting. The conceit is evident from the first sentence of the first of these tales: "I am Candaules, King of Lydia, a little country situated between Ionia and Caria, in the heart of that territory which centuries later will be called Turkey."[139] Although the first-person narrator presents himself as the king of an ancient kingdom, his reference to Turkey reveals that this he is pretending to be someone from a distant past.

The self-satisfaction that Don Rigoberto feels about possessing his wife is transformed into a voyeuristic fantasy loosely set in an ancient kingdom. In

Vargas Llosa's narrative, Candaules invites Gyges, his minister, to observe his wife undressing. The fantasy is loosely faithful to Herodotus's version of the story of Candaules and Gyges.[140] The narrative in Vargas Llosa's novel follows the free associations of a prurient imagination rather than the classical sources. In the painting Candules is standing behind Gyges observing the nude woman, but in the narration Candules also gives Gyges permission to spy on him, without her knowledge, while the couple is together in bed.[141] The narrative contradicts what is observable in the reproduction of the painting. The Jordaens painting shows two masculine figures: a bearded man with a crown, and a beardless man. The first wears a proud expression, the second a lascivious one. The crown enables the viewer to distinguish the king from the other man. Vargas Llosa confuses the characters as they are described in the narrative and depicted in the painting. In the painting the king is bearded and his expression is somber, but in the narration the king is beardless and his expression is lascivious. While the painting highlights Gyges excitation, Vargas Llosa's story highlights the king's. Although based on the painting, the story narrated by Vargas Llosa has been thoroughly modified and transformed to fit Rigoberto's erotic fantasy and his wandering thoughts.

The episodes based mainly on Don Rigoberto's fantasies are the ones that include reproductions of paintings by Jacob Jordaens and Francis Bacon. In each of these narrations allusions are made to Don Rigoberto's household and to the escalating sexual tensions among the novel's protagonists. The chapter based on "Head I," a painting by Francis Bacon, is about a hideous monster whose body is rotting but whose active sexual organ makes him irresistible to men and women. This represents the celebratory apotheosis of Don Rigoberto's self-contentment with his sexuality. Here again, Vargas Llosa adds elements to the painting. The painting represents an emotionally charged distorted face that suggests intense pleasure or pain, but it does not represent details of any other area of his body.

In the playfully ironic final section of the novel, which takes place after Don Rigoberto has abjured his sexual activities, Vargas Llosa includes a reproduction of Fra Angelico's San Marco fresco of the Annunciation. The narrative suggests the religious conversion of Don Rigoberto among other possibilities. The innocence and surprise of the Virgin Mary could be interpreted both as a preparation for the divine conception or as the beginning of a seduction by the angel:

> How handsome he was! . . . I felt a warm dawn on my face. Can this be, if magnified throughout the body, what young girls feel when they fall in love?

He is gone now and has left my head full of doubts. Why did he address me as señora if I am still an unmarried girl? Why did he call me queen? Why did I discover a gleam of tears in his eyes when he prophesied that I would suffer? Why did he call me mother if I am a virgin? What is happening? What is going to become of me after this visit?[142]

Thus the "Annunciation" painting can be interpreted either as narrative inspired by a religious meditation by Don Rigoberto, or it could also be interpreted as the uneasiness of a woman (it could be either Lucrecia's or Justiniana's) who is confused by a charismatic angel.

The narration based on Titian's "Venus with Cupid and a Musician" (from the Prado Museum) is ambiguous because it can be attributed—for different reasons—either to Don Rigoberto or to Lucrecia. The chapter on Titian's painting narrates a woman's preparation for an encounter with her husband. The musician and the angel stir up Venus's imagination before she meets a character who is not represented in the painting: an African merchant called "Don Rigoberto." In this fantasy, the first-person narrator who pretends to be the angel of the painting, seems to express the wishes of Don Rigoberto: "You will not be Lucrecia today but Venus, and today you will change from a Peruvian woman into an Italian one and from a creature of this earth into a goddess and a symbol."[143] The obvious allusion to Alfonso suggests that the narrator is creating a story inspired in his character's sexual fantasy, rather than reporting his character's fantasy. For at this stage in the novel, Don Rigoberto does not know about the sexual tensions between Lucrecia and his son.

The chapters that include the paintings by Boucher and Szyszlo are narrations based on Lucrecia's domestic life and on her feminine fantasies. Boucher's mythological painting represents two nudes, Diana on the right and her servant on the left. The female narrator begins with the description of a scene: "That one, the one on the left, is me, Diana Lucrecia. . . . On my right, bending over, gazing at my foot, is Justiniana, my favorite. We have just bathed, and are about to make love."[144] Someone who is not depicted in the painting is observing them from behind. His visual field is therefore different from the painting's perspective: "The main character is not in the picture. Or rather, he is not in sight. He is there in the background, hidden in the shady grove, spying on us."[145]

As elsewhere in the novel, prurient voyeurism plays an important role in stimulating the character: "[Fonsín, the young angel that spies on us knows] that this delights us and adds zest to our sport."[146] In this section there is a fantasy within a fantasy. While making love with her servant, Diana imagines she is seducing the angel whose name Fonsín, a diminutive associated to Alfonso:

"I smell him, I caress him, I press him to by bosom and make him disappear within me."[147]

While Boucher's painting appears before Lucrecia and Alfonso have consummated their relations, the narration based on Szyszlo's painting appears afterwards. This narration is based on a fantasy Lucrecia had after Alfonso, in the previous chapter, told her that the abstract painting in their living room is a depiction of her. Lucrecia's fantasy is based on Foncito's comments about the painting.

It should not be surprising that the chapter based on the Szyszlo painting is the most successful one in terms of combining keen insights on painting with the narrative elements of the story. Vargas Llosa has written some of the most important essays about Fernando de Szyszlo's painting. In one of them he offers an interpretation of the series of paintings that includes "Camino a Mendieta 10," the painting reproduced in the novel. According to Vargas Llosa's interpretation the painting evokes and portrays an immolation or sacrificial ceremony at a primitive altar. During this barbarous ritual, somebody bleeds to death and perhaps also feels intense pleasure. A mysterious masculine figure, like a totem, appears next to the altar. This figure is an obscure and frequently recurring character in Szyszlo's painting as described by Vargas Llosa:

> Something is always happening in [his pictures], something that is more than form and colour: a spectacle that is difficult to describe, although not to feel; a ceremony that seems at times to be a funeral pyre or a sacrifice celebrated on a primitive altar; a barbarous and violent rite in which someone bleeds, disintegrates, surrenders and also perhaps enjoys something which, in any event, is not intelligible, which we must apprehend through the tortuous route of obsession, nightmare and vision. My memory often suddenly conjures up that strange totem, visceral debris or monument covered with disturbing offerings—ligatures, spurs, suns, splits, incisions, shafts—which has long been a recurring character in Szyszlo's canvases. And I have asked myself the same question on countless occasions: Where does it come from? Who, what is it?[148]

The female narrator in the chapter with the Szyszlo painting imagines she is the victim of the mysterious masculine figure about which Vargas Llosa has written. The fantasy is an allegory of Lucrecia's dilemma: to experience pleasure she must sacrifice herself. The fantasy based on Szyszlo's painting is for Lucrecia what the fantasy based on Bacon's painting is for Rigoberto—the height of titillation. Lucrecia's erotic awakening depends on a transgression that will threaten her marriage. The third-person narrator comments on this transgression with a question phrased in the terminology of Georges Bataille: "Was that what sovereignty was?"[149]

TOWARD A DOMESTICATED BATAILLE

By sovereignty Bataille means a human being's claim to the erotic, to desire and pleasure.[150] Vargas Llosa follows Bataille in assuming that true and fulfilling pleasure is impossible without transgression and that any individual seeking fulfillment is faced with the following dilemma: sovereignty is an affront to collective life, but faultless adherence to social norms stifles the individual.[151] Bataille's solution to the dilemma, as summarized by Vargas Llosa, is precarious:

> Through a precarious, polemical balance between the social whole and the individual, society controls, but does not kill, the spirit of rebellion and the desire for rupture—for waste, for excess—because this would imply man's return to an animal state. This spirit can live on in man, fighting to achieve sovereignty, without ever fully achieving it, because to achieve it would bring with it the holocaust. This is the implacable warning contained in Bataille's work: in each of us, muzzled and tied by the conventions of the community that surrounds us, there lurks, panting at the boys with golden locks, brandishing a dagger, one hand on his flies, a secret Gilles de Rais.[152]

Vargas Llosa took Bataille's doctrines to heart in the conception of the novel as well as the conscious thoughts of his characters. Don Rigoberto seems to take Bataille's ideas seriously when he expresses his desire to withdraw "momentarily from the base decadence and the civil servitudes of the social order, the abject conventions of the herd, in order to attain, for one brief parenthesis per day, a sovereign nature."

Lucrecia also rehearses Bataille's ideas when she thinks about the transgression that has provided her with joy:

> She preferred to bow to this contradictory situation, in which her acts challenged and violated her principles as she pursued that intense, dangerous rapture that happiness had become for her. One morning, on opening her eyes, the phrase "I have won sovereignty" came

to her. She felt fortunate and emancipated, but could not have said what it was that she had been freed from.[153]

In Praise of the Stepmother illustrates Vargas Llosa's personal answer to Bataille's contention that pleasure and transgression are interrelated, that human beings need to find innocuous activities where they can diffuse the dangerous potentialities of their desires. Vargas Llosa has commented explicitly on the matter:

> The impulse toward violence and excess is part of what it means to be human. It is important, therefore, to channel this impulse toward activities that are harmless to others and to oneself.[154]

In writing *In Praise of the Stepmother*, it is clear that Vargas Llosa drew inspiration not only from Bataille's ideas but also from his novels where relentless transgressions of social norms and moral taboos unleash his characters' most destructive instincts, culminating in paroxysms of incest, necrophilia, suicide, and murder. Bataille's novels exemplify his claim that "there is in [erotic behavior] an element of disorder and excess which goes as far as to endanger the life of whoever indulges in it."[155] Bataille's ideas resonate with those of César Moro, who celebrated activities "with unforeseeable, dangerous and vertiginous consequences, such as soporiferous masturbation or luminous incest"[156] and who wrote poems such as the one Vargas Llosa chose to provide the epigraph for *In Praise of the Stepmother*, which begins, "One must wear one's vices like a royal mantle, with poise."[157]

Moro's poem is an ironic commentary on *In Praise of the Stepmother* because a moderate indulgence in an ostensibly private and measured personal vice ruins the marital and family life of Don Rigoberto and Lucrecia. In Bataille's literature, on the other hand, Moro's epigraph would not be ironic because Bataille's characters pursue their vices to their ultimate consequences. As one of Bataille's characters comments:

> Vice, in my view, is like the mind's dark radiance, which blinds and of which I am dying. Corruption is the spiritual cancer reigning in the depths of things. As fast as I debauch myself I sense my lucidity grow, and the steady breakdown of my nerves is nothing else in me than a havoc whose source is my innermost thinking.[158]

This celebration of vice comes from *Ma mère*, a novel that impressed Vargas Llosa:

It is difficult not to feel moved when Bataille describes the passionate and destructive relation between a mother and the son whom she corrupts, and the complicated combinations into which the insatiable appetite for depravation, shared by both, is expressed.[159]

Hélene, the protagonist of Bataille's novel, seems to exemplify Moro's exhortations. At various times she tells her son that she is not ashamed of her desires or her vices and does not intend to hide them: "I'll not change my desires. You shall respect me such as I am; I am not going to hide anything of myself from you. No more pretences: that at last is over with, and I am glad."[160]

In Praise of the Stepmother is influenced by *Ma mère*, a novel that explores a scandalous love triangle involving a woman who habitually yields to the erotic fantasies of her husband, who, like Don Rigoberto, stimulates his sexual imagination with erotic images.[161] The wife, whose sexuality and eroticism are more intense than her husband's, embarks on the slow but relentless seduction of her own son. As in Vargas Llosa's novel, prurient voyeurism also contributes to heightening the characters' sexual desires.[162]

Bataille considers transgression the essence of eroticism. In *Ma mère*, the transgression that excites the young boy and his mother are their incestuous feelings for each other. However, they never consummate the sexual act that would eliminate that which most excites them—the sexual tension of their forbidden desire:

> Had we translated our trembling madness into the barren acts of copulation, the cruel game we played with our eyes would have ceased: I would have ceased seeing my mother ecstatic at the sight of me, my mother would no longer have seen me beholding her in ecstasy. We'd have exchanged the purity of the unattainable for a mess of pottage, to satisfy our immediate greed.[163]

In her relation with her son, Hélene seeks a pleasure "so thoroughgoing that death alone could terminate it."[164] True to her own persuasion that death is the ultimate consequence of her impulses, Hélene commits suicide with the satisfaction that she has pushed her desire to the limit. She confesses it in her last letter:

> Your corruption was my handiwork: I gave you what was purest and most intense in me, the desire to love that which tears the clothes off my body, and that alone. This time, they are all my clothes.[165]

Both *Ma mère* and *In Praise of the Stepmother* are novels that illustrate Bataille's ideas about the relationship between pleasure and transgression. Both are centered in a sexual taboo, but *In Praise of the Stepmother* has domestic controls absent in *Ma mère*. Bataille's protagonists do not seek a balance between transgression and sociability. They are more instinctive and dangerous to themselves and their fellow human beings than Vargas Llosa's. While in Bataille's novel the sexual impulse culminates in death, in Vargas Llosa's novel this impulse is checked when it threatens Don Rigoberto's personal sense of moral comfort with the behavior of his wife.

THE NOTEBOOKS OF DON RIGOBERTO

Vargas Llosa's most recent novel, *Los cuadernos de don Rigoberto* (The notebooks of Don Rigoberto (1997), a sequel to *In Praise of the Stepmother*, is also indebted to the ideas of Bataille, but it emphasizes a different aspect, namely, the notion that the morality of those who embrace their darker side can be superior to conventional morality.[166] In the original, Don Rigoberto was attempting to find a balance between his private vices and his personal sense of right and wrong in order to embrace the mediocrity of everyday life. In the sequel Don Rigoberto feels increasingly uneasy with the negative connotations of the words normally used to refer to his private behavior ("how should I call [my phobias and manias] without doing harm to them: eccentricities? private desires?"[167]) because he believes that "a rich and healthy mental life requires curiosity, a bit of malice, and unfulfilled desires—that is to say, a 'dirty' mind."[168] In the sequel Don Rigoberto is willing to forgive his wife for her affair with his son, which means that he is also willing to reconsider the parameters of his personal morality.

The novel is made up of nine chapters and an epilogue. Every chapter has four sequences according to the following pattern: the first sequence tells the story of the meetings between Fonchito and Lucrecia, which are kept secret from Don Rigoberto until the family is back together in the epilogue of the novel; the second is an essay in epistolary form that Don Rigoberto expresses his views and opinions on a range of topics from ecology to homosexuality; the third is based on one of the sexual fantasies that Don Rigoberto elaborated during his separation from Lucrecia; and the fourth sequence is a short anonymous letter—drafted perhaps by Fonchito—that expresses erotic feelings intended to seduce the recipient. Chapter 2 includes a fifth sequence based on Don Rigoberto's sexual fantasies.

For readers familiar with *In Praise of the Stepmother*, the beginning of the sequel seems awkward. Fonchito comes to visit Lucrecia's home and, without many preliminaries, is forgiven. A sense of complicity is rapidly reestablished between the boy, his stepmother, and Justiniana, her maid. In their conversations Fonchito—who seems to be following in Don Rigoberto's footsteps in the realm of art appreciation—discusses his fascination and sense of personal identification with the Viennese painter Egon Schiele as he titillates Lucrecia and Justiniana while exploring the connections between vice and art. The other topic of their conversations is the possible reconciliation of Lucrecia and her estranged husband—she has been receiving and is responding to anonymous letters she assumes have been written by Don Rigoberto.

While these meetings are taking place, Don Rigoberto seems to divide his private time between two kinds of activities: he continues to peruse his collection of art prints in pursuit of erotic arousal, and he writes down his thoughts and ideas on the notebooks that give the name to the title of the novel. Don Rigoberto's epistolary essays are stylized and slightly hyperbolic versions of ideas Vargas Llosa has expressed in his journalistic articles. The theme informing all of them is a defense of individualism and a condemnation of collectivism. With irony, and sometimes with contempt, Don Rigoberto criticizes ecologists, feminists, sport fans, the rotary clubs and other civic associations, patriotism, and bureaucrats for constraining the liberty of individuals in the name of their collective ideals. In other entries he expresses his ideas about the transformation of sexuality into a creative act, and in others he complains about sexually explicit magazines because he does not think they are conducive to the spiritual dimension he seeks in his own erotic experiences:

> My contempt for *Playboy* and *Penthouse* is not unwarranted. That kind of magazine is a symbol of the debasement of sex, of the disappearance of those beautiful taboos that used to surround it, and thanks to whom the human spirit could rebel, exercising individual liberty, affirming the singular personality of each, and creating, little by little, the sovereign individual in the secret and discreet elaboration of rituals, conducts, cults, fantasies, ceremonies that transcend the animality of the act of love, conferring to it an ethical nobility and an aesthetic dimension so that, progressively, it becomes a creative act.[169]

Ostensibly, the sections devoted to his erotic fantasies exemplify Don Rigoberto's attempts to transcend his sexuality as he affirms it, but they are mostly expressions of sexual longing for the woman who had willingly participated in the acting out of his earlier fantasies. In his current fantasies Don Rigoberto imagines Lucrecia playing a number of roles and situations: she rekindles an old flame in an adulterous tryst in elegant circumstances; she has a comic encounter with an old seducer; she is willing to titillate a man who was castrated; she seduces a prudish university professor; and she participates in a wife-swapping experience. Many of the details of Don Rigoberto's fantasies are inspired by his collection of art prints, and at least two of them are inspired by works of literature, including Juan Carlos Onetti's novel *A Brief Life* and Calderon de la Barca's classic play *Life is a Dream*.

It is clear from Don Rigoberto's musings and from the conversations between Fonchito and Lucrecia that the couple is ready for a reconciliation, which takes place through the intervention of Fonchito. The young man was the author of the anonymous letters to both Lucrecia and to his father as part of a surreptitious plan to rekindle their relationship. For the reader, the scene of reconciliation is ambiguous because it can be read as one of Don Rigoberto's fantasies. It takes place in a hotel where Lucrecia plays the part of a prostitute as Alfonso, along with a young woman, participates in the events that lead to a sexual encounter between the estranged spouses.

In the epilogue of the novel the family is finally together again in their old home, and Don Rigoberto has lost some of his moral scruples. Lucrecia tells him that she continues to have sexual feelings for his stepson ("if he does not leave this house, if he continues living with us, it will happen again"[170]), but Don Rigoberto no longer seems to mind. Whether Fonchito will remain at home is left open at the end of the novel. What is patently clear, however, is that the bounds of acceptable behavior have expanded for Don Rigoberto. In his own home he is able to tolerate what in the original novel had been intolerable, and he expresses sympathy for many behaviors and practices he has not personally experienced.

In the original novel Don Rigoberto's sexual fantasies were presented as an innocuous alternative to his previous enthusiasm for social utopias, but in the sequel the fantasies preceded and played a decisive role in his disenchantment with social utopias:

> Discovering the central role of fetishism in the life of the individual was decisive in my disenchantment with social utopias (the idea that happiness, goodness, and ethic or aesthetic values could be arrived at collectively) as I became an agnostic, and as I embraced the conviction that since men and women cannot live without utopias, the only realistic way to come to terms with them is to shift them from the social to the individual level.[171]

The differences between the original and the sequel are subtle but significant. Manias and perversions are no longer mere alternatives to the dangerous propensities of social utopias; they have come into the foreground as the constitutive elements of human individuality: "There is no mania or phobia that lacks a measure of greatness. This constitutes the originality of a human being, the best expression of his sovereignty."[172]

In the earlier novel Don Rigoberto's perversions are presented as an escape valve, as an acceptable and successful way to tame those utopian inclinations that could otherwise endanger the basis for peaceful coexistence among human beings. This message was one solution Vargas Llosa had offered as an alternative to the human proclivity toward violence evinced by the willingness of his most fanatic characters to wreak havoc and destruction on their fellow human beings in the name of their utopian ideals. Don Rigoberto may have lost the balance between his private utopia and his personal morality, but his failure, unlike the failures of the military, political, and religious fanatics of novels like *The War of the End of the World*, did not risk endangering his society. Don Rigoberto has at least managed to direct his utopian inclinations from the social to the private, and in so doing he is like the novelist-narrators of *The Real Life of Alejandro Mayta* and *The Storyteller* who avoid the temptations of their protagonists by writing fiction.

The theme uniting all of Vargas Llosa's novels of the 1980s is the importance of imagination and fantasy in curbing those irrational elements that can endanger social coexistence. *The Notebooks of Don Rigoberto* is a corrective to his earlier work because, in this novel, the irrational elements that motivate human behavior may never be fully tamed. Unlike *In Praise of the Stepmother* where Don Rigoberto was able to sacrifice his private utopia when it began to offend his sense of right and wrong, in the sequel a number of his moral convictions are undermined by his irrational inclinations, notwithstanding his full awareness that this has taken place.

The Notebooks of Don Rigoberto suggests that Vargas Llosa is moving away from the themes of his 1980s novels, in which the irrational propensities of his characters could be effectively contained within the realm of the private. When *The Notebooks of Don Rigoberto* is seen in connection with *Death in the Andes* (1993) (as we will do in the conclusion of this book), it becomes clear that Vargas Llosa is reorienting his literary works to emphasize the inevitability of irrational propensities that are, perhaps, beyond control.

CONCLUSION

NOTES

BIBLIOGRAPHY

INDEX

CONCLUSION

In Praise of the Stepmother was the last novel Vargas Llosa wrote before he lost the Peruvian presidential elections in June 1990. Since then he has been as prolific as ever. He has published numerous articles and several books including *A Fish in the Water*, a memoir of his experiences during the presidential campaign with chapters about his childhood and youth that offer biographical insights about his political motivations; *Desafíos a la libertad* (Challenges to freedom), a collection of political articles originally published in newspapers; *La utopía arcaica* (The archaic utopia), a study of the life and literary works of José María Arguedas; and two plays: *El loco de los balcones* (The madman of the balconies) about a man intent on preserving the charms of Lima's neglected Viceroyal architectural heritage, and *Ojos bonitos, cuadros feos* (Beautiful eyes, ugly paintings), a play about a frustrated art critic's impact in the lives of a young couple. He has also published two novels: *Death in the Andes* and *The Notebooks of Don Rigoberto*. Any conclusions about a living writer as active and productive as Vargas Llosa can only be tentative. It is possible, however, to make general observations about the novels he has published to date and to underscore new tendencies in his most recent work.

I have argued throughout much of this book that Vargas Llosa's moral and political convictions have resonated in his fiction. He began his literary career as a socialist whose novels diagnosed the corruption of capitalist society in Latin America. After his break with the Latin American Left his novels have often explored the dangers of fanaticism and utopian thinking. In these two periods of his literary career, social problems and human suffering were, for Vargas Llosa, needless at some level because they were the result of human propensities toward corruption or fanaticism that could be tamed. Both in the socialist and in the neoliberal period, therefore, Vargas Llosa was an optimist who felt that violence and exploitation could be redressed by the appropriate kind of political action. Since losing the Peruvian elections, however, he has been expressing unprecedented pessimism about his own role as a political activist and skepticism about politics in general:

> Real politics, not the kind that one reads and writes and thinks about—the only sort that I had been acquainted with—but the politics that is lived and practiced day by day, has little to do with ideas, values and imagination, with long-range visions, with notions of an ideal society, with generosity, solidarity or idealism. It consists almost exclusively of maneuvers, intrigues, plots, pacts, paranoias, betrayals, a great deal of calculation, no little cynicism and every variety of con game.[1]

Notwithstanding his reservations about political activity, Vargas Llosa has been as keen as ever to study and to interpret political events in Peru. He believes that the Peruvian people acted against their own best interest when they rejected his presidential bid. He has been insistent in expressing his opinion that president Fujimori's behavior is dictatorial, and he feels a measure of surprise that he has been the "object of strident recriminations in Peru and not only by the regime, the traitorous military leaders, and the journalists in their hire but also by many well-intentioned citizens."[2] He resents the suggestion that his criticisms of President Fujimori's policies are "dictated not by convictions and principles but by the bitterness of having suffered a defeat."[3]

Although one cannot yet say where exactly Vargas Llosa is heading, his most recent work is pointing to a new direction in his narrative fiction and in his general attitude toward political issues. His contempt for authoritarianism continues, but he appears to be more pessimistic about the possibilities of political action and more conciliatory about the frailties of those with whom he disagrees, because he is beginning to detect fallibilities in all political persuasions:

> There are many kinds of idiocy: the sociological and the historical; the political and the journalistic; the leftist and the rightist; the social-democratic, the Christian-democratic, the revolutionary, the conservative and—alas!—the liberal as well.[4]

His conciliatory tone and his pessimistic outlook may be two sides of the same coin in that he seems resigned to the inevitability of human frailty. Conciliation is one of the themes of *The Notebooks of Don Rigoberto* and pessimism is patent in *Death in the Andes* (as well as in *Ojos bonitos, cuadros feos,* his most recent play). His latest novels reflect a change in his literary vision, much in the way that *Captain Pantoja and the Secret Service* and *Aunt Julia and the Scriptwriter* signaled a turn away from the novels of the socialist period while exploring themes more fully developed in the neoliberal period. Vargas Llosa's novels of the 1980s presented social and political situations explicitly addressed in his stern but optimistic political essays. In their distinct ways these writings argue that corruption and political fanaticism are problems that need to be resolved for the establishment of a better social order. His most recent works of fiction, however, evince a growing pessimism about man's ability to overcome his frustrations and a sense that the threat of violence is always in the offing. One gets the sense that Vargas Llosa's demons are becoming less metaphorical and that he might embrace their literary representation with less reserve or offer a new vision, perhaps a religious one, with which to oppose them. But speculations of this kind must be fraught with uncertainty. One can say with certainty only that in his most recent literary works Vargas Llosa is becoming increasingly pessimistic about the human condition.

Pessimism is evident in *Ojos bonitos, cuadros feos,* where all of the characters are either pitiable or crass. Eduardo Zanelli, the protagonist of the play, is an art critic who feels frustrated because he has not been fully able to define his sexual identity or to become an artist.[5] When he writes a scathingly malicious review of Alicia Zúñiga's first exhibition, he shatters the life of the young artist, who has nurtured a pathetic admiration of Zanelli; and Rubén Zevallos, her philistine boyfriend, is willing to go to sadistic lengths to humiliate the man who inadvertently ruined his relationship with Alicia.

Death in the Andes also reflects the pessimistic tone evinced in *Ojos bonitos, cuadros feos.* As in the novels of the 1980s, political fanatics produce unnecessary violence, and fantasy and eroticism are compensations for the mediocrity of life. But *Death in the Andes* offers elements that point to an unprecedented turn in Vargas Llosa's fiction. For the first time the violent instincts of some characters no longer have any rational explanation whatsoever; violence just happens. It is no longer an instrument of those who exploit or the result of political fanaticism.

In *Death in the Andes* the manifestations of violence are variegated. The novel is set in the heart of the Andes where the Shining Path guerrillas are taking over towns, destroying private property, and killing those they perceive to be their enemies. Violence also arises from other sources, such as crimes of passion, perceived or real threats, and bizarre ritualistic practices. Most disturbingly, violence occurs without reason. To understand the new turn in Vargas Llosa's literary treatment of violence, one must understand his views about the Shining Path movement in Peru because *Death in the Andes* is, first of all, Vargas Llosa's literary response to the terrorist group.

Vargas Llosa has not hidden his disgust for the leaders and militants of groups such as the Shining Path whom he considers fanatics willing to apply terror and commit murder to establish their utopian dreams.[6] That being said, however, his position on the guerrilla movement is not straightforward. Even though he no longer shares the socialist ideals or violent means of the leftist revolutionary groups he supported in the 1960s, he continues to agree with the main contention used to justify the armed struggle in the Peruvian Andes: something must be done to address the misery of the indigenous populations in the Andes who have been exploited for centuries and whose civil and human rights are still neglected by Peru's political and military authorities. From Vargas Llosa's perspective the revolutionaries are responsible for their crimes, but in the final analysis the Peruvian government is responsible for the neglect of the Andean population and for the social climate wherein groups such as the Shining Path can flourish. For Vargas Llosa, therefore, the Shining Path movement is a tragic sideshow that has added to the misery of a neglected population. His concern about the plight of the Peruvian peasants in the Andes, however, is qualified. He believes that the indigenous populations have also had a long history of brutal violence and barbaric practices, some of which are remnants of their pre-Columbian past.[7] In short, Vargas Llosa has been critical of both the guerrilla movement and the Peruvian authorities, but he is also weary of the violent tendencies of the local populations. In Vargas Llosa's analysis all of the parties involved are prone to violence and all have committed crimes. A feeling of mistrust of the military, the guerrilla movement, and the indigenous population also pervades *Death in the Andes*.

Vargas Llosa first analyzed this situation and expressed his surprise at the violent practices of the Peruvian peasants in 1983 in connection with the investigation of the murder of a group of journalists in the village of Uchuraccay. He was particularly dismayed at the religious rituals with which the local population massacred the journalists whom they mistook for enemies. Although Vargas Llosa did not find the murder of the journalists excusable, he did find it understandable because the local population had good reason to feel threatened by both the terrorists and the military authorities.

In the 1990s Vargas Llosa has continued to be adamant about condemning the Shining Path's use of violence and terror, and he believes that they act with what he calls "'technological' efficiency and a cold, unscrupulous mentality."[8] But he is equally convinced that the movement would have been short lived had it not been for the incompetence and the irresponsibility of the political and military authorities in Peru. The Peruvian government has generally ignored the activities of the Shinning Path, allowing for the breakdown and collapse of civil authority in the interior of the country; and when the military has intervened it has not respected the human rights of the peasants. In Vargas Llosa's analysis the indigenous populations in the interior of the country have been the victims of both the guerrilla movement and of the military. Vargas Llosa has accused the military of many shortfalls and of crimes against the villagers, including unjustifiable arrests, torture, rape, and murder.[9] Rather than helping matters, the military, in Vargas Llosa's view, has actually encouraged local populations to support the guerrilla movement: "They have generated fear and resentment that has favored the Shining Path and have neutralized the negative reaction that may have been generated by the local population against the terrorist group."[10]

Vargas Llosa has been adamant about the need to repress the guerrilla movement within the rule of law. He made this point in many speeches during his presidential campaign. After he lost in his bid to become the president of Peru in 1990, Vargas Llosa continued writing essays in which he has criticized the inability of Peruvian political authorities to take seriously the breakdown of civil authority in the Andes and to insure that the military act efficiently within the bounds of the law while respecting the human rights of the terrorists and peasants alike. Vargas Llosa has criticized the military's failure to support the efforts of local populations who have been struggling against the terrorists.[11] He has been especially concerned with the fact that local authorities and police have abandoned their posts and closed local jails in precisely those areas where the guerrilla movement has been most active.

Vargas Llosa's feelings of disenchantment with Peru's capacity to deal with the Shining Path turned to anger in 1992 when President Alberto Fujimori argued that it was necessary to dissolve the Peruvian constitution, the congress, and the supreme court in order to fight corruption and terrorism in Peru. In Vargas Llosa's view authoritarian practices encourage the growth of revolutionary groups.[12] Therefore, even after the capture of Shining Path leader Abimael Guzmán in 1993 and the apparent unraveling of the terrorist group, Vargas Llosa continues to expect that Peru is likely to explode in violence. He believes that the conditions accounting for the rise and success of the Shining Path have worsened because he considers Fujimori to be a dictator.[13]

Vargas Llosa's analysis of the Shining Path movement and his frustration over Peruvian authorities' indifference to the breakdown of the rule of law in the interior of Peru inform *Death in the Andes*. The novel is set in the heart of the Andes in the fictional town of Naccos. The conceit of inventing a fictional town as a representative microcosm of the social troubles and violence in the

Andes is as old, in the history of the Peruvian novel, as *Birds without a Nest* (1889), in which Clorinda Matto de Turner invents a town called Killac to expose the corruption of civil and religious authorities, which she and other nineteenth century Peruvian intellectuals had criticized in their journalistic and political essays. In Matto de Turner's novel the corruption and the violence of men in power prove insurmountable to the handful of enlightened characters who attempt to redress situations of social injustice. Vargas Llosa's Naccos, like Matto de Turner's Killac, is also a mining region where human potential is wasted because of corruption and social strife.[14] The lost opportunities of the mining industry, in both novels, are emblematic of the impediments to progress and civilization in the Andean region.

As *Death in the Andes* begins, the mine that used to be the economic motor of Naccos has been abandoned. The only authorities representing the government in Naccos are the elusive lieutenant Pancorvo and two civil guards under his command, Lituma and his assistant, Tomás Carreño. The guards are charged with investigating the disappearance of three individuals: a man known as Demetrio Chanca, which may be the assumed identity of the governor of Andamarca, Medardo Llantac, whose life was saved by happenstance when Shining Path terrorists took over his town; Casimiro Hurcaya, an albino Indian peasant who has romantic ties to a girl who has become a Shining Path terrorist; and Pedro Tinoco, the mute vicuña shepherd who was tortured by lieutenant Pancorvo, the highest ranking military official in the area, when he mistook the boy for a Shining Path terrorist.

The story of Pedro Tinoco deserves a brief parenthesis because it is perhaps one of the most beautiful and moving episodes in Peruvian narrative fiction. It rivals the pathos of the most intense moments in José María Arguedas's *Deep Rivers* where Ernesto, a boy brought up by Indians, is placed in a boarding school. He is shunned by his classmates because he behaves like an Indian and by the Indians because he looks and dresses like their oppressors. He lives in hell as Northrop Frye has defined it: "a human construct on the surface of the earth [where] there are other people but there is no community; there is solitude but no individual space."[15]

In Vargas Llosa's novel Pedro Tinoco will also experience hell on the surface of the earth. He has no family, friends, or anyone who cares about his well-being. He has found in his love for his herd of vicuñas, however, a fulfilling compensation for the neglect and indifference of the people who have ignored and abandoned him. In a scene of extraordinary emotion Pedro is unable to stop the massacre of his herd by a group of "terrucos" (a slang term used to refer to the Shining Path guerrillas) who consider the boy one of the people they are fighting for and the vicuñas the property of their enemies:

He went from one to the other, trying to kiss their hands, pleading with them, going down on his knees. Some moved him away gently, others with repugnance.

"Have a little pride, have some dignity," they said. "Think about yourself instead of the vicuñas."

They were shooting them, chasing them, killing off the wounded and dying. It seemed to Pedro Tinoco that night would never come.[16]

Death in the Andes has many small episodes such as the story of Pedro Tinoco, but the novel is conceived around two major story lines: Lituma and Carreño's investigation of the missing people; and the romantic adventures of Tomás Carreño from the time he murders a drug kingpin he had been hired to protect until his arrival to Naccos to become Lituma's assistant.

Like most of Vargas Llosa's novels with several plot lines *Death in the Andes* is an intricate web of characters and situations that are organized in a methodical pattern. The novel consists of ten chapters, 1–4 making up part one, 6–9 part two, and chapter 10 serving as the epilogue of the novel. Each chapter is divided into three sections. In part one the first section of each chapter involves the investigation of the disappearance of the three characters by Lituma and his assistant.

Lituma, the protagonist of *Death in the Andes*, is the most recurrent character in Vargas Llosa's fiction. The original Spanish title of the novel, *Lituma en los Andes,* underscores the significance of the character for Vargas Llosa. As Vargas Llosa's everyman, Lituma is best remembered as the protagonist of *The Green House,* but he has made important appearances in *Who Killed Palomino Molero? La Chunga, Aunt Julia and the Scriptwriter,* and *The Real Life of Alejandro Mayta.* As in his other appearances he is originally from Piura, a coastal town in the north of Peru. He is therefore an outsider in the Andes, as he was in the setting of the Peruvian jungle of *The Green House. Death in the Andes* is ostensibly set after the events of the short story "a Visitor" and of *Who killed Palomino Molero?* where he plays roles in assisting criminal investigators.

The novel adds an important episode in the life of the character, but it does not tie up all the loose ends of his biography, as Vargas Llosa had hinted he would like to do in a novel. On the contrary, it complicates matters.[17] Lituma in *Death in the Andes* has not been to the Peruvian jungle, makes specific references to the events of the play *La Chunga* (where he was a sexually starved young man from Piura who has not yet joined the Peruvian armed forces), and is involved as a military officer in criminal investigations and as a terrorist hunter, as he was in previous incarnations in *The Cubs, Who Killed Palomino Molero?* and *The Real Life of Alejandro Mayta.*

In more generic terms Lituma in *Death in the Andes* fits into a character type of Vargas Llosa's novels: the military man who is committed to his duty in an adverse and corrupt environment. In this particular story, the criminal investigation is quixotic because the Peruvian government seems indifferent to the activities of the Shining Path guerrillas. As in *Who Killed Palomino Molero?* the criminal investigators are convinced that the uncooperative locals know more than they let on about the crimes. For their part, the Andean villagers distrust the criminal investigators, know what has happened, and are unwilling to cooperate, perhaps because some of them have played some role in the crimes.

But if Lituma in *Who Killed Palomino Molero?* faces the mistrust of his own people in Piura, in this novel he also has to interact with a population he finds bizarre. It is disconcerting to him that the locals worship the Apus, or spirits of the Andean mountains as in pre-Columbian times, and that they have developed strange beliefs, the most curious of which is the existence of "pishtacos." The pishtaco is not an invention of Vargas Llosa but a cultural phenomenon that has been noted by anthropologists. The engaging Enrique Mayer has defined the pishtacos as

> feared figures, believed to be white marauders who capture Indians and kill them to obtain human grease needed to cast specially sonorous bells for sale abroad, to run complex machinery (space craft, for example), or to pay Peru's international debt. . . . Pishtaco fears have increased remarkably since political violence has reigned in the highlands. . . . Pishtacos are coherent and historically mythologized versions of the real threat of externally perpetrated violence against which collective outrage is one possible outlet.[18]

In his thought-provoking article on Vargas Llosa's analysis of the Uchuraccay massacre, Mayer suggests that some of the journalists may have been perceived as pishtacos by their killers. Vargas Llosa did not address the pishtaco issue in his essays about Uchuraccay, but he later incorporated the theme into *Death in the Andes*, where some people are willing to take revenge upon those they perceive to be pishtacos. In the novel there are also indications that the local population is involved in violent sacrificial practices. Vargas Llosa's depiction of the climate of violence in the Andes includes most of the elements that Shining Path historians such as Gustavo Gorriti and anthropologists such as Enrique Mayer have discussed in their scholarly papers and books.[19] But Vargas Llosa does not stop with the information gathered from his own investigation of the Uchuraccay massacre or from his study in the writings of historians and anthropologists. He invents characters and situations that embrace Dionysian rites, and he adaptively alters the Greek myths that involve Dionysus. It is no coincidence that Naccos, the name of the town in which the novel is set, so closely resembles Naxos and that Naccos's most visible citizens are the amoral tipsy barman Dionisio (whose name is identical to Dionysus in Spanish) and his wife Adriana, whose name is an anagram of Ariadna.[20] In some sections of the novel, Vargas Llosa recreates the climate of irrational violence suggested by the most Dionysian of Euripides' plays, the *Bacchae*.

The third section of each chapter of part one is based on a series of ongoing conversations in which Tomás Carreño tells Lituma about his love affair and adventures with the prostitute Mercedes. Tomás had been an army officer stationed in Piura with the dubious task of protecting a drug trafficker known as the Hog. Having fallen in love with Mercedes, Tomás killed the Hog because he thought he had caught the drug trafficker abusing Mercedes during one of their sexual encounters. After deserting the army and vowing opposition to the drug traffickers, Tomás escaped from Piura to Lima, with Mercedes as his reluctant companion. Mercedes becomes Carreño's lover, but she refuses his relentless marriage proposals. Lituma becomes convinced that Mercedes is Meche, the woman from Piura who seems to draw excessive sexual desire from both male and female characters in Vargas Llosa's fiction. There are allusions to Meche in both *Who Killed Palomino Molero?* and in the play *La Chunga*, where the sexually starved Lituma has fantasies in which Meche rejects his marriage proposal because he cannot support her. Carreño's story, developed through these recurring conversations, seems to placate Lituma's feelings of sexual longing.

The middle sections of each chapter in part one recount the unexpected encounter by one or more individuals with the terrucos who act with military discipline and carry out their missions with cold and impersonal ruthlessness. In one of these sections two young French tourists are captured and killed by the terrorists; and in another, two ecologists are captured and killed after they are judged in the kind of popular trial Vargas Llosa has elsewhere called "juridical aberrations."[21] The other three incidents involve the individuals whose disappearance is under investigation: Pedrito Tinoco, don Medardo Llantac, and Casimiro Hurcaya.

At the end of part one, therefore, the mystery of the novel appears to be solved. It remains to be seen whether Lituma will find out what the reader has been led to suspect, namely, that the terrucos have captured and killed the three missing people. But the novel takes a surprising turn when Lituma becomes convinced that they were actually the victims of human sacrifice by the local population. Lituma's conclusions bring to mind the Uchuraccay investigation. Even though many had assumed that the journalists were killed by Shining Path terrorists, Vargas Llosa and the other members of the investigative commission discovered that they had actually been killed in accordance with a religious ritual by the local peasants.

Part two is also made up of chapters that are each divided into three sections according to a predictable pattern: the first section of each chapter tells how Lituma is distracted from the investigation by a call from Esperanza, a nearby mining town that has been attacked by the Shining Path guerrillas. The mining engineers who call Lituma are under no illusion about the civil guard's ability to capture or punish the terrorists. They simply need a police report that will assist them in filing insurance claims. Each first section of each chapter in part two tells the story of Lituma's visit to Esperanza. On his return home he experiences a huayco (a sudden muddy flood or avalanche) that nearly wipes out Naccos. The natural disaster, ironically, does not produce particularly strong feelings of fear in a town that has been so abused by human violence.

As in part one, the third section of each chapter in part two continues the dialogues between Lituma and Tomás Carreño about his adventures with Mercedes. The couple makes it to Lima where Tomás looks to his uncle Iscariote for help. The ironically named uncle offers his nephew a way to escape from the drug traffickers and to regain his good status in the army. He manages to convince his friend Pancorvo to admit Carreño into one of the least desirable military posts, an antiterrorist unit in an area where the Shining Path guerrillas have made important gains.[22] While Iscariote helps Tomás resolve practical matters, he develops a sexual interest in Mercedes. She rejects Iscariote's sexual advances as well as the marriage proposals of her lover. Notwithstanding her refusal, Tomás insists that Mercedes take his life savings before leaving for the military post in the Andes where he will meet and work for Lituma.

The second section of each chapter in part two is constituted of first-person narratives by Doña Adriana, many of which have supernatural themes. She tells several stories about pishtacos, including one involving Timoteo Fajardo, Adriana's first husband. This story reads like an intentionally grotesque retelling of the myth of Theseus and Ariadne. Fajardo abandons Adriana in Naccos after killing the pishtaco who plays the role of the Minotaur in the Andean labyrinth. As in the Greek myth, the abandoned Adriana will be saved by the mysterious Dionisio who has been accompanied by frolicking women in the Andes. In Adriana's stories about pishtacos it becomes apparent that Casimiro Hurcaya, also known as the Albino, has been taken as a pishtaco by the local population.

Throughout part two Lituma is convinced that the three characters who disappeared were not killed by terrorists but actually sacrificed by the local population, and he becomes certain that Adriana and Dionisio were involved in the killings. Vargas Llosa does not bother to explain either Lituma's thought process or the evidence he considers to solve the crimes. However, the reader must accept Lituma's conclusion in order to follow the final sections of the novel.

Chapter 10, the epilogue, also has three sections. In the first, Mercedes comes to Naccos in search of Tomás whose relentless wooing pays off in the end. Even though Lituma remembers Mercedes as the Meche he had seen in Piura, she does not seem to recognize him when she finds the modest military post where Lituma and Carreño have been stationed. In the second section of this chapter Lituma visits Dionisio and Adriana's bar to give the young couple some privacy in the tiny quarters he shares with Tomás. It is obvious that Adriana and Dionisio were involved in the ritual massacres of the missing people and that they show no signs of guilt or remorse for their savagery. In the third section—the final episode of the novel—Lituma walks out of the bar with an unnamed character, referred to as "the blaster," who was also involved in the sacrificial practices. In the concluding pages of the novel Lituma hopes he will get some insight into what motivated this man and others to participate in the ritual sacrifice of the disappeared men. Lituma asks:

> Did you sacrifice them so there wouldn't be a huayco? So the terrucos wouldn't come to kill anybody or take people away? so the pishtacos wouldn't dry out any laborers? What was the reason?[23]

What is most surprising and disturbing about the blaster's response is that he has no idea why he participated in ritual sacrifices or why he partook in cannibalistic rites. Unlike Dionisio and Adriana, the blaster seems tormented by his memories of the sacrifices and by the taste of the human organs he ate, but he does not know why he participated in the killings. Lituma feels disgust for the man, but he does not want to pursue the matter any further. In fact he regrets he had been so keen to solve the crimes: "I'm sorry I tried so hard to find out what happened to them. I'd be better off just suspecting."[24]

In previous Vargas Llosa novels violence always had an explanation or a rationalization, such as passion, rebellion, or vengeance. In his socialist period, violence was inherent to the inhumanity of capitalist society, and in his neoliberal period it was the result of a fanatic's utopian dreams for a better world. In *Death in the Andes,* some participate in the most depraved acts of murder and cannibalism for no apparent reason at all. The brutal massacre of the three people is therefore more disturbing and perverse than the killings of the Shining Path guerrillas, who justify violence as a means toward military and political aims, or the murder that Tomás Carreño commits when he thought his loved one was being tortured by the Hog. In *Death in the Andes* evil seems a real presence, ubiquitous and eager to spring whenever the rule of law is slackened, and its most brutal expressions are inexplicable.

Death in the Andes' literary representations of irrational violence, as well as its many direct and indirect allusions to Dionysian themes, are an invitation to reflect upon E. R. Dodds's books on the Greeks and the irrational.[25] Dodds meditates on the Nietszchean idea that "we ignore at our own peril the demand of the human spirit for Dionysiac experience."[26] Dodds takes this idea to an almost exquisite level of moral refinement when he argues that the most profound aspect of the Greek view of irrational violence, as evinced in the plays of Euripides, occurs when those carried away by actions they are unable to control know that the evil comes from within and not from without:

> This is what gives Euripides' studies of crime their peculiar poignancy: he shows us men and women nakedly confronting the mystery of evil, no longer as an alien thing assailing their reason from without, but as a part of their own being.[27]

The "Daemon" of the Greeks, as analyzed by Dodds, is not simply an external force that takes over the rational mind; it "is a carrier of man's . . . actual guilt."[28] In Vargas Llosa's novel, however, there is no sense that the evil is coming from within, and no one, not even the blaster, who feels haunted by the memories of the violence in which he participated, expresses any sense of personal guilt or responsibility for his acts.[29]

In other Vargas Llosa novels, criminal investigators, such as Gamboa in *Time of the Hero* or Silva in *Who Killed Palomino Molero?* are frustrated by a corrupt milieu. They feel troubled that their sense of justice has been violated. This is no longer the case with Lituma in *Death in the Andes*. Lituma is one of many criminal investigators in the literature of Vargas Llosa who is confronted with corruption, but he is the most cynical. From the beginning, he had been indifferent to Carreño's murder of the Hog, and notwithstanding his disgust at the horrendous deeds he has uncovered, he regrets he had so desired to understand the motivation of the criminals. In the context of the novel, his detachment seems warranted, because the brutality of the terrucos pales in comparison to the bestiality of the local population, and the civil and military authorities appear to be indifferent.

The inexplicable violence in *Death in the Andes* is a disturbing new theme in Vargas Llosa's fiction, but it is not at odds with Vargas Llosa's most consistently held belief, that irrational forces determine important aspects of human behavior. This notion has been the touchstone of his ideas about the nature of artistic creation, and it has been one of his oldest and most recurrent literary themes.

As an insight about artistic creation, the doctrine of the demons is a way of asserting a writer's creative freedom and of exonerating the creative artist from any responsibility for the content of artistic works. In his own essays of literary criticism, Vargas Llosa relies on the notion of irrational obsessions to determine the origin of a writer's inspiration. According to his doctrine of the demons of artistic creation, a writer is not responsible for his literary themes, and his personal convictions may contradict the contents and messages of his literary works.

Whatever the general merits of Vargas Llosa's literary doctrine of the writer's demons, it does not clarify the connection between his convictions and his own novels: they could have been written as conscious attempts to exemplify his own political and moral views. To be sure, Vargas Llosa has had no qualms about transforming historical and biographical events to fit his literary purposes. But these transformations (as well as the inventions of his imagination) have invariably contributed to exemplify or to embellish rather than to betray his political and moral convictions. In fact, the political content of his novels happens to coincide with his most passionately held political beliefs. When he was a socialist in the 1960s, the themes of his novels reflected his conviction that capitalism was beyond reform. When he embraced free-market democratic liberalism in the 1980s his novels underscored the dangers of fanaticism and utopian thinking that can undermine the stability of an open society.

The political messages and the literary techniques of Vargas Llosa's novels changed significantly after he distanced himself from socialism, and they justify a division of Vargas Llosa's literary trajectory according to the vicissitudes of his political convictions. It is useful to think of his socialist period and of his neoliberal period as distinct, and *Death in the Andes* may be pointing to a new, third direction in his narrative fiction. Through all his phases, however, Vargas Llosa has consistently pursued the important literary theme of the individual's dissatisfaction with his own society. His most memorable characters, including Lieutenant Gamboa, Pedro Camacho, and Antonio the Counselor, are individuals whose hopes are not fulfilled because their expectations about reality are too optimistic. Vargas Llosa's most important characters almost always fail in their aims and aspirations, and they sometimes contribute to the failures of others. These failures exemplify the central message of Vargas Llosa's novels from *Time of the Hero* to *The Notebooks of Don Rigoberto:* the hopes and desires of an individual are always greater than his or her ability to fulfill them. Unhappiness and suffering are therefore as inevitable as the two responses with which individuals try to cope with their unavoidable feelings of dissatisfaction—rebellion and fantasy.

During his revolutionary period Vargas Llosa considered that this situation was temporary because humans would realize their true aspirations with the advent of socialism. After his disenchantment with Marxist-Leninist doctrines, Vargas Llosa has argued that dissatisfaction is part and parcel of the human condition. In his socialist period, the root cause of his characters' feelings of dissatisfaction was the corruption of capitalist society; in his neoliberal period dissatisfaction explains why many are drawn to fanaticism and violence. The theme of human dissatisfaction is oriented and reoriented in Vargas Llosa's novels to illuminate whatever he, at the time, considers to be the most pressing political problems and moral dilemmas.

Jean-François Revel has called Vargas Llosa a moralist because his novels can be read as protests against the injustices caused and suffered by human beings. This has been the case in both his socialist and his neoliberal period, and a great deal of his prestige as a world-class writer has rested on the moral implications of his finely crafted novels. Several of the most important literary awards he has received—including the Jerusalem prize in 1995 and the Frankfurt Peace Prize in 1996—have stressed the moral significance of his novels. There is indeed an important ethical dimension to Vargas Llosa's novels because his greatest literary characters, from a moral point of view, are those who make extraordinary personal sacrifices to avoid contributing to corruption and injustice.

Vargas Llosa has been pleased to point out the political significance and the moral implications of his literary works, but he has steadfastly denied that these literary intentions have been conscious.[30] This refusal to admit that the moral aspects of his own literary works are anything but a happy accident is consistent with his belief in the existence of irrational forces that determine important aspects of human experience. In Vargas Llosa's essays and in his fiction, he invariably embeds an appeal to the irrational as the ultimate source of human motivations. Morality, from this perspective, is an effort to check man's base instincts for the sake of civility.

Vargas Llosa has had no qualms about expressing his outrage at corruption, violence, and exploitation, and his novels have exemplified his moral views. He has not, however, ventured into the most complex theme in moral literature, the recognition by an individual of his personal guilt or responsibility for his own suffering or that of others. Vargas Llosa has not explored this theme in his novels, but it would be unfair to single him out from the company of other Latin American writers, like Gabriel García Márquez and Carlos Fuentes, who have also made strong claims about the moral and political significance of Latin American literature. For over three decades Spanish American writers have used a plethora of literary devices, their fantasy, and sometimes even their wild imaginations to diagnose sick societies, condemn injustices, or lament solitudes, but they have seldom explored the theme of the individual who comes to terms with his most troubling limitations. In the history of the Latin American novel such grandeur has perhaps only been reached by Brazil's Machado de Assis.

The late Angel Rama once claimed that the highest standards in the contemporary Latin American novel have been set by Vargas Llosa.[31] One might add that in the field of Hispanic literature today, Mario Vargas Llosa is his own rival. Few Spanish-language authors are in a position to surpass the literary quality he has achieved.

NOTES

Introduction

1. José Miguel Oviedo, "Entrevista con Mario Vargas Llosa," in *Espejo de escritores*, ed. Reina Roffé (Hanover, New Hampshire: Ediciones del Norte, 1985), 160. All translations from Vargas Llosa's work and from other sources not available in English in published form are my own unless otherwise specified. In some cases, I have deviated from precisely literal translation to convey more clearly the spirit of the original.

2. The term *neoliberal* in Latin American has some of the same connotations as the term *neoconservative* in the United States, suggesting a commitment to free-market democracy. I am using it to refer to Vargas Llosa's break with socialist and collectivist solutions that lead to his commitment to free-market democracy. It should be stressed that Vargas Llosa's neoliberalism (or neoconservatism) comes with a strong anti-authoritarian stance. Chapter 4 will explore this facet of Vargas Llosa's political views in the context of his intellectual biography.

3. *Los Cuadernos de don Rigoberto* (Madrid: Alfaguara, 1997) is Vargas Llosa's most recent novel. It is not yet available in English translation.

4. I have been inspired and indebted by my readings of Hans Georg Gadamer's *Warheit und Methode,* where I learned about the significance of reconsidering general interepretations in the light of details, and vice versa. Nelson Goodman, Richard Wollheim, and E. H. Gombrich (whom I cite below) have helped me to think about the conditions, devices, and methods that go into the formation of particular works of art. (See Wollheim's *Art and Its objects* and Goodman's *Languages of Art*).

5. Gombrich, E. H., "Expression and Communication," *Meditations of a Hobby Horse and Other Essays on the Theory of Art* (Chicago: University of Chicago Press, 1963), 69.

6. This is a central insight of Bloom in *The Anxiety of Influence* (New York: Oxford University Press, 1973) and of George Steiner's *Real Presences* (Chicago: University of Chicago Press, 1989).

7. See chapter 2, 34–37.

8. See chapter 5, 142–143 and 150.

Chapter 1

1. Mario Vargas Llosa, "El regreso a Satán," in *Contra viento y marea,* vol. 1 (1962–1972) (Barcelona: Seix Barral, 1986), 263. (Many essays from *Contra viento y marea* have appeared in a splendid translation by John King in *Making Waves* [New York: Farrar, Strauss & Giroux, 1996]. Wherever possible I have used the English version.) Cf. his book *García Márquez: Historia de un deicidio* (Barcelona: Barral Editores, 1971); and the interview with R. Cano Gaviria, *El buitre y el ave fénix: Conversaciones con Mario Vargas Llosa* (Barcelona: Editorial Anagrama, 1972), 50–51. See also Mario Vargas Llosa's *Fiction: The Power of Lies* (Melbourne: Antipodas, 1993).

2. "I believe that those unconscious, obsessive elements that I have called a writer's 'demons' (Goethe had already done so, hadn't he?) are what almost always determine the subject of a work, and that a writer can exercise little or no rational control over them" (Vargas Llosa, "Luzbel, Europa y otras conspiraciones," *Contra viento y marea,* 1 (1962–1972): 233).

3. See the conversations with Eckerman (on March 2, 8, 18 and 30, 1831) in which Goethe discusses the demonic. Cf. Johann Wolfgang von Goethe, *Goethes Gespräche.* Vol. 4, *Gesamte Ausgabe* (Leipzig: Bierderman, 1910), 338–358.

4. For an engaging psychoanalytic interpretation of the theory of the Demon in Vargas Llosa, see Roy Boland, *Mario Vargas Llosa: Oedipus and the 'Papa' State* (Madrid: Editorial Voz), 1988.

5. Victor Hugo considered literary inspiration to be a supernatural phenomenon: "The thoughts of a poet should take place at a supernatural level." He believed that it had revolutionary implications: "The literary force has always been, and is in our day more than ever, a revolutionary force" (translated from Christiane Ledouppe, *Victor Hugo et la création littéraire: Guide systématique pour la connaissance des idées de l'écrivain* [Liège: Mémoires, 1980], 31–32).

6. George Bataille, *Literature and Evil,* trans. Alastair Hamilton (New York: Marion Boyars, 1985), 197.

7. The short story about a seminarian with sexual obsessions was published in French in 1924, some fifty years after it was written, at the insistence of André Breton and Louis Aragon. Vargas Llosa translated it into Spanish in 1960. The translation remained unpublished until 1989. Arthur Rimbaud, "Un corazón bajo la sotana," prologue and translation by Mario Vargas Llosa (Lima: Jaime Campodónico, 1989).

8. Vargas Llosa, Garcia Márquez: *Historia de un deicidio.* Barcelona: Seix Barrel: 1971), 86.

9. Cf. Vargas Llosa, "Sebastián Salazar Bondy and the Vocation of the Writer in Peru," in *Making Waves*, 59–69.

10. In an interview, Vargas Llosa stated, "Liberal democracies recognize the principle of artistic freedom, and on this point (but only on this point) they are absolutely right." "Once preguntas claves a Mario Vargas Llosa," *Caretas* (Lima), August 29, 1967: 56.

11. *Cuadernos de Marcha* (Montevideo) 49, May 19, 1971, 20.

12. Vargas Llosa, "José Carlos Mariátegui," *Cultura Peruana* 94 (1956). Vargas Llosa's essay is published in four parts, without page numbers.

13. Cf. Sebastián Salazar Bondy, "Mao Tse Tung entre la Poesía y la Revolución," *Literatura* (Lima) 1 (February 1958): 22.

14. Interview with Mario Vargas Llosa, *Caretas* (Lima), August 29–September 10, 1967. In additon, in 1968 he said: "The recognition of Marxism as the official philosophy of the revolution does not preclude, until now at least, other ideological viewpoints which can be freely expressed. Castro's statement to the Congress of Cuban Writers—'Within the revolution everything; against the revolution, nothing'—is being put into practice in a rigorous manner. In art and literature this is very obvious: there is no official aesthetic" (Vargas Llosa, "Chronicle of the Cuban Revolution," in *Making Waves*, 73.

15. Mario Vargas Llosa, "La novela," *Cuadernos de literatura* (Montevideo) 2 (December 1968): 13.

16. "Conferencia de Mario Vargas Llosa," *Primer encuentro de narradores peruanos* (Lima: Latinoamericana Editores [1968], 1986), 163. The lecture was given in 1965.

17. Participation by Vargas Llosa in *Mario Vargas Llosa y Gabriel García Márquez: Diálogo* (Lima: Milla Batres, 1967), 42.

18. "I believe that literature allows a society's underlying problems to become visible, especially when that society is corrupt." (Jean-Michel Fossey, "Mario Vargas Llosa," *Galaxia latinoamericana [siete años de entrevistas]* [Las Palmas de Gran Canaria: Inventarios Provisionales, 1973], 119).

19. In *Contra viento y marea*, 1 (1962–1972): 179.

20. Vargas Llosa, "José Carlos Mariátegui, *Cultura Peruana* 16:93–96, additional unnumbered pages.

21. Vargas Llosa, "José María Arguedas," *El Comercio: Suplemento Dominical* (Lima) 4 (September 1955): 8.

22. Cf. José María Arguedas, *Formación de una cultura nacional indoamericana*, ed. and with prologue by Angel Rama (Mexico City: Siglo XXI, 1975).

23. Vargas Llosa, "José Carlos Mariátegui," *Cultura Peruana* (Lima), 16 (1956): 95.

24. With the exception of Arguedas, Vargas Llosa criticized those Peruvian authors who tried to offer realistic depictions of the Peruvian Indian: "Although they have generous feelings for the Indians, they could not speak about them with authority. Their nativism was intellectual and emotional; it was not backed up with a direct and intimate knowledge of the reality of the Andeans" (Mario Vargas Llosa, "José María Arguedas y el índio," *Casa de las Américas* 4, no. 26 [1964]: 141). Vargas Llosa claimed

that only someone like Arguedas could attempt the literary portrayal of the Indian. Others, including himself, should, therefore, avoid the theme: "It could be that one of the reasons for which I so admire José María Arguedas is not only because he is a great writer, but also because he managed to portray that Andean world for so many Peruvians, such as myself, who have no direct experience of the Indian world—it is a world . . . that responds to another mentality, that has another historic tradition, where another language is spoken, a language that I don't understand, that has a landscape which is exotic for me" (Mario Vargas Llosa, in *Semana de Autor: Mario Vargas Llosa*, ed. Instituto de Cooperación Iberoamericana [Madrid: Ediciones Cultura Hispánica, 1985], 31).

25. Ariel Dorfman, "Mario Vargas Llosa y José María Arguedas: Dos visiones de una sola América," *Casa de las Américas* 10, no. 64 (1971): 12.

26. Sebastián Salazar Bondy, *Lima la horrible* (Lima: Populibros Peruanos, 1964), 11–12.

27. Sebastián Salazar Bondy, letter to Mario Vargas Llosa, July 6, 1962, Correspondence, box 1, Mario Vargas Llosa Collection, Firestone Library, Princeton University.

28. Ibid.

29. Angel Rama, "*Lima la horrible* de Sebastián Salazar Bondy," *Casa de las Americas* 4, no. 27 (1964): 117.

30. Ibid.

31. Vargas Llosa, "Un mito, un libro y una casta," in *Contra viento y marea*, 1 (1962–1972): 41.

32. Salazar Bondy, letter to Mario Vargas Llosa, April 5, 1964, Correspondence, box 1.

33. José María Arguedas, letter to Mario Vargas Llosa, September 26, 1967, Correspondence, box 4.

34. José María Arguedas, letter to Mario Vargas Llosa, Correspondence, box 1, folder 1.

35. Jean Michel Fossey, "Mario Vargas Llosa," 124.

36. Jean Paul Sartre, *What Is Literature?* trans. Bernard Frechtman (New York: Philosophical Library, 1949), 70.

37. Vargas Llosa, "Sebastián Salazar Bondy y la vocación del escritor en el Perú," in *Contra viento y marea*, 1 (1962–1972): 120.

38. Mario Vargas Llosa, "César Moro en París," *Caretas* 10, no. 198 (March 25–June 8, 1960): 23.

39. An English translation of his prologue to the Exposición International de Surrealismo along with other documents appears in a special issue on Latin American surrealism edited by Alfred MacAdam in *Review: Latin American Literature and Arts* 51 (1995): 7–8.

40. Cf. Julio Ortega, "La poesía de César Moro," *La imaginación crítica: Ensayos sobre la modernidad en el Perú* (Lima: Peisa, 1974), 150–152; and James Higgins, *The Poet in Peru*, (Liverpool: Francis Cairns, 1982), 134–140.

41. Moro, "Los anteojos de azufre," 95.

42. "*Rebellion* and *subversion* could be understood as the signs of this verbal activity that passes from the voice to the performance of Moro, in the word" (Alberto Escobar, *El imaginario nacional: Moro-Westphalen-Arguedas, una formación literaria* [Lima: Instituto de Estudios Peruanos, 1989], 33).

43. In an interview Breton recalls that the manifesto "Pour un art révolutionnaire indépendant" expresses his agreement with Trotsky on "the conditions that art and poetry ought to meet, from a revolutionary point of view, so that they can participate in the fight for political emancipation, while doing it entirely their own way" (André Breton, *Entretiens* [Gallimard: Paris, (1952) 1969], 190).

44. For Moro's participation in the surrealist movement see Julio Ortega, "La poesía de César Moro," *La imaginación crítica: Ensayos sobre la modernidad en el Perú* (Lima: Peisa, 1974), 145–159; and Julio Ortega, "Moro: Nobre y renombre," *Crítica de la identidad; la pregunta por el Perú en su literatura* (Mexico City: fondo de Cultura Económica, 1988). In his short book on Moro, Coyné recalls that Moro was offended that Diego Rivera signed the manifesto drawn up by Breton and Trotsky. Cf. André Coyné, *César Moro* (Lima: Torres Aguirre, 1956); and his article "César Moro entre Lima, París y México," in *César Moro: Obra poética* (Lima: Instituto Nacional de Cultura, 1980).

45. César Moro, "El uso de la palabra," an essay written in 1939, in *Los anteojos de azufre,* 16.

46. The narrator of the novel recalls that in the 40s, "Trotsky's ideas were brought to Peru by a handful of surrealists who had come back from Paris—Pablo de Westphalen, Abril de Viveo [*sic*], and César Moro" and suggests that the oldest member of Mayta's cell was one of the first trotskyites of Peru (Vargas Llosa, *The Real Life of Alejandro Mayta,* trans. Alfred MacAdam [New York: Farrar, Straus & Giroux, 1986], 32)

47. Vargas Llosa, *The Real Life of Alejandro Mayta,* 271.

48. César Moro, "Carta a Xavier Villaurrutia," *Los anteojos de azufre,* 96.

49. Vargas Llosa, "César Moro en París," 23.

50. The poem "Viaje hacia la noche" is dated: "Lima the horrible, July 24 or August, 1949." César Moro, *La La tortuga ecuestre y otros poemas, 1924–1949* (Lima: Talleres Gráficos "D. Miranda," 1957), 63. The posthumous poetry has since been published, edited by André Coyné and Ricardo Silva-Santisteban. It was written in his second period, when, as Coyné points out, "the divorce between Moro and the milieu in which he lived many years of his life was absolute" (André Coyné [in a note with which he introduces an untitled text by Moro], *Los anteojos de azufre: Prosas reunidas y presentadas por André Coyné* [Lima: Talleres Gráficos "D. Miranda," 1958], 136). Coyné also recalls with lyricism, "In his last years Moro had drawn a very heavy line between those hours that he wasted earning a living by teaching French classes in the four corners of an out-of-the-way city, and those, when he took off his mask, daring marvelous tempests, and proudly submerging himself in desperation until the sun

looked over the night, laughing at him while grinding his heart" ("César Moro entre Lima, París y México," 22).

51. Vargas Llosa, "Nota sobre César Moro," *Literatura* (Lima) 1 (February 1958). Pedro Lastra was the first to call attention to the similarity between Professor Fontana of *The Time of the Hero* (173) and the profile that Vargas Llosa gave of the poet in the text just quoted. See Pedro Lastra, "Un caso de elaboración narrativa de experiencias concretas en *La ciudad y los perros*," in *Relecturas hispanoamericanas* [Santiago de Chile: Editorial Universitaria, 1987], 111–15).

52. Ibid.

53. Vargas Llosa translated the brief article "La bazofia de los perros," included in *Los anteojos de azufre*, 12–13.

54. Vargas Llosa, "Nota sobre César Moro" 5–6. Moro had also rejected the *indigenista* movement with arguments that prefigured those of Vargas Llosa. Cf. César Moro, "A propósito de la pintura en el Perú," in *La tortuga ecuestre y otros textos*, ed. Julio Ortega (Caracas: Monte Avila, 1973), 101–106.

55. César Moro, "Los anteojos de azufre," in *La tortuga ecuestre y otros textos*, 95.

56. Ibid., 96.

57. Higgins, *The Poet in Peru* (Liverpool: Francis Cairns, 1982), 124.

58. James Higgins, *A History of Peruvian Literature*, (Liverpool: Francis Cairns, 1987), 188–189. Moro's poetry makes many references to the satanic, the damned, and the infernal:

> ". . . gime tras el olor de tu paso
> De fuego de azufre de aire de tempestad
> De catastrofe intangible y que merma cada día
> Esa porción en que se esconden los designios nefastos."

> (. . . it screams behind the odor of your step
> of fire of sulfur of air of storm
> of intangible catastrophe and shrinks each day
> that portion in which are hidden the nefarious designs.)

(César Moro, "La leve pisada del demonio nocturno," in *La tortuga ecuestre y otros poemas,* 25–27.)

59. Higgins, *The Poet in Peru*, 133.

60. English trans. Helen Lane, *In Praise of the Stepmother* (New York: Farrar Straus Giroux, 1990). The poem "A vista perdida" can be found in *La tortuga ecuestre y otros textos,* 25–27.

61. César Moro, "Objeción a todos los homenajes a Paul Eluard," in *La tortuga ecuestre y otros textos,* 136.

62. The ideas of Vargas Llosa on *indigenismo* coincide with those of César Moro: "It is easy to see that *indigenismo* is not limited merely to painting; these intellectuals

in Peru want to build the new walls that will isolate us from Europe" (Moro, "A propósito de la pintura en el Perú," *Los anteojos de azufre*, 17–18).

63. Moro, "Carta a Villaurrutia," in *La tortuga ecuestre y otros textos*, 133.

64. "Nota sobre César Moro," 6.

65. Vargas Llosa, "¿Es útil el sacrificio de la poesía?" *Literatura* (Lima) 3 (August 1959): 45.

66. Ibid.

67. Cf. Mario Vargas Llosa, "Carta de batalla por Tirant lo Blanc," prologue to *Tirant lo Blanc*, by Joanot Martorell and Martí Joan de Galba, (Madrid: Alianza, 1969c, 1988), 19–53. This essay has been included in *Carta de batalla por Tirant lo Blanc* (Barcelona: Seix Barral, 1991).

68. In his essay Dámaso Alonso says that he sees Martorell "as a contemporary. He is tired, disillusioned, very sensual, sad, and humorous, like a European of our time." See "*Tirant-lo-Blanc*, Novela Moderna," *Primavera temprano de la literatura europea* (Madrid: Guadarrama, 1961), 201–253. On Vargas Llosa's first reading of Martorell, cf. Luis Harss and Barbara Dohmann, *Into the Mainstream*, (New York: Harper & Row, 1967), 362.

69. *Carta de batalla por Tirant lo Blanc*, 24. It might be relevant to mention that in his essay on Martorell's realism, Dámaso Alonso did not call attention to the formal and literary elements of the novel, upon which Vargas Llosa focuses persistently.

70. *Carta de batalla por Tirant lo Blanc*, 26.

71. See, for example, the essay "Tirant lo Blanc: Las palabras como hechos," *Carta de batalla por Tirant lo Blanc*.

72. Vargas Llosa, in Ricardo A. Setti, . . . *sobre la vida y la política: Diálogo con Mario Vargas Llosa* (Buenos Aires: Intermundo, 1989), 43.

73. The quotation comes from the interview: "Once preguntas claves a Mario Vargas Llosa," *Caretas*, August 29–September 10, 1967.

74. Vargas Llosa, "El papel del intelectual en los movimientos de liberación nacional," in *Contra viento y marea*, 1 (1962–1972): 105–106.

75. "'*The Making of a Hero* bored me and . . . I liked *The Castle*'" (Vargas Llosa, *Conversation in the Cathedral*, trans. Gregory Rabassa [New York: Harper & Row, 1974], 91).

76. "I have always had problems justifying my admiration for Borges" (Vargas Llosa, *Mario Vargas Llosa y Gabriel García Márquez: Diálogo*), 40.

77. Angel Rama and Vargas Llosa engage in a polemic in the magazine *Marcha* (Montevideo) May 5, 1972. Vargas Llosa's part in the polemic also appears in *Contra viento y marea*, 1 (1962–1972): 263–284, and the entire text has been published in book form (Angel Rama and Mario Vargas Llosa, *García Márquez y el problema de la novela* [Montevideo: Corregidor-Marcha, 1973]).

78. Vargas Llosa, "La insurrección permanente," *Contra viento y marea*, 1 (1962–1972): 109. This argument recalls Sartre's claim that literature will continue to be subversive even in a free and classless society: "Literature is, by its very nature, the

subjectivity of a society in permanent revolution" (Sartre, *What is Literature?* trans. Bernard Frechtman [New York: Philosophical Library, 1949], 159.

79. R. Cano Gaviria, *El buitre y el ave fenix,* 41–42.

80. "El papel del intelectual en los movimientos de liberación nacional, in *Contra viento y marea,* 1 (1962–1972): 105.

81. Albert Camus, "The century of fear" (*Combat* [November 1948]), *Moral y política* (Madrid: Alianza, 1978), 84.

82. Vargas Llosa, "Revisión de Albert Camus," in *Contra viento y marea,* 1 (1962–1972): 17. "Camus's tragic dilemma, when confronted with the war in Algeria, is the best proof of the purely rhetorical nature of his doctrine" ("Revisión de Albert Camus," in *Contra viento y marea,* 1 (1962–1972): 20).

83. Mario Vargas Llosa, "Génesis de *La ciudad y los perros,*" *Studi di letteratura ispano-americana* 3 (1971): 84.

84. Ibid. Vargas Llosa explains that the inspiration for the novel was the time that he passed as a cadet in the Colegio Leoncio Prado, an institution where the cadets were obligated to judge life "by a system of Peruvian military values, which is the same as saying 'by deformed values.'" Mario Vargas Llosa, "Génesis de *La ciudad y los perros,*" *Studi di letteratura ispano-americana* 3 (1971): 84.

85. Participation by Vargas Llosa in Luis Agüero, Juan Larco, et. al., "Sobre *La ciudad y los perros* de Mario Vargas Llosa," *Casa de las Américas* 5, no. 30 (May–June 1965): 77.

86. Vargas Llosa was in Cuba during the Bay of Pigs events and he wrote a testimony for the French Press that is reproduced in both Spanish an French in *Contra viento y marea,* 1 (1962–1972): 21-29.

87. See "Carta al vocero del partido comunista peruano," in *Contra viento y marea,* 1 (1962–1972): 182–83, and "La censura en la URRS y Alexander Solzhenitsyn," in *Contra viento y marea,* 1 (1962–1972): 189–194.

88. Vargas Llosa, "El papel del intelectual en los movimientos de liberación nacional," in *Contra viento y marea,* 1 (1962–1972): 103–104.

Chapter 2

1. I am deliberately alluding to a phrase by Jorge Luis Borges because of its affinity with Vargas Llosa's understanding of Flaubert: "Flaubert was the first to consecrate (I use the word with all its etymological rigor) the creation of a purely esthetic work *in prose*" (Jorge Luis Borges, "Flaubert y su destino ejemplar," *Discusión* [Madrid: Alianza, (1932) 1986], 126).

2. Vargas Llosa states: "What I also find admirable in Flaubert is the complete authority he assumes over the material he uses, which is what distinguishes him from the novelists that preceded him" (in Luis Harss and Barbara Dohmann, *Into the Mainstream* [New York: Harper & Row, 1966] 359).

3. Flaubert, letter to Louise Colet, September 13, 1852, *Oeuvres complètes de Gustave Flaubert* (Paris: Club de l'Honnête Homme, 1974), 13:236. In another letter

Flaubert declares: "I believe . . . that one can be interested in every subject. As to making something beautiful out of them, I also think that is possible, theoretically at least, but I am less sure" (Letter to Louise Colet, September 16, 1853, *Oeuvres complètes de Gustave Flaubert* 13:409). Vargas Llosa follows Flaubert in thinking that any subject can be worthy of a literary work.

4. "The author, in his work, should be like God in his creation—invisible and all powerful: he must be everywhere felt, but never seen. Art being a second nature, the Creator of that nature must behave similarly. In all its most minute particles, in all its aspects, let there be a hidden and infinite impassivity. The effect for the spectator must be a kind of amazement. 'How is this done?' we should ask, and we should feel overwhelmed without knowing why" (Letter to Louise Colet, December 9, 1852, *Oeuvres complètes de Gustave Flaubert* 13:265.

5. "[Flaubert] was the first modern writer" (Vargas Llosa, in Harss and Dohmann, *Into the Mainstream*, 359).

6. Vargas Llosa, *The Perpetual Orgy: Flaubert and* Madame Bovary, trans. Helen Lane (New York: Farrar, Straus & Giroux, 1986), 168.

7. Ibid., 218.

8. Ibid., 60.

9. Ibid., 218.

10. Vargas Llosa in Ricardo A. Setti, . . . *sobre la vida y la política: Diálogo con Vargas Llosa* (Buenos Aires: Intermundo, 1989), 76.

11. In a note to *Los ríos profundos* (Caracas: Biblioteca Ayacucho, 1978), Vargas Llosa says, "Taking literally what José María Arguedas said about what he has written has caused many—including myself, at one time—to think that the merit of his books is in having shown the reality of the Indian with more truth than any other writer" (191). Solzhenitsyn's novel is, for Vargas Llosa, the book that brought to world-wide attention "that brutal contradiction implicit in the chimera of the socialist paradise" (*La verdad de las mentiras* [Barcelona: Seix Barral, 1990], 223).

12. Vargas Llosa, "Novela primitiva y novela de creación en América Latina," *Revista de la Universidad de México* 23, no. 10 (June 1969): 29.

13. Ibid.

14. Ibid., 30.

15. "In contrast to the primitivists, there is no common denominator either in matter or style or procedure with the new novelists; their similarity is in their diversity. They no longer try to express 'a reality,' but rather personal visions and obsessions—'their' realities.' The worlds that they create are fictions, and they have value as such before you notice that they are also versions, approaches from different angles, and representations (psychological, fantastic or mythic) of Latin America. Some of the new novelists, I am thinking of the Mexican Juan Rulfo, the Brazilian João Guimarães Rosa, or the Peruvian José María Arguedas in *Los ríos profundos* (1959), have utilized the very topics of the primitive novel. But in the new novels these themes are means not ends, experiences that the imagination renews and objectifies by means of the word" (Vargas Llosa, "Novela primitiva y novela de creación en América Latina," 31).

16. Ibid., 31.

17. Vargas Llosa, *The Perpetual Orgy*, 85.

18. Ibid., 225.

19. In *Aunt Julia and the Scriptwriter* (New York: Farrar, Straus, & Giroux, 1982), Varguitas exemplifies this process: "I wanted it to be a funny story, and to learn the techniques of writing humor, I read—on jitneys, express buses, and in bed before falling asleep—all the witty authors I could get my hands on, from Mark Twain and Bernard Shaw to Jardiel Poncela and Fernández Flórez" (97).

20. For an in-depth interpretation of Vargas Llosa's life and works from a psychological point of view, see Roy Boland's *Mario Vargas Llosa: Oedipus and the 'Papa' State.* See also Carlos Alonso's "La tía Julia y el escribidor: The Writing Subject's Fantasy of empowerment," *PMLA* 106 (January 1991): 46–59, for an analysis of the oedipal situation in Vargas Llosa with a poststructuralist twist.

21. His assessment of the *Tirant lo Blanc* by Martorell is typical: "A novel is something more than an objective document; it is, above all, a subjective testimony of the reasons that brought the author who wrote it to become a radical rebel. And this subjective testimony always consists of a personal addition to the world" ("Martorell y el 'elemento añadido' en *Tirant lo Blanc*, 26, see note 68, chapter 1).

22. See José Miguel Oviedo, "Entrevista con Mario Vargas Llosa," in *Espejo de escritores*, notes and prologue by Reina Roffé (Hanover, N. H.: Ediciones del Norte, 1985), 164.

23. In English the stories of *Los jefes* are included with the translation of *Los cachorros* (The Cubs) in *The Cubs and Other Stories*, trans. Gregory Kolovakos and Ronald Christ (New York: Harper & Row, 1979). I will use the English titles of the short stories, but to avoid confusion I will use the Spanish title *Los jefes* to refer to the first collection of stories and the title *The Cubs* to refer to *Los cachorros*.

24. Vargas Llosa, in Harss and Dohmann, *Into the Mainstream*, 346.

25. "Los jefes" appeared for the first time in the magazine *Mercurio peruano* 38, no. 358 (February 1957): 93–110. An explanatory note states that it was written in 1955.

26. Guadalupe Fernández Ariza has demonstrated an important connection between *The Cubs* and *Conversación en La Catedral.* She has also shown that many characters in the novel reappear as well in *Aunt Julia and the Scriptwriter.* Consult her fine edition of *The Cubs (Los Cachorros)* (Madrid: Catedra, 1987).

27. For example: "'el Chispas' was a character who was scarcely sketched out in *Los cachorros.* In *Conversación en La Catedral* he is the brother of Santiago Zavala" (Fernández Ariza, in "Introducción" in *Los cachorros).*

28. Vargas Llosa, *The Cubs and Other Stories* (New York: Harper & Row, 1979), 43.

29. "They came from all parts of Peru. They had never seen each other before but they were all together now, lined up in front of the cement hulks whose insides they had not yet seen" (*The Time of the Hero*, trans. Lysander Kemp (New York: Harper & Row, 1979), 50.

30. Vargas Llosa, *A Writer's Reality*, ed. Myron I. Lichtblau (Syracuse, N.Y.: Syracuse University Press), 39. In her useful introduction to the life and works of

Vargas Llosa Sara Castro-Klarén offers an insight about why the editors may have used the word "hero" in the English title. The novelist had used it for the title of an earlier draft: "The young writer had more or less finished a version of the novel he was working on, but he was still not satisfied with it. Its intended title was *La morada del heroe* (The Hero's Dwelling)." In *Understanding Mario Vargas Llosa* (Columbia: University of South Carolina Press, 1990), 10. The other tentative title in Spanish before the definitive *La ciudad y los perros* was *Los impostores* (The impostors).

31. Setti, . . . *Sobre la vida y la política: Diálogo con Vargas Llosa* (Buenos Aires, Intermundo, 1989), 18. "Perhaps the most enduring learning experience of my years at the university was not what I learned in the lecutre halls, but what I discovered in the novels and stories recounting the saga of Yoknapatawpha County. I remember how dazzling it was to read—pencil and paper in hand—*Light in August, As I Lay Dying, The Sound and the Fury*, and the like, and to discover in these pages the infinite complexity of shade and allusion and the textual and conceptual richness that the novel could provide. I also learned that to tell a story well required a conjuror's technique. The literary models from my youth have paled, like Sartre, whom I can no longer read. But Faulkner continues to be a major writer for me, and every time that I read him I am convinced that his work is a novelistic *summa* comparable to the great classics" ("The Country of a Thousand Faces," in *Making Waves,* 10).

32. "For Joe, the problem of whether he is white or black is a question that keeps him restless, a question that cannot be put to sleep. For him it is inextricably bound up with the question, 'Who am I?' Joe's identity crisis is permanent" (Cleanth Brooks, *William Faulkner: First Encounters* [New Haven: Yale University, 1983], 173).

33. We continue to use the terminology that José Miguel Oviedo gives to the brief narrative sections that are the elemental unities with which Vargas Llosa constructs his novels. Cf. his book *Mario Vargas Llosa: Invención de una realidad.*

34. Mary E. Davis has pointed out the relationship between Boa's interior monologues and those of *Absalom, Absalom!* Cf. "La elección del fracaso: Vargas Llosa y William Faulkner," in Oviedo, *Mario Vargas Llosa: El escritor y la crítica* (Madrid: Taurus, 1981), 42.

35. The first draft of the novel can be found in a notebook in box D, folder 1, of the Mario Vargas Llosa Collection, Firestone Library, Princeton University.

36. Jorge Luis Borges, *Antiguas literaturas germánicas* (Mexico City: Fondo de Cultura Económica, 1951), 72.

37. See Alberto Escobar, " Impostores de sí mismos," *Patio de letras* (Caracas: Monte Avila, 1971), especially 360; the first edition of *Patio de letras*, published in 1965, does not include the essay on Vargas Llosa.

38. Vargas Llosa, *The Time of the Hero,* 108–109.

39. The cinema is mentioned more than a hundred times in the novel. All the novel's characters frequent the cinema, and the novel tells of the cinematic experiences of most of them. There are references to the Western, to horror films, to Mexican melodramas, etc. The novel also mentions the names of Hollywood stars and of famous characters from the movies. For example, the cadets compare the eyes of an

effeminate professor to those of Rita Hayworth (175), one of Teresa's suitors yells like Tarzan to impress her (323), the standards for physical beauty come from the cinema (225), etc.

40. "When I'm seeing a good movie I forget everything else. It's like I'm in another world" (*The Time of the Hero*), 104.

41. See Sara Castro-Klaren, *Mario Vargas Llosa: Analisis introductorio* (Lima: Latinoamericana Editores, 1988), 38, for a discussion "machismo" in the novel.

42. In *The War of the End of the World*, for example, the myopic journalist, who has inhibitions with women of his own class and social world, takes Jurema, a woman of the backlands, as a lover.

43. Vargas Llosa, *The Time of the Hero*, 363.

44. Ibid., 364.

45. Ibid., 378.

46. Ibid., 372–373.

47. Juliaca is one of the most inhospitable places in the literary world of Vargas Llosa. A character in *La Casa Verde* compares the jungle (puna) with the arid highlands of Juliaca and prefers the jungle, also called "montaña" (mountain) in Peru: "Shorty had spent a year in Juliaca, and the mountains were tougher than the jungle" (*The Green House*, trans. Gregory Rabassa [New York: Harper & Row, 1968], 110). On the measures that Gamboa could have taken to keep his post, see *The Time of the Hero*, 374–375.

48. Vargas Llosa, *The Time of the Hero*, 387.

49. The Jaguar lies, for example, about the theft of the exam, with which the novel begins, to protect the secrets of "the Circle" to which he belongs. Cf. *The Time of the Hero*, 40.

50. For example, Harss and Dohmann, *Into the Mainstream*, 350; Carlos Fuentes, *La nueva novela hispanoamerican* (Mexico City: Joaquín Mortiz, 1969), 41.

51. See *The Time of the Hero*, 93–94 and 371–372.

52. Ibid., 385.

53. Ibid., 230–231.

54. Ibid., 398–399.

55. Ibid., 398–399.

56. Vargas Llosa, in Harss and Dohmann, *Into the Mainstream*, 352–353.

57. "It was a vestige from the golden age of the jungle (the end of the last century and the beginning of this one), during the 'rubber fever.' This epoch was long gone. The 'bosses' were by this time poor and even miserable, barefoot, nearly illiterate, with primitive customs. Rubber and animal skins had ceased to be 'good business.' In the Alto Marañón the exploitation of man by man was bestial, but the beneficiaries of that horror did not gain wealth or even well being: they just barely survived" (Mario Vargas Llosa, *Historia secreta de una novela* [Barcelona: Tusquets, 1971], 40–41).

58. Mario Vargas Llosa, "Crónica de un viaje a la selva," *Cultura Peruana* 17, no. 123, no page numbers.

59. Eduardo Neale-Silva, *Horizonte humano: Vida de José Eustasio Rivera* (Mexico City: Fondo de Cultura Económica, 1960), 274–275.

60. Vargas Llosa, *The Green House*, 305.

61. Luis Loayza, "Los personajes de *La Casa Verde*," *Amarú* 1, 1967.

62. "There has been so much talk in Piura about the original Green House, that first building, that no one knows for sure any more what it was really like or the authentic details of its history. The few survivors from that period argued with and contradicted one another, and they have ended up confusing what they saw and heard with their own inventions. And the witnesses are so decrepit now, and their silence so obstinate, that it is no use questioning them. In any case, the original Green House no longer exists" (*The Green House*, 85).

63. Vargas Llosa, *The Green House*, 209.

64. Emir Rodríguez Monegal, "Madurez de Vargas Llosa," an interview with Vargas Llosa in *Mundo Nuevo* (Paris) 3 (1966): 68.

65. Vargas Llosa, "Crónica de un viaje a la selva."

66. Ibid.

67. "When I read the novels of Dumas which spoke of the Court of Miracles, I thought of this neighborhood; I don't know if it still exists" (Vargas Llosa in Rodríguez Monegal, "Madurez de Vargas Llosa," 67).

68. José Emilio Pacheco, "Lectura de Vargas Llosa," *Revista de la Universidad de México* 22, no. 8 (1968): 33.

69. José Emilio Pacheco has written, "Vargas Llosa would say that he doesn't write for those who are going to read him but rather for those who are going to re-read him" ("Lectura de Vargas Llosa," 28; Pacheco's observation is particularly relevant to *The Green House*).

70. Vargas Llosa, *The Green House*, 146–148 and 168–169.

71. Ian Watt, *Conrad in the Nineteenth Century* (London: Chatto & Windus, 1980), 276ff.

72. Vargas Llosa, *The Green House*, 12. A complex but important clue is lost in the English version, which translates "churres" as "kids."

73. Ibid., 4.

74. Ibid., 6.

75. Vargas Llosa, "La ciudad y el forastero," *Casa de las Américas* 426, no. 26 (October–November 1964): 97. The quote is actually about Don Anselmo. It illustrates the way in which regionalisms were explained in an earlier version of the novel. In the novel no such explanations are offered.

76. As in *The Time of the Hero* it is a transgression that sets the plot in motion. In the first novel it is the robbery of the exam. In *The Green House* it is the liberation of the pupils by Bonifacia.

77. Fuentes, *La nueva novela hispanoamericana*, 44.

78. "One of the keys of *The Green House* and one of its riskiest and most attractive aspects: the acceptance of melodrama as one of the axes of Latin American existence.

To say it provocatively, it would be possible to film *The Green House* as a bad Mexican film" (Fuentes, *La nueva novela hispanoamericana,* 47).

79. Vargas Llosa, *The Perpetual Orgy,* 17.

80. Vargas Llosa, "En torno a *Los Miserables,*" in *Contra viento y marea,* vol. 1 (1962–1972) (Barcelona: Seix Barral, 1986), 50.

81. Vargas Llosa, *Historia secreta de una novela,* 54–55.

82. "Anselmo would carry away Antonia and would carry her to live in the Green House, where the girl would die: this, besides, has Faulknerian resonances and Faulkner for me was the epitome of the novelist (he still is)" (*Historia secreta de una novela,* 55).

83. William Faulkner, *Light in August* (New York: Random House, 1932c, 1972), 111.

84. Ibid., 134.

85. Vargas Llosa, *The Green House,* 323.

86. Ibid., 348.

87. Ibid., 394.

88. See José Oviedo, *Mario Vargas Llosa: La invención de una realidad* (Barcelona: Seix Barral, 1982), 132–133.

89. In *Historia secreta de una novela,* 64, Vargas Llosa says that Fushía's illness is leprosy, although the word is not mentioned in the novel. He adds that he wanted to allude to Flaubert's voyage to the Orient, the chronicle of which includes an encounter with a leper colony.

90. Vargas Llosa, *The Green House* 22.

91. Ibid., 118.

92. Luis Harss has pointed out affinities between *Heart of Darkness* and *The Green House* in "Juego de espejos en *La Casa Verde,*" in *Mario Vargas Llosa,* ed. José Miguel Oviedo (Madrid: Taurus Ediciones, 1981), 143–155.

93. Joseph Conrad, *Heart of Darkness,* ed. Robert Kimbrough (New York: Norton, 1988), 56.

94. Vargas Llosa, *The Green House,* 244.

95. See for example the story "Fushía," box F, folder 12, in the Mario Vargas Llosa Collection, Firestone Library, Princeton University.

96. José Emilio Pacheco, "Lectura de Vargas Llosa," *Revista de la Universidad de México* 22, no.8 (1968): 33.

97. "It has always been characteristic of Joyce to neglect action, narrative, drama, of the usual kind. . . . There is tremendous vitality in Joyce, but very little movement. . . . [T]hough Joyce almost entirely lacks appetite for violent conflict or vigorous action, his work is prodigiously rich and alive. His force, instead of following a line, expands itself in every dimension (including that of Time) about a single point" (Edmund Wilson, *Axel's Castle* [New York: Scribner's, 1931], 168, 169). For the significance of Joyce in Latin American literature see Gerald Martin's *Journey through the Labyrinth: Latin American Fiction in the Twentieth Century* (London: Verso, 1989).

98. Cano Gaviria, *El buitre y el ave fénix,* 100.

99. My own translation of "En este país el que no se jode, jode a los demás" (Mario Vargas Llosa, *Conversación en La Catedral* [Barcelona: Seix Barral, 1969], 1:166).

100. Sebastián Salazar Bondy, prologue to the collective work *La encrucijada del Perú* (Montevideo: Arca, 1963), 7–8.

101. "If they're offered a little something, the Apristas would be willing to come to terms with the government" (*Conversation in the Cathedral*, trans. Gregory Rabassa [New York: Harper & Row, 1974], 384).

102. My own translation of : "Lo peor, era tener dudas. . . . Se había dado cuenta que a veces hacía trampas en el círculo . . . decía creo o estoy de acuerdo y en el fondo tenía dudas. . . . Cerrar los puños, apretar los dientes, Ambrosio, el Apra es la solución, la religión es la solución, el comunismo es la solución, y creerlo. Entonces la vida se organizaría sola y uno ya no se sentiría vacío" (*Conversación en La Catedral*, 1:117).

103. Vargas Llosa, *Conversation in the Cathedral* 1:139. I modified the translation slightly .

104. Ibid., 139.

105. Mary E. Davis, "La elección del fracaso: Vargas Llosa y William Faulkner," 42.

106. William Faulkner, *Absalom, Absalom!* (New York: Vintage, 1936c, 1987), 424. There are also, in Vargas Llosa's novel, resonances with a character from *Les Misérables*. Marius is an orphan who rejects his bourgeois grandfather and prefers poverty to his family's money, which he considers responsible for the human misery that only a revolutionary change can rectify.

107. "Tell me about the south. What's it like there. Why do they live there. Why do they live at all" (*Absalom, Absalom!* 218).

108. Vargas Llosa, *Conversation in the Cathedral*, 261.

109. In *Aventurera* (1946), a film by Alberto Gout, a son discovers that his mother whose reputation and social status appear impeccable is leading a double life. She is the madam of a brothel and she functions brutally in a world of criminals and assassins who obey her.

110. Vargas Llosa, *Conversation in the Cathedral*, 143.

111. Ibid., 52.

112. Ibid., 353.

113. Ibid., 156.

114. Ibid., 598. "[Y]ou're not your papa, son."

115. Vargas Llosa, Ibid., 3. Translation slightly modified.

116. Vargas Llosa, Ibid., 601.

117. Vargas Llosa in Harss and Dohmann, *Into the Mainstream*, 352.

118. Victor Hugo, *Les Miserables* (Philadelphia: University LIbrary Association, n.d.). The first part of the quote is on p. 125, the second on p. 124.

119. Hugo, *Les Misérables*, 379.

120. *Les miserables*, 42.

121. Ibid., 156.

122. *The Time of the Hero*, 23.

123. Vargas Llosa, in Harss and Dohmann, *Into the Mainstream* 351.

124. Rolf Kloepfer and Klaus Zimmermann are right when they point out that the Peruvian world represented in Vargas Llosa's first novels is not one where individuals express their free will: "It is rather a world in which individuals do not determine or alter the historical situation" (Rolf Kloepfer and Klaus Zimmermann, "Mario Vargas Llosa," in *Lateinamerikanishche Literatur der Gegenwart,* ed. Wolfgang Eitel (Stuttgart: Alfred Kröner Verlad, 1978), 478.

125. Sebastián Salazar Bondy, "Mario Vargas Llosa y un mundo de rebeldes," *El Comercio* (Lima), October 4, 1959, 5.

126. Sebastián Salazar Bondy, letter to Mario Vargas Llosa, July 6, 1962, Correspondence, box 1, folder 23, Mario Vargas Llosa Collection, Firestone Library, Princeton University.

127. Mario Benedetti, "Vargas Llosa y su fértil escándalo," in *Letras del continente mestizo* (Montevideo: Arca 1967), 183.

128. Benedetti, "Vargas Llosa y su fertil escándalo," 201.

129. Jean Franco, "Lectura de *Conversación en La Catedral,*" *Revista Iberoamericana* 37, nos. 76, 77 (July–December 1971): 766.

130. Franco, "Lectura de *Conversación en La Catedral,*" 767.

131. Ibid., 764.

132. Ariel Dorfman ("Mario Vargas Llosa y José María Arguedas: Dos visiones de una sola América," *Casa de las Américas* [Havana] 11, no. 64 [1971]: 18) states that "Vargas Llosa breaks myths, breaks conventions, makes the reader uncomfortable; Arguedas constructs myths." For Dorfman, *Todas las sangres,* Arguedas's most political novel, is a presage of the Latin American revolution: "A situation exactly like that in *Todas las sangres* has not occurred and will not occur, although the novel may well be imitating the structure of the entire situation of Latin America: the liberation of the oppressed peoples by means of revolutionary action" (14).

133. "The only positive person in the novel is Lieutenant Gamboa; he is the most human of the characters, paradoxically, because he submits voluntarily and decidedly to an inhuman discipline" (Washington Delgado, "Mario Vargas Llosa. La ciudad y los perros," *Letras* (Lima) 36, nos. 72, 73 [1964]: 314). Joseph Sommers uses Delgado's argument to suggest that Vargas Llosa secretly admires the authoritative military order. Cf. Joseph Sommers, "Literatura e ideología: la evaluación novelística del militarismo en Vargas Llosa," *Hispamérica* 4, no. 1 (1975): 118–129.

134. Jorge Lafforgue, "*La ciudad y los perros,* Novela moral," *Nueva novela latinoamericana* (Buenos Aires: Paidós, 1969), 123. The title of Lafforgue's essay borrows an idea from Delgado: "*La ciudad y los perros* . . . is fundamentally a novel of moral problems" ("Mario Vargas Llosa, *La ciudad y los perros,*" 313).

135. Lafforgue's article contains a "post-script" in which he indicates that his essay was written before he was aware that important critics of the left, such as Angel Rama, considered Vargas Llosa to be a progressive novelist. Lafforgue may be referring to Rama's reviews of *La ciudad y los perros* (*Marcha,* February 21, 1966, 29–39) and of *La Casa Verde* (*Marcha,* August 13, 1966, 30–31) where he celebrates the leftist optimism implicit in novels that bitterly criticize the status quo.

Chapter 3

1. Vargas Llosa, *The Real Life of Alejandro Mayta*, trans. Alfred MacAdam (New York: Farrar, Straus & Giroux, 1986), 298.

2. In an interview Vargas Llosa recalls the conversation with Alejo Carpentier in which he rejected the Cuban proposition: "[Carpentier] showed me a letter by Haydée Santamaría [editor of the Cuban literary journal *Casa de las Américas*]. The letter was probably not written by her, it was just not her style. . . . I told Carpentier: 'How can Haydée make such a proposition? It offends me greatly. If they tell me: 'Donate the prize,' I will decide whether I donate it or not. But don't tell me: 'Go through the farce of donating the prize because you will not lose anything, you will keep the money.' This is not how one treats a writer who has self-respect" (Ricardo A. Setti, . . . *sobre la vida y la política: Diálogo con Vargas Llosa* (Buenos Aires: Intermundo, 1989), 148–149.

3. "La literatura es fuego," in *Contra viento y marea*, vol. 1 (1962–1972) (Barcelona: Seix Barral, 1986), 179.

4. Vargas Llosa, "La censura en la URSS y Alexander Solzhenitsin," in *Contra viento y marea*, 1 (1962–1972): 192, 193, 189.

5. Vargas Llosa, "El socialismo y los tanques," in *Contra viento y marea*, 1 (1962–1972): 219.

6. Oscar Collazos, Julio Cortázar, and Mario Vargas Llosa, *Literatura en la revolución y revolución en la literatura* (Mexico City: Siglo XXI, 1970), 102.

7. Ibid., 20.

8. A transcript of the round-table conference in which Roberto Fernández Retamar participated, "Diez años de Revolución: El intelectual y la sociedad," was published in the journal *Casa de las Américas* 10, no. 56 (1969): 7–52.

9. This letter was published in *Le Monde* (Paris), April 9, 1971, 32. For a detailed account of the "Padilla case" consult Seymour Menton, *Prose Fiction of the Cuban Revolution* (Austin: University of Texas Press, 1975). See also Lourdes Casal (ed.), *El Caso Padilla* (Miami: Ediciones Universal, 1971).

10. Heberto Padilla, "Intervención en la unión de escritores y artistas de Cuba el martes 27 de abril de 1971," *Casa de las Américas* 10, nos. 65–66 (1971): 191–192.

11. Vargas Llosa, "Carta a Fidel Castro," in *Contra viento y marea*, 1 (1962–1972): 250–51.

12. *Casa de las Américas* 11, nos. 65, 66, (March–June 1971): 27–28.

13. Vargas Llosa, "Letter to Haydée Santamaría," in *Making Waves* (New York: Farrar, Strauss & Giroux, 1996), 105.

14. Haydée Santamaría, "Respuesta a Mario Vargas Llosa," published as an unnumbered supplement to *Casa de las Américas* 11, nos. 65–66 (1971). The letter is published again in the following issue of *Casa de las Américas* 11, no. 67 (1971): 140–142.

15. Cf. *Casa de las Américas* 11, no. 67 (1971): 145.

16. Juan Marinello's text appears in *Casa de las Américas* 11, no. 68 (1971): 45.

17. Mario Benedetti, "Las prioridades del escritor," *Casa de las Américas* 12, no. 68 (1971): 75.

18. Carlos Rincón, "Para un plano de batalla de combate por una nueva crítica literaria en Latinoamérica," *Casa de las Américas* 11, no. 67 (1971): 57, 46, 45, 47.

19. Rincón, "Para un plano de batalla," 48.

20. Ibid, 55.

21. Ibid, 55.

22. Ibid, 59.

23. "The *nouveau Roman*. A movement Vargas Llosa has treated tenaciously, as a way of marking his own development . . . but with which his work shares many structural and technical similarities, despite the difference of the goals for each type of writing" (Rincón, "Para un plano de batalla," 51); "The definition of Lukács' esthetic are no different than those of the bourgeois esthetic," (53).

24. Rincón, "Para un plano de batalla," 39.

25. Ibid., 59.

26. "Es überraschte den Autor nicht, daß die herrsechenden Kreise seinen Roman [*La ciudad y los perros*] durch einen öffentlichen Skandal zu diskreditieren suchten. Vargas Llosa hatte mit diesem Roman der peruanischen Wirklichkeit jeden falschen Schein genommen und von einem konsequent antioligarchischen Standpunkt aus in der Erziehungsanstalt Leoncio Prado das Abbild eines Peru der strengsten Klassenhierarchie, der militärischesn Mythologie un des moralischen Verfalls gestaltet. Vargas Llosa, der die Lektüre Flauberts, Tolstois un Sartres zu seinen entscheidene Bildungserlebnissen rechnet, hat in dieser Geschichte eigene Jugenderfahrungen verarbeitet." My translation of the German, from Gisela Leber and Carlos Rincón, "Einige Grundzüge des Lateinamerikanisches Roman der Gegenwart," ed. Werner Bahner *Zur Gegenwartsliteratur in den romanischen Ländern: Studien und Berichte 1/2* (Berlin: Akademie-Verlag, 1968), 71.

27. "Die Gewalt des Stoffes über den Leser hat Vargas Llosa durch eine Vielzahl literarischer Techniken innerhalb des Buches zu vermitteln versucht. . . . Mit der Gewalt seiner einfachen Lebensschicksale hat Vargas Llosa das nationale Gewicht der peruanischen Volksklassen aufgespürt. Er hat sie der Anonymität entrissen, als positive Kraft dargestellt und in die Weltliteratur eingegliedert. Die Frage nach der Perspektive dieser Gesellschaft durchzieht einen Roman wie "Das grüne Haus" völlig" (Gisela Leber and Carlos Rincón "Grundzüge des Lateinamerikanischen Roman der Gegenwart," 73).

28. "Wenn der sozialkritische Roman der 30er Jahre vor allem durch sein politisches und soziales Pathos überzeugte, so gestalten ein Carpentier, Fuentes, Rulfo, oder Vargas Llosa in ihren Werken ein vertieftes Gesellschaftsbild, das von der Durchdringung kollektiver sozialer und moralischer Normen in ihrem historischen Prozeß getragen wird. . . . Für diese .Romanliteratur, die zu einer immer tieferen Erfassung der Wirklichkeit fortschreitet, verbietet sich eine Wertung, die auf dem Gegensatz von Erzählen und Beschreiben beruht, den Lukács fixiert, um den realistischen Roman vom naturalistischen zu unterscheiden" (Gisela Leber and Carlos Rincón "Grundzüge des Lateinamerikanischen Roman der Gegenwart," 60).

29. Vargas Llosa's declaration was published in an issue of *Cuadernos de Marcha* 49 (May 1971): 20, dedicated to the discussion of the Padilla case and of Cuban's new cultural policies. Vargas Llosa repeated his defense of Cuba in other published statements and interviews including "Entrevista exclusiva a Vargas Llosa (por César Hildebrandt)" published in *Caretas* and reappearing in *Contra viento y marea,* 1 (1962–1972): 169–173. "I have not done anything other than protest against those events that contradict that which I have always admired in the Cuban Revolution: it showed that social justice is possible without disparaging the dignity of individuals, without political or esthetic dictatorship. I think that what has happened in these last weeks damages the exemplary image of Cuba and has evoked energetic protests around the world. I speak only, of course, of the protests of the left such as the letter to Fidel by 61 writers and artists—Sartre and José Revueltas among them, whom no one would dare call reactionaries, and who have made the revolution their cause from the first moment of the Cuban Revolution," 254.

30. Santamaría, "Respuesta a Mario Vargas Llosa," 141.

31. Vargas Llosa, "Entrevista exclusiva a Vargas Llosa (por César hildebrant)," in *Contra viento y marea,* 1 (1962–1972): 255. Originally published in *Caretas* June 1971.

32. Angel Rama, "El fin de los demonios," *Marcha,* July 28, 1972, 30.

33. Ibid., 30.

34. Ibid., 30.

35. José Miguel Oviedo, *Mario Vargas Llosa: La invención de una realidad* (Barcelona: Seix Barral, 1982), 346.

36. Cornejo Polar, *La novela peruana* (Lima: Horizonte, 1989), 272.

37. Ibid., 270–271.

38. Ibid., 272.

39. Mirko Lauer, *El sitio de la literatura: Escritores y política en el Perú del siglo XX* (Lima: Mosca Azul, 1989), 110.

40. Ibid., 111.

41. Ibid., 116.

42. Ibid., 99–100.

43. Jorge Edwards, *Persona Non Grata: An Envoy in Castro's Cuba,* trans. Colin Harding (New York: Pomerica Press, 1976), 152–153.

44. Edwards, *Persona Non Grata,* 167.

45. Vargas Llosa, "Un francotirador tranquilo," in *Contra viento and marea,* 1:289.

46. Ibid., 298–299.

47. Vargas Llosa, *The Perpetual Orgy: Flaubert and Madame Bovary,* trans. Helen Lane. (New York: Farrar, Straus & Giroux, 1986), 43.

48. Vargas Llosa, *The Perpetual Orgy,* 13–14.

49. Ibid., 89–90.

50. Ibid., 88.

51. Ibid., 126.

52. Ibid., 232.

53. Ibid., 230–231.

54. Ciro Alegría, José María Arguedas, et al. *Primer encuentro de narradores peruanos* (Lima: Latinoamericana Editores, 1986), 164.

55. Vargas Llosa, *The Perpetual Orgy* 231.

56. Ibid., 32. In *The Perpetual Orgy* there remain vestiges of views he would soon abandon about literature as a rebellious act against a given society, or a given historical period: "[Literature is] at once a cause and an effect of human dissatisfaction, an occupation thanks to which a man in conflict with the world finds a way of living that suits him, a creation that examines, questions, profoundly undermines the certainties of an era" (*The Perpetual Orgy,* 239).

57. Letter by Flaubert quoted in *The Perpetual Orgy,* 236.

58. Vargas Llosa, *The Perpetual Orgy* 36.

59. Vargas Llosa, *Captain Pantoja and the Special Service,* trans. Gregory Kolovakos and Ronald Christ (New York: Harper & Row, 1978), 104.

60. José Miguel Oviedo, *Mario Vargas Llosa,* 127.

61. "I used the acotaciones to present all necessary description in the novel" (*A Writer's Reality* [Syracuse, N.Y.: Syracuse University Press, 1991], 96). Note that Vargas Llosa uses the Spanish "acotaciones" to refer to the annotations that accompany dialogue in the narrative.

62. Vargas Llosa, *Captain Pantoja and the Special Service,* 184.

63. Ibid., 133, 116, 122.

64. The first draft of the novel can be found in Notebook [E-1], box 3, folder 3 of the Mario Vargas Llosa Papers at Princeton University's Firestone Library. According to a note in Vargas Llosa's handwriting he used the notebook between 1971 and 1972.

65. The rough drafts can be consulted at the Mario Vargas Llosa Collection in Princeton University's Firestone Library.

66. Vargas Llosa, *Captain Pantoja and the Special Service,* 53. Brother Francisco appears for the first time in a draft of 1973 (Mario Vargas Llosa Archive, Firestone Library, Notebook [E-4], box 3, folder 6.) and was therefore conceived after Vargas Llosa's first reading of da Cunha's *Rebellion in the Backlands.*

67. Vargas Llosa, *Captain Pantoja and the Special Service,* 152.

68. Vargas Llosa, *The Storyteller,* trans. by Helen Lane (New York: Farrar, Straus & Giroux, 1989), 184.

69. William Faulkner, *Light in August,* (New York: Random House, 1932c, 1972), 434.

70. Ibid., 428.

71. Ibid., 432.

72. Martín de Riquer and Mario Vargas Llosa, *El combate imaginario: Las cartas de batalla de Joanot Martorell* (Barcelona: Barral, 1972).

73. "Per ço que tal maldat e deslealtat per vós feta no romanga a sens punició, si lo contrari del dessús dit per vós és negat, yo a tota ma requesta, . . . vos offir combatre a tota ultrança, mon cors contra lo vostre" (Riquer and Vargas Llosa, *El combate imaginario,* 40).

74. Vargas Llosa, *Captain Pantoja and the Special Service*, 124.

75. Ibid., 243.

76. Ibid., 1.

77. Gustave Flaubert, *The Temptation of Saint Anthony*, trans. Kitty Mrosovsky (Ithaca, N.Y.: Cornell University Press, 1981), 223.

78. Vargas Llosa had expressed his admiration for *The Temptation of Saint Anthony* years before writing *The Perpetual Orgy*. Cf. "*La tentación de San Antonio* en el teatro," *Caretas*, no. 353, May 29–June 9, 1967, 37–38.

79. Mario Vargas Llosa Papers, Notebooks, [E-1] box 3, folder 3, Firestone Library, Princeton University.

80. Taking the novel as a version of their courtship and marriage, Ms. Urquidi Illánez wrote a book to present her side of the story: *Lo que Varguitas no dijo* (La Paz: Khana Cruz, 1983). She points out many exaggerations and fabrications and is unhappy that her role in assisting Vargas Llosa's literary career is not adequately treated. As Sara Castro-Klarén has pointed out, Ms. Urquidi Illánez did not appreciate *Aunt Julia and the Scriptwriter*'s "daring mix of chronicle, mock autobiography, realistic novel, and parody of the sentimental Romance" (*Understanding Mario Vargas Llosa*, 161).

81. José Miguel Oviedo, "Entrevista con Mario Vargas Llosa," in *Espejo de escritores*, ed. Reina Roffé (Hanover, N.H.: Ediciones del Norte, 1985), 156–157.

82. Vargas Llosa, "*Los Miserables*: El último clásico," *Cielo Abierto* (Lima) 8, no. 23 (January–March 1983).

83. Joanot Martorell and Martí Joan de Galba, *Tirant lo Blanc* vol. 2, (Madrid: Alianza Editorial, 1984), chap. 258, 600.

84. Vargas Llosa, *Aunt Julia and the Scriptwriter*, trans. Helen R. Lane (New York, Farrar, Straus & Giroux, 1982), 161.

85. "In preparing to write *Aunt Julia and the Scriptwriter*, I did not listen to soap operas. For ideas I did not need to hear or watch soap operas, but only to look inside myself. As a writer one of my problems is that I have many projects and not enough time to have them all materialize. I know that I will never have enough time to write all the stories I want to write. In addition, I have always had a secret perversion—a fascination with melodrama, grotesque stories of adventure, the distortion of reality that melodrama represents. I am deeply sensitive to this literary perversion. And so in this novel I found a way to solve both problems. I used several of my projects, any one of which could have become a novel, for the stories in *Aunt Julia*, using Pedro Camacho as a pretext for a melodramatic style" (*A Writer's Reality*, 119–120).

86. Marie-Madeleine Gladieu, *Mario Vargas Llosa* (Paris: L'Harmattan, 1989), 33–36.

87. Vargas Llosa, *Aunt Julia and the Scriptwriter*, 129.

88. Ibid., 99.

89. Ibid., 69.

90. Ibid., 127.

91. Ibid., 55.

92. Ibid., 85.

93. Gustave Flaubert, *Sentimental Education*, trans and with and introduction by Robert Baldrick (Harmondsworth, Middlesex, England: Penguin, 1964), 416.

94. Vargas Llosa, *Aunt Julia and the Scriptwriter*, 360.

95. Ibid., 159.

96. Ibid., 372.

97. Ibid., 368.

98. Ibid., 6–7.

99. Ibid., 343.

Chapter 4

1. See chapter 3, 69–81.

2. Ricardo A. Setti, . . . *sobre la vida y la política: Diálogo con Vargas Llosa* (Buenos Aires: Intermundo, 1989), 143–144.

3. "The only legitimate manner to criticize the 'errors' of socialism, the 'deficiencies' of Marxism, the 'dogmatism' of the Communist Party, is to first affirm total solidarity with those who—the USSR, the Marxist philosophy, the pro-Soviet parties—incarnate the cause of progress in spite of everything" (Vargas Llosa, "Prologo a *Entre Sartre y Camus*," in *Contra viento y marea*, vol. 1 (1962–1972) (Barcelona: Seix Barral, 1983), 13.

4. Vargas Llosa, "Revisión de Albert Camus," in *Contra viento y marea*, 1 (1962–1972): 20.

5. "Albert Camus y la moral de los límites," in *Contra viento y mare*, 1 (1962–1972): 2l.

6. Ibid., 334. Vargas Llosa is alluding to the following thought by Camus: "Henceforth, violence will be directed against one and all, in the service of an abstract idea" (*The Rebel*, trans. Anthony Bower [New York: Vintage, 1956], 161).

7. "Moreover, it is impossible to understand twentieth-century revolutionary thought if we overlook the fact that unfortunately it derived a large part of its inspiration from a philosophy of conformity and opportunism" (*The Rebel*, 147).

8. "Since nothing is either true or false, good or bad, our guiding principle will be to demonstrate that we are the most efficient—in other words, the strongest" (*The Rebel*, 5). For Camus's criticism of the Leninist ideal of the programmed society, see *The Rebel*, 214.

9. "Revolution consists in loving a man who does not yet exist. But he who loves a living being, if he really loves, can only consent to die for the sake of the being he loves" (*The Rebel*, 96).

10. Albert Camus, "El testigo de la libertad" (*La Gauche*, December 20, 1948); *Moral y política* (Madrid: Alianza, 1978), 139.

11. Albert Camus, *Carnets*, vol. 2 (Madrid: Alianza Editorial, 1985), 283.

12. "Albert Camus y la moral de los límites," in *Contra viento y marea*, 1 (1962–1972): 322–325.

13. See the historical footnote to Popper's *The Poverty of Historicism* (London: Routledge & Kegan Paul, 1957), vii.

14. "Isaiah Berlin: Un heroe de nuestro tiempo," in *Contra viento y marea*, vol. 2 (1972–1983) (Barcelona: Seix Barral, 1986), 263.

15. "Dogmatic revolutionaries easily become oppressive tyrants: this then is common to Sorel and the anarchists. Camus revived it in his polemic with Sartre. Force, by definition represses; violence directed against it, liberates" (Isaiah Berlin, *Against the Current: Essays in the History of Ideas* [New York: Viking, 1980], 321).

16. Albert Camus, "Diálogo en favor del diálogo" (*Défense de l'Homme* [July 1949]; *Moral y política*, 139.

17. Isaiah Berlin, *Vico and Herder: Two Studies in the History of Ideas* (London: Hogarth, 1976), 153.

18. Berlin, *Against the Current*, 74–75

19. Ibid., 248; "So long as one ideal is the true good, it will always seem to men that no means can be too difficult, no price too high, to do whatever is required to realize the ultimate goal. Such certainty is one of the greatest justifications of fanaticism, compulsion, persecution" (*Against the Current*, 78).

20. "Isaiah Berlin: Un héroe de nuestro tiempo," in *Contra viento y marea*, 2 (1972–1983): 265.

21. "The Country of a Thousand Faces," in *Making Waves* (New York: Farrar, Strauss & Giroux, 1996), 14.

22. *Contra viento y marea*, vol. 3 (19764–1988) (Barcelona: Seix Barral, 1990).

23. For example, Jean-François Revel, with the assistance of Branko Lazitch, *How Democracies Perish*, trans. William Byron (New York: Perennial Press, 1985).

24. "The most counterrevolutionary alliance that can possibly exist in the Third World is that of socialism with the past. Taken together, they have the effect of perpetuating economic stagnation while justifying political dictatorships" (Jean-François Revel, *Without Marx or Jesus: The New American Revolution Has Begun*, trans. J. F. Bernard (Garden City, New York: Doubleday, 1971), 68.

25. Ibid., 68, 110.

26. Vargas Llosa's essay on Revel, "La socieda abierta y sus enemigos," can be found in *Contra viento y marea*, 3 (1964–1988): 493–499. Vargas Llosa has recalled the following: "*The Open Society and Its Enemies* had come to my attention in 1980" (Vargas Llosa, "A Fish Out of Water," *Granta* 36 [Summer 1991]: 56).

27. Karl Popper, *The Open Society and its Enemies* (Princeton, N.J.: Princeton University Press, 1962c, 1966), 2:215.

28. "A system is to be considered scientific only if it makes assertions which may clash with observations; and a system is in fact, tested by attempts to produce such clashes, that is to say by attempts to refute it. Thus testability is the same as refutability, and can likewise be taken as a criterion of demarcation" (Popper, *The Open Society*, 2:256).

29. Ibid., 1:57.

30. Karl Popper, *The Poverty of Historicism* (London: Routledge & Kegan Paul, 1957), vii.

31. "That the Utopian method, which chooses an ideal state of society as the aim which all our political actions should serve, is likely to produce violence can be shown thus. Since we cannot determine the ultimate ends of political actions scientifically, or by purely rational methods, differences of opinions concerning what the ideal state should be like cannot always be smoothed out by the method of argument. They will at least partly have the character of religious difference. And there can be no tolerance between these different Utopian religions. Utopian aims are designed to serve as a basis for rational political action and discussions, and such action appears to be possible only if the aim is definitely decided upon. Thus the Utopianist must win over, or else crush, his Utopianist competitors who do not share his own Utopian aims, and who do not profess his own Utopian religion. But he has to do more. He has to be very thorough in eliminating and stamping out all heretical competing views. . . . The use of violent methods for the suppression of competing aims becomes even more urgent if we consider that the period of Utopian construction is liable to be one of social change. . . . What may have appeared to many as desirable at the time when the Utopian blueprint was decided upon may appear less desirable at a later date. . . . The only way to avoid such changes of our aims seems to be to use violence, which includes propaganda, the suppression of criticism, and the annihilation of all opposition" (Karl Popper, "Utopia and Violence," in *Conjectures and Refutations: The Growth of Scientific Knowledge* [London: Routledge & Kegan Paul, 1963], 359–360); and "Only if we give up our authoritarian attitude in the realm of opinion, only if we establish the attitude of give and take, of readiness to learn from other people, can we hope to control acts of violence inspired by piety and duty" ("Utopia and Violence," 356–357).

32. Popper, *The Open Society*, 2:238.

33. Jesús Mosterín, "Entrevista con Karl Popper," *Arbor* 133, no. 522 (June 1989): 32–33. See also Popper, *The Open Society*, 2:234.

34. Mosterín, "Entrevista con Karl Popper," 33

35. Popper, *The Poverty of Historicism*, 155.

36. "La cultura de la libertad," in *Contra viento y marea*, 2 (1972–1983): 433.

37. "Matones en el país de la malaria," in *Contra viento y marea*, 3 (1964–1988): 410.

38. Mario Vargas Llosa, prologue to *The Other Path: The Invisible Revolution in the Third World*, trans. June Abbot (New York: Harper & Row, 1989), xvi; "La revolución silenciosa," in *Contra viento y marea*, 3 (1964–1988): 340–341.

39. José Carlos Mariátegui, *Seven Interpretative Essays on Peruvian Reality*, trans. Marjory Urquidi (Austin: University of Texas Press, 1974), 58, 171.

40. Vargas Llosa, prologue to *The Other Path*. The prologue also appears in *Contra viento y marea*, 3 (1964–1988): 335–348.

41. Vargas Llosa, "Entre la libertad y el miedo," in *Contra viento y marea,* 3 (1964–1988): 484.

42. Lola Díaz, "Entrevista con Mario Vargas Llosa," *Cambio 16,* January 4, 1988, 74, and prologue to foreword to *The Other Path:* "At the same time that the mercantilist system condemns a society to economic impotence and stagnation, it imposes relations between citizens and between citizens and the state that reduce or eradicate the possibility of democratic politics" (xvii).

43. Mario Vargas Llosa, "Carta a Günther Grass," *Vuelta* 117 (August 1986): 59. The letter to Günther Grass also appears in *Contra viento y marea,* 3 (1964–1988): 394–400.

44. "In Latin America, with few exceptions, our intellectuals continue to practice moral paralysis which consists of condemning the iniquities of military dictatorships and the abuses of democratic states while keeping an ominous silence when the perpetrators are socialist regimes" (*Vuelta* 117 [1986]: 58); and "For reasons at times noble and at times ignoble—the fear of being unfairly labeled as reactionary, for example—many Latin American intellectuals have aided in the collapse of our democratic experiments" (*Vuelta* 117 [1986] 59).

45. Vargas Llosa, "Entre tocayos," *Contra viento y marea,* 2 (1972–1983): 409.

46. Ibid., 410.

47. Vargas Llosa, *Vuelta* 117 (1986): 60.

48. Vargas Llosa published "A Fish Out of Water," a testimony of his political experiences, in *Granta* 36 (Summer 1991): 15–75 which grew into a major book, *A Fish in the Water* (New York: Penguin, 1995). Alvaro Vargas Llosa, his son and spokesman for the campaign, wrote an account of the electoral campaign. Cf. *El diablo en campaña* (Madrid: Ediciones El País, 1991).

49. Vargas Llosa, *Acción para el cambio* (Lima: Industrial, 1989), 18.

50. Ibid., 9.

51. Vargas Llosa, "A Fish Out of Water," 56.

52. Vargas Llosa, "La cultura de la libertad," in Mario Vargas Llosa et al., *Libertad: Primer ciclo de conferencia* (Lima: Pro-Desarrollo, 1988), xlii.

53. Vargas Llosa, "La cultura de la libertad," xxxix.

54. Vargas Llosa, "Hacia un gran cambio," in *Libertad: Primer ciclo de conferencias,* lxxxvi.

55. Vargas Llosa, "Mensaje al país," in *Libertad: Primer ciclo de conferencias,* xxiii.

56. Ibid., xxv.

57. Vargas Llosa, "Isaiah Berlin: A Hero of Our Time," in *Making Waves,* 147.

58. "Men are different from animals in that they observe laws, but laws are ambiguous. They observe them, but they also violate them" (Bataille, *La littérature et le mal* (Paris: Gallimard, 1957), 157. This text does not appear in the English translation.

59. Bataille, *Literature and Evil,* trans. Alastair Hamilton (New York: Marion Boyars, 1985), 29.

60. "Bataille or the Redemption of Evil, in *Making Waves,* 118.

61. "We do not take pleasure in evil except to the extent that it is indecent" (Bataille, *La littérature et le mal,* 197; this is another note that is not translated in the English version).

62. *Literature and Evil,* ix.

63. Setti, . . . *sobre la vida y la politica,* 117.

64. "The Truth of Lies," in *Making Waves,* 327.

65. Karl Popper, *Realism and the Aim of Science* (Totowa, N.J.: Rowman & Littlefield, 1983), 27.

66. Popper opposes the irrationalist position to his "belief in the authority of objective truth indispensable for a free society based on mutual respect" (*Conjectures and Refutations,* 375) because "The irrationalist insists that emotions and passions rather than reason are the mainsprings of human action" (*The Open Society,* 2:233).

67. Popper, *The Open Society,* 2:234.

68. Ibid., 2:235.

69. Popper asserts that irrationalism is an "intellectual misunderstanding" when it is assumed to be in opposition to dogmatism or authoritarianism (*Conjectures and Refutations,* 375).

70. Popper, *The Open Society,* 2:232.

71. Ibid., 2:240.

72. From "Vargas Llosa habla de su nueva novela," an interview conducted by José Miguel Oviedo in *Mario Vargas Llosa,* ed. José Miguel Oviedo (Madrid, Taurus), 314.

73. "El teatro como ficción," in *Kathie y el hipopótamo* (Barcelona: Seix Barral, 1983), 10; see also "Un escritor y sus demonios," *La nación* (Buenos Aires), May 12, 1985, section 4d 1.

74. Mario Vargas Llosa, *La verdad de las mentiras* (Barcelona: Seix Barral: 1990), 22.

75. Ibid.

76. Ibid., 85.

77. Vargas Llosa, *A Writer's Reality* (Syracuse, N.Y.: Syracuse University Press, 1991), 3.

78. Ibid., 10.

79. Ibid.

80. Ibid., 16.

81. Mario Vargas Llosa, "*Los miserables*: El último clásico," *Cielo Abierto* (Lima) 7, nos. 23 (January–March 1983): 33.

82. Ibid., 33.

83. Ibid., 40.

84. These are ideas that Vargas Llosa has expressed in an article on Karl Popper in which he says that real history defies the rational and intellectual intentions of comprehension" ("Historia y novela," *El país* (Opinión 11), April 1, 1991.

Chapter 5

1. José Miguel Oviedo, *Mario Vargas Llosa: La invención de una realidad* (Barcelona: Editorial Seix Barral, 1982), 333.

2. I am quoting Notebook [B-4], box 1, folder 8, of the Mario Vargas Llosa Papers, Firestone Library, Princeton University.

3. In "War Dogs" Epaminondas was the owner of the ranch.

4. "Vargas Llosa habla de su nueva novela," *Mario Vargas Llosa*, ed. José Miguel Oviedo, (Madrid: Taurus Ediciones, 1981), 309.

5. Leopoldo Bernucci, *Historia de un malentendido: Un estudio transtextual de* La guerra del fin del mundo *de Mario Vargas Llosa* (New York: Peter Lang, 1989), 24.

6. Bernucci makes a series of observations (*Historia de un malentendido: Un estudio transtextual de La guerra del fin del mundo de Mario Vargas Llosa* [New York: Peter Lang. 1989]), in which he insists that the reading of *The War of the End of the World* supposes, in the reader, a previous knowledge of *Rebellion in the Backlands*. For example, he asserts that "The disposition of the episodes and the temporal structure that Vargas Llosa adopts for his work cannot be totally understood without taking into account the book by the Brazilian author" (219); and "Observe the narration *in media res* in the opening of the novel and the absence of the name of the counselor in the phrase 'the man was tall and so skinny that he always appeared in profile' which supposes immediately the existence of a character that is not given by the novel but rather by the previous text" (24).

7. Angel Rama, "*La guerra del fin del mundo:* Una obra maestra del fanatismo artístico," *Eco* 246 (1982): 604.

8. Euclides da Cunha, *Rebellion in the Backlands*, trans. with an introduction by Samuel Putnam (Chicago: The University of Chicago Press, 1944), xxix.

9. Cf. Dain Borges, "'Puffy, Ugly, Slotheful, and Inferior': Degeneration in Brazilian Social Thought 1880–1940," *Journal of Latin American Studies* 25 (1993): 235–256.

10. Da Cunha considers both Antonio the Counselor and Moreira César to be suffering from psychologial pathologies. The following is his assessment of the Counselor: "'Indifferent paranoiac' is, possibly, an expression that is not wholly applicable to him. With an insane temperament marked by an obvious ideational retrogression, he was, certainly, a notable case of intellectual degenerescence" (*Rebellion in the Backlands,* 120). And he argues that Moreira César is an unbalanced individual prone either to heroism or to criminality, 233–324.

11. For the links between the individual and the social pathology in *Rebellion in the Backlands,* see Dain Borges, "El reverso fatal de los acontecimientos: dos momentos de degeneración en la literatura brasileña," in *La voluntad de humanismo: Homenaje a Juan Marichal,* ed. B. Ciplijauskaité and C. Maurer (Barcelona: Anthropos, 1990), pp.121–133. See especially 125–126.

12. Da Cunha, *Rebellion in the Backlands,* 280.

13. "It was the very core of our nationality, the bedrock of our race, which our troops were attacking" (da Cunha, *Rebellion in the Backlands,* 464).

14. In *Myth and Archive,* a major statement on the origins of the Latin American narrative, Roberto González Echevarría has persuasively argued that *Rebellion in the Backlands* "exceeds the scope of the prosaic positivistic doctrine that guides [Euclides da Cunha]" (*Myth and Archive: A Theory of Latin American Narrative* [Cambridge: Cambridge University Press, 1990, 126]. Swerving from da Cunha, Vargas Llosa made it a point to avoid references to any positivist doctrine in crafting his version of the Canudos events.

15. Ibid., 192.

16. See Christine Arkinstall, "La guerra del fin del mundo: unas prot(o)gonistas olvidadas," *Antipodas* 1 (December 1988): 105–113.

17. Vargas Llosa, *The War of the End of the World,* trans. Helen R. Lane (New York: Avon Books, 1985), 22.

18. Ibid., 14.

19. Ibid., 48.

20. Ibid., 231–232.

21. See Arkinstall, "La guerra del fin del mundo," 108.

22. Vargas Llosa, *The War of the End of the World,* 129.

23. Ibid., 137.

24. Ibid., 145.

25. Ibid., 379.

26. Ibid., 380.

27. Ibid., 415.

28. Tolstoy, *War and Peace,* trans. with an introduction by Rosemary Edmonds (Harmondsworth, Middlesex, England: Penguin, 1957), 1:357.

29. Tolstoy, *War and Peace* 2:1168, and 1:512.

30. Ibid., 2:1162.

31. Isaac Berlin, *Russian Thinkers* (London: Penguin, 1979), 73.

32. Tolstoy, *War and Peace,* 2:1286–1287.

33. Berlin, *Russian Thinkers,* 76.

34. Ibid., 81.

35. Vargas Llosa, "Isaiah Berlin, un heroe de nuestro tiempo," in *Contra viento and marea,* 2 (1972–1983): 261.

36. "Vargas Llosa schreibt weder gegen eine bestimmte Geschichtsphilosophie (etwa die von da Cunha) noch für eine andere. Er schreibt ihn gegen Geschichtsphilosophie *als solche*" (Thomas M. Scheerer, *Mario Vargas Llosa, Leben und Werk: Eine Einführung* [Frankfurt: Suhrkamp, 1991], 119).

37. Rama, "*La guerra del fin del mundo*: Una obra maestra del fanatismo artístico," 638.

38. Vargas Llosa, *The War of the End of the World,* 568.

39. Ibid., 455.

40. The newspaper articles Vargas Llosa used are to be found under the entry "Historia de Mayta" in the Vargas Llosa Papers at Princeton. The names of Vallejos

and Mayta appear, for instance, in an article in the Lima newspaper *La prensa*, May 31, 1962.

41. In Spanish the headline reads, "Golpe encaja en plan fidelista" (*Ultima hora*, May 30, 1962).

42. Cf. José Miguel Oviedo, "*Historia de Mayta* (Una reflexión política en forma de novela)," *Atenea* 457, 1988; and Antonio Cornejo Polar, "Historia de Mayta," *La novela peruana* (Lima: Editorial Horizonte, 1989).

43. Salman Rushdie, "The Real Life of Alejandro Mayta," *Imaginary Homelands: Essays and Criticism 1981–1991*. (London: Granta Books, 1991), 314.

44. Cornejo Polar, "Historia de Mayta," 250.

45. "It was not for money that this man who was the first to pass was coming to kill those upstairs who were still alive, it was for an idea, for a faith" (André Malraux, *Man's Fate*, trans. Haakon M. Chevalier [New York: Modern Library (1934) 1961], 292). And the assassin of a minister in *Under Western Eyes* justifies his act in the name of his ideals: "This is not murder—it is war, war. My spirit shall go on warring in some Russian body till all falsehood is swept out of the world" (*Under Western Eyes* [London: Penguin, 1989], 69.

46. Conrad, *Under Western Eyes*, 273. See also 118–119.

47. Ibid., 127; Razumov also criticizes "the dream-intoxication of the idealist incapable of perceiving the reason of things, and the true character of men. It was a sort of terrible childishness" (77).

48. "I truthfully do not know why Mayta's story intrigues and disturbs me" (*The Real Life of Alejandro Mayta*, trans. Alfred MacAdam [New York: Farrar, Straus & Giroux, 1986], 44).

49. Ibid., 67.

50. Ibid., 287. The narrator echoes Vargas Llosa's ideas about literary creation as they have appeared in essays and interviews. His novel can be read as a fictional exemplification of those ideas. See, for instance, the chapter devoted to *Mayta* in *A Writer's Reality* where he quotes the narrator of the novel to underscore his own literary intentions: "To be persuasive as a novelist in most cases you are obliged to transform, to distort reality, to lie, to invent something that is not true—that is the only way fiction can be persuasive. I did so not to be objective, exact, truthful to reality, but, as the narrator of Mayta's story says: 'Para mentir con conocimiento de causa.' I do not like the translation of this phrase into English as it appears in the novel. What it really means is that one lies or distorts knowing that one is distorting" ([Syracuse, N. Y.: Syracuse University Press, 1995], 151).

51. Vargas Llosa, *The Real Life of Alejandro Mayta* 276.

52. Ibid., 288.

53. Oviedo, "*Historia de Mayta* (Una reflexión política en forma de novela)," 172.

54. See for instance, *The Real Life of Alejandro Mayta*, 26, 35, 58.

55. Ibid., 200–201.

56. The narrator reflects about "how mysterious and unforeseeable the ramifications of events are, the unbelievably complex web of causes and effects, reverberations

and accidents that make up human history" (165). *The Real Life of Alejandro Mayta* is a close relative of Conrad's *Under Western Eyes,* where a character observes: "Events started by human folly link themselves into a sequence which no sagacity can foresee and no courage can break through" (*Under Western Eyes),* 118.

57. Vargas Llosa, *The Real Life of Alejandro Mayta,* 82.

58. In this case I prefer my own translation of "Mayta: su cara aparece y desaparece, es un fuego fatuo" (*Historia de Mayta),* 90.

59. Vargas Llosa, *The Real Life of Alejandro Mayta,* 14.

60. See for example Ibid., 243–44 and 254.

61. See for example Ibid., 22, 39, 63.

62. Ibid., 154.

63. Ibid., 273.

64. "Sometimes among moralists and novelists one finds the mystery of ideological crystallization portrayed in all of its awesome plenitude. It is hardly necessary to mention certain well-known classic works on the subject—the story of the Grand Inquisitor in Dostoevsky's *Brother's Karamozov,* or *The Possessed.* There are also some precious insights to be found in the 'Genealogy of Fanaticism' in Emil Cioran's *Précis de décomposition* and in his *Histoire et Utopie.* Or again, in Mario Vargas Llosa's *The Story of Mayta,* the superb, stifling portrayal of the birth and growth of a terrorist ideology in a certain group. The novelist makes us relive from within a concrete case of a delirious and at the same time carefully reasoned vision, experienced and above all translated into acts by specific individuals. It could be the story of the founders of the Peruvian 'Shining Path' movement, those professors of Maoist philosophy who (like the Khmer Rouge of Cambodia) are persuaded that they have the right to kill all those who oppose their plans" (Jean-François Revel, *The Flight from Truth: The Reign of Deceit in the Age of Information,* trans. Curtis Cate [New York: Random House, 1991]), 167.

65. In Paris he remembers having been "with a group of café revolutionaries" (*The Real Life of Alejandro Mayta,* 128).

66. Ibid., 128.

67. Ibid., 299.

68. André Malraux, *Man's Fate,* 355.

69. "El terroristmo en Ayacucho," in *Contra viento y marea,* vol. 3 (1964–1988) (Barcelona: Seix Barral, 1990), 131.

70. See "Informe sobre Uchuraccay," in *Contra viento y marea,* 3 (1964–1988): 123.

71. Cf. The three articles by Vargas Llosa appear in "El periodismo como contrabando," in *Contra viento y marea,* 3 (1964–1988): 193–198, "Respuesta a Bo Lindblom," 211–214, and "Contra los estereotipos," 215–219.

72. Roy Boland, "Demonias y lectores: Génesis y reescritura de ¿Quién mató a Palomino Molero?" *Antipodas* 1 (December) 1988, 160–182.

73. See Vargas Llosa's article "Updating Karl Popper," *PMLA* 105 (1990): 1018–1025.

74. Popper argues that the concept of truth is provisional. A theory that attempts

to solve a problem, if it is the best available theory, counts as truth "until, all of a sudden, another theory emerges, 'falsifying' the previous one, and what seemed the firm consistency of the predecessor crumbles like a castle of cards in a gale" ("Updating Popper," 1018).

75. *Who Killed Palomino Molero*, 86.

76. Vargas Llosa, *The Green House*, trans. Gregory Rabassa (New York: Harper & Row, 1968), 232.

77. Vargas Llosa, *Who Killed Palomino Molero?* (New York: Farrar, Straus & Giroux, 1987), 13.

78. Ibid., 38.

79. Ibid., 54.

80. Ibid., 63.

81. Ibid., 86.

82. Ibid., 105.

83. Ibid., 110.

84. Ibid.

85. Ibid., 112.

86. Ibid., 123.

87. The story of a Massacre," in *Making Waves* (New York: Farrar, Strauss & Giroux, 1996), p. 197.

88. Vargas Llosa, *Who Killed Palomino Molero?*, 128

89. Vargas Llosa, "El nacimiento del Perú," in *Contra viento y marea*, 3 (1964–1988): 377.

90 Vargas Llosa, "Crónica de un viaje a la selva," *Cultura peruana* 123, no page numbers.

91. Vargas Llosa, "The Story of a Massacre," in *Making Waves*, 197. Under the title "Sangre y mugre en Uchuraccay," Vargas Llosa dedicates an important section of the third volume of *Contra viento y marea* to this matter that marked and disturbed him because of the atrocity of the event and because of the accusations that he suffered, like this one from Mirko Lauer: "More dead, fewer dead, is a dynamic similar to that of the lightning-quick investigation of the massacre of Uchuraccay, after his fleeting presence in the place where the journalists were murdered, where Vargas Llosa didn't even separate the peasants under investigation to compare their stories. With this action, which can be seen in restrospect as part of the intensification of the Dirty War in Peru, Vargas Llosa found a niche for his participation" (*El sitio de la literatura: Escritores y política en el Perú del siglo XX* [Lima: Mosca Azul Editores, 1989], 103). Vargas Llosa recalls with bitter irony that the hundreds killed in Uchuraccay after the massacre did not move the intellectuals who criticized him for his role in the investigation of the murder of the eight journalists: "Since then, hundreds of peasants have been exterminated during the revolutionary war without provoking the least reaction, either nationally or internationally" (Vargas Llosa, "Une culture du métissage," *Magazine littéraire* 296 [February 1992]: 60).

92. Vargas Llosa, "The Story of a Massacre," 198.

93. Vargas Llosa, "José María Arguedas: entre la ideología y la arcadia," *Revista Iberoamericana* 47, nos. 116, 117 (1981): 33–46. This article was the starting point of Vargas Llosa's *La Utopía Arcaica: José María Arguedas y las ficciones del indigenismo* (Mexico, D.F.: Fondo de Cultura Económica, 1996).

94. For a careful analysis of the roles of narrator and storyteller in Vargas Llosa's novel, see "Facing the Author: Telling Stories in Mario Vargas Llosa's El Hablador," in Lucille Kerr's splendid book *Reclaiming the Author: Figures and Fictions from Spanish America* (Durham: Duke University Press, 1992), 134–159.

95. See Roy Boland, "Padres e hijos en las novelas de Mario Vargas Llosa," in *Love, Sex and Eroticism in Contemporary Latin American Fiction*, ed. Alun Kenwood (Mellbourne and Madrid: Voz Hispanica, 1992), 85–97.

96. Vargas Llosa, *The Storyteller* (New York: Farrar, Straus & Giroux, 1989), 25.

97. Ibid., 243.

98. Ibid., 78.

99. Ibid., 99–100.

100. Ibid., 78.

101. Ibid., 18. Fidel Pereira is a valuable informer for Andrés Ferrero, *Los machiguengas* (Salamanca: Caltrava, 1967). See, for example, 38–39.

102 Vargas Llosa, *The Storyteller*, 15.

103. Ibid., 33.

104. Ibid., 99.

105. Ibid., 36.

106. Ibid., 35.

107. Vargas Llosa, *Captain Pantoja and the Special Service* 44.

108. Vargas Llosa, "Crónica de un viaje a la selva," no page numbers.

109. Cf. Wayne Snell and G. Baer, "An Ayahauasca Ceremony among the Matsigenka (Eastern Peru)," *Zeitschrift für Ethnologie* 99, nos. 1–2 (1974); and Betty Elkins de Snell, *Machiguenga: Fonología y vocabulario breve* (Pucalpa: Instituto Lingüistico de Verano, 1974), and *Kenkitsatagantsi Matsigenka: Cuentos folkloricos de los machiguenga* (Pucalpa: Instituto Lingüistico de Verano, 1976). I thank Héctor Villaseñor, who called my attention to the publications of the Summer Institute of Linguistics and who gave me a copy of Betty Elkins de Snell's collection of folktales.

110. Vargas Llosa, *The Storyteller*, 85.

111. Ibid., 85–86.

112. Joaquín Barriales, *Matsigenka* (Madrid: Secretariado de Misiones Dominicanas, 1977), 71.

113 Vargas Llosa, *The Storyteller*, 86

114. Barriales, *Matsigenka*, 70–71.

115. Vargas Llosa, *The Storyteller*, 47.

116. "Cuando el Sol se apague o El fin del mundo," in Snell, *Cuentos folklóricos de los machiguenga,* 73).

117. See also "Un viaje alrededor del mundo (Ineantavageirgira)," in Snell, *Cuentos folklóricos machiguenga,* 88–89).

118. Vargas Llosa, *The Storyteller*, 38–39.

119. Ibid., 59.

120. Ibid., 203.

121. Ibid., 244.

122. In "Pierre Menard, Author of the *Quixote*," the protagonist knows that his literary enterprise is impossible, but he discards uninteresting ways to accomplish it: "the undertaking was impossible from the start, and of all the impossible means of carrying it out, this one was the least interesting" (Jorge Luis Borges, *Ficciones*, trans. Anthony Bonner, ed. with an introduction by Anthony Kerrigan [New York: Grove, 1962], 49).

123. Jorge Luis Borges, "The Anthropologist," in *In Praise of Darkness*, trans. Norman Thomas di Giovanni, (New York: E. P. Dutton, 1974), 49.

124. Borges, "The Anthropologist," 49.

125. Vargas Llosa, *In Praise of The Stepmother*, trans. Helen Lane (New York: Farrar, Straus & Giroux, 1990), 103.

126. Ibid., 54.

127. Ibid., 62.

128. Ibid., 60.

129. Ibid., 6–7.

130. See *Aunt Julia and the Scriptwriter*, trans. Helen R. Lane (New York, Farrar, Straus & Giroux, 1982), 52.

131. Vargas Llosa, *In Praise of The Stepmother* 7–8

132. Ibid., 39.

133. Vargas Llosa, *Who Killed Palomino Molero?* 146; *Aunt Julia and the Scriptwriter*, 270–71.

134 "My days and nights for one great joy, / One only, fooling womenkind, / Ruining, and leaving them behind!" (Tirso de Molina, *The Love-Rogue*, trans. Harry Kemp (New York: Leiber & Lewis, 1923), 97.

135. Vargas Llosa, *In Praise of The Stepmother*, 134

136. Ibid., 148.

137. Ibid., 149.

138. In an unpublished essay, Damián Bayón considers Vargas Llosa's comments on Bacon in the ninth chapter of the novel illuminating, from a strictly artistic point of view.

139. Vargas Llosa, *In Praise of The Stepmother*, 13.

140. The story is told in the first two or three pages of book 1 of the *History*.

141. "And as I contemplated her and thought of Gyges doing the same, that perverse complicity that united us suddenly made me burn with desire. Without a word I advanced upon her, pushed her onto the bed, and mounted her. As I caressed her, Gyges' bearded face appeared to me and the idea that he was watching us inflamed me even more, seasoning my pleasure with a bittersweet, piquant condiment hitherto unknown to me" (*In Praise of the Stepmother*, 21).

142. Ibid., 136, 140.

143. Ibid., 75.

144. Ibid., 45.

145. Ibid., 46.

146. Ibid., 46.

147. Ibid., 49.

148. "Szyszlo in the labyrinth," in *Making Waves,* 269. A different translation of this essay appears in Mario Vargas Llosa et al., *Fernando de Szyszlo* (Cali: Ediciones Alfred Wild, 1991). See also the untitled essay by Vargas Llosa in *Fernando de Szyszlo,* ed. Werner Lang and José Antonio de Lavalle (Lima: Santiago Valverde, 1979), 11–36.

149. Vargas Llosa, *In Praise of the Stepmother,* 116

150. This is how Vargas Llosa defined the concept of sovereignty, in an interview with Thomas M. Scheerer. Cf. *Mario Vargas Llosa, Leben un Werk: Eine Einführung* (Frankfurt: Suhrkamp, 1991), 165.

151. "Bataille or the the Redemption of Evil," in *Making Waves,* 125–126.

152. Vargas Llosa, *In Praise of the Stepmother,* 98.

153. Ibid., 109–110.

154. Lola Díaz, "Entrevista con Mario Vargas Llosa," *Cambio,* January 4, 1998, 78.

155. Bataille, *Literature and Evil,* trans. Alastair Hamilton (New York: Marion Boyars, 1985), 121.

156. César Moro, "El uso de la palabra," in *Los anteojos de azufre: Prosas reunidas y presentadas por André Coyné* (Lima: Talleres gráficos "D. Miranda., 1958), 16.

157. Vargas Llosa, *In Praise of the Stepmother,* ix.

158. Georges Bataille, *My Mother* (London: Marion Boyars, 1989), 121.

159. "Bataille o el rescate del mal," in *Contra viento y marea,* 2 (1972–1983): 26

160. Bataille, *My Mother,* 38.

161. Ibid., 40.

162. The son discovers his father's erotic engravings and feels strong emotions: "I sensed that I was damned, I defiled myself before the filth in which my father—and perhaps my mother too—had wallowed" (*My Mother,* 41).

163. Ibid., 87–88.

164. Ibid., 86.

165. Ibid., 133.

166. See the section of chapter 4 on Bataille's notion of "hypermorality," 116–117.

167. *Los Cuadernos de Don Rigoberto,* 207.

168. Ibid., 128.

169. Ibid., 284.

170. Ibid., 373.

171. Ibid., 211.

172. Ibid., 205.

Conclusion

1. "A Fish Out of Water," *Granta* 36 (Summer 1991): 74.

2. *A Fish in the Water: A Memoir,* trans. Helen Lane (New York: Farrar, Straus & Giroux), 529. He continues to believe that his political and economic program was a way out of what he has called Peru's "authoritarian tradition, the reason behind our

backwardness and barbarism" (*A Fish in the Water* [New York, Penguin], 526). He feels that the Peruvian people voted against their best interests in voting against him: "The program for which I had sought a mandate and which the Peruvian people refused to give me proposed placing public finances on a sound footing, putting an end to inflation, and opening the Peruvian economy to the world, as part of an integral plan to dismantle the discriminatory structure of society" 526–527).

3. *A Fish in the Water*, 529.

4. "El perfecto idiota latinoamericano," Vargas Llosa's prologue to Apuleyo Mendoza, Plinio, Carlos Alberto Montaner, and Alvaro Vargas Llosa, *Manual del perfecto idiota latinoamericano... y español* (Barcelona, Plaza y Janes, 1996), 13.

5. "My lucidity has screwed my life. It has frustrated me as a gay and as an artist. . . . My intelligence has revealed to me that I am surrounded by imbeciles and, in exchange, it closed the doors to physical pleasure and it frustrated my artistic vocation" (*Ojos bonitos, cuadros feos*, Lima, Peisa, 1996, 43.

6. See for example "El Perú en llamas," in *Desafíos a la libertad* (Madrid: El País, 1994), 37–41.

7. "Those who express dismay about the crimes and cruelties of the conquistadores against Incas and Aztecs have good reason to feel solidarity for those people who suffered in the past. They should, however, be equally outraged about the crimes and cruelties of Incas and Aztecs against the thousands of peoples they subjugated. But they are not. Academics have been itemizing every single crime committed by Europeans with reamarkable meticulousness, but they have not shed a single tear for the thousands, the hundreds of thousands, perhaps millions of Indian men and women who were sacrificed in wars of conquest and in barbarous Inca, Maya, Aztec, Chipcha, or Tolteca ceremonies" ("The Disputed Legacy of Christopher Columbus," *Bostonia* (Summer 1992): 47.

8. "The Story of a Massacre," in *Making Waves* (New York: Farrar, Strauss & Giroux, 1996), 183.

9. "The abuses they committed multiplied: arbitrary arrest, torture, rape, robbery, wounding, and even killings" ("The Story of a Massacre," in *Making Waves*, 183).

10. "This created a climate of fear and resentment in the poorer sectors which in turn helped Sendero Luminoso, since it tended to neutralize what might otherwise have been a rejection of their own activities," ("The Story of a Massacre," in *Making Waves*, 183).

11. See "El Perú en llamas," in *Desafíos a la libertad*, 38.

12. See "Regreso a la barbarie," in *Desafíos a la libertad*, 109–110.

13. After Vargas Llosa finished *Death in the Andes*, Abimael Guzmán, the leader of the shining path was captured and Alberto Fujimori took credit for the capture. Vargas Llosa wrote an article in which he objected to the violation of Guzman's human rights and he warned that the capture of Guzmán was tantamount to relieving a symptom but not the illness because the conditions that accounted for the rise of the Shining Path movement have not been altered. Vargas Llosa argued that president Alberto Fujimori's leadership was conducive to political violence and terrorism." See "El preso, 1,509," in *Desafíos a la libertad*, 152.

14. For a Marxist version of this theme see César Vallejo's novel *Tungsten*.

15. Frye, Northrop, *Words with Power* (San Diego: Harcourt, Brace, Jovanovich, 1992), 230.

16. *Death in the Andes,* 44–45.

17. Before *Death in the Andes* the events of Lituma's life in Vargas Llosa's fiction were consistent with the life story as originally presented in *The Green House*: a soldier from Piura sent to a military post in the Peruvian jungle returns home with a wife who will become a prostitute in the bar of La Chunga. The events of Lituma's jungle adventures in Vargas Llosa's fiction, including his marriage to Bonifacia, are ostensibly set in the 1950s. But in *Death in the Andes,* set in the late 1980s or early 1990s, Lituma is a bachelor and his transfer to a military post in the Peruvian jungle will occur after the end of the novel.

18. Mayer, Enrique, "Peru In Deep Trouble: Mario Vargas Llosa's 'Inquest in the Andes' Reexamined," *Cultural Anthropology* 6 no.4 (November 1991): 472–473.

19. Gorriti Gustavo, *Historia de la guerra milenaria en el Perú* (Lima: Editorial Apoyo, 1990).

20. As in the Greek myth, the novel makes allusions to Dionisio's birth associated with the death of his mother by lightning. Of course Vargas Llosa plays with the myth by offering strange twists. In *Death in the Andes* Dionisio promised that he would engage in homosexual sex with the keeper of the cemetery where his mother was burried. He finds an unusual way to keep his promise when he marries after the keeper's death.

21. "El preso 1,509," in *Desafíos a la libertad,* 153.

22. The theme of the young men who enroll in antiterrorist units as a means to enhance their military careers is also developed in the most important Peruvian film inspired by the Shining Path, Lombardi's *La boca del lobo.*

23. *Death in the Andes,* 272–273.

24. Ibid., 275.

25. His critical editon of the *Bacchae,* with a long introduction and extensive notes, and his famous book *The Greeks and the Irrational* both quoted below.

26. I quote from E. R. Dodds's introduction to his edition of Euripides' *Bacchae* (New York: Oxford University Press, 1960), xlv.

27. Dodds, T*he Greeks and the Irrational* (Berkeley: University of California Press, 1968), 186.

28. Ibid., 153.

29. I am grateful to my colleague Katherine King for pointing out that the blaster's feeling haunted is an indication of an innate repugnace to violence, which is in tension with his propensity for it. Her point is illuminating. I would only add that in either case the blaster is not conscious of his motivations.

30. When he received the prestigious Romulo Gallegos prize in 1965 for *The Green House* (see my comments on Vargas Llosa's acceptance speech in chapter 1, pp. 7–8), Vargas Llosa stressed the significance of his own novels as a denunciation of the evils of capitalism in Latin America, and more recently he has claimed that novels such as *The*

Real Life of Alejandro Mayta have offered what amounts to a realistic portrayal of Peru during the rise of terrorist groups ("Violencia y Ficción," in *Desafíos a la libertad,* 143).

31. The high standards reached by Latin American literature in the last few decades have been raised by [*The War of the End of the World*]. There may be novels that become more popular than this one, but it will be difficult to surpass it in the sort of fusion between the popular novel and literary art that was established by this novel's only rival, [Gabriel García Márquez's] *One Hundred Years of Solitude*" ("La Guerra del fin del mundo: Una obra maestra del fanatismo artístico,", *Eco* 45/6, no. 246, [1982]: 600).

BIBLIOGRAPHY
(works by Vargas Llosa listed in chronological order)

Works by Mario Vargas Llosa in Spanish

Narrative

Los jefes. Barcelona: Editorial Rocas, 1959.
La ciudad y los perros. Barcelona: Seix Barral, 1963
"La ciudad y el forastero," *Casa de las Américas* (Havana) 4, no. 26 (1964): 94–98.
La Casa Verde. Barcelona: Seix Barral, 1966.
Los cachorros. Pichula Cuéllar. Barcelona: Editorial Lumen, 1967.
Conversación en La Catedral. Barcelona: Seix Barral, 1969.
Pantaleón y las visitadoras. Barcelona: Seix Barral, 1973.
La tía Julia y el escribidor. Barcelona: Seix Barral, 1977.
La guerra del fin del mundo. Barcelona: Seix Barral, 1981.
Historia de Mayta. Barcelona: Seix Barral, 1984.
¿Quién mató a Palomino Molero? Barcelona: Seix Barral, 1986.
El hablador. Barcelona: Seix Barral, 1987.
Elogio de la madrastra. Barcelona: Tusquets, 1988.
Lituma en los Andes. Barcelona: Planeta, 1993.
Los cuadernos de don Rigoberto. Madrid: Alfaguara, 1997.

Drama

La señorita de Tacna. Barcelona: Seix Barral, 1981
Kathie y el hipopótamo. Barcelona: Seix Barral, 1983.

La Chunga. Barcelona: Seix Barral, 1986.
El loco de los balcones. Barcelona: Seix Barral, 1993.
Ojos bonitos, cuadros feos. Lima: Peisa, 1996.

Essays

Historia secreta de una novela. Barcelona: Tusquets, 1971.
García Márquez: Historia de un deicidio. Barcelona: Seix Barral, 1971.
La orgía perpetua: Flaubert y Madame Bovary. Barcelona: Seix Barral, 1975.
Contra viento y marea. Vol. 1 (1962–1972). Barcelona: Seix Barral, 1986.
Contra viento y marea. Vol. 2 (1972–1983). Barcelona: Seix Barral, 1986.
Contra viento y marea. Vol. 3 (1964–1988). Barcelona: Seix Barral, 1990.
La verdad de las mentiras. Barcelona: Seix Barral, 1990.
Carta de batalla por Tirant lo Blanc. Barcelona: Seix Barral, 1990.
El pez en el agua: Memorias. Barcelona: Seix Barral, 1993.
Desafíos a la libertad. Madrid: El País, 1994.
La utopía arcaica: José María Arguedas y las ficciones del indigenismo. Mexico, D.F.:
    Fondo de Cultura Económica, 1996.

Articles, Lectures, and Declarations

"José María Arguedas." *El comercio* (Lima), September 4, 1955.
"José Carlos Mariátegui." *Cultura Peruana* (Lima) (1956): 93–96.
"Nota sobre César Moro." *Literatura* (Peru) (1958): 1.
"*Carta de Amor*, de César Moro." *Literatura* (Peru) (1958): 2.
"Crónica de un viaje a la selva." *Cultura Peruana* (Lima) (1958): 123.
"¿Es útil el sacrificio de la poesía?" *Literatura* (Lima) (1959): 3.
"César Moro en París." *Caretas* (Camana, Peru) 198 (1960).
"José María Arguedas y el índio." *Casa de las Américas* (Havana) 4, no. 26 (1964):
    139–147.
Alegría, Ciro, José María Arguedas, et. al. Lecture by Mario Vargas Llosa. *Primer
    encuentro de narradores peruanos*, 1965.
"*La tentación de San Antonio* en el teatro." *Caretas* 353 (1967): 37–38.
"La novela." *Cuadernos de literatura* (Montevideo) 2 (1968).
"Novela primitiva y novela de creación en América Latina." *Revista de la Universidad
    de México* 23 (1969): 10.
"Carta de batalla por Tirant lo Blanc." Prologue to Joanot Martorell and Martí Joan
    de Galba, *Tirant lo Blanc*. Madrid: Alianza, 1969.
"Génesis de *La ciudad y los perros*." *Studi di letteratura ispano-americana* (Milan) 3
    (1971): 77–85.
Declaration in favor of the Cuban Revolution after the Incidents Regarding the
    Padilla Case. *Cuadernos de Marcha* (Montevideo) 49, May 19, 1971.
"Martorell y el elemento añadido en Tirant lo Blanc." Prologue to *El combate imagi-*

nario: Las cartas de batalla de Joanot Martorell. Barcelona: Seix Barral, 1972. 9–28.

"Ensoñación y magia en *Los ríos profundos.*" Prologue to José María Arguedas, *Los ríos profundos.* Caracas, Biblioteca Ayacucho, 1978.

"La utopía arcaica." Cambridge, England: Centre of Latin American Studies, 1978.

"Fernando de Szyszlo." *Fernando de Szyszlo.* Lima: Santiago Valverde, 1979.

"José María Arguedas. Entre la ideología y la arcadia." *Revista Iberoamericana* 47 (1981): 116–117.

"El teatro como ficción." *Kathie y el hipopótamo.* Barcelona: Seix Barral, 1983.

"*Los Misérables:* El último clásico." *Cielo abierto* 7 (1983): 23.

"Un escritor y sus demonios" (lecture). Buenos Aires, *La nación,* May 12, 1985.

"Carta a Günther Grass." *Vuelta* 117 (August 1986): 58–60.

Vargas Llosa, et al. *Libertad. Primer ciclo de conferencias.* Lima: Pro-Desarrollo, 1988.

Acción para el cambio: El programa de gobierno del Frente Democrátic. Lima, 1989.

"Historia y novela." *El país,* April 1, 1991.

"Szyszlo in the labyrinth." In Mario Vargas Llosa et al., *Fernando de Szyszlo.* Bogotá: Ediciones Alfred Wild, 1991.

"El perfecto idiota latinoamericano," Prologue to Plinio Apuleyo Mendoza, Carlos Alberto Montaner, and Alvaro Vargas Llosa. *Manual del perfecto idiota latinoamericano . . . y español.* Barcelona: Plaza y Janes, 1996.

Interviews and Dialogues

Agüero, Luis, Juan Larco, Mario Vargas Llosa, et. al. "Sobre *La ciudad y los perros* de Mario Vargas Llosa." *Casa de las Américas* 5, no. 30 (1965): 63–80.

Harss, Luis, with Barbara Dohmann. "Mario Vargas Llosa." In *Into the Mainstream.* New York: Harper & Row, 1966.

Rodríguez Monegal, Emir. "Madurez de Vargas Llosa." *Mundo nuevo* 3 (1966).

"Once preguntas claves a Mario Vargas Llosa." *Caretas* 29 (1967).

Mario Vargas Llosa y Gabriel García Márquez: Diálogo. Lima: Carlos Milla Batres, 1967.

Cano Gaviria, Ricardo. *El buitre y el ave fénix: Conversaciones con Mario Vargas Llosa.* Barcelona: Anagrama, 1972.

Fossey, Jean-Michel, "Entrevista con Mario Vargas Llosa." *Galaxia Latinoamericana (siete años de entrevistas).* Las Palmas de Gran Canaria: Inventarios provisionales, 1973.

Oviedo, José Miguel, "Entrevista con Mario Vargas Llosa." *Espejo de escritores.* Ed. Reina Roffé. Hanover, N. H.: Ediciones del Norte, 1985.

Altares, Pedro, Manuel Andújar, Mario Vargas Llosa, et. al. *Semana de Autor. Mario Vargas Llosa.* Madrid: Ediciones cultura hispánica, 1985.

Díaz, Lola. "Entrevista con Mario Vargas Llosa." *Cambio 16,* January 4, 1988, 74-85.

Setti, Ricardo A. *. . . sobre la vida y la política. Diálogo con Mario Vargas Llosa.* Buenos Aires: Intermundo, 1989.

Boland, Roy, "Interview: A Citizen of the World," *Island* 58 (Autumn 1994): 22–27.

Unpublished Material in the Mario Vargas Llosa Papers (Firestone Library, Princeton University) Cited in This Book

Letter from José María Arguedas dated October 11, 1964. Box 1, folder 1.
Letters from Sebastián Salazar Bondy dated February 16, 1962, July 6, 1962, and May 5, 1964. Box 1, folder 23.
Letter from José María Arguedas dated September 26, 1967. Box 4, under Letter A.
First draft of *La ciudad y los perros*. Notebook (D-1), box 3, folder 11.
First draft of *Pantaleón y las visitadoras*. Notebook (E-1), box 3, folder 3. ; also contains his first notes for the elaboration of *La tía Julia y el escribidor*.
The version of *Pantaleón y las visitadoras* in which the character of Brother Francisco appears for the first time. Notebook (E-4) box 3, folder 6.
Vargas Llosa's notes for a course in Latin American literature that he taught at the University of Columbia between 1975 and 1976; in particular his notes on Euclides da Cunha, *Los sertones* (The Spanish translation of *Os sertoes* [*Rebellion in the Backlands*]). Notebook (B-4), box 1, folder 8.
Stories that are the embryonic material for *La Casa Verde:* "Anselmo," "La aventura," "Jum, Alcalde de Urakusa," "Los Manganches," and "Fushía." Box 9.
"La guerra de Canudos" and "Los perros del infierno," (The Dogs of Hell), the unfilmed screenplay that is the embryonic material for *La guerra del fin del mundo*.

Works by Mario Vargas Llosa Available in English Translation

Narrative

The Green House. Trans. of *La Casa Verde* by Gregory Rabassa. New York: Harper & Row, 1968.
Conversation in the Cathedral. Trans. of *Conversación en La Catedral* by Gregory Rabassa. New York: Harper & Row, 1974.
Captain Pantoja and the Special Service. Trans. of *Pantaleón y las visitadoras* by Gregory Kolovakos and Ronald Christ. New York: Harper & Row, 1978.
The Time of the Hero. Trans. of *La ciudad y los perros* by Lysander Kemp. New York: Harper & Row, 1979.
The Cubs and Other Stories. Trans. of *Los cachorros* by Gregory Kolovakos and Ronald Christ. Also contains "The Leaders," a translation of "Los jefes." New York: Harper & Row, 1979.
Aunt Julia and the Scriptwriter. Trans. of *La tía Julia y el escribidor* by Helen R. Lane. New York: Farrar, Straus & Giroux, 1982.
The War of the End of the World. Trans. of *La guerra del fin del mundo* by Helen R. Lane. New York: Avon Books, 1985.
The Real Life of Alejandro Mayta. Trans. of *Historia de Mayta* by Alfred MacAdam. New York: Farrar, Straus, & Giroux, 1986.

Who Killed Palomino Molero? Trans. of *¿Quién mató a Palomino Molero?* by Alfred MacAdam. New York: Farrar, Straus & Giroux, 1987.

The Storyteller. Trans. of *El hablador* by Helen Lane. New York: Farrar, Straus & Giroux, 1989.

In Praise of the Stepmother. Trans. of *Elogio de la madrastra* by Helen Lane. New York: Farrar, Straus & Giroux, 1990.

Death in the Andes. Trans. of *Lituma en los Andes* by Edith Grossman. New York: Farrar, Straus & Giroux, 1996.

Drama

Three Plays. The Young Lady from Tacna. Kathie and the Hippopotamus. La Chunga. Trans. by David Graham-Young. London: Fabar & Faber Ltd., 1990.

Essays, Articles, Lectures, and Declarations

The Perpetual Orgy: Flaubert and Madame Bovary. Trans. of *La orgía perpetual: Flaubert y* Madame Bovary by Helen Lane. New York: Farrar, Straus & Giroux, 1986.

"Updating Karl Popper." PMLA 105 (1990): 1018–1025.

"A Fish out of Water." Trans. by Helen Lane. *Granta* 36 (1991): 15–75.

A Writer's Reality. Edited with an introduction by Myron I. Lichtblau. Syracuse: Syracuse University Press, 1991.

Fiction: The Power of Lies. Bundoora, Victoria, Australia: La Trobe University, 1993.

A Fish in the Water: A Memoir. Trans. of *El pez en el agua. Memorias* by Helen Lane. New York: Farrar, Straus & Giroux, 1994.

Literature and Freedom. Foreword by Roy Boland. The Center for Independent Studies (Australia) Occasional papers, 1994.

Making Waves. Essays edited and translated by John King. New York: Farrar, Straus & Giroux, 1996.

Works on Vargas Llosa

Alonso, Carlos J. "*La tía Julia y el escribidor:* The Writing Subject's Fantasy of Empowerment." PMLA 106 (January 1991): 46–59.

Benedetti, Mario. "Vargas Llosa y su fertil escándalo." In *Letras del continente mestizo.* (Montevideo: Arca, 1967).

———. "Las prioridades del escritor." *Casa de las Américas* 12, no. 68 (1971): 70–79.

Bernucci, Leopoldo. *Historia de un malentendido: Un estudio transtextual de* La guerra del fin del mundo *de Mario Vargas Llosa.* New York: Peter Lang, 1989.

Boland, Roy. "Demonios y lectores: Génesis y reescritura de ¿Quién mató a Palomino Molero?" *Antipodas* 1 [Special issue on Mario Vargas Llosa edited by Roy Boland] (December 1988): 160-182.

—————. *Mario Vargas Llosa: Oedipus and the "Papa" State. A Study of Individual and Social Psychology in Mario Vargas Llosa's Novels of Peruvian Reality*. Madrid: Editorial Voz, 1990.

—————. "Ni de derecha ni de izquierda: la visión moral de Mario Vargas Llosa," *Antipodas* 8–9 (1996-1997): 230-240.

—————. "Padres e hijos en las novelas de Mario Vargas Llosa," in Kenwood, Alun, ed. *Love, Sex and Eroticism in Contemporary Latin American Fiction*, Madrid: Voz Hispanica, 1992: 85-97.

—————, ed. *Mario Vargas Llosa. Antipodas* (special issue) 1 (December) 1988.

Castro, Fidel. "Discurso de clausura del primer congreso nacional de educación y cultura." *Casa de las Américas* 11, nos. 65–66 (1971): 21–33.

Castro-Klaren, Sara. *Mario Vargas Llosa: Analisis introductorio*. Lima: Latinoamericana Editores, 1988.

—————. *Understanding Mario Vargas Llosa*. Columbia: University of South Carolina, 1990.

Collazos, Oscar, Julio Cortázar, and Mario Vargas Llosa. *Literatura en la revolución y revolución en la literatura*. Mexico City: Siglo XXI, 1970.

Cornejo Polar, Antonio. *La novela Peruana*. Lima: Horizonte, 1989.

Davis, Mary E. 1981. "La elección del fracaso: Vargas Llosa y William Faulkner." In *Mario Vargas Llosa*. Ed. José Miguel Oviedo. Madrid: Taurus, 1981.

Dorfman, Ariel. "Mario Vargas Llosa y José María Arguedas. Dos visiones de una sola América." *Casa de las Américas* 11, no. 64 (1971): 6–19.

Delgado, Washington. "Mario Vargas Llosa: *La ciudad y los perros*." *Letras* 36 (1964): 72–73.

Edwards, Jorge. *Persona Non Grata: An Envoy in Castro's Cuba*. Trans. Colin Harding. New York: Pomerica, 1976.

Escobar, Alberto. *Patio de letras*. Caracas: Monte Avila, 1971.

Fernández Ariza, Guadalupe. Introduction and notes to Mario Vargas Llosa, *Los cachorros*. Madrid: Catedra, 1987.

Fernández Retamar, Roberto. Participation in a round table conference "Diez años de Revolución: El intelectual y la sociedad." *Casa de las Américas* 10, no. 56 (1969): 7–52.

Franco, Jean. "Lectura de *Conversación en La Catedral*." *Revista Iberoamericana* 37 (1971): 76–77.

Fuentes, Carlos. *La nueva novela hispanoamericana*. Mexico City: Joaquín Mortiz, 1969.

Gladieu, Marie-Madeleine. *Mario Vargas Llosa*. Paris: L'Harmattan, 1989.

Harss, Luis. "Espejos de *La Casa Verde*." *Mario Vargas Llosa*. Ed. José Miguel Oviedo. Madrid: Taurus, 1981.

Harss, Luis, and Barbara Dohmann. *Into the Mainstream*. New York: Harper & Row, 1967.

Kerr, Lucille. *Reclaiming the Author: Figures and Fictions from Spanish America*. Durham and London: Duke University Press, 1992.

Kloepfer, Rolf and Klaus Zimmerman, "Mario Vargas Llosa." in *Lateinamerikanische Literatur der Gegenwart*. Ed Wolfgang Eitel. Stuttgart: Alfred Kröner, 1978.

Kristal, Efraín. "Mario Vargas Llosa y la función social de la literatura." In *La voluntad del humanismo: Homenaje a Juan Marichal*. Ed. Biruté Ciplijauskaité and Christopher Maurer. Barcelona: Antropos, 1990.

Lafforgue, Jorge. "*La ciudad y los perros:* Novela moral." *Nueva novela latinoamericana*. Buenos Aires: Paidós, 1969.

Lastra, Pedro. "Un caso de elaboración narrativa de experiencias concretas en *La ciudad y los perros*." In *Relecturas hispanoamericanas*. Santiago, Chile: Editorial Universitaria, 1987.

Lauer, Mirko. *El sitio de la literatura: Escritores y política en el Perú del siglo XX*. Lima: Mosca Azul, 1989.

Loayza, Luis. "Los personajes de *La Casa Verde*." *Amaru* (Lima) (1967): 1.

Marinello, Juan. "Literatura y revolución." *Casa de las Américas* 12, no. 68 (1971): 40–47.

Mayer, Enrique. "Peru in Deep Trouble: Mario Vargas Llosa's 'Inquest in the Andes' Reexamined." *Cultural Anthropology* 6, no. 4 (November 1991): 472–473.

Oviedo, José Miguel. *Mario Vargas Llosa. La invención de una realidad*. Barcelona: Seix Barral, 1982.

———. "*Historia de Mayta* (Una reflexión política en forma de novela)." *Atenea* (1988): 457.

———, ed. *Mario Vargas Llosa*. Madrid: Taurus, 1981.

Pacheco, José Emilio. "Lectura de Vargas Llosa." *Revista de la Universidad de México* 22 (1968): 8.

Rama, Angel. "De como sobreviene lo humano." *Marcha*, February 21, 1964.

———. "Vargas Llosa. Las arias del virtuoso." *Marcha*, August 13, 1966.

———. "Vade retro." *Marcha*, May 5, 1972.

———. "El fin de los demonios." *Marcha*, July 28, 1972.

———. "*La guerra del fin del mundo:* Una obra maestra del fanatismo artístico." *Eco* 40 (1982): 246.

Rama, Angel and Mario Vargas Llosa. *García Márquez y el problema de la novela*. Montevideo: Corregidor-Marcha, 1973.

Revel, Jean-François. *The Flight from the Truth: The Reign of Deceit in the Age of Information*. Trans. Curtis Cate. New York: Random House, 1991.

Rincón, Carlos. "Para un plano de batalla de un combate por una nueva crítica en Latinoamerica." *Casa de las Américas* 11, no. 67 (1971): 39–59.

Rincón, Carlos and Gisela Leber. "Einige Grundzüge des Lateinamerikanishces roman der Gegenwart." *Zur Gegenwartsliteratur in en romanishchen Ländern: Studien und Berichet 1/2*. Ed. Werner Bahner. Berlin: Akademie-Verlag, 1968.

Rodríguez Rea, Miguel Angel. *Tras las huellas de un crítico: Mario Vargas Llosa*. Lima: Pontificia Universidad Católica del Peru, 1996.

Romualdo, Alejandro, et. al. "Llamamiento de los premios nacionales de literatura del Perú a los intelectuales de la América Latina." *Casa de las Américas* 11, no. 67 (1971): 145.

Rushdie, Salman. "The Real Life of Alejandro Mayta." *Imaginary Homelands: Essays and Criticism, 1981–1991*. London: Granta, 1991.

Salazar Bondy, Sebastián. "Mario Vargas Llosa y un mundo de rebeldes." *El comercio*, October 4, 1959.

Santamaría, Haydée. "Respuesta a Mario Vargas Llosa." *Casa de las Américas* 11, nos. 65–66 (1971): 140–142.

Scheerer, Thomas M. *Mario Vargas Llosa, Leben und Werk: Eine Einfürung*. Frankfurt: Suhrkamp, 1991.

Sommers, Joseph. "Literatura e ideología: La evaluación novelística del militarismo en Vargas Llosa." *Hispamérica* 4, no. 1 (1975): 83–117.

Tusell, Javier. *Retrato de Mario Vargas Llosa*. Barcelona: Círculo de lectores, 1990.

Urquidi Illánez, *Lo que Varguitas no dijo*. La Paz: Khana Cruz, 1983.

Vargas Llosa, Alvaro. *El diablo en campaña*. Madrid: Ediciones El País, 1991.

General Bibliography

Alegría, Ciro, José María Arguedas, et. al. *Primer encuentro de narradores peruanos*. Lima: Latinoamericana Editores, 1986. The meeting took place in 1965. Its proceedings were published for the first time in 1969.

Alonso, Dámaso. "*Tirant lo Blanc*, Novela Moderna." In *Primavera de la literatura europea*. Madrid: Guadarrama, 1961

Arguedas, José María. *Formación de una cultura nacional indoamericana*. Selection and prologue by Angel Rama. Mexico City: Siglo XXI, 1975.

Barriales, Joaquín. *Matsigenka*. Madrid: Secretariado de Misiones Dominicanas, 1977.

Bataille, Georges. *La littérature et le mal*. Paris: Gallimard, 1957.

———. *Ma mère*. Paris: Jean-Jacques Pauvert, 1966.

———. *Literature and Evil*. Trans. Alastair Hamilton. New York: Marion Boyars, 1985.

———. *My Mother; My Mother; Madame Edwarda; and, The Dead Man*. Trans. Austryn Wainhouse. New York: Marion Boyars, 1989.

Berlin, Isaiah. *Vico and Herder: Two Studies in the History of Ideas*. London: Hogarth, 1976.

———. *Russian Thinkers*. London: Penguin, 1979.

———. *Against the Current: Essays in the History of Ideas*. Reprint. London: 1989.

Borges, Jorge Luis. *Antiguas literaturas germánicas*. Mexico City: Fondo de cultura Económica, 1951.

———. *Ficciones*. Edited with an introduction by Anthony Kerrigan. New York: Grove, 1962.

———. *In Praise of Darkness*. Trans. Thomas di Giovanni. New York: E. P., 1974.

———. *Discusión*. Madrid: Alianza, 1986.

Breton, André. *Entretien*. Paris: Gallimard, 1969.

Brooks, Cleanth. *William Faulkner: First Encounters*. New Haven, Conn.: Yale University Press, 1983.

Camus, Albert. *L'homme revolté*. Paris: Gallimard, 1951.

———. *The Rebel.* Trans. by Anthony Bower. New York: Vintage, 1956.

———. *Moral y política.* Madrid: Alianza, 1978.

———. *Carnets.* Madrid: Alianza, 1985.

Conrad, Joseph. *Heart of Darkness.* New York: Norton, 1988.

———. *Under Western Eyes.* London: Penguin, 1989.

Coyné, André. *César Moro.* Lima: Torres Aguirre, 1956.

———. "César Moro entre Lima, París y México." *Obra poética.* Ed. Ricardo Silva-Santiesteban, 1980.

Cunha, Euclides da. *Rebellion in the Backlands.* Translated with an introduction by Samuel Putnam. Chicago: University of Chicago Press, 1944.

Dodds, E. R. *Bacchae.* By Euripides. Edited with an introduction and commentary by E. R. Dodds. Oxford: Oxford University Press, 1960.

———. *The Greeks and the Irrational.* Berkeley: University of California Press, 1968.

Elkins de Snell, Betty. *Machiguenga: Fonología y vocabulario breve.* Pucalpa: Instituto lingüístico de verano, 1974.

———. *Kentkitsatagantsi Matsigenka: Cuentos folklóricos de los machigueng.* Pucalpa: Instituto lingüístico de verano, 1976.

Escobar, Alberto. El imaginario nacional. In *Moro-Westphalen-Arguedas: Una formación literaria.* Lima: Instituto de estudios peruanos, 1989.

Faulkner, William. *Absalom, Absalom!* 1936. Reprint. New York: Vintage, 1987

———. *The Wild Palms.* New York: Random House, 1939.

———. *Light in August.* 1932. Reprint. New York: Random House, 1972.

Ferrero, Andrés. *Los machiguengas.* Salamanca: Calatrava, 1967.

Flaubert, Gustave. *Sentimental Education.* Trans. with an introduction by Robert Baldrick. Harmondsworth, Middlesex, England: Penguin, 1964.

———. *Oeuvres complètes de Gustave Flaubert.* Paris: Club de l'Honnête Homme, 1974.

———. *The Letters of Gustave Flaubert, 1830–1857.* Selected, edited and translated by Francis Steegmuller, Cambridge, Massachusetts: Harvard University Press, 1980.

———. *The Temptation of Saint Anthony.* Trans. Kitty Mrosovsky. Ithaca, New York: Cornell University Press, 1981.

Frye, Northrop. *Words with Power.* San Diego, Calif.: Harcourt, Brace. Jovanovich, 1992.

Goethe, Johann Wolfgang. *Goethes Gespräche.* Vol. 4, *Gesamte Ausgabe.* Leipzig: Biederman, 1910.

Goldenberg, Isaac, *The Fragmented Life of Don Jacob Lerner.* trans. Robert S. Picciotto. New York: Persea, 1976.

González Echevarría, Roberto. *Myth and Archive: A Theory of Latin American Narrative.* Cambridge University Press, 1990.

Gorriti, Gustavo. *Historia de la guerra milenaria en el Perú.* Lima: Editorial Apoyo, 1990.

Gout, Alberto, director. *Aventurera.* Producciones Calderon S.A., 1946.

Higgins, James. *The Poet in Peru*. Liverpool: Francis Cairns, 1982.

———. *A History of Peruvian Literature*. Liverpool: Francis Cairns, 1987.

Hugo, Victor. *The Man who Laughs*. Trans. Isabel Florence Hapgood. New York: T. Y. Crowell & Co., 1888.

———. *Les Miserables*. Vol. 6. *The Works of Victor Hugo in Sixteen Volumes*. Translator unnamed. Philadelphia: University Library Association, n.d.

Kafka, Franz. *The Metamorphosis*. Trans. Willa and Edwin Muir. Harmondsworth, Middlesex, England: Penguin Books, 1949.

Ledouppe, Christiane. *Victor Hugo et la création littéraire. Guide systématique pour la connaissance des idées de l'écrivain*. Liège: Memoirs, 1980

Malraux, André. *Man's Fate*. Trans. Haakon M. Chevalier. 1934. Reprint. New York: Modern Library, 1961.

Mariátegui, José Carlos. *Seven Interpretive Essays on Peruvian Reality*. Trans. Marjory Urquidi. Austin: University of Texas Press, 1971.

Martorell, Joanot, and Martí Joan de Galba. *El Tirant lo Blanc*. Madrid: Alianza Editorial, 1984.

Matto de Turner, Clorinda. *Aves sin nido*. Prologue by Antonio Cornejo Polar, with notes by Efraín Kristal and Carlos García Bedoya, and chronology and bibliography by Efraín Kristal. Caracas: Biblioteca Ayacucho, 1994.

Menton, Seymour. *Prose Fiction of the Cuban Revolution*. Austin: University of Texas Press, 1975.

Moro, César. *La tortuga ecuestre y otros poemas (1924–1949*. Lima: Talleres gráficos "D. Miranda," 1957.

———. *Los anteojos de azufre: Prosas reunidas y presentadas por André Coyné*. Lima: Talleres gráficos "D. Miranda," 1958.

———. *La tortuga ecuestre y otros textos*. Ed. Julio Ortega. Caracas: Monte Avila, 1973.

———. *Obra poética*. Ed. and trans. Ricardo Silva Santiesteban. Lima: Instituto nacional de cultura, 1980.

Mosterín, Jesús. "Entrevista con Karl Popper." *Arbor* 133, no. 522 (1989): 9–35.

Neale-Silva, Eduardo. *Horizonte humano: Vida de José Eustasio River*. Mexico City: Fondo de Cultura Económica, 1960.

Ortega, Julio. *La imaginación crítica: Ensayos sobre la modernidad en el Perú*. Lima: Peisa, 1974.

———. *Crítica de la identidad: La pregunta por el Perú en su literatura*. Mexico: Fondo de Cultura Económica, 1988

Padilla, Heberto. "Intervención en la unión de escritores y artistas de Cuba, el martes 27 de abril de 1971." *Casa de las Américas* 11, nos. 65–66 (1971).

Popper, Karl. *The Poverty of Historicism*. London: Routledge & Kegan Paul, 1957.

———. *Open Society and its Enemies*. New Jersey: Princeton University Press, 1962.

———. "Utopia and Violence." In *Conjectures and Refutations: The Growth of Scientific Knowledge*. London: Routledge & Kegan Paul, 1963.

———. *Realism and the Aim of Science*. Totowa, N.J.: Rowman & Littlefield, 1983.

Rama, Angel. "*Lima la horrible* de Sebastián Salazar Bondy." *Casa de las Américas* 4 (1964): 27.

Revel, Jean-François. *Without Marx or Jesus: The New American Revolution Has Begun.* Trans. J. F. Bernard (Garden City, N.Y.: Doubleday, 1971).

Revel, Jean-François, and Branko Lazitch. *How Democracies Perish.* Trans. William Byron. New York: Perennial Library, 1985.

Riquer, Martín de, and Mario Vargas Llosa, eds. *El combate imaginario: Las cartas de batalla de Joanot Martorell.* Barcelona: Barral, 1972.

Rimbaud, Arthur. *Un corazón bajo la sotana.* Prologue and translation by Mario Vargas Llosa. Lima: Jaime Campodónico, 1989.

Salazar Bondy, Sebastián. "Mao Tse Tung entre la Poesía y la Revolución." *Literatura* (1958): 1.

―――. *Lima la horrible.* Populibros peruanos, 1963.

―――. Prologue to *La encrucijada del Perú.* Montevideo: Arca, 1963.

Sartre, Jean Paul. *What Is Literature?* Trans. Bernard Frechtman. New York: Philosophical Library, 1949.

Snell, Wayne, and G. Baer. "An Ayahuasca Ceremony among the Matsigenka (Eastern Peru)." *Zeitschrift für Ethnologie* 99, nos. 1, 2 (1974): 63–77.

Soto, Hernando de. *The Other Path: The Invisible Revolution in the Third World.* Trans. June Abbot. Foreword by Mario Vargas Llosa. New York: Harper & Row, 1989.

Stendhal. *The Charterhouse of Parma.* Trans. with an introduction by Margaret R. B. Shaw. Harmondsworth, Middlesex, England: Penguin, 1958.

Tirso de Molina. *The Love-Rogue.* Trans. Harry Kemp. New York: Leiber & Lewis, 1923.

Tolstoy, Leo. *War and Peace.* Translated and with an introduction by Rosemary Edmonds. Harmondsworth, Middlesex, England: Penguin Books, 1957.

Watt, Ian. *Conrad in the Nineteenth Century.* London: Chatto & Windus, 1980.

Wilson, Edmund. *Axel's Castle.* New York: Scribner's, 1931.

INDEX

alienation, xi, 8, 12; from nature,
101–102
Allende, Salvador, 80
Alonso, Carlos, 210 n.20
Alonso, Dámaso, 20, 207 nn.68, 69
Althusser, Louis, 75
Aragon, Louis, 202 n.7
Arguedas, José María, xvi, 9–11, 26, 68,
142, 158, 185, 203 n.24, 209 n.11,
209n.15, 216n.132; works: *Deep
Rivers* (*Los ríos profundos*), 209 n.11;
Todas las sangres, 216 n.132
Arkinstall, Christina, 130, 132
artistic freedom, 6, 203 n.10, 203 n.14;
and socialism, 70

Bacon, Francis, 171, 172, 174, 233 n.138
Bakhtin, Mikhail, 75
Barral, Carlos, 72
Barriales, Joaquín, 164
Barthes, Roland, 75
Bataille, Georges, xvi, 53; and hyper-
morality, 117; and literature of evil

(transgression), 3, 4, 81–82,
115–117, 119, 120, 169; and political
literature, 18; and sovereignty, 172,
175–178; works: *The Accursed Share,*
18; *Literature and Evil,* 4; *Ma mère,*
176–178
Baudelaire, Charles, 3
Bay of Pigs invasion, 23, 208 n.86
Bayón, Damián, 233 n.138
Belaúnde Terry, Fernando, 56, 57, 151
Benedetti, Mario, 67, 68, 74, 112
Benjamin, Walter, 75
Berlin, Isaiah, xvi, 102–106, 114–115,
120, 136–137; work: *Against the
Current,* 102–103, 109
Bernucci, Leopoldo, 127; work: *Historia
de un malentendido: Un estudio trans-
textual de La guerra del fin del mundo
de Mario Vargas Llosa,* 227 n.6
Beyle, Marie-Henri [pseud. Stendhal],
124, 135; work: *The Charterhouse of
Parma,* 135
Blake, William, 4

Boland, Roy, 151, Bloom, Harold, xv
Borges, Dain, 128
Borges, Jorge Luis, 19, 21, 37, 121–122,
    207 n.76, 208 n.1; works: "The
    Ethnographer," 168; "Pierre Menard,
    Author of Don Quixote," 168; *In
    Praise of Darkness,* 168
Boucher, Auguste-Gaspard-Louis, 173,
    174
Bowles, Paul, 51; work: *The Sheltering
    Sky,* 51
Braudel, Fernand, 109, 114; work:
    *Civilisation materielle, Economie it
    Capitalisme XVe-XvIII Siécle,* 109
Brecht, Bertold, 75, 82
Breton, André, 13, 14, 15, 202 n.7,
    205 n.43; work: "For an independent
    revolutionary art," 14
British Museum, 126
Bronzino, Agnolo, 170

Calvino, Italo, 72
Camus, Albert, xvi, 22, 100–103,
    208 n.82, 222n.6, 223 n.15; works:
    Carnets, 102; *The Rebel,* 22, 100, 108
Canudos rebellion, 86, 124–125, 138,
    228 n.14
Caretas, 71, 219 n.29
Carpentier, Alejo, 70, 76, 113, 217 n.2
Casa de las Américas (organization), 72
Casa de las Américas, 49, 73, 74, 77
Castro, Fidel, 8, 69, 70–73, 80, 99, 100,
    113, 140, 203 n.14
Castro-Klarén, Sara, 211 n.30, 221 n.80
Cioran, Emil, 230n.64; works: *Précis de
    décomposition,* 230n.64; *Histoire et
    Utopie,* 230 n.64
Collazos, Oscar, 71, 74
Comas, Juan, 43
Congress of Cuban Writers, 203 n.14
Conrad, Joseph, 28, 49, 142; works: *The
    Heart of Darkness,* xv, 47, 54–55, 214,
    92; *The Secret Agent,* xv; *Under*

Western Eyes, xv, 142–143, 150,
    229 nn. 45, 56
Cornejo Polar, Antonio, 78, 141–142
Coyné, André, 14, 15, 205nn. 44, 50
La Crónica, 93
Cuadernos de Marcha, 219 n.29
Cuban revolution, 8, 97; and artistic
    freedom, 6; as model, 5; and Vargas
    Llosa, 67, 71–81, 83, 219n.29
Cunha, Euclides da, 86, 128–130,
    227 n.10; work: *Rebellion in the
    Backlands,* 86–87, 125, 126–130, 139,
    227 nn.6, 11, 228 n.14
Czechoslovakia: invasion of, 70–71, 73, 99

Dagens Nyheter (Stockholm), 151
Davis, Mary E. 58
de Assis, Machado, 27, 199
de Beauvoir, Simone, 72
de la Barca, Calderon, 180; work: *Life is
    a Dream,* 180
de Soto, Hernando, 110–112; work: *The
    Other Path: The Invisible Revolution
    in the Third World,* 110, 111
Debray, Regis, 112
Delgado, Washington, 68,
    216 nn.133–134
Dodds, E. R., 196
Dorfman, Ariel, 10, 68, 216 n.132; work:
    "Mario Vargas Llosa y José María
    Arguedas: Dos visiones de una sola
    América," 216 n.132
Dostoevsky, Fyodor, M., 230 n.64
Doyle, Sir Arthur Conan, 153
Dumas, Alexandre, 19, 47

Eco, Umberto, 90
Edwards, Jorge, 79–80, 109; work:
    *Persona Non Grata: An Envoy in
    Castro's Cuba,* 80
Elkins de Snell, Betty, 163, 166–167
Elkins-Snell, Betty. *See* Elkins de Snell,
    Betty

Eluard, Paul, 17
Engels, Friedrich, 75
Enzensberger, Hans Magnus, 72
Escobar, Alberto, 13, 37
Euripides, 193, 196; work: *Bacchae,* 193
Eustasio Rivera, José, 27, 43; work: La
    vorágine, 27, 43, 162

fanaticism, 89, 187, 197, 223 n.19; and
    Bataille, 119; of Camacho, Pedro,
    94–97; and Camus, 101–102; and
    Faulkner, 87; military, 134; religious,
    87, 134; and utopias, 97. *See also*
    Vargas Llosa, Mario: and fanaticism
Faulkner, William, xv, 26, 28, 52, 87;
    works: *Absalom, Absalom!* 58–59, 63,
    211 n.34; *As I Lay Dying,* 211 n.31;
    Light in August, xv, 34–37, 52, 54, 58,
    87, 211nn.31–32; *The Sound and the
    Fury,* 59, 211 n.31; *The Wild Palms,*
    51, 55
Fernández Ariza, Guadalupe, 31,
    210 n.26
Fernández Retamar, Roberto, 71, 74,
    217 n.8
First National Congress of Education
    and Culture (Cuban), 72
Fischer, Ernst, 75
Flaubert, Gustave, xiii, xvi, 3, 5, 19,
    25–26, 28, 75, 76, 90, 208 nn.1, 2,
    209 nn.3, 5; works: *Madam Bovary,*
    81–83; *The Sentimental Education,*
    90, 92, 95–96; *The Temptation of
    Saint Anthony,* 90
Foucault, Michel, 75
Fra Angelico, 172
Franco, Jean, 68
Frankfurt Peace Prize, 198
free market. *See* Vargas Llosa, Mario:
    and the free market
Freud, Sigmund, 106
Frye, Northrop, 190
Fuentes, Carlos, xi, 27, 50, 72, 76, 198

Fujimori, Alberto, 186, 189, 235 n.13

Gadamer, Hans Georg, 201 n.4; work:
    Warheit und Methode, 201 n.4
García Márquez, Gabriel, xi, 21, 27, 113,
    198; work: *One Hundred Years of
    Solitude,* xi, 237 n.31
García, Alan, 113, 114
Gladieu, Marie-Madeleine, 93
Glumplowics, Ludwig, 128
Goethe, Johann Wolfgang, 3–4, 25
Goldemberg, Issac, 160; work: *The
    Fragmented Life of Jacob Lerner,* 160
Goldmann, Lucien, 75
Gombrich, E. H., xiv, 201 n.4
Góngora, 48
González Echevarría, Roberto,
    228 n.14; work: *Myth and Archive: A
    Theory of Latin American Narrative,*
    228 n.14
Goodman, Nelson, 201 n.4
Gorriti, Gustavo, 192
Gout, Alberto, 215 n.109; Film:
    Adventurera, 215 n.109
Grass Günther, 112
Guerra, Rui, 86, 87, 125
Guevara, Che, 70, 73
Guimarães Rosa, João, 209.n15
Guzmán, Abimael, 189, 235 n.13

Hamsun, Knut, 44; work: *Mysteries,* 44
Harss, Luis, 30
Hemingway, Ernest, 28
Herodotus, 172
Higgins, James, 13, 17
historicism, 108, 117–118; and Cunha,
    128–130
Hobbes, Thomas, 128
Hugo, Victor, xv, 3, 4, 26, 66, 91–92,
    121–122, 202 n.5; works: *The Man
    Who Laughs,* 46, 51; *Les Misérables,*
    26, 51, 54, 64–65, 122, 215 n.106
Huidobro, Vicente, 13, 16

indigenismo, 9–10, 18, 31, 158, 206 nn.54, 62

irrationalism, 117–123, 226 nn.66, 69

James, Henry, 121
Jerusalem prize, 198
Jordaens, Jacob, 171, 172
Joyce, James, 26, 55, 214 n.97: *Ulysses,* 55

Kafka, Franz, 21; work: *Metamorphosis,* 160
Kerr, Lucille, 232 n.94
King, Katherine, 236 n.29
King, John, 202 n.1
Kloepfer, Rolf, 216 n.124
Koestler, Arthur, 101

Lacan, Jacques, 75
Lafforgue, Jorge, 68, 78, 216 nn.134, 135
Lastra, Pedro, 206 n.51
Lauer, Mirko, 78–79, 231 n.91
Leber, Gisela, 75–76
Left (Latin American), xiii, xiv, xvi, 10, 69–81, 99–100, 111–113, 138–139, 185
Leoncio Prado school, 15, 23, 26, 32, 75, 208 n.84
Lezama Lima, José, 27
Literatura, 6, 15, 18
literature: autonomy of, 19–24, 70, 121; definition of, 12; of evil, 3, 4, 13, 116, 226 n.61 (*see also under* Bataille, Georges, and Moro, César); and politics, xi–xii, 5–8, 12–24, 69–98, 205 n.43; and Marxism, 77–78; narrator in, 91–92; and the open society, 117; purpose of, 19; role of, 4, 12, 20–21, 72, 74, 81; and socialism, xii, 6–8 19, 21–23; as subversive activity, 17, 19–20, 207 n.78; and transgression, 4, 53, 81, 116, 213 n.76, 225 n.58.
Loayza, Luis, 44

Lombardi: Film: *La boca del lobo,* 236 n.22
Lukács, George, 75, 76, 218 n.23

Machiavelli, Niccoló, 103–104
Malraux, André, 57, 142; works: *The Human Condition,* 57–58; *Man's Fate,* 142, 145, 149, 150
Machiguenga Indians, 157–158, 164–167
Mao Zedong, 6
Mariátegui, José Carlos, 6, 8–9, 10, 11, 111, 158; work: *Seven Interpretive Essays on Peruvian Reality,* 8–9, 111
Marinello, Juan, 74
Mario Vargas Llosa Collection, Firestone Library, Princeton University, xv, 11, 36, 45, 55, 141
Martorell, Joanot, xv, 20, 26, 88, 207 nn.68, 69; work: *Carta de batalla por Tirant lo Blanc,* 19, 74, 92, 207 n.69, 210 n.21
Marx, Karl, 75, 105, 106
Matto de Turner, Clorinda, 190; work: *Birds without a Nest,* 190
Mayta Mercado, Vicente, 140
Mayer, Enrique, 192
Milton, John, 4
Monsivais, Carlos, 72
Moro, César, xvi, 205 n.42, 44, 50; and *indigenismo,* 206 nn.54, 62; and influence on Vargas Llosa, 12–19, 53, 81, 115, 119; and literature of evil, 3–4, 176–177; and surrealist movement, 205 n.44; work: "La bazofia de los perros," 16

Neale-Silva, Eduardo, 43
Neruda, Pablo, 113
neoconservative, xii–xiv, 109, 201 n.2
neoliberal, xiii, xiv, 109–110, 201 n.2. *See also* Vargas Llosa, Mario: neoliberal period

nouveau roman movement, 218 n.23
novel (the), 25–28, 78; Latin American, 27–28; modern, 26–28; primitive, 26–27; realist/naturalist, 76. See also *nouveau roman*

Odría, 56–57
Onetti, Juan Carlos, 180; work: *A Brief Life*, 180
Ortega, Julio, 13
Orwell, George, 101
Oviedo, José Miguel, 6, 35, 53, 78, 84, 119, 141, 145, 211 n.33

Paz, Octavio, 109
Pacheco, José Emilio, 47, 55, 213 n.69
Padilla case, 71–81, 99–100, 219 n.29
Padilla Herberto, 71, 73, 81, 99–100
Peruvian Communist Party, 8
Piñon, Nélida, 126
pishtacos, 192
poètes maudits, 3, 5
Popper, Karl, xvi, 102, 106–109, 114–115, 117, 120, 152–153; and demarcation, 107, 223 n.28; and irrationalism, 226 n.66, 69; and irrefutable theories, 106–107; and truth, 107, 117–118, 152, 153, 230 n.74; and utopias, 108–109, 224 n.31; works: *The Open Society and its Enemies*, 107, 114, 118; *The Poverty of Historicism*, 107, 108; "Utopia and Violence," 108

Rama, Angel, 11, 21, 68, 77–78, 127, 138, 199, 216 n.135
realism, 37, 207 n.69; and reality, 122; socialist, 7; of Tolstoy, 137; of Vargas Llosa, xvii, 37
Revel, Jean-François, 102, 105–106, 109, 114, 148, 198
Revueltas, José, 219 n.29
Rimbaud, Arthur, 3, 5

Rincón, Carlos, 74–77
Riquer, Martín de, 88; work: *The Imaginary Combat*, 88
Riva Agüero, José de la, 78
Rivera, Diego, 205 n.44
Romualdo, Alejandro, 18
Rómulo Gallegos prize, 7, 70, 73, 236 n.30
Rulfo, Juan, 72, 76, 209 n.15
Rushdie, Salman, 141

Salazar Bondy, Sebastián, xvi, 6, 10, 16, 57, 67; work: *Lima la horrible*, 10, 11
Salomón, Raúl, 90
Santamaría, Haydée, 73, 76, 217 n.2
Sartre, Jean Paul, xvi, 12–13, 19, 22, 81, 207 n.78, 211 n.31, 219 n.29, 223 n.15; work: *What is Literature?* 12
Sartre, Jean-Paul, 72, 76, 79, 100
Scheerer, Thomas, 138
Schiele, Egon, 179
Shining Path, 144, 188–189, 230 n.64, 235 n.13, 236 n.22; and the Uchuraccay incident, 151, 157, 192–193
Snell, Wayne, 163
solidarity, xi
Solzhenitsyn, Alexander, 27, 100, 142; work: *A Day in the Life of Ivan Denisovich*, 27, 209 n.11
Sommers, Joseph, 216 n.133
Sontag, Susan, 72
sovereignty, 116–117, 175, 234 n.150. *See also* Bataille, Georges: and sovereignty
Stendhal. *See* Beyle, Marie-Henri
Steiner, George, xv
Summer Institute of Linguistics, 43, 232 n.109
surrealism, 4, 13–15, 205 n.44
Le surrealisme au service de la révolution, 14
Szyszlo, Fernando de, 171

Times (London), 151

Tirso de Molina, 170

Titian, 171, 173

Tolstoy, Leo, xv, 76, 124, 135, 137–138;
    work: *War and Peace,* 126, 135, 137

transgression, 115–119, 169, 175–176;
    and eroticism, 53, 116, 117–118; and
    fanaticism, 119; and pleasure,
    176–178. *See also* literature: and
    transgression

Trotsky, Leo, 14, 205 nn.43, 44; work:
    "For an independent revolutionary
    art," 14

Uchuraccay massacre, 150–151, 188,
    192, 231 n.91; Investigatory
    Commission, 150, 151, 157

Urquidi Illánez, 221 n.80; work: *Lo que
    Varguitas no dijo,* 221 n.80

Vallejos Vidal, Francisco Guillermo, 140

Vargas Llosa, Alvaro, 225 n.48

Vargas Llosa, Mario: and artistic free-
    dom, 6, 12, 15, 19, 22, 23, 70, 100,
    197; and break with the Left,
    109–115, 185, 225 n.44; and Camus,
    99–102; and the cinema, 29, 37, 46,
    50, 60, 88, 125–126, 211 n.39; con-
    demnation of, 71–81; and delayed
    decoding, 49; and "demons," 3–4, 7,
    13, 17, 21, 22–23, 115, 119, 120, 122,
    187, 197, 202 n.2; and fanaticism,
    124, 129 138–139, 149–150, 186, 187,
    188, 197; and the free market,
    109–114; and human frailty,
    186–187, 198; literary conceptions
    of, 28–30, 77, 197, 211 n.31, 221 n.85;
    and literary (artistic) creation, 4,
    119–120, 144, 197, 209 nn.3–4,
    210 n.20, 229 n.50; and literature and
    revolution, 6–9, 19–24, 220 n.56;
    moral vision of, 63–68; and Moro,
    12–19; neoliberal period of, xiii, xiv,

xvi, 186–187, 198; and the novel,
    25–30, 209 n.15, 210 n.21, 211 n.33;
    presidential bid of, 113–114; 185,
    186, 189, 234 n.2; revolutionary peri-
    od of, 198; short stories of, 30–32;
    socialist period of, xiii, xiv, 4, 5–6,
    12, 14, 23, 25, 63, 158, 186, 198,
    222 n.3; and telescoping dialogues,
    53–54; transition period of, 69–98;
    and truth, 20, 82–83, 91–92, 103,
    105, 115, 117–118, 120, 122–123,
    153; and transgression, 31, 38–39,
    41, 42, 53, 115, 164, 169, 174–175,
    213 n.76; and violence, 186, 187–188;

fictional characters (selected):

Alfonsito (Alfonso) (Fonchito),
    170–171, 173–174, 178–180;

Antonio the Counselor, 86–87, 89,
    126, 129, 130–131, 133–134, 138,
    139, 197, 227 n.10;

Arana, Ricardo (the Slave), 33,
    35–36, 38–41, 67,84, 152;

Camacho, Pedro, 29, 90–91, 93–97,
    197, 221 n.85;

Cuéllar, Pichula, 31–32, 60;

Fernández, Alberto, 33, 36, 37–42, 56;

Gall, Galileo, 125–127, 129–134, 139;

Gamboa, 33, 38–41, 65–67, 84, 87,
    89, 152, 197 212 n.47, 216 n.133;

Gonçalves, Epaminondas, 125, 126,
    132–134, 139, 227 n.3;

Jaguar, 33, 35, 36–42, 54, 56, 65,
    212 n.49;

Jurema, 125–126, 129–130, 132,
    212 n.42;

Lituma, 29, 31, 45–51, 94, 145,
    151–156, 191–196, 236 n.17;

Lucrecia, 170, 173–176, 178–180;

Mayta, 14, 69, 141, 143–150, 152,
    162, 169, 205 n.46, 228 n.40,
    229 nn.48, 50;

Rigoberto, Don, 169–181;

Rufino, 125–126;
Silva, 140, 145, 151–156;
Teresa, 33, 38, 41, 130;
Tinoco, Pedro, 190–191;
Zavala, Santiago, 21, 29, 31, 38,56–63, 66–67, 84, 169, 210 n.27;
Zuratas, Saúl (Mascarita), 29, 159, 160, 161–162, 168

works:

Acción para el cambio, 113
"Albert Camus and the Morality of Limits," 100–101
Aunt Julia and the Scriptwriter, xiv, 90–98, 210 n.19, 221 n.80; and use of alternating narratives, 169; and interconnectedness of, 29, 191, 210 n.26; as melodrama, 221 n.85; narrator of, 144, 159; as transition novel, xiii, 187
Los cachorros (The Cubs), 31–32, 60, 210 nn.23, 26, 27
Captain Pantoja and the Special Service, xiii, 84–86, 94, 98, 152, 163, 187
La Chunga, 29, 152, 191, 193
"La ciudad y el forastero," 49
La ciudad y los perros. See Vargas Llosa, Mario; works: *The Time of the Hero*
Contra viento y marea, 102, 105, 202 n.1, 231 n.91
Conversation in the Cathedral, 31, 54, 56–63; and corrupt society, 30, 65, 68; and interconnectedness of, 29, 210 nn.26, 27; and literature vs. politics, 21; as melodrama, 88; as socialist period novel, xiii; and social class, 38
Los cuadernos de don Rigoberto. See Vargas Llosa, Mario; works: The Notebooks of Don Rigoberto

The Cubs and Other Stories. See Vargas Llosa, Mario: works: *Los cachorros* and *Los Jefes*
Death in the Andes, xiv, xvii, 29, 181, 187, 189–197, 236 nn.17, 20
Desafíos a la libertad, 185
Entre Sartre y Camus, 102
A Fish in the Water, 112, 185, 225 n.48
"A Fish Out of Water," 114, 225 n.48
García Márquez: Historia de un deicidio, 77
The Green House, xi, xv, 7, 29, 42–47, 105, 130, 149, 212 n.47, 213 n.78, 214 n.92, 216 n.135, 236 n.17; and corrupt society, 65, 57, 166; form of, 47–51; and interconnectedness of, 31,152, 153, 191, 235 n.17; literary fusions in, 51–56; socialist period novel, xiii, 76; and space, 61–62, 76
Historia secreta de una novela, 214 n.89
The Imaginary Combat, 88
Los impostores (The Impostors), 11, 210 n.30 (*see also* Vargas Llosa, Mario; works: *Time of the Hero*)
Los jefes, 30, 31–32, 36, 45, 67, 152, 210 n.23; "The Challenge," 31, "The Grandfather, 30, "The Leaders," 30; "On Sunday, 31, "A Visitor," 31, 45, 152, 191, "The Younger Brother," 31
Kathie y el hipopótamo, 29, 120
"La literatura es fuego" (Literature is Fire), 7, 70
Lituma en los Andes, 152, 191 (*see also* Vargas Llosa, Mario; works: *Death in the Andes*)
El loco de los balcones, 185
Making Waves, 202 n.1
The Notebooks of Don Rigoberto, xiv, xvii, 29, 178–181, 187, 201 n.3

Vargas Llosa: **works** (*continued*)
Ojos Bonitos, Cuadros Feos, xii, 185, 187
"On the Role of the Intellectual in National Liberation Movements," 21
The Perpetual Orgy: Flaubert and Madame Bovary, 81–83, 220 n.56
In Praise of the Stepmother, 13, 17, 29, 119, 169–178, 181
The Real Life of Alejandro Mayta, 69, 140–150, 181; influences on, xv, 14, 230 n.56; and interconnectedness of, 152, 191; and revolutionary theme, 140, 159, 162, 230 n.64, 237 n.30
La señorita de Tacna, 29
"La sociedad abierta y sus enemigos," 106
The Storyteller, 29, 87, 156–169, 181
Time of the Hero, xi, xiv, 5, 32–42, 45, 64, 130, 197, 210 n.30, 213 n.76; critics of, 68, 75, 79, 216 nn.134, 135; influences on, xv, 15, 206 n.51; inspiration for, 29; and revolutionary theme, 11; and social corruption, 30, 54, 56, 65, 67, 68, 152, 196; as socialist period novel, xiii, 22–23
"The Truth of Lies," 117

"¿Es útil el sacrificio de la poesía?" 18
La utopía arcaica: José María Arguedas y las ficciones del indigenismo, 185
"War Dogs," 125
"The War of Canudos, 125
The War of the End of the World, xiv, 84, 102, 123, 140, 212 n.42, 237 n.31; critics of, 138, 236; form of, 130–135; historical setting of, 124–127, 137; influences on, 129–130, 138–139, 227 n.6; as neoliberal period novel, xvii; and religious fanaticism, 87, 89–90, 119, 181
Who Killed Palomino Molero?, 29, 150–156, 160, 191–193, 196
A Writer's Reality, 84, 229 n.50

Villaseñor, Héctor, 232 n.109

Watt, Ian, 49
Wilson Center, Washington D.C., 126
Wilson, Edmund, 56
Wollheim, Richard, 201 n.4
Woolf, Virginia, 26

Zimmerman, Klaus, 216 n.124

EFRAÍN KRISTAL, a native of Peru, is author of *The Andes Viewed from the City* (1987) and is currently professor of Spanish and comparative literature at UCLA.

TEMPTATION OF THE WORD

was composed electronically using
Minion types, with displays
in City Light, Medium, and Bold.
The book was printed on 60# Booktext Natural acid-free,
recycled paper and was Smyth sewn and cased in Pearl Linen
by BookCrafters.
The dust jacket was printed in three colors by
Vanderbilt University Printing Services.
Book and dust jacket designs are the work of Tom Ventress.
Published by Vanderbilt University Press
Nashville, Tennessee 37235

Temptation of the Word
The Novels of Mario Vargas Llosa

EFRAÍN KRISTAL

TEMPTATION OF THE WORD is an ambitious and careful reading of the creative process—the origin of themes and the development of literary techniques—that Mario Vargas Llosa has brought to each of his novels, published through 1997. To understand the novelist's intellectual environment, Kristal analyzes the entire corpus of Vargas Llosa's writings (including his many books of essays and his plays), his literary influences in several languages, his intellectual biography, and his polemical activism in contentious times, all in the light of the evolution of his political views and concept of literature.

Kristal's analysis of each of the novels sheds light on how literary techniques, themes, and character types appear, recur, and are transformed over the four decades Vargas Llosa has been active as a writer of narrative fiction. In turn, Kristal's close readings are enriched by other sections of the book that offer insights into the intellectual currents and the political ideas that are addressed in Vargas Llosa's novels. This method brings to bear the most pertinent contextual debates, such as a discussion of the way his works borrow from, and sometimes rewrite, masterpieces by Conrad, Faulkner, Flaubert, Malraux, Stendahl, and Tolstoy, as well as exemplary works in the Latin American narrative tradition.

Kristal also identifies an irrationalist streak in the writings of Vargas Llosa and explores its implications in the novelist's literary conceptions and ethical views. While the political content of Vargas Llosa's novels has never betrayed his convictions, he has successfully avoided the temptation—fatal, according to Flaubert—of reproducing rather than recreating reality. Kristal concludes that the central concern of Vargas Llosa's novels is a premise that the hopes and desires of individuals are always greater than their ability to fulfill them.